WELCOME TO THE JUNGLE

Welcome

THE WHY BEHIND

ST. MARTIN'S GRIFFIN 🙢 NEW YORK

to the Jungle

"GENERATION X"

Geoffrey T. Holtz

WELCOME TO THE JUNGLE. Copyright © 1995 by Geoffrey T. Holtz. All rights reserved. Printed in the United States of America. No part of this book may be used or reproduced in any manner whatsoever without written permission except in the case of brief quotations embodied in critical articles or reviews. For information, address St. Martin's Press, 175 Fifth Avenue, New York, N.Y. 10010.

Design by Sara Stemen

LIBRARY OF CONGRESS CATALOGING-IN-PUBLICATION DATA

Holtz, Geoffrey T.
  Welcome to the jungle / Geoffrey T. Holtz.
       p.   cm.
       ISBN 0-312-13210-7
  1. Generation X.   2. Young adults—United States—Social
                                     conditions.   I. Title.
     HQ799.7.H63   1995   95-7938
     305.23′5—dc20   CIP

First St. Martin's Griffin Edition: June 1995

10 9 8 7 6 5 4 3 2 1

TO MY PARENTS

CONTENTS

Introduction: The Free Generation   1

PART ONE
THE GENERATION THAT RAISED ITSELF

1. Reconsidering Childhood   9
   Home Sweet Home • 9   The Population Bomb Explodes • 12
   Defusing the Bomb • 15   The End of the Boom? • 16

2. Family Deconstruction   19
   A White One for Twenty-One Days, a Pink One for Seven • 19
   How Much Is One of Those Things? • 20   Sexy Young Things • 22
   Living in a Box • 24   It's a Mad, Mad, Mad, Mad World • 24
   Breaking Up Isn't So Hard to Do • 26   On Our Own • 29
   After the Fall • 30   The Disappearance of the Father • 31
   Hey Dad, How About a Little Help? • 33   Meet Your New
   Family • 36

3. It's 3:00 P.M. Do You Know Where Your Parents Are?   39
   The Organization Woman • 39   The Warehouse Generation • 42
   Two Breadwinners, Only One Mom • 44

4. The Youthful Face of Poverty   45
   A Historical First • 45   Tight Budgets • 47   Robin Hood,
   American Style • 49

5. Peers Over Parents   51
   Quality Time • 51   That's What Friends Are For • 53
   Becky Bell • 56   The Halloween Sadist • 57   The
   Child-Stealing Bogeyman • 58   Look Homeward, Angel • 62

6. A Growing Pessimism   63
   The Adult Child • 63   Too Fat, Too Thin • 65   Way Beyond
   Candy Cigarettes • 67   Babies Having Babies • 69   Thrill
   Seekers • 73   The Ultimate Self-Destructive Act • 76

7. New Extremes of Discipline   80
   Brave New World • 80   Birth of a Disease • 81   SOMA
   Holiday • 82   Is There a Doctor in the Classroom? • 83
   The Living Dead • 84   Short and Sweet • 86   I Was

Bad Because You Forgot to Give Me My Pill • 87   Mother's Little Helper • 88   We Just Don't Want You to Hurt Yourself • 88

8. Home Away from Home ... 92
Running to Stand Still • 92   The Crime Roller Coaster • 94
Adult Crimes, Adult Penalties, Child Criminals • 96   Eye for an Eye • 98

9. What a Difference Twenty Years Makes ... 100
Pop-Culture Icons Then and Now • 100

PART TWO
THE BLACKBOARD JUNGLE

10. Schools Without Walls ... 105
Teach Your Children Wrong • 105   Down with the Teacher, Up with the Bureaucrat • 106   The Decline of the Teacher • 108
The End of the Funding Party • 109   School Deconstruction • 110
The Feel-Good School • 112   Spontaneous Education • 114
Get Out While You Can • 115   Fallout from the "Movement" • 115
Majoring in "Other" • 116   If Only They Had Asked the Students • 117   Everybody Is Above Average • 118   Results of the Experiment • 120

11. College ... 122
The $100,000 Education • 122   The Six-Year Undergraduate • 124
College or Bust • 125   College *and* Bust • 126
Get a Job • 128   The High-Schoolization of the University • 130
Anxiety U. • 131   The "Movement" and the Curriculum • 132
The Absent Professor • 136   In Loco Parentis Revisited • 137

PART THREE
THE IMPOVERISHED GENERATION

12. Working More for Less ... 143
Child Labor • 143   Hard Times • 147   Monkey on the Back • 147
The Disappearing Job • 149   McJobs and Temps • 151
The Government's Closed-Door Policy • 153   Two Tiers: The High-Paying One and the Free One • 154   Out of Work, Out of Luck • 155

13. Low Incomes and Expensive Homes ... 158
    The Incredible Shrinking Paycheck • 158   Trickling Down • 161
    Social Insecurity • 163   True Tax Reform • 166   The Housing
    Pot o' Gold • 166   The Ponzi Scheme Comes to an End • 167
    Deregulation and Protecting the Haves • 171   Rent Forever • 174
    The Boomerang Effect • 174

PART FOUR
THE FREE GENERATION TODAY AND TOMORROW

14. Free-Style Families ... 179
    Winds of Change • 179   Love and Marriage (Well, Maybe
    Just Love) • 180   The Free as Parents? • 183

15. A New Political Force ... 187
    A Wasted Generation? • 187   Taking Nothing for Granted • 189
    Free Thinking • 191   An End to Politics as Usual? • 194   Positive
    Thinking? • 195   No Free Ride • 198   Inside Joke • 199
    Long Live Rock and Roll (and Hip Hop, Punk, New Wave,
    Rap . . .) • 200

16. Looking Ahead ... 202
    War Between the Generations? • 202   Waking Up? • 205
    The Cynical Generation—Pro and Con • 206   Mixin' It Up • 207
    An Eye to the Future • 208

Notes ... 209

Index ... 277

WELCOME TO THE JUNGLE

INTRODUCTION: THE FREE GENERATION

The generation of Americans born during the 1960s and 1970s remains, to many, an enigma. *Time* magazine referred to them in 1990 as "an unsung generation, hardly recognized as a social force or even much noticed at all." The size of this unheralded generation? A mere seventy-five million teenagers and young adults—nearly one American out of every three. They are now coming of age and beginning to assume a broader position in the public spotlight, but until now, the media's depiction of them has been disturbingly consistent:

"The Doofus Generation" (The *Washington Post*)
"The Tuned-Out Generation" (*Time*)
"A generation of animals" (The *Washington Post*)
"The Numb Generation" (The *New York Times*)
"The Blank Generation" (The *San Francisco Examiner*)
"This is a generation without a soul" (A West Coast radio talk-show host)
"The Unromantic Generation" (The *New York Times*)
A "generation of self-centered know-nothings." (Pollster Andrew Kohut)

Not the most flattering of portrayals. Born just after the magnificent baby boom, we are forever cast in the shadow of that pig-in-the-python that has dominated our nation's attention from its members' sheer numbers as infants in the fifties, their vociferous social and political exploits in the sixties, their epic quests for self-fulfillment in the seventies, and their drive toward materialistic gain in the eighties. In the wake of this group, we have often had to fight to be noticed at all, let along to be judged by fair standards or to be understood.

We are, perhaps more than any previous generation, a product of the societal trends of our times and of the times that immediately preceded us. The years in which we were born and raised—the sixties, seventies, and eighties—saw unprecedented changes in the political, social, and economic environment that, for the first time in American history, have made the future of society's young members uncertain. In many cases, these troubling and sometimes appalling trends have since been scaled back or reversed, so that Americans born in the eighties and after do not face the same dire conditions. But for the 75 million of us immediately in the baby boom's wake, the uphill battle to overcome preexisting obstacles remains.

The birth dates that differentiate these two generations are somewhat debatable, and thus need to be defined. For purposes of this book, the term Baby Boomer (a name that is appropriate given their vast numbers) refers to those

Americans born between 1943 and 1960. I use these dates rather than the more popular boundaries of 1946 and 1964 for reasons proposed by historians Neil Howe and William Strauss; this defines a group with a more consistent peer personality. After all, those born in the early sixties weren't even born when the first Americans were killed in Vietnam, and had hardly entered kindergarten classes when Woodstock took place. The boundaries that define this outspoken generation's births are the year in which it became apparent that the American effort in World War II would likely be rewarded with victory—1943—and the year in which the man who epitomized our nation's youth obsession, John F. Kennedy, was elected president—1960. This generation is forever associated with the post-war optimism, the "boom," that extended to so many aspects of American society following our military triumph. (Since these adults are now in their late thirties to early fifties, and many are grandparents, and not "babies," hereafter, I'll refer to them as simply "Boomers.")

As for the generation that *follows* the Boomers, the defining moment—the event that would mark their first year—came, with what would be characteristic irony, by default: In late 1960, the G.D. Searle Drug Company of Skokie, Illinois, marketed the first commercially produced birth control pill, Enovid 10. Never before was it so easy to *not* have children. America's attitude toward its youth would undergo a great transformation in the following two decades. As the true children of the 1960s, this generation would grow up in the midst of what Tom Wolfe dubbed the "Third Great Awakening," a time when the young adult Boomers were experiencing a tremendous euphoria through "the moment" in the universities, "finding" themselves in various self-help groups, and living the "sexual revolution." As children, we were unable to participate directly in these endeavors, but many of us experienced them as a nightmarish breakdown of political leadership, a troubling dissolution of family structures, and a chaotic education in schools with confusing, directionless objectives.

As for the closing boundary: By 1980, when the Boomers had begun having children of their own in greater numbers, Ronald Reagan was elected president, and the country would once again undergo an extreme transformation. This time, however, the change would be back toward tradition and away from experiment. And thus a generation—in some senses by default—was created.

The next question is what to call this now-infamous group of young people. The past few years have seen many attempts to tag us with a number of cute, catchy, or derisive monikers. Given the tremendous diversity of the group, it has proved no simple task. Most demographers have referred to us as the "baby-bust generation," but the term is inappropriate, primarily because it is simply too derivative. It defines us solely in terms of the generation whom we just happen to follow, the Boomers. Some have called us a new "lost generation," likening us to the select group of disenfranchised Americans who came of age in the 1920s. While there are many similarities in the social norms and the sense of anomie under which the two groups came of age, it once again denies us any identity of our own.

Historians Strauss and Howe give us the tag "13er" since we're the thirteenth generation to call ourselves American citizens. "It's a name they can see as a gauntlet, a challenge, an obstacle to be overcome," they explain in their 1991 book, *Generations*. Thanks, but no thanks. The label is too generic, and it imparts a sense of fatalistic misfortune that is not really relevant.

The now almost omnipresent name coined by novelist Douglas Coupland—Generation X—with its use of the mathematical symbol for the unknown, pays homage to this generation's disdain for accepting any single definition. However, while this designation does capture a certain spirit of anonymity, and serves the characters in his novel very well, this much-hyped, slightly derogatory label seems to be nearly universally disliked among the members of the young generation whom it is supposed to define.

I'm proposing a new name, at least for the remainder of these pages—a name that speaks to the individualistic, multifaceted, difficult-to-define nature of this group. "The Free Generation." *Free* in the sense of liberated or emancipated: We have grown up in a world that offers more choices than have ever before been available (though many of these are certainly less than optimal). With the breakdown of many gender-based traditions and racial stereotypes, we enjoy a much broader ranger of lifestyle and career choices than any generation which preceded us.

We're also free of any defining event or experience. Whereas the Great Depression, each of the world wars, the Vietnam War, and Woodstock offered previous generations a definitive, powerful touchstone for group identity, we have nothing like this in which we can all share.

But the term *Free* has other pertinent connotations as well. It can mean extra, loose, or spare. From our infancy during the days of the "swinging single" and the popularity of the idea of zero population growth, to our adolescence and young adulthood when the media virtually ignored us, society has long found us somewhat superfluous, if not bewildering or outright inscrutable.

Free also suggests a group that is unchecked, uninhibited, carefree or careless—as in "free spirit." The generation that popularized bungee jumping, "extreme skiing," and Japanese superbike motorcycles capable of doing 150 miles an hour certainly warrants such a designation. A recent Gallup poll indicates that 73 percent of Americans agree that we are more reckless than our counterparts were twenty years ago—more reckless, that is, than even the radical, free-loving members of the sixties generation were in their youth. There are many reasons for the potentially self-destructive, risk-taking conduct many of us have sought, and these are explored in detail throughout the book.

In a similar vein, *Free* can indicate a state of drifting, rootlessness—"free-floating," a condition that can be either liberating or terrifying depending on one's point of view.

The Free Generation grew up in a time when other members of society were also beginning to discover and act upon newfound freedoms in onerous ways. Our mothers and fathers exercised their freedom to divorce to the tune of over one million a year, triple the rate of their own parents. Schools demonstrated their freedom to test out a variety of new, often ill-conceived curricula on us. Politicians and other policy makers felt free to conduct new experiments in spending and in funding government operations—alarmingly often by means that benefitted the old at the expense of the young. And as we've seen, the media have considered themselves free to chide and ridicule us.

There is, without a doubt, also an ironic aspect to the name "the Free." Just as we are unencumbered by many of what William Blake called the "mind-forged manacles" that shackled members of previous generations, we also find our opportunities to exercise these newfound freedoms drying up. Higher education is being priced out of reach for a growing number. Job and income prospects are dismal. And the dream of owning a home is slipping away from all but a dwindling few. The chances that we'll surpass our parents' standards of living are minimal. In fact, as the pages to follow will illustrate, to call us "the Free" may seem a cruel joke. To cite one concrete example, in unprecedented numbers the mind-forged manacles have been replaced by actual, steel ones: The Free are already the most incarcerated generation ever. (Perhaps they should call us the "baby bust" after all!)

Lastly, as most of us have already learned, with freedom comes tremendous responsibility. It means having to decide one's own course of action, exercising "free will," and being held accountable for any consequences. And, contrary to many of the media reports so far, most of us have faced up to our responsibilities. In fact, as we've struggled with the untoward legacy that's been handed us, we've had little choice but to create our *own* opportunities. This book details that legacy, putting into focus the many and varied obstacles in our paths—that is, the social, political, and economic trends and events of the 1960s, 1970s, and 1980s that set the stage for the America we would know.

For those who may not be familiar with the Free, or can't understand how this young generation could be struggling so, consider a cross-section of this vast and diverse group:

The woman behind the department store perfume counter. Not the elegant older woman who went to work to earn wardrobe money after her kids all left home. Rather, the twenty-three-year-old working to pay her rent who, with every sale, has to fight the urge to scream in disbelief that someone can pay thirty-five dollars for a half-ounce bottle of *eau de toilette*.

The two young guys who, after a day of working in the record store ringing up Crosby, Stills and Nash CDs for nostalgic forty-five-year-olds, have to borrow the store's demo copy of the newest Snoop Doggy Dogg disk to tape at home because they can't afford to shell out four hours' worth of wages to buy it.

The twenty-eight-year-old woman who handles the western regional sales for the Fortune 500 pharmaceutical company—not a bad job, but she knows she can't get promoted for another ten years because everyone above her on the company's organizational chart is between thirty-five and fifty years old, and unlikely to retire for a long, long time.

The guy who can hardly keep his eyes open in his college British Literature class—not because he's bored, but because he had to work until midnight the previous night at the fast-food restaurant to help pay the tuition that's more than doubled in the past ten years. (He'll also need six years to complete school because, working thirty hours a week, he has no time for more than twelve units per semester.)

The twenty-five-year-old laid-off auto worker who still lives at home and who knows he'll never be recalled because, with production moving overseas, there are five thousand other laid-off auto workers with more seniority than he.

The recent history Ph.D. graduate who has little chance of actually teaching at the university level in the near future, due both to drastic staff cutbacks in colleges across the country and to an overabundance of tenured faculty hired during the sixties and seventies.

Contrary to popular belief, we're not a generation of malcontents, underachievers, and complainers. Such stereotypes indicate a lack of understanding of the forces that have shaped this diverse group. There are signs, however, that the negative characterizations are starting to soften. President Clinton, notably the first Boomer to sit in the Oval Office, told UCLA students in the spring of 1994, "Americans of my generation have been bombarded by images on television shows, and even one book, about the so-called Generation X filled with cynics and slackers. Well, what I have seen today is not a generation of slackers, but a generation of seekers." There may be 75 million answers to the question of what, exactly, we are seeking, but comments like these may indicate that older generations are finally giving us a little "slack," and even some credit. Such credit is certainly due. As the history and analysis detailed in this book will show, for 75 million of us, it's a jungle out there.

Part One

THE GENERATION THAT RAISED ITSELF

1

RECONSIDERING CHILDHOOD

Magazines that ran articles in 1970 concerning coerced population control: *Science, Life, Reader's Digest, The New Republic, Discussion, Parents, Bulletin of the Atomic Scientist, Newsweek, Time, Science Digest, Look, Mademoiselle, The New York Times Magazine*

Fertility Rate of American Women
(Expressed as the average number of children born per woman)

1957: 3.8

1977: 1.8

SOURCE: *VITAL STATISTICS OF THE UNITED STATES*

HOME SWEET HOME

Lois and Stephen Wolfson welcomed the birth of their first child in September, 1975—a son they named Adam. They brought their infant home to the Marina Del Rey, California, apartment where they had resided for a year and a half and where they had planned to keep on living. But not long after this happy occasion, they were informed by the manager of the apartment complex that they would be unable to renew their lease. The reason? Adam.

A year before Adam's birth, in October of 1974, Marina Point Apartments had changed its rental policy to exclude all families with children. Although they did allow those children who currently resided in the complex to remain, they would no longer rent to new families with children, nor to pregnant women. Although the Wolfsons had lived at Marina Point since February of that year, before the policy was adopted, the arrival of their son apparently rendered them ineligible to remain in their home. Because they were having a difficult time finding a new place to live, the apartment manager granted them a short extension before they would be forced to vacate. But soon after this, the manager took the Wolfsons to court to evict them.

The new parents, feeling that they were being unlawfully discriminated against—as the sole reason for their eviction was the presence of their son—decided to defend their position in court. In the municipal court trial, the manager justified her no-children policy on the grounds that the apartment complex had no facilities for children or any place suitable for them to play. The fact that there were sixty-six families with children living in the complex at the time the new policy was adopted didn't seem to enter into the case. "Expert" evidence was presented to argue that children *generally* cause more wear and tear on property than do adults. Therefore, the argument went, the increased maintenance costs associated with children justified excluding them.

Lois and Stephen Wolfson offered testimony from both their upstairs and next-door neighbors that Adam's presence was in no way annoying to them. Furthermore, the manager presented no evidence whatsoever that the little boy had been disruptive or had damaged property in any way. During the trial, the judge conceded that, from the evidence, the court was satisfied that Adam had created no problems on the apartment premises. His ruling? The Wolfsons would have to move. Whatever the evidence, there were simply no laws protecting the rights of children against discrimination in rental properties. The couple appealed the decision to the California court of appeals, and the ruling was upheld. The presence of the infant justified eviction.

The Wolfsons were not alone in their predicament. In the seventies and early eighties, 70 to 90 percent of all newly constructed apartments in large cities such as Dallas, Houston, and Denver were strictly adults-only. In Dallas's case, a 1978 study showed that more than half of *all* apartment complexes, new and old, flat-out refused to accept children. Another 12 percent only accepted them with certain restrictions (not above or below a certain age, no more than one child per household, etc.). Thus a family with children in Dallas, the nation's ninth-largest city, had only a third of the available apartments from which to choose.

The situation in the fast-growing Los Angeles area, where the Wolfsons resided, was even worse. A study conducted in 1979 showed that seven apartment complexes in ten excluded children. An additional 15 percent allowed children only within certain age ranges. That left only one apartment in eight available to families with children of any age in the Los Angeles area. To add to the predicament, the problems were even more acute in newly constructed complexes. Across the nation, apartments constructed during the seventies were 60 percent *more* likely to exclude children than older units. Newer units also tended to be of higher quality and located in better neighborhoods than older ones, shutting families out of much of the more desirable housing in our cities.

The California study also showed that median rents for apartments that allowed children were *higher* than for equivalent units that excluded them. So not only were parents forbidden from seven out of eight Los Angeles apartments, they had to pay more for the paltry choices given them. This price premium might illustrate nothing more than supply and demand, but the driving force was certainly a lack of supply, with parents paying the penalty. The judges in the Wolfson case even recognized that families with children have a more difficult time finding housing. Yet they justified their decision by noting that, after all, not *all* apartments have no-child policies.

Nationwide, the policies regarding apartment availability to families with children were similarly hostile. Only about one rental unit in four was available with no restrictions. In larger complexes, fewer than one unit in five was available unconditionally to parents with children. While some apartment managers have always excluded children for a variety of reasons, the number who decided these reasons were justifiable rose by 50 percent during the seventies. And these managers were not out of line with public sentiment. A 1980 study by the University of Michigan for HUD found that 40 percent of renters in buildings that maintain explicit no-children policies chose to live there specifically because of those policies. Even with single-family detached homes, one in five rentals was strictly off-limits to children.

Would not the building frenzy of that time, combined with lower birth rates, still have left families with adequate choices for good housing? Unfortunately not. The Michigan survey showed that nearly half of the respondents with children reported that when last looking for a place to live, they had found a suitable apartment but were forbidden to rent it because of the policies regarding children. This dilemma crossed all boundaries of race, income, gender of the head of household, and size of the apartment in question. This was not a problem of the poor or of minorities. It was simply a problem for all those who decided to raise a family. The obstacles faced by these parents included limited access to quality schools and day-care centers because they could not rent in their preferred area. Other families in the Michigan investigation reported having to choose apartments without convenient access to public transportation or in areas that forced them to make an undesirably long commute to work—a restriction that put strains on the family by making the time available for parents to spend with their children more limited than they would have liked.

Forbidding children wasn't a policy that was limited to cantankerous landlords. In fact, many communities, eager to tap the growing expendable income of single yuppies and increasingly wealthy senior citizens, actively encouraged adult-only construction by offering a variety of incentives to builders. The growth of one- and two-person households during these years insured that there would be a big enough market for such developments. Cities allowed developers to build higher-density complexes in exchange for no-children restrictions. The rationale was that not only would higher-income adults, paying higher taxes as well, be attracted to their area, but the cities could also avoid providing expensive municipal services for children, such as schools and parks. It was a win-win situation for all involved. Except for children and their parents, who weren't involved at all.

One might think that such exclusionary policies would be considered a blatant disregard for the law. This is America—you can live wherever you want. The Fair Housing Act, passed by Congress in 1968 and amended in 1974, prohibited discrimination in the sale or rental of housing on the basis of race, color, religion, sex, or national origin. Other legislation protected the rights of the elderly. These acts, however, as the Wolfsons discovered, did not address child discrimination. Perhaps as a result of the fact that children can't vote, and are unlikely to form political action committees to pump funds into the treasuries of congressmen, they simply hadn't received the protection that other groups had.

The problem became acute enough in the West that nine different bills concerning the topic were introduced to the California state legislature between 1975 and 1981. All failed. Before 1980 only eight states had any regulations specifically prohibiting bias against renting to families with children, and only Massachusetts enforced them. San Francisco was the only large city that truly protected tenants with children.

This was a new problem. Never before had families suffered widely from discrimination in housing, and this predicament is just one manifestation of society's sea-change in its attitude toward the newest generation.[1]

THE POPULATION BOMB EXPLODES

The experiences of families trying to find a place to live with their children were not the only indicators of a transformation in national mood. Nor was this situation merely a rare aberration from America's general love affair with its children. Whereas historian Richard Hofstadter commented in the fifties that the United States was becoming the land of the "overvalued child," now, in the

---

[1] Indicating how society's regard toward its children slowly began to change in the eighties, the California Supreme Court overturned the Wolfson decision in 1982. And in 1988, Congress passed an extension to the Civil Rights Act of 1968 and rendered housing discrimination against families with children illegal.

1960s, after twenty years of escalating birth rates known as the "baby boom," America began to reevaluate its attitudes toward children. The pendulum had begun to swing wildly in the opposite direction.

The British biologist Thomas Malthus wrote in 1798 that "population, when unchecked, increases in a geometrical ratio. Subsistence only increases in an arithmetical ratio." It's interesting to note that Malthus used the explosive population growth in the American colonies in researching his thesis, because 160 years later his concept was heartily embraced across the Atlantic. In 1968, Paul Ehrlich, a biologist from Stanford University, looked up from his petri dishes, decided there were too many people around, and wrote a small book called *The Population Bomb*. An instant best-seller, it gave readers a somewhat scientific confirmation of the growing belief that our planet and our nation were bursting at the seams.

In the book, Ehrlich presents a number of overpopulation-induced scenarios. In the first, he depicts a riot-torn U.S. in the early eighties, with citizens starving to death because of food shortages and beef an unattainable luxury at twelve dollars a pound (in 1970 dollars!). The second scenario is filled with imaginary doomsday headlines of the near future with a resulting one and a half billion people perishing worldwide from disease, starvation, and pandemic-related "civil disorder." All this by 1974. In the third, he foresees a 1980 UN-mandated "International Survival Tax" of 8 percent of America's GNP (about 90 billion 1970 dollars). To prevent these dire projections, Ehrlich suggests a number of baby-prevention measures: luxury taxes on cribs, diapers, and expensive toys; "responsibility prizes" awarded to each couple for every five years they remain childless; and a "special lottery" with tickets going only to the childless.

How seriously were these premonitions taken? As Gertrude Himmelfarb wrote in a 1960s reprinting of Malthus's work, "The 'Population Bomb' is beginning to usurp the place of the H-Bomb in the public imagination and conscience." Each child born was supposedly akin to a tiny nuclear explosion, with a devastating cumulative effect. Young-adult Boomers in particular embraced this idea, and a year after publishing his book, Ehrlich founded an organization for them, Zero Population Growth, Inc. (ZPG), dedicated to the idea that we absolutely must stem the rate at which men and women have children. Our very existence depended on it. ZPG grew rapidly, with its membership reaching over 700,000 by the eighties. *The Population Bomb* spawned a host of imitators all signaling the same dire alarms: *Too Many Americans; Famine, 1975!; The Hungry Future; Breeding Ourselves to Death; The Case for Compulsory Birth Control*—all these, among myriad other books, painted a gloomy picture of the near future unless extreme, often outrageous, measures were taken.

Although Ehrlich's work achieved the most widespread notoriety, it wasn't the first, or most dramatic, to address overpopulation concerns. A scientist in Rockville, Maryland, John Calhoun, decided to test Malthus's original premise by allowing rats to breed out of control in a pen in 1963. What ensued was a nightmarish vision of hell in the land of Rodentia. The rats became severely pathological, with some turning aggressive and cannibalistic while others became bisexual and sadistic; female rats were unable to carry pregnancies, and the rearing of their young was disrupted (certainly sounds like America in the 1970s, doesn't it?). Calhoun called the breakdown of all social order a "behavioral sink" and tied his conclusions to the future of humanity, citing "analogous problems confronting the human species." The future sounded like a David Lynch movie.

Surprisingly, only a few years earlier, *Life* magazine ran an article proclaiming that children were the *answer* to all our economic ills, because of their inherent need for more housing, more appliances, and more jobs. KIDS: BUILT-IN RECESSION CURE, headlined the 1958 cover story in the nation's most popular magazine. "The four-year-olds shown trying out the swings on the cover of this issue represent a backlog of business orders that will take two decades to fill!" excitedly proclaimed the article. A decade later, though, children represented only a worsening of our social ills. They signified a drain on our already overtaxed supply of food and energy, on our tax funds, and on our employment resources. They denoted a compounding of the problems of pollution, crowded cities, and environmental degradation. *Life* responded to this dire viewpoint by launching the new decade with the cover story "Squeezing into the Seventies," commenting that, lest anybody mistakenly believe that the affluent United States could handle a growing populace even if third-world nations could not, "each American baby represents fifty times as great a threat to the planet as each Indian baby."

To illuminate the universal nature of the population problem, biologist Garret Hardin developed the allegory of "The Tragedy of the Commons" in a 1968 *Science* magazine essay. In this parable, a village has made a patch of grazing ground available to all members of the community. The parcel has enough grazing for one cow per household, but Hardin anticipates that a few people will send two cows to the area in order to increase their yield. As more and more follow suit, the commons becomes overgrazed, and all the cattle die. The implied message is that the earth was becoming "overgrazed" by *other people's* children.

As historian John Sommerville described the sentiment of the times, "Babies are the enemy. Not your baby or mine, of course. Individually they are all cute. But together they are a menace." In what was called the "more mouths to feed" argument, it was asserted that many of the costs of rearing children, especially the costs associated with education, are social rather than private costs.

They are costs borne by society rather than by the parents alone. We "bind individuals to pay for the education of other people's children," complained demographer Judith Blake Davis. Parents who chose to have children, went the belief, were not only selfish; they were a threat to society and, more specifically, to "me." A Columbia University sociologist, Lincoln Day, put the point succinctly. In America, he said, "we must inevitably be faced with a choice between quantity and quality: vast numbers of people living poorly at necessarily low levels of living, or fewer people, but with those fewer living well." Day added that "the couple with more than three [children] is contributing to the population disaster. It is, in this sense, *socially irresponsible,* the more so the more numerous the children." *Newsweek* ran an article titled "Make Love, Not Babies." The general spirit of the times was captured in the popular slogan "The Population Explosion Is Everybody's Baby."

Observing this sentiment, a wave of popular films showed children in a most unchildlike light. In *Paper Moon* (1973), *The Bad News Bears* (1976), *Bugsy Malone* (1976), *Taxi Driver* (1976), and *Pretty Baby* (1978), kids were foulmouthed, devilish little con artists, criminals, and whores. In *Rosemary's Baby* (1968), *The Exorcist* (1973), *It's Alive!* (1974), *Demon Seed* (1977), *The Boys from Brazil* (1978), and *The Omen* parts I (1976), II (1978), and III (1981), they were literally the devil (or at least der Fuehrer). Not only were movies about children centered on such degenerate themes; movies *for* children all but disappeared. The percentage of G-rated movies fell by 70 percent from the late sixties to the late seventies.

The Germans have a word for this prevailing anti-child sentiment: *Kinderfeindlichkeit,* meaning "hostility to children." An American term was given to the problem—"popullution." A 1971 survey indicated that two thirds of the general public agreed that it was a serious problem in the U.S. As the authors of one book put it, babies were looked upon "like headaches, things you take pills not to have."

DEFUSING THE BOMB

So how to deal with this predicament? How could we keep people from having so many darn kids? A variety of solutions were proposed in addition to Ehrlich's. Kenneth Bouling, an economist, suggested government licensing of children as the only solution offering a "maximum of individual liberty and ethical choice." Childbearing permits, he recommended, should be issued like housing permits. The *Bulletin of the Atomic Scientist* even checked in with an article called "Licensing: For Cars and Babies." Senator Robert Packwood proposed removing the tax exemption for any child beyond the second. This particular measure was actually enacted to a certain degree (see chapter four). Others wanted to deny college loans to those with large families. Possibly the most extreme measure discussed (fortunately never enacted) was a Tufts Medical School professor's idea of putting fertility-depressing chemicals in municipal water supplies. (Perhaps they could have just mixed it in with the flouride?)

The Nixon administration responded to society's concerns in 1970 by forming the Commission on Population Growth and the American Future. The commission concluded, after two years of deliberation, that "population growth is one of the major factors affecting the demand for resources and the deterioration of the environment in the United States." The final report added that "there are no advantages from further growth of the population beyond the level to which our past rapid growth has already committed us. Indeed we would be considerably better off over the next thirty to fifty years if there were a prompt reduction in our population growth rate." Want to be patriotic? Don't have any children.

The media joined the fray with their own rash of publications and articles on how to get out of this predicament. A number of new books—*The Case Against Having Children, Life Without Birth, The Baby Trap*—espoused the benefits of childlessness. A group of voluntarily childless couples was formed in 1971: NON, the National Organization for Non-Parents, offered support for those who decided to live childless. People wore buttons bearing the slogans "None Is Fun" and "Jesus Was an Only Child." Betty Rollin summed up the arguments neatly in her 1970 *Look* magazine article "Motherhood: Who Needs It?"

Into this environment a somewhat unheralded generation was born.[2]

THE END OF THE BOOM?

What is perhaps the most intriguing element of all this consternation about U.S. overpopulation is that by the time the Nixon commission was formed, the birth rate had already been falling precipitously for a dozen years.

Even though the rate of fertility—the number of children the average woman could expect to have during her lifetime—was cut in half from the late fifties to the midseventies, the *average* annual number of babies born during the Free's birth years was only 6 percent lower than during the Baby Boom, when the "procreation ethic" prevailed. So the term "baby-buster" is somewhat of a misnomer. While the *rate* of births by the early seventies was much lower, the

---

[2]Further indication of the recent change in popular sentiment, Paul Ehrlich's 1989 rehash of *The Population Bomb*, entitled *The Population Explosion*, went virtually unnoticed. Meanwhile, Ben Wattenberg's 1987 book, *The Birth Dearth*, which asserted that Americans weren't having *enough* children, hit the best-seller list and sparked a great deal of discussion.

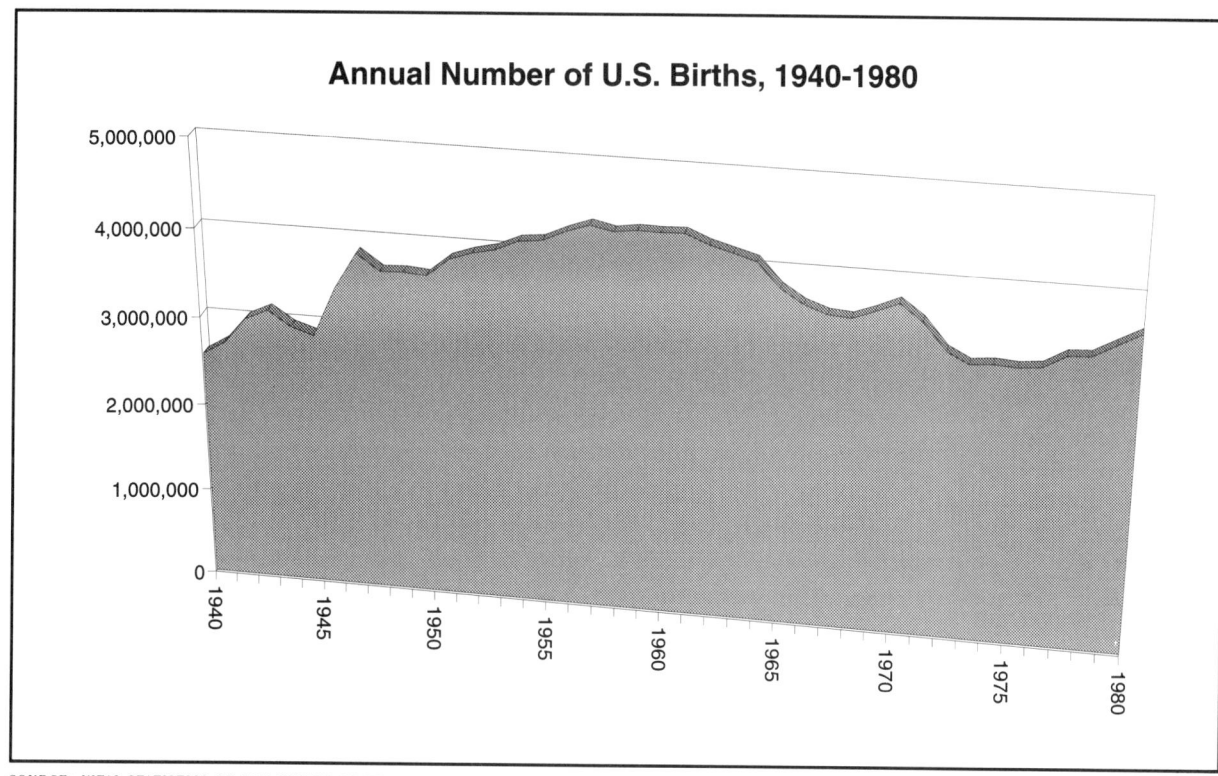

SOURCE: *VITAL STATISTICS OF THE UNITED STATES*

number of women of childbearing age was much higher. The bust wasn't so much a drop in numbers of births as in percentages. Of course, as a proportion of the population as a whole, the Boomers in their youth filled a much larger share than do the Free.

For many of the institutions that deal with children, from maternity wards to schools, having expanded to meet the numbers of births during the peak years meant that even a 6 percent decrease in real numbers was dramatic. Thus, the drop appeared bigger than it actually was, furnishing the idea of a "baby bust." The news was full of stories on plummeting school enrollments. The Cupertino, California, school district saw its student population fall from 23,000 in 1970 to 10,300 in 1986. New York City closed sixty schools between 1975 and 1980. Although the overall numbers of students did decline, of course, the drop wasn't as universal or as steep as such examples would have one believe. After all, eight states in the South and West saw an increase of children under the age of five in the early seventies. In Utah, the gain was 36 percent over the baby-boom days. Added to this overreporting of the issue was the psychological effect of a general decline in births from year to year rather than a rising trend as was seen during the boom. As the vociferous Boomer youth gave way to quieter kids, it simply seemed as if there were a lot fewer children than there actually were.

So why was there not an even bigger baby boom than the original, with so many Boomers reaching peak childbearing years during the sixties and seventies? Fueled by the hostile environment toward children, the number of young couples who remained childless during these years swelled by 75 percent (the term actually mutated from "childless" to "child-free"). During this period, despite the huge increase of young Boomer adults, the number of couples with children increased by only 8 percent. Among those parents who did risk public disapproval by bringing into the world another mouth to be fed, one or two children was usually the limit. In only fifteen years, the odds that a woman with two children would have a third declined by 50 percent. At the same time, the proportion of married women with fewer than two children rose by 40 percent.

Also contributing to the unwelcomeness of children was the birth of the "swinging single." Record numbers of adults simply chose to postpone or forgo marriage. They certainly weren't sticking around Mom and Dad's house though; they were setting out on their own and having fun. Encouraged by a flourishing economy, they were leaving home at an unprecedented young age. The average male in 1970 left the house at nineteen. But this was the generation that came of age during the child-loving fifties, and despite leaving home early, they weren't in any hurry to grow up. Bob Dylan promised them they would stay "Forever Young," and they believed it (Jerry Rubin seconded the idea with his somewhat less eloquent assertion that "we ain't never, never gonna grow up!"). From singles' bars to singles' magazines to the singles' apartment complexes noted at the beginning of chapter one, Boomers were not about to ruin a good thing by having a bunch of kids around. The cult of the child had become the cult of the young adult. Having a kid would spoil all the fun.

2

FAMILY DECONSTRUCTION

1974
Chances that a child is living in poverty:

If living with both parents 8.3%

If living with mother only 51.5%

SOURCE: U.S. BUREAU OF THE CENSUS

Each baby that did manage to be born during these years of *Kinderfeindlichkeit* overcame overwhelming odds simply by coming into existence. The 1960s were also years of great advances in the development and usage of new, efficient birth-control methods. Four years after it was first made available, in late 1960, the first oral contraceptive was already used regularly by 10 percent of married couples. And the numbers rose steadily until, by 1980, one fourth of women of reproductive age were relying on the pill. In the most extreme development in birth control, over a million Americans a year had themselves surgically sterilized during the seventies, a procedure that was almost unheard of just a decade earlier. During the seventies 10 million people made sure that they would never have another child. America's love affair with its children was, at least for now, a thing of the past.

While the debate over abortion has in recent years become an issue over a woman's right to control her own body, and even pro-choice advocates generally disapprove of the use of abortion as purely a contraceptive measure, the atmosphere affecting the Supreme Court's 1973 *Roe v. Wade* decision had another dimension. Before California became the first state to adopt limited abortion rights in 1967, reform on the issue had been proceeding slowly. Two years after this, Planned Parenthood, an influential organization that had worked for the liberalization of contraceptive laws, but that had previously opposed abortion, reversed its stance on this issue. It's speculated that Zero Population Growth wielded

A WHITE ONE FOR TWENTY-ONE DAYS, A PINK ONE FOR SEVEN

some influence in this decision. The tide then began to turn. In 1970, the New York state legislature, by a one-vote margin, enacted the most liberal abortion measure to that time, enabling women to undergo the procedure up until the twenty-fourth week of pregnancy. Then, in 1972, the final report of Nixon's Commission on Population Growth and the American Future—a group committed solely to population concerns—urged that "present state laws restricting abortion be liberalized along the lines of the New York State statute, such abortions to be performed on request by duly licensed physicians under conditions of medical safety."

The commission also recommended that both public funds and private health-insurance benefits be made available to fund abortion services. So while the Supreme Court did rule on the case based on constitutional rights, it appears that some of the lobbyists pressing for the decision had the mere limiting of the number of babies born on their minds as well. In 1973, some wanted abortion not to be, as President Clinton has proposed, "safe, legal, and rare," but rather for it to be safe, legal, and widespread.

HOW MUCH IS ONE OF THOSE THINGS?

With the general feeling of antipathy toward bringing children into the world, one would suppose that to have a baby in this era must imply that the child was truly wanted; to risk such public disapproval, new parents must have treasured their babies. Ann Landers ran a survey in 1975 asking parents to respond to the question "If you had to do it all over again, would you have had children?" The fact that a nationally syndicated columnist would ask this question at all speaks volumes about the country's state of mind, but most disturbing is that out of fifty thousand responses, 70 percent answered "No!"

Parents magazine saw its circulation plummet from 2.1 million in 1971 to 1.4 million in 1979, a 33 percent drop. This decline might be easily dismissed by looking at how the annual number of births dropped by as much as 25 percent compared to the peak of the baby boom. But during the seventies, the total number of parents actually went *up* slightly. One explanation for the declining interest in this magazine is the corresponding decline in the interest in parenting itself.

Gone as well was the American maxim that one should make sacrifices, in both time and money, for the sake of one's children. Indicative of mothers' and fathers' ostensible concern for their children, membership in Parent Teacher Associations began a twenty-five-year decline in membership. And in a series of studies on the American family carried out by Yankelovich, Skelly, and White in the 1970s for General Mills, it was discovered that two-thirds of those with children felt that "parents should be free to live their own lives even if it means spending less time with their children." On top of that, half agreed that "parents should not sacrifice in order to give their children the best." An even higher number endorsed the view that they had the right to live well now and spend what they had earned "even if it means leaving less to the children."

Whereas in the early sixties, an annual survey had shown that children were the number-one priority for gaining happiness, by the early eighties they had dropped to number four. Right behind automobiles. Meryl Streep's character in the 1979 film *Kramer vs. Kramer* captures the spirit of the times. "I have gone away because I must find some interesting things to do for myself in the world," she writes her bewildered eight-year-old little boy. "Everybody has to and so do I. Being your mommy was one thing but there are other things. . . ." A liberating experience for her. A devastating one for the child. David Elkind, a Tufts University expert on child development, writes that this particular film became a minor cult hit among young teenagers at the time, "because the father pays attention to his kid."

The more vocal element of the burgeoning feminist movement made children one of its first proscriptions. "Down with childhood!" cried Shulamith Firestone in her 1970 book, *The Dialectic of Sex.* She argued that the whole concept of childhood being distinct from adulthood was a mere social invention intended only to oppress and subjugate women. Betty Friedan called the traditions of marriage and motherhood a "comfortable concentration camp" for women. Kate Millet suggested that parenthood be completely taken over by specialists through collective professionalization of the task. Paid, efficient child-care workers would replace mothers and fathers. Going one step further, Germaine Greer recommended the founding of a huge baby farm in Italy where children would be raised by a "local family" and could occasionally be visited by mothers and fathers jetting over during pauses in their busy work schedules. Children were essentially a necessary, but unpleasant, burden.

Another popular topic of discussion in the seventies was the "cost" of raising a child. Factoring in the "opportunity costs" of a woman's lost wages and the price of a college education, *U.S. News & World Report* put the total figure in 1977 at $326,000. Apparently, each child left unborn fattened the wallets of the prospective parents by this amount. With the "return on investment" of children questioned for the first time, rising "opportunity" and social costs made the yield appear meager indeed.

Parents had other reinforcements in their attitudes toward their kids. The early seventies saw a number of writers insist that treating children as, well . . . children was not only a burden to adults, but was also unfair to the young ones. In his 1974 book *Birthrights,* Richard Farson argued that child-labor laws have not been beneficial to children, but rather have "successfully prevented the child from fulfilling his economic needs and . . . therefore, kept him in a helpless and dependent position." He called for an end to such "ageism," describing the superior fashion by which other cultures treat their youngsters: "As soon as they can toddle, the children of the East African Chaga are at work looking after smaller babies, carrying water or firewood, helping to prepare food, cleaning animal quarters, sweeping the yard, cutting fodder, and thatching the house." John Holt wrote in *Escape from Childhood* that children, by "exploiting their cuteness," are not the innocent little creatures that we've all been duped into believing, and adults who fawn all over them only encourage this subterfuge. "Some five-year-olds and younger, as much as any adult, are uptight, guarded, devious, calculating . . . manipulators and con men," Holt asserted. They "do almost everything they do, including smile and laugh, to get an effect or reward." He advocated a sort of children's bill of rights including the rights to vote, work, choose their own guardian, have a guaranteed income, control their own learning, and drive. He added, "I don't think we should 'protect' children against whatever drugs their elders use." Although these books masqueraded as champions of children's rights, most of the prescribed "rights" were actually added duties. Their underlying message is that children are burdensome and should pull their own weight.

SEXY YOUNG THINGS

One trend that illustrates the blurring distinction between childhood and adulthood seen during the Free's youth was the late-seventies' fad of young models and actresses assuming not-so-young roles. Jodie Foster began this craze with her stunning portrayal of a twelve-year-old prostitute in the 1976 film *Taxi Driver*. Even though the character's sexually explicit scenes were played by a double—Foster's older sister, Connie—the audience didn't know this. To prepare for the part, it was unblushingly circulated that the thirteen-year-old Foster spent a month of her summer vacation in satin hot pants and six-inch platforms walking a beat on Manhattan's Lower East Side. (No, she was not picked up.)

Brooke Shields did her own nude scene as the preteen prostitute in Louis Malle's 1978 film *Pretty Baby*. In one scene, Shields was carried on a platter into a room and auctioned off as "the finest delicacy New Orleans has to offer." Although a number of magazines expressed outrage at the film's premise previous to its release, most of these articles were also accompanied by seductive photographs of the young girl.

Brooke Shields also led the trend toward increasingly younger models. *Time* magazine proclaimed her face "the look of the eighties" when she was all of sixteen years old. In a series of print and television ads for Calvin Klein blue jeans, the young model titillated consumers with her declaration that "nothing comes between me and my Calvins." Klein himself proclaimed the ads "a major statement." Shields was not an isolated phenomenon. When an advertisement ran in the *Village Voice* seeking young models, parents showed up in droves, dragging their daughters along. On one episode of the television show "The Facts of Life," a character lied about her age to a modeling agent so that he wouldn't fire her. She told him she was thirteen when she was really fifteen. The real-life ads that featured these young girls were not geared for readers of *Tiger Beat*. The girls were usually made up and dressed in very adult outfits that belied their youth. In 1981, Shields became the youngest model ever to grace the cover of *Cosmopolitan*.

While some of these ads and films were unquestionably in bad taste (if not outright cases of child exploitation), the issue of sexual depictions of children had exploded by 1981. On May 12 of that year, New York State's highest court ruled that the state could *not* prohibit the use of children in portrayals of sexual activity in books, films, photographs, or plays. The exception? The work had to be judged "obscene." By requiring the finding of obscenity, the court of appeals, in a five-to-two vote, made it considerably more difficult to obtain a conviction in a child-pornography case. The judges weren't discussing showing a baby's bottom in a diaper commercial; the law that was oveturned in the decision had been directed at stopping those who use children in such conduct as "actual or simulated sexual intercourse, deviate sexual intercourse, sexual bestiality, masturbation, sadomasochistic abuse or lewd exhibition of the genitals." Because the interpretation of obscenity is determined on an individual basis, with standards varying from one community to the next, the rights of children would not necessarily be safeguarded.

Ironically, on the same day, the same court ruled unanimously that a person who forces another to touch his genitals may be found guilty of sexual abuse in the first degree. Apparently child actors and models didn't deserve the same protection. In citing two United States Supreme Court decisions that allowed states to prohibit the sale of sexual materials to children, the two dissenters of the kiddie-porn ruling wrote, "It would seem clear that the state's interest in the prevention of abuse of children in the creation of sexually exploitive literature involving children is at least as compelling as the interest in preventing them from reading it." The majority apparently didn't think so. In these years of childhood often becoming increasingly perilous, even the courts were disinclined to offer relief.

LIVING IN A BOX

To illustrate the degree to which the pendulum of the view of children had swung from one generation to the next, one can look at the work of B. F. Skinner. The renowned behavioralist published a best-selling book in 1971 titled *Beyond Freedom and Dignity*, advocating the idea that society can no longer tolerate freedom in mankind and this must be replaced by control over his conduct and his culture. The book espoused the belief that humans are akin to machines or Pavlovian dogs, and that they can and should be raised with a strict "interchange between control and countercontrol." Children should be reared in a manner akin to programming a computer, with the ultimate goal being to reform society according to the ideals of a sagacious leader (presumably Skinner). The behavioralist raised his own daughter literally in a glass box for her first two and a half years. Around one thousand of these so-called air cribs were in use in 1971. The *New York Times* called *Beyond Freedom and Dignity* the most important book of the year. *Time* magazine ran a cover story on Skinner and his theories asserting that he "is the most influential of living American psychologists."

It's interesting to note that Skinner had published the same ideas, in even less emphatic terms, in his 1953 book, *Science and Human Behavior,* and in a 1948 fictional depiction of his theories in action, *Walden Two*. At that time, however, his robotic notions of raising children received relatively little attention, the public apparently not finding his ideas too palatable. Skinner himself describes this phenomenon in the introduction to a reprinting of *Walden Two*. "The public left [the book] alone for a dozen years. Then it began to sell, and the annual sales rose steadily on a compound interest curve." By the mid-seventies, the previously ignored book had sold a million and a half copies. Clearly something had changed.

IT'S A MAD, MAD, MAD, MAD WORLD

Perhaps because of America's tribulations and ultimate defeat in Vietnam, perhaps as a reaction to a decade of devastating political assassinations, perhaps as a repercussion of the Watergate scandal which brought about the demise of a president, by the seventies, Americans had seemed to completely lose faith in "the system." In a 1979 speech, President Carter addressed the "national malaise" that had swept the country. Whatever its origins, people simply didn't consider the world a very pleasant place anymore, and their children absorbed this sentiment.

As David Elkind wrote at the time in his best-seller *All Grown Up with No Place to Go,* "Society no longer seems to regard children as innocent or to see innocence as a positive characteristic." It was widely presumed that allowing children to be exposed to the hostility, corruption, and injustices that are so prevalent in the adult world would somehow protect them from these evils and enable them to succeed in this world where nice guys finish last. Perhaps we wouldn't be raising a generation of saints, went the idea, but at least our kids would have the necessary survival tools. Like the benefits of a woman taking a self-defense course or a banker being taught how to deal with a robbery, the assumption was that a "streetwise" kid was a safe kid.

Judy Blume, in defense of her hyperrealistic books written for Free adolescents, wrote, "I hate the idea that you should always protect children. They live in the same world we do." A divorced New York mother told Marie Winn in her book *Children Without Childhood* that children "might as well find out sooner than later that life can be complicated and unfair and infuriating." Alayne Yates advised parents in her 1982 book *Sex Without Shame* that at seven years of age, if your "child is not yet masturbating he should be." She went on to give tips on how to encourage this. "Brothers and sisters may experiment with each other," she suggested. "Most sibling incest doesn't cause emotional damage." There wasn't much encouragement for allowing children to do what comes naturally—act like children.

Annie Gottlieb, in her groovy Boomer chronicle, *Do You Believe in Magic?*, casually excused this open parental attitude toward children by, in essence, blaming Boomers' own parents for being "overprotective." "We had enormous security as kids," said one man interviewed in her book. But this was not something to be grateful for. "We couldn't breathe," he complained. Because of this horrible childhood background of their own, he noted that this group, now parents themselves, actively "tried to suppress our instinctive protectiveness." Observing the new parent-child relationships, one therapist confessed, "Sometimes I think I'm too old-fashioned to practice in today's world. Half the time the children act like adults and the adults behave like children."

The children who grew up in such an environment did bear a certain burden of accepting a forced maturity. The fact is that children simply can't absorb some of the horrible realities of the world as easily as adults. While this is common sense to most, the idea was twisted around profoundly in the midst of our "national malaise."

Children absorb the values, morals, and attitudes of the adults who are closest to them. If parents present the world as a positive place, their kids grow up with this view. If parents present the world as a dangerous, undesirable place, their kids assimilate this idea. During the Free's youth many may have considered it hypocritical to keep some of the more unpleasant details of the adult world from their children. But without knowing that adults can control their impulses, without learning that self-discipline and commitment can breed success, and without a clear understanding of right from wrong, children have a hard time seeing any hope or promise in adulthood. And you wondered where gangsta rap and Guns N' Roses came from.

BREAKING UP ISN'T SO HARD TO DO

When billionaire banker Seward Prosser Mellon and his wife, Karen Leigh Boyd Mellon, divorced in 1974, they were riding the crest of a divorce wave that had begun a decade and a half earlier. Custody of the couple's two little girls—Catherine, age seven, and Constance, age five—was awarded to the father by a Pennsylvania court. But in December 1975, when the girls were visiting their mother, she decided she didn't want to give them back, and she took them to New York and obtained a court order there that granted *her* sole custody of the girls. A few months later, however, Mr. Mellon had Catherine and Constance abducted on their way to school and brought back to Pennsylvania, where he had originally been given custody. In turn, Mrs. Mellon sought help from New York authorities in enforcing her own court order and having the girls returned, but the district attorney determined after investigating the situation that there were no grounds for prosecution. Since their father had legal custody of the girls according to the original Pennsylvania ruling, he had the right to keep them while in that state. As their parents fought a battle in a society that wasn't yet equipped to handle all the consequences of divorce, the little girls were run through an emotional wringer.

In 1972, Judith Wallerstein began what would be a fifteen-year study of the effects of divorce on sixty families in California. She arranged to meet the legendary anthropologist Margaret Mead for a few clues as to what she might expect to find. "Judy," Mead lamented, "I don't think anybody can predict what you will find." As Wallerstein began this pioneering investigation, the divorce rate had already been skyrocketing for a decade and was at a peak level, where it would remain for the next fifteen years. Yet the effects of the dissolution of a family on the children involved were virtually unknown. The experiment had begun.

In 1961, when the first of the Free were coming into the world, America saw 375,000 divorces involving a half-million children—a statistic that had been steady for a few decades. Ten years later, the yearly rate had risen to 650,000 divorces affecting nearly a million children. Within another five years, the rate had spiraled higher yet, and 1975 saw a million married couples split up, with more than 1.1 million children touched by the social phenomenon. A similar number of the Free saw their parents' marriage dissolve *each year* from that point on. It's

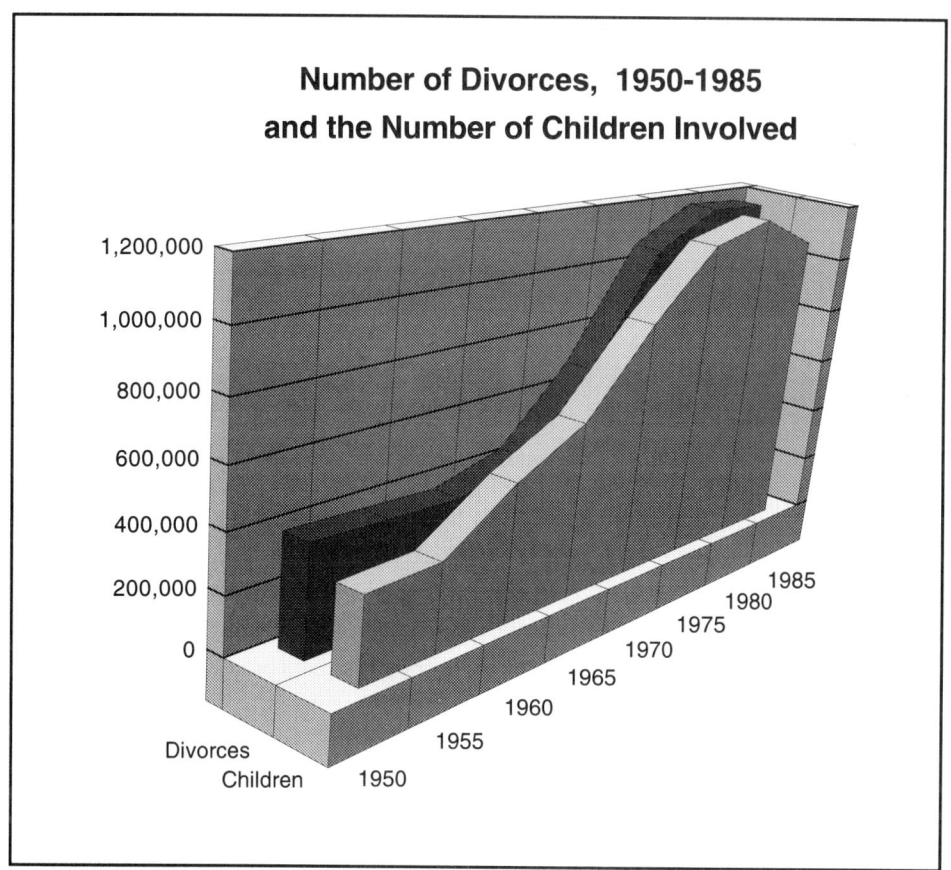

Number of Divorces, 1950-1985 and the Number of Children Involved

SOURCE: U.S. DEPARTMENT OF EDUCATION

estimated that more than 40 percent of the Free at present are children of divorce, compared to only 11 percent of those born during the fifties. In addition, the number of unwed mothers also doubled in only two decades, making the chances about fifty-fifty that today's young adults spent at least some time living with a single parent. Yet the first widespread studies showing the effects of this drastic shift in parenting didn't appear until the early eighties. Too little, too late. In the fifties, Ward and June Cleaver fretted over whether or not to allow Beaver to play with the son of divorced parents. Making that decision thirty years later would have been much easier. If they were to disallow contact with children of divorced parents, the Beav wouldn't have had too many friends.

Before comprehensive studies began to appear, sentiment toward children had changed so much that in the early seventies it was simply assumed that what was good for parents was good for kids. Wallerstein writes that "the adult who sees di-

FAMILY DECONSTRUCTION 27

vorce as the remedy to a conflict-ridden marriage and hopes for an improved family life expects, not unreasonably, that the child, too, will share the parent's relief and hope for a brighter future." Many even espoused the belief that divorce will invariably improve the relationships between parents and children because the interactions would now be free from the pain and friction of the marriage.

If what was good for Mom and Dad was good for Junior, then there was no question in society's eyes about the benefits of divorce. One *Newsweek* writer observed in a 1967 article, "Divorce may be evolving—at least in the fashion and society pages—into something of a status symbol. The stereotype of the gay New York divorcee has never seemed more in vogue. Having deposited the children at the Hewitt School, we are told, she flits from Kenneth's to Kounovsky's Gym to Henri Bendel; lunch is spent at La Grenouille with the sorority, dinner on the patio with 'the new man.'" With the publication of Betty Friedan's *The Feminine Mystique* and, much more significant, the rise of the self-fulfillment movement and the general disdain for "the system," divorce became almost a moral and political imperative. After all, marriage and family were just further examples of the "oppressive institutions" that shackled us all. Asserted one popular book on divorce, "The parents who take care of themselves will be best able to take care of their children." Of course children benefited from these new freedoms. They would have to.

Even if one empathized with the difficulties that children experienced in the face of divorce, it was assumed that children "bounce back." They are "flexible" and "resilient." They easily "adapt." In his 1974 book, *Creative Divorce: A New Opportunity for Personal Growth*, Mel Krantzler naively assured parents that "children can survive *any* family crisis without permanent damage—and grow as human beings in the process . . ." (my italics). In other words, any problems children endured as a result of divorce were really no problem at all.

The results of this enormous experiment are coming in, and it looks like the original hypotheses were more than a little off. While divorce is typically a liberating experience for the couple involved—80 percent of the divorced parents in Wallerstein's study reported being happy about their decision—the needs of their kids have been largely ignored. Krantzler's 268-page self-help book for divorcing couples, for example, devoted only a single, short chapter to the well-being of the children. The parents of the Free widely believed the assumption that children are very perceptive in noticing their parents' marital problems and therefore the dissolution of a marriage is typically not a great shock. Because of this misconception, as Wallerstein's study shows, 80 percent "of the youngest children studied were not provided with either an adequate explanation or assurance of continued care. In effect, they awoke one morning to find one parent gone." She also found that the big announcement, when made at all, was too brief and did not include any assurances for the children that their needs were being considered. In not a single case in this study was adequate attention given to the child's concerns or to instilling a sense of security about what the future might bring.

An indication of the difference in the way the parents and the children perceived the pre-divorce family situation is that a year and a half after their parents' divorce, two-thirds of the children in Wallerstein's California study saw no improvement in their family life. Only one child in five fully approved of their parents' decision after this period of time. Even after five years, while four out of five of the parents considered their post-divorce life to be better than before, more than half of their kids still reported little or no improvement. And nearly a third continued to strongly disapprove of the split.

The initial problem that children in most studies faced when experiencing a divorce was that their parents often stopped parenting. The children had to confront the sorrows and pressures of the divorce without a great deal of adult support. Wallerstein writes that "parental care often diminishes, not because parents are necessarily less loving or less concerned with their children during divorce, but because the radical alterations in their lives tend to focus their attention on their own troubles." During the period immediately following a breakup, Wallerstein found that only about one in ten of the children felt that their parents were empathetic and sensitive to their concerns.

Even with the rising popularity of no-fault divorce laws, a couple, particularly where children are involved, generally agonizes over the decision to divorce, and it is not surprising that they find themselves preoccupied with their own problems. Paradoxically, however, a child who sees his mother and father split up most likely needs a parent's comfort more than ever. As Wallerstein notes, the family structure "supports [children's] psychological, physical, and emotional ascent into maturity. When that structure collapses, the children's world is temporarily without supports."

Writer Barbara Dafoe Whitehead notes that following a divorce, "all too often the adult quest for freedom, independence, and choice in family relationships conflicts with a child's developmental needs for stability, constancy, harmony, and permanence in family life." Divorce often means not only the loss of one parent, but in many ways, the loss of both. Especially in the months immediately following divorce, but sometimes lasting for a period of years, Wallerstein's study showed, some children not only had to take care of themselves, but they had to look after the distraught parent as well. The wave of parent-child role-reversal movies in the late seventies and eighties—*Freaky Friday* (1977); *Like Father, Like Son* (1987); *Vice Versa* (1988)—reflects this profound and unprecedented shift in many children's lives.

AFTER THE FALL

Divorce often causes upheaval in a child's life beyond simply seeing his family break apart. One study showed that within the first three years following the divorce, two-thirds of the children had been forced to change their place of residence. A substantial number had to move three or more times. Typically, the move was prompted by economic needs—cheaper housing, jobs, better child care. When a child has to leave behind friends, neighbors, and family, it's traumatic enough. Coming on the heels of his parents' splitting up, it can be overwhelming.

Contrary to Mel Krantzler's assertion that "children can survive any family crisis," English psychiatrist Michael Rutter has demonstrated that children usually can absorb a *single* stressful experience without much risk, but the same isn't true of additional stresses. Multiple shocks such as the divorce itself, moving, changing schools, mother going to work for the first time, and new child-care arrangements all add up to increasingly adverse effects. Notes Whitehead, "Anyone who knows children knows they are deeply conservative creatures. They like things to stay the same." As a model of stability preserved, the Free adored the Brady Bunch, two shattered families who were able to come together and form a new family, a replacement that was in every way as desirable as the original. The television parents and children melded seamlessly into their new situation with a wonderful lack of pain, distress, and grief. The Bradys were a comfortable reminder of the way things used to be, the way children felt things *should* be. The series retains a cult popularity to this day. In the world outside the television, though, the decision to divorce usually marks the beginning of a troubling, rather than trouble-free, time. What's more, the increasing numbers of children of never-married mothers experienced many of the same difficulties as children of divorce.

Such tumult can have a variety of detrimental psychological effects. A 1988 survey by the National Center for Health Statistics found that children in single-parent families were two to three times as likely to have emotional and behavioral problems as children living with both parents. A number of studies have found that the populations of clinics that treat such problems tend to have an overrepresentation of children of divorce. This experience is not something that is easily left behind, and a number of the Free have sought help years after the split. Given the consequences of increasingly frail parent-child ties, the tremendous growth of the therapeutic industry comes as no surprise.

A more easily measured immediate effect for most children with a single parent is their financial well-being. Children living with only one parent are five times as likely to be poor as those in two-parent families. Since the great majority of children go with their mother following a divorce, when she is poor, they are poor. After tracking the effects of divorce from the mid-sixties to the mid-eighties in a study titled "5,000 Families," economists Saul Hoffman and Greg Duncan have determined that a woman can expect a 30-percent decline in her standard of living following the split. This is one area in which divorce costs all of society—divorce is the single most commonly given reason for a person's going on welfare.

Notwithstanding the obvious consequences of a serious income decline—inadequate housing and medical care, for example—the emotional aspects of a child's sudden immersion in a less solid financial situation can be just as damaging. "Children of divorce feel less protected economically," writes Wallerstein. "From an early age, these children are aware of money." As if the Free didn't already have enough adult responsibilities thrust upon them, money worries added to the overall anxiety. Unfortunately, the decline in living standards is usually a condition that remains a permanent part of post-divorce childhood. A staggering 75 percent of single-parent children spend some time below the poverty level before they reach age eighteen, and more than one in five spend seven years or more in this dire financial situation. Although a 1977 study by the Carnegie Council on Children had presumed that "the greater availability of jobs for women means that more middle-class children today survive their parents' divorce without a catastrophic plunge into poverty," such a rosy conclusion has clearly proven to be greatly mistaken. With the turns the economy has taken, not only two parents but two incomes have become a necessity for a growing number of families.

THE DISAPPEARANCE OF THE FATHER

A number of studies indicate that losing one parent puts children at other long-term disadvantages compared to those living in intact families. The first area in which parents often notice deterioration is a child's schoolwork. A report by the National Association of Elementary School Principals noted a significant discrepancy in the educational achievements of children from intact and single-parent families. Children living with just one parent were nearly twice as likely to be low achievers. Other studies have shown a direct link between SAT scores and family status. In general, the condition of our schools, as discussed in later chapters, was hardly adequate to compensate for the dissolving family.

The problems of keeping children in school at all also seem to be exacerbated by divorce. A University of Michigan study showed that children who had gone through a divorce were five times more likely than other students to be either expelled or suspended, and were also twice as likely to repeat a grade. Children in disrupted families also dropped out of high school altogether at nearly twice the rate of those in intact families. As educational debate in the seventies centered around topics such as curriculum reform, racial desegregation, and self-esteem building, an underlying, close-to-home problem continued to fester.

Barbara Ehrenreich has noted that divorce doesn't affect men and women the same way. "The result of divorce," she says, "in an overwhelming number of cases, is that men become singles and women become single mothers." Studies on the Free have shown that after divorcing, fewer than half of their fathers maintained an active parental role. In most cases, divorce truly did indicate the loss of one parent.

A large-scale study by University of Pennsylvania sociologists, for instance, following a national sample of one thousand children of disrupted families between 1976 and 1987, found that 42 percent had not seen their fathers at all in the last year. And only *one in five* had slept over at their father's house in the previous month. Boomers liked to complain that their *Organization Man* fathers were emotionally distant men who devoted all their energy to their work, came home only to eat and sleep, and had little left to offer the kids. For many of the Free, having a father at all was worthy of appreciation. While single mothers were struggling to make ends meet, the absence of a father was having far-reaching effects on the kids.

A long-term study conducted by Dr. Mavis Hetherington in the seventies compared teenage girls from divorced homes living with only their mothers with those from intact families. The study, controlling for factors such as birth order and economic situation, determined that girls from broken homes were much more aggressive and forward with boys. They were more likely to seek attention and approval from males and tended to hang out in places that boys frequent. While on the surface the girls might seem to have gained assertiveness and self-assurance, the researchers found that the girls' aggressive behavior was simply a response to low self-esteem. The girls themselves reported more feelings of insecurity around boys and men, and less control over their lives in general, than those from intact families. The girls weren't self-assured at all; they were desperate for affection. The problems seemed to be more acute if a girl's parents divorced when she was very young.

These conclusions were supported when Hetherington contacted the girls a number of years later. Those with divorced parents had been more likely to marry at an earlier age and also to be pregnant at the time of marriage. In addition, the husbands of these women typically had achieved a lower level of education and career attainment, and were also more likely to be in trouble with the law. What's more, other studies have shown that daughters of single parents are nearly twice as likely as others to dissolve their own marriages. Whether the benefits of living with both parents were due to the example of seeing a lasting relationship, or due to factors such as the added discipline of having two caregivers, those from an intact family apparently had something that gave them the confidence and discretion to avoid unhealthy relationships.

For boys, the price of a missing father often seems to be delinquency. Nationwide, more than 70 percent of all juveniles in state reform institutions come from homes where there was no father present. Even when income discrepancies are taken into account, boys from single-mother homes are substantially more likely to commit a crime and wind up in the courts. Those from fatherless homes are also more likely to be repeat criminals. *Fortune* writer Myron Magnet concludes, "Ominously, the most reliable predictor of crime is neither poverty nor race but growing up fatherless." The million children a year affected by divorce and the hundreds of thousands who were born without a father during the seventies may help to explain the skyrocketing crime rates of the Free a decade later, as discussed in chapter eight.

Some research indicates that children of divorce and single-parenthood have troubles making other long-term commitments as well. A study of Peace Corps volunteers, for example, found that those who were raised in single-parent families were much more likely not to complete their scheduled overseas tours than those from intact families. Other studies showed that boys with divorced parents are more likely to choose instant gratification over being patient for a more substantial reward. They tend to live for the present at the expense of future benefits.

Of course, it's impossible to generalize about all children of divorce, but looking at the Free Generation as a whole does seem to support some of these unfortunate conclusions. The Free, for example, are marrying at a lower rate and a later age than ever before. Educational and economic attainments are both down. And living for the moment has become a credo for a significant number of young adults today—often with dangerous consequences (see chapter six). No one can say exactly how great a factor the frequency of divorce has been in these developments, but there does seem to be more than pure coincidence at work.

HEY DAD, HOW ABOUT A LITTLE HELP?

When pollsters asked fathers in 1976 whether providing for children was a "life goal," the number that answered yes was less than half the number who answered yes to the same question in 1957. If nothing else, one must commend their candor.

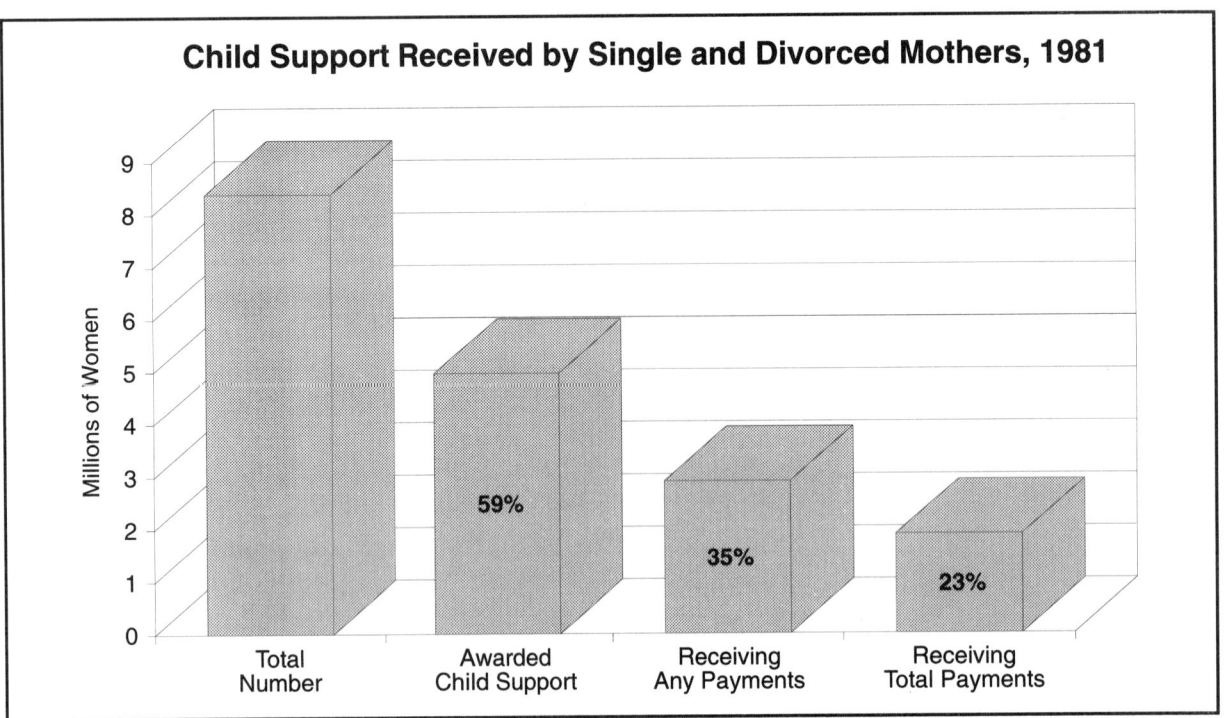

Child Support Received by Single and Divorced Mothers, 1981

	Millions of Women
Total Number	~8.4
Awarded Child Support	59%
Receiving Any Payments	35%
Receiving Total Payments	23%

SOURCE: U.S. BUREAU OF THE CENSUS

Greatly contributing to the economic woes of post-divorce children—and their mothers—is the high probability that the fathers were negligent in their child-support obligations. The typical child-support payment the Free's fathers were ordered to pay was surprisingly low; in 1983, the average award was only $1,430 a year per child—about $120 a month—only half of what a parent would need to keep the child fed, clothed, housed, and cared for at a *poverty-level* standard of living. For black mothers, the average amount was a meager $322 a year. What's more, a 1981 Census Bureau study determined that of the roughly 9 million women raising children without the father present, only 59 percent had even been awarded support payments (see chart above). Yet only one in three was actually receiving any payments at all, and a third of these were not receiving all of the modest amount that had been mandated. So only about one child in five was receiving full support payments from his father after a divorce. What's more, the women most likely to receive court-ordered support were those who were educated and employed, not those most in need, and unwed mothers were almost guaranteed not to be awarded *any* child support. Small wonder that in the divorce-plagued seventies, children became the most impoverished segment of our society.

Adding to the financial woes from the skyrocketing divorce rates, the likelihood of children receiving support payments actually declined from the sixties to the eighties. Perhaps the myth that a single mom's income was now adequate to raise a family convinced fathers that their help was not needed or wanted. Between 1978 and 1985 alone, the average amount of child support that men paid fell by nearly 25 percent. In the eighties, men were more likely to meet their car payments than their child-support payments, even though, according to one study, for two thirds of them their monthly car payment was *higher* than the amount owed to their children! To top it off, many states lowered the top age that children were granted support from twenty-one to eighteen, absolving fathers from contributing toward college costs, and even allowing them to cut off support to some children still in high school. Yet some still referred to the eighties as "the Daddy Decade," or what author Kyle Pruett called the age of *The Nurturing Father*.

If divorced men had been as poor as their former wives, one might have been able to empathize with the high default rates of child-support payments. Yet a study by Martha Hill found that in only 10 percent of the cases where the mother was in poverty was the father also poor. And in only one case in fifty would the father have become poor had he been forced to devote a high enough percentage of his income to equalize his children's living standard with his own. Cases of fathers owing tens of thousands of dollars in back support were not rare. It wasn't that men weren't paying their share because they couldn't; they weren't paying because they *wouldn't*.

One might expect rigid enforcement of child-support payments in the face of such widespread negligence, but before the mid-eighties there was little a mother could do to compel the father of her children to pay his share. In response to the situation, national legislation was passed in 1984, giving states more tools for enforcing such payments, but by 1988, only $5 billion of the $25 billion in back child support had been collected. And a federal audit completed that year found that thirty-five states weren't even complying with the federal laws. In the fall of 1988, Congress passed welfare-reform legislation that finally gave states the ability to garnish back support payments from the paychecks of deadbeat dads beginning in 1994. In addition, support amounts will be determined by state standards rather than the often capricious determinations of individual judges.

It is notable that fathers fighting for some custody have in recent years become the rule rather than the exception in divorce court. Of course, this may reflect little more than the fact that Free men are increasingly the *fathers* involved, rather than the children, as they were in the seventies. Perhaps experience has taught them that children need both a mother and a father, and they are determined not to repeat so many of their parents' mistakes.

MEET YOUR NEW FAMILY

The final consequence of the exploding divorce rate of the Free's parents was the ensuing growth in the number of stepfamilies. Once merely the villainous antagonists of fairy tales, stepmothers and stepfathers became common enough to the Free Generation to engender the clarifying expressions "my real mother" and "my real father." While a second marriage often gave everyone involved a chance at a fresh start, as with most social developments of the times, the situation was not without its own set of problems.

By the late eighties, 6.8 million kids—20 percent of all children in married-couple families—were stepchildren. While divorced parents can look upon a second marriage as an antidote to the problems associated with a divorce, the children don't usually see it in such a simple way. A second marriage did usually bring another income into the family and could alleviate some of the financial difficulties, but children could see this new parent in a number of lights, ranging from a welcome source of stability to an unwelcomed sign that their parents' break was now final. In many cases, the stepfather's arrival, in the child's eyes, primarily meant the loss of the mother.

University of Pennsylvania sociologist Frank Furstenberg cautions, "One of the consistent findings in research is that stepparenthood does not re-create the nuclear family." In Wallerstein's study, more than half of the children resented their stepfathers and 90 percent felt that their lives weren't improved by their having a stepfather. Older children were especially unlikely to develop a good relationship with their stepfather. Those between nine and fifteen seemed to handle the new situation the poorest. Of all relationships created in a stepfamily, the most difficult seems to be that between stepmother and stepdaughters. Psychoanalyst and author Dr. Esther Menaker has found that "at best stepmothers and stepdaughters have a nothing relationship." A second marriage is certainly no cure-all for the problems created by a divorce.

As a group, say psychologists, stepchildren also have more developmental, emotional, and behavioral problems than children in intact families. They are also more likely to be victims of child abuse, particularly sexual abuse, than other children. In fact, a study by Canadian researchers Martin Daly and Margo Wilson found that preschool children in stepfamilies are *forty times* as likely as children in intact families to suffer from physical or sexual abuse. (Most of the abuse wasn't done by the stepparent but by a neighbor, male friend of the stepparent, or other acquaintance.) To top it off, second marriages are even 20 percent more likely to fail than first marriages, once again sending the children on the emotional roller coaster.

As studies of divorce have shown, a good relationship between a child's parents after the breakup is of the utmost importance. But in researcher Glynnis Walker's 1986 survey of divorced families, only 14 percent of the children who lived in new families said they felt good about the relationship between their natural parents and their stepparents. The new family can also adversely affect children's relationships with their "real" parents. A woman whose father had remarried told author Deidre S. Laiken that "I felt like a carry-over, a leftover from a life my father wanted to forget. Every time he looked at me, he saw my mother . . . I was a living reminder of what had failed." Dr. Alan Roland agrees that "in the second marriage, it is not unusual for the father to link the original child with the mother." Some have offered this fact as one reason that fathers seem so unwilling to pay child support.

As the number of stepfamilies continued to climb in the seventies and eighties, many elements of society were slow in responding to the new circumstances of the children involved. In some cases, stepparents were assumed to be equal to biological parents, and in others they were given few parental rights at all. A stepparent's legal right to authorize medical treatment for a stepchild, for example, was not always certain, and few companies included stepchildren in an employee's sick-leave policy. On the other hand, in many cases a college's criteria for financial aid would include a stepparent's income even if the stepparent was unlikely to provide any support for the student's education. A significant portion of the Free were caught in this gap between family reconstruction and society's refusal to adjust.

On the positive side, the presence of a stepfather can check some of the negative effects of a divorce, particularly on boys. One 1972 study found that when a boy's mother remarried, especially if he was younger than five years old, the adverse consequences of his natural father's absence could be reversed. For instance, boys in remarried families are less likely to drop out of school than boys in single-parent families. Unfortunately, however, the converse is true for girls. Of course, the new bonds formed when a divorced man or woman with children remarries aren't necessarily deleterious and can offer needed stability and support. It doesn't come automatically, however. As the authors of a 1989 *Newsweek* article reported, "Happy endings mean hard work from everybody. The commitment begins with the couple." Now that stepfamilies are increasingly common, and we have much more information regarding their possible difficulties, maybe some of the poor consequences can be avoided.

It would be impossible to analyze the Free Generation and leave out the growing problem of the breakup of the family. The phenomenon shows up repeatedly as a factor in a variety of social trends throughout this book and is certainly something that society jumped into with little regard for possible repercussions. Sociologist David Popenoe, who has devoted much of his career to the study of families, sums up the results as follows:

> In three decades of work as a social scientist, I know of few other bodies of data in which the weight of evidence is so decisively on one side of the issue: On the whole, for children, two-parent families are preferable to single-parent and stepfamilies.

Certainly every case of divorce and single-parenthood doesn't result in children who are worse off than those in intact families. But an enormous number of the Free Generation were profoundly affected by the growing dissolution of the family. Although evidence of its consequences is now mounting, a generation has come of age with a greatly altered sense of how to pattern a family, and this will continue to pose challenges to a society that is often slow to adapt.

3

IT'S 3:00 P.M. DO YOU KNOW WHERE YOUR PARENTS ARE?

> 1983 median weekly salary:
>
> Bartenders—$172
> Janitors—$191
> Child-care workers—$63
>
> SOURCE: BUREAU OF LABOR STATISTICS

THE ORGANIZATION WOMAN

Before the 1960s, American women had few opportunities to establish a career. Few jobs outside of teaching or nursing were considered acceptable work for a woman, and even these were widely expected to be ceded once children came along. Future Supreme Court Justice Ruth Bader Ginsberg couldn't land a position other than as a secretary upon graduating from law school in the late fifties. But soon after this, an unprecedented wave of Boomer women graduating from college began to demand better. One of the greatest benefits to arise from the social developments originating in the sixties was that women began to eke out the same freedom to earn a living as men had always enjoyed. Actually, women with children weren't only given the right to go to work; in the overcompensating mind-set of the seventies it became almost an obligation. Mothers who may have desired to stay home to raise a family were made to feel not only guilty about their decision, but also inadequate and undervalued—too incompetent to get "a real job." As former director of the Economic Policy Council Sylvia Ann Hewlett observed, anything was better than being labeled " 'just a housewife'—the contemporary nonperson."

The days of the stay-home mother were, for the majority of the Free, a relic of the past, something to watch while sitting home alone after school on television reruns of *Leave It to Beaver* or the fifties-nostalgia sitcom *Happy Days*. While a small percentage of mothers have always had to work, usually driven by economic need (12 percent of mothers with preschool children worked in 1950), historically nearly all had been at home while their kids were young, and had been home for older children when they returned from school. By 1970, how-

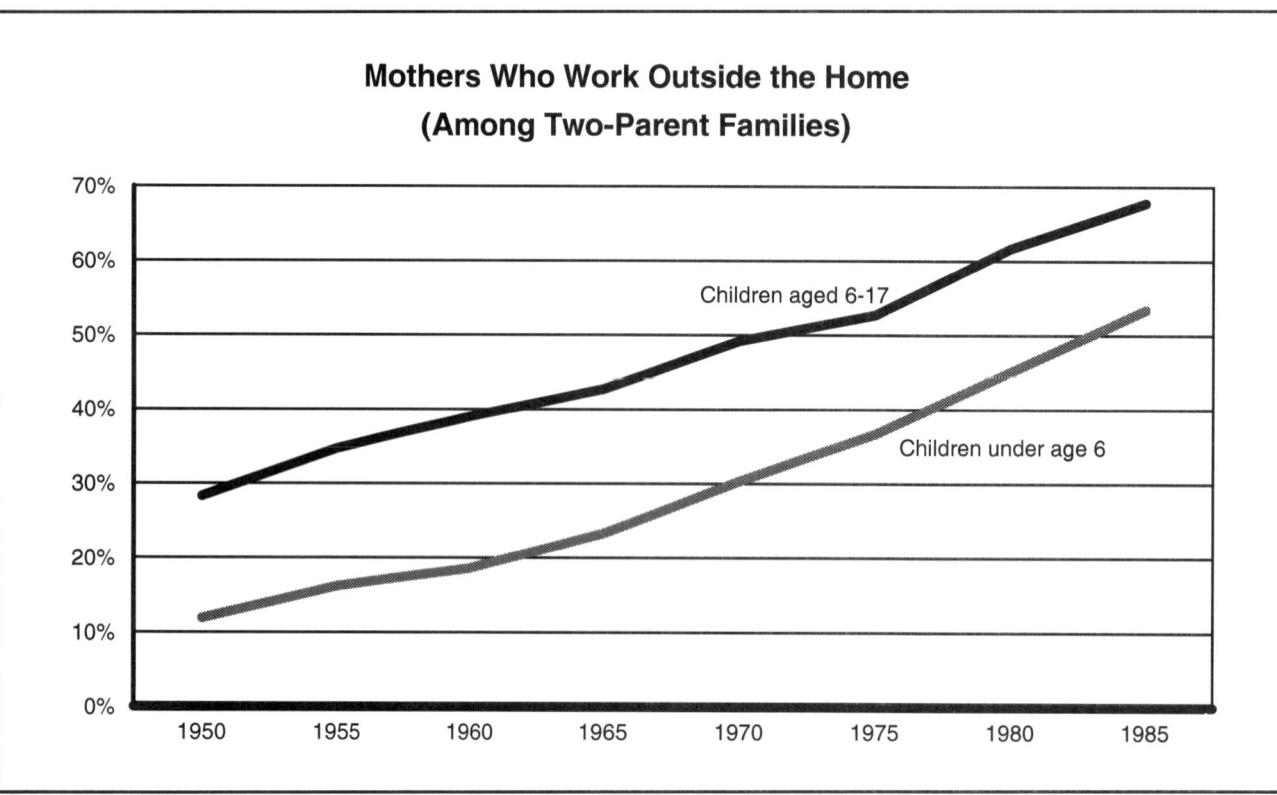

Mothers Who Work Outside the Home
(Among Two-Parent Families)

[Line graph showing two trend lines from 1950 to 1985. "Children aged 6-17" rises from about 28% in 1950 to about 68% in 1985. "Children under age 6" rises from about 12% in 1950 to about 53% in 1985.]

SOURCE: BUREAU OF LABOR STATISTICS

ever, 40 percent of mothers with children were in the workforce, a figure that climbed rapidly, reaching 61 percent by 1985. By the late seventies, a majority of even those mothers with children aged three to five, as well as 39 percent of those with infants under the age of *one*, were working. And these figures represent mothers who were married and living with their husbands; among divorced women with children, a fast-growing segment of society, 80 percent were in the job market.

Despite the growing numbers of working mothers, resistance to making any changes to assist the children who were left at home came from both ends of the political spectrum. The right wing, for the most part, felt that women simply should not be working at all but should stay home for their children. And even women's groups on the left felt that any new programs to benefit children, such as maternity leave for new mothers, were taboo. As management consultant Felice Schwartz recalls, "In the mid-1970s the senior management team at IBM called me in to talk about maternity provisions. My feeling then was . . . we can't talk about it—it would be detrimental to women." Economist Barbara Bergmann wrote that "a policy requiring employers to give such paid leaves has important disadvantages for women. If the employer must pay a woman's salary for a long maternity leave, employers will have a further incentive to keep women out of the high-paying fields." She added that "another disadvantage of long paid maternity leaves for child-rearing is that they reinforce the idea that child-care, and the other family service chores that women do when they stay home, are women's work."

The way we regarded our children underwent a profound change during these years. Rather than doing whatever one could to protect and nourish children, a growing number of parents chose a much more self-centered approach. "Decisions aren't made on the basis of what's best for the child, but what can the child tolerate," complained James Garbarino, a researcher in child development. "With infants, it's how soon can they go to day care so the parents can go to work. With eight- or nine-year-olds, it's how soon can they come home alone. It's all designed to make the participation of adults in the workforce easier." There was a lot of talk about the psychological effects on parents as they left their children to go to work, but not much about the effects on the children.

Naturally there were consequences. As society moved to allow mothers to hold a job—indeed, forced them to do so as the economy changed[1]—it didn't move to accommodate the children that were left behind. Pennsylvania State psychologist Jay Belsky, who has been researching the effects of outside child care for decades, has argued that working parents simply have too much stress in their lives to devote much energy to their children. After a day at the office one wants to relax, not take care of the kids. Even the more direct relationships between parent and child, and between the two parents, suffered from the halfway approach to dealing with the situation. While divorce is certainly a major impetus in forcing women into the workplace, a major study by the Census Bureau has determined that when added to the chores of child care and taking care of the household, the additional stresses that go along with both parents working add to the possibility of a couple's divorcing in the first place! Based on surveys that tracked twenty-four thousand people between 1984 and 1988, researchers found that the rate of divorce or separation in families in which both parents work full-time is 60 percent higher than for other families. Also notable is that the very highest rates were among those families in which *only* the mother works. As *San Francisco Chronicle* writer Torri Minton explains, "You work all day and you come home to a million loose ends—your children need attention, your children need to be fed, your children need to do homework. We didn't ex-

---

[1] A 1986 Gallup poll showed that only 13 percent of working women with dependent children wanted to work full-time. A 1990 survey by Yankelovich, Clancy and Shulman reported that 80 percent of women would quit their jobs or reduce their work hours if they didn't need the money.

actly learn how to balance all this, and the kids too, growing up." The imbalance apparently drove many families apart.

Certainly the answer to the problem wasn't a return to the "good old days" when women had no choice but to stay at home. A 1978 study, for instance, concluded that women who worked outside the home enjoyed greater self-esteem and suffered less anxiety than women who stayed home all day to mind the house and kids. What was (and still is) obviously required to complete the trend of the emerging class of career mothers was additional options for taking care of the children involved. For newborns, as late as 1990 only 44 percent of employers offered even *unpaid* parental leave beyond the disability period, even though the benefits of offering additional benefits are well documented. A Bureau of Labor Statistics study found that between 1981 and 1985, 70 percent of women with paid leave or other benefits returned to work within six months of childbearing, while only 44 percent of those without benefits did so. Additionally, the great discrepancies in pay for men and women that exist also contribute to the fact that many mothers might be working more hours than they would prefer—throughout the seventies, the median pay for women was still only about 60 percent of men's. Correcting this disparity alone would go a long way to freeing up time for parents to spend with their children. For a significant portion of the Free Generation, such reforms would have been welcome indeed.

THE WAREHOUSE GENERATION

In 1971, Congress seemed to be making a real attempt at addressing the issue when it passed the Child Development Act. This piece of legislation was truly revolutionary, providing for government-funded day care for nearly every child in the country who needed it. However, congressional passage was merely a symbolic gesture and would never have gone through were it not for the certainty that President Nixon would veto the bill. After the veto, there was no serious attempt to override it, even though the legislation had originally passed both houses by more than the two-thirds majority that would have been required. With the failure to enact anything a little more realistic in scope, the federal government let the issue slide for the next two decades. In fact, despite the low availability of good day care, Reagan nevertheless slashed Title XX funding, which supports day-care centers, in both the 1981 and 1983 budgets.

A lot of the Free were taken care of by someone other than their parents. Even with birth rates falling from the mid-sixties to the mid-seventies, the number of day-care centers more than doubled. In 1977 two-thirds of those whose mothers worked were looked after by an outside caretaker. The early "expert" opinion outside day care was that there were no ill effects on children. In fact, assertions were even made that children who were out of the home at an early age developed a stronger sense of independence and made friends more easily than others. "We believe that quality infant day care is not only a valuable supplement to exclusive home care," wrote the authors of the 1972 book *Day Care for Infants,* "but in fact may be an improvement over typical home care because it stimulates an infant's physical, emotional, social, and intellectual development." While the studies that came to such conclusions weren't necessarily flawed, they were most often conducted in the most ideal locations—in university-sponsored centers where the child-care workers were frequently students preparing for careers as teachers.

As the authors of a 1978 book on child care explained, the consequences of growing up under the care of a supervisor other than a family member were actually unknown. Explaining their failure to cite concrete studies, the writers admitted that "there *are* no answers about what will happen in the long run to group-reared children." Nevertheless, parents were greatly reassured by early reports, and sent their kids off to baby-sitters and day-care centers that had begun to sprout up from coast to coast. While later studies have confirmed that high-quality day care does not necessarily bring about any harmful consequences in children, and in fact can be beneficial to children from the most deprived backgrounds, this is only half the story. The problem with relying on such studies was that most of the day care available at the time was not high-quality.

In the summer of 1970, the National Council of Jewish Women visited 431 licensed and unlicensed day-care centers across the country that cared for approximately twenty-four thousand children to assess how well the nation's next generation was being cared for. The results were alarming to say the least. Of those centers that were for profit, only 1 percent were rated as "superior" and another 15 percent as "good." Another 35 percent were considered "fair"—indicating that they provided only custodial care—and *half* were rated as "poor." The nonprofit centers, typically government- or church-supported, were better, but half were still only considered "fair" and 10 percent were "poor." In addition, it was estimated that only about 5 percent of the children being cared for outside the home were in licensed centers, meaning that 95 percent were kept under whatever conditions the caretakers happened to determine on their own were adequate.

As Meryl Frank, a consultant on family issues, has succinctly observed, "Good day care may be good for kids, but bad day care is bad for kids." To see how outside care might affect children down the road, UCLA researchers looked at how eighty preschoolers who had been enrolled in day care as infants adjusted to kindergarten. "Children who entered low-quality child care as infants," wrote Carollee Howes, "had the most difficulty with peers as preschoolers." She noted that teachers said the children were easily distracted, less task-oriented, and more hostile. Researcher Jay Belsky has come to similar conclusions. Although he was one of those who originally claimed in the seventies that outside care had no adverse effects, Belsky later reversed his opinion. He now concludes that infants who spend more than twenty hours per week in a day-care center, in another family's home, or in the home being cared for by a nanny, housekeeper, or baby-sitter are at greater risk of developing emotional problems. Nobody can replace Mom and Dad.

TWO BREADWINNERS, ONLY ONE MOM

If one were to name a person responsible for the negative developments associated with so many women joining the workforce, it would have to be the husbands. While women adjusted to the new demands of society and the economy by going to work, thus taking on some of the traditional male role of breadwinning, many men refused to assume some of the traditional female roles of housekeeping and child care.

In 1965, for example, surveys showed that men averaged about nine hours a week doing household chores and caring for children, while women spent about twenty-nine hours in such activities. A decade later, with half of all mothers now in the workplace, women had pared their housekeeping and child-care activities down by four hours, but men had only picked up an additional forty minutes of such work per week. Women and their children were run ragged by these developments, but men's lives changed hardly at all. The Free's fathers weren't so much thoughtless as they were simply slow in adjusting. A 1987 Boston University study found that three-fourths of fathers felt that they *should* share child-care chores equally with the mother, but only 13 percent actually did so.

One additional item of note: Despite the diminished parental availability that resulted from two-career families, the Free don't begrudge their parents this development. Whereas in 1976, 63 percent of high-school seniors felt that "a preschool child is likely to suffer if the mother works," by 1986, only 46 percent felt so (interestingly, a *Fortune* magazine survey of working parents the same year found that more *parents* felt that the children suffered from this situation than the children themselves thought).

Although they were the ones most affected by this trend, the Free seem to have understood that, in this case, their parents were only doing what they felt was necessary to provide for the family. There certainly were some benefits to this trend to counter some of the disadvantages. Seeing Mom go off to work alongside of Dad undoubtedly offered girls a healthier perspective on the opportunities available to them. Perhaps not coincidentally, since 1980 women have outnumbered men on college campuses, and income discrepancies are finally narrowing. With the two-career family now almost an absolute economic necessity, the Free can appreciate the pioneering efforts of their mothers, despite the negative consequences that may have resulted.

4

THE YOUTHFUL FACE OF POVERTY

Taking into account all sources of
income and benefits, in 1983, the age group with:

The lowest percentage living in poverty:
Over 65

The highest percentage living in poverty:
Under 18

1983 Ratio of federal government spending
on the elderly vs. children:
11 to 1

SOURCE: U.S. BUREAU OF THE CENSUS AND *SCIENTIFIC AMERICAN*, DECEMBER 1984

A HISTORICAL FIRST

In 1974, the Free Generation assumed a dubious title from the elderly so-called Lost Generation, those born around the turn of the century, to whom they've often been compared. This newly achieved distinction was that of the most impoverished generation in America. The title was passed directly from the oldest Americans to the very youngest, without ever touching the three generations in between. In this way, the Free are unique. As Senator Daniel Patrick Moynihan has put it, the United States had become "the first society in history in which a person is more likely to be poor if young rather than old." They weren't the poorest children the world has seen in absolute terms, but they were the poorest in relation to the affluence of the rest of the society. Much has been said about "the feminization of poverty" in the U.S. over the last two decades, but even more poignant has been the "youthification" of poverty. That the U.S. allowed its children—its future—to become the poorest members of the community goes a long way in explaining why so many of the Free have developed a disturbing sense of anomie and cynicism about the future.

**Poverty Rate by Age Group
1967-1987**

SOURCE: U.S. BUREAU OF THE CENSUS

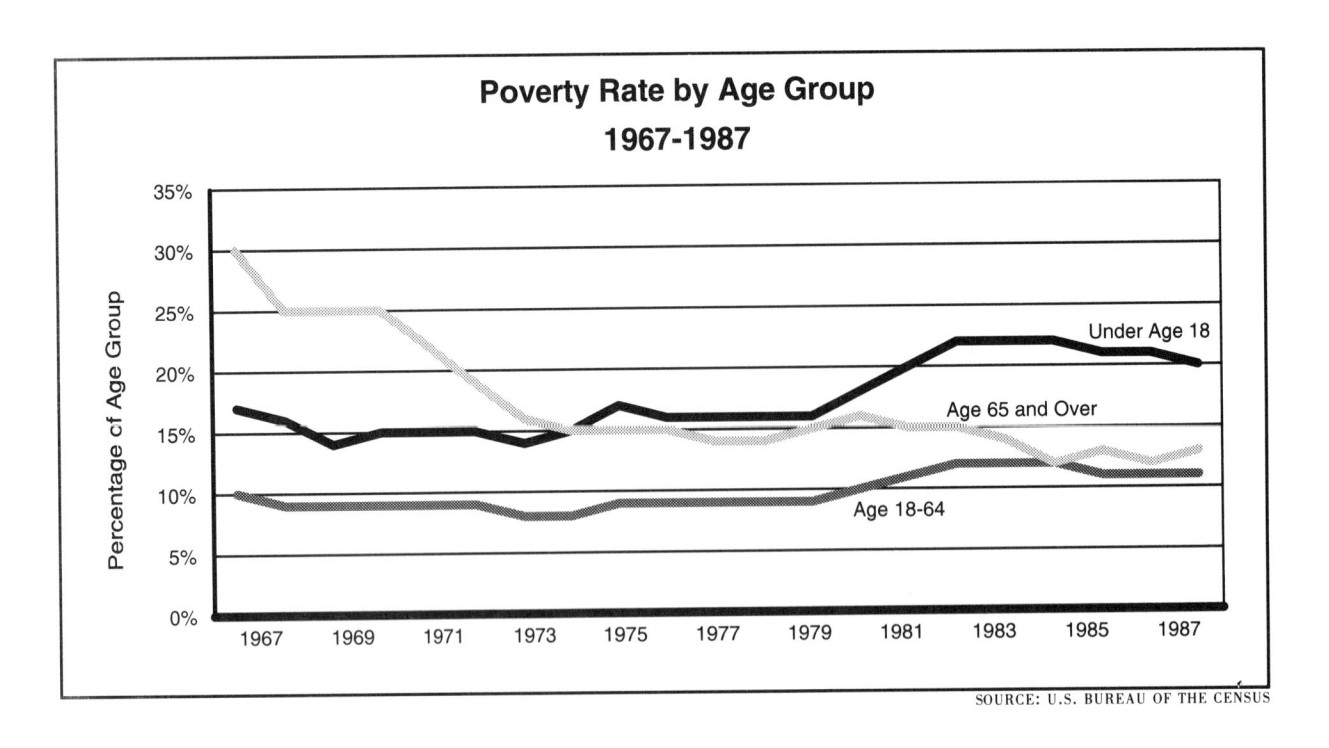

The widespread dissolution of the family was certainly a great contributor to the impoverishment of the Free; David Eggebeen and Daniel Lechter of Penn State have estimated that half of the child poverty rate increase is attributable to higher divorce rates and unwed mothers. But these troubled circumstances were due to specific government actions as much as to any changes in demographics and social trends.

How many poor? Between 1973 and 1984, the percentage of children living below the poverty line increased by nearly two thirds. By the latter date, more than one American child in five under the age of eighteen was poor. The youngest of the Free suffered the most. In 1983, the Census Bureau reported that a staggering 25 percent of those children below the age of six were in this predicament—a total of 13 million children growing up in poverty. For many, the situation was truly dire; *Newsweek* estimated in 1989 that 500,000 of these kids were without even a home. Not since the Great Depression had homeless children been seen begging in the streets of our major cities as they were beginning to in the mid-eighties. It's tempting to explain away this situation as an unfortunate manifestation of a generally poor economy, but what is most striking about these developments is that during these same years the poverty rates for other age groups *fell*—dramatically, in the case of the elderly. The great strides in eliminating child poverty made in the fifties and sixties had been erased, and replaced by great strides in eliminating *everyone else's* poverty.

TIGHT BUDGETS

The downward spiral may have had its origins in events that took place in 1969. That year, President Richard Nixon, advised by Moynihan, proposed the Family Assistance Plan (FAP), a truly revolutionary, comprehensive approach to aiding impoverished families. The program was to include a base of financial support for all poor families regardless of marital or employment status. The FAP was designed to replace the basic Aid to Families with Dependent Children (AFDC), which had always been a clumsy program with erratic, often contradictory eligibility requirements. Congress squabbled over the FAP, the far left and far right unwilling to compromise, and moderates keeping their mouths shut. Eventually the bill was killed, and Southern conservatives controlling the Senate Finance Committee proceeded to tighten the eligibility and employment restrictions on existing programs to an extreme that stunned the liberals who had killed the FAP in the first place. What remained was a hodgepodge of programs that were inconsistent from one state to the next and generally forced intact families to either split up or cheat.[1] Children paid for the congressmen's inability to compromise.

In the two decades after 1970, grants for AFDC recipients fell 40 percent behind cost-of-living increases, and with housing costs skyrocketing even beyond the inflation rate, the real effect of this decline is steeper yet. The result of these cuts was that a large number of families who were on the threshold of poverty slipped beneath it.

By way of comparison, the maximum AFDC benefit in a typical state in 1960 paid 63 percent of the poverty-level income for a family of four. Twenty years later, AFDC was only providing 43 percent of this minimum amount. That critical 20 percent often meant the difference between good nutrition and hunger, satisfactory health care or none. By the mid-eighties, only 12 percent of welfare recipients were actually being lifted out of poverty by the benefits. While one can argue about the necessity or method of implementing welfare reform, it's clear that by this time the system was not doing what it was intended to do.

Not only were the appropriations smaller; the number of children receiving them also shrank dramatically. From 1973 to 1982 the proportion of impoverished children receiving welfare benefits fell by 40 percent. The drop was steady

---

[1] At this time, all fifty states denied welfare payments to families, no matter how poor, in which the father was both working full-time and living at home.

over this period of time, but cuts made by Ronald Reagan early in his administration accelerated the decline. His 1981 Omnibus Budget Reconciliation Act slashed $1 billion off of a total AFDC budget of $7 billion with a single pen stroke. All in all, when budget cuts, program eliminations, and tightened eligibilities are added up, benefits for children and families suffered more than a $50 billion decline from 1980 to 1986. Even basics such as programs to feed people took a painful hit during these years. Among those affected by these cuts were the million people who lost their food stamps, and 2 million kids who were dropped from school lunch programs, as well as all children—to the extent that ketchup suddenly was declared an adequate vegetable in school lunches.

Cuts in welfare weren't the only legislation working against the Free in their youth. The Children's Defense Fund reports that children's share of Medicaid payments, which subsidize health care for the needy, fell from 18 percent in 1972 to 12 percent a decade later. This drop occurred despite a rise in the proportion of children among those eligible for the program. One very visible consequence of this trend is that the United States's ranking among nations in infant mortality worsened from sixth place in the mid-fifties to twentieth place thirty years later. The odds of the youngest Free baby born in the United States making it to his first birthday in 1980 were lower than those of his counterparts in Costa Rica, Romania, and the Soviet Union.

Another area of assistance that was curtailed was in federal housing support, which saw a tremendous drop. Thirty-two billion dollars in federal aid went to families in low-income housing subsidies in 1978. Ten years later the figure had dropped to less than $10 billion—an 80 percent drop in assistance, accounting for inflation. Only one in three renting households below the poverty line were receiving housing aid by the early eighties. Who knows how many of the less fortunate two-thirds ended up on the streets?

Children and families who were poor were not the only ones affected by changes in government policy; the middle class took a hit as well. Whether or not they were fueled by the overpopulation fears of the late sixties and the tax penalties suggested to deal with the problem, families with children saw dramatic increases in their tax bite while childless families saw their taxes remain steady through the seventies and eighties. Although no actual child penalty was imposed, the method by which taxes were adjusted over time amounted to exactly that. In fact, from 1960 to the early eighties, the average family of four experienced a tax increase of more than 200 percent. The federal tax deduction for dependent children saw only one modest increase over a twelve-year period, undergoing a true inflation-adjusted decline of 43 percent.

The tax policies enacted early in the Reagan administration only worsened this trend. Between 1979 and 1982 alone, a family of four earning poverty-level wages watched the percentage of its already low income paid to the federal treasury rise from 2 percent to 10 percent. And despite the fact that two thirds of mothers were in the workforce by the mid-eighties, including as many as 80 percent of single mothers, tax policy at this time still favored married couples with only one worker. In fact, it severely penalized any other family type. This may have been due to a conservative yearning for a return to "family values," or it may have simply been bad policy. Either way, the result was less after-tax income available to the Free, and now to the children of the Free.

These examples deal only with the manner in which children have been affected by tax and social policy in the last few decades. Now that most of the Free are in the workforce, tax changes have affected us to an even more startling degree. This topic is discussed in chapter thirteen.

ROBIN HOOD, AMERICAN STYLE

In the mid-sixties, a number of poverty-busting programs aimed at the elderly were instituted. There was certainly a need for such legislation; in 1967, for example, nearly 30 percent of the over-sixty-five population was living below the poverty line. What happened in the decades to follow, however, is baffling. While the programs that targeted children and young families were allowed to dwindle, those that transferred funds to the elderly—needy or not—expanded at ever-increasing rates. In fact, the one surviving element of the failed 1969 Family Assistance Plan that had originally targeted poor children was the Supplemental Security Income program, which provided further assistance to *elderly* poor. As a result, by the end of the eighties, with all sources of income and benefits considered, the poverty rate for children had risen to *seven times* that of the elderly, who had the lowest rate of any age group. And by that time, the federal government was spending eleven times as much on the elderly as it was on children—a total of $356 billion a year, equivalent to $11,300 for each person over sixty-five, and greater than the total spent on national defense.

In contrast to children's programs, which have seen toughened eligibility requirements in the last two decades, Social Security is still distributed with little or no regard for need. Economist Philip Longman has noted that only 17 percent of these payments are made to families who are actually poor. In addition, health care, which is becoming increasingly unaffordable for the rest of the nation, has become increasingly available and affordable to the elderly, thanks to huge government subsidies.

While it's wonderful that our society has enabled the elderly to live longer and healthier lives than ever before, this hasn't come without a cost. Despite what lobbyists for the elderly claim, the old and the young *are* in direct competition for the limited social-welfare dollars the government spends.

One indication of who won this battle was the 33 percent drop in children's share of Medicaid funds during the seventies. Over the same ten-year period, the elderly's share of Medicaid rose significantly. The fact that the elderly comprise such a powerful electoral group, while children can't vote for themselves, likely contributed to this disparity. "In many cases, Congress quite consciously cut programs for children and young families more than those serving the elderly," noted Robert Greenstein, director of the Center on Budget and Policy Priorities, a private research group in Washington. The result of this transfer of health-care funds is that *one-third* of the hundreds of billions spent annually on health care goes to the elderly, who comprise only 12 percent of the population.

While our international ranking for infant mortality has plummeted, 28 percent of the massive Medicare budget is spent on patients who are in the final year of life. Minnesota senator David Durenberger put the point succinctly when he observed that "society doesn't pay for the education of most children beyond high school. Yet it shovels out free health care for elderly millionaires." The willingness of society to increasingly invest in those at the end of their lives, while at the same time demonstrating a growing *un*willingness to invest in those at the beginning, speaks volumes about the cultural environment into which the Free were born and in which they grew up.

With their wealth and well-being increasing dramatically over the last two decades, it's no surprise that the elderly find the situation to their liking. A 1982 Gallup poll showed that 71 percent of those age sixty-five or over reported being highly satisfied with their standard of living—by far the greatest level of satisfaction of any age group. As one sixty-nine-year-old Beaverton, Oregon, resident told *U.S. News & World Report*, "This is the best time to be a senior citizen there ever could be." While it's wonderful that society has enabled the golden years to be so rewarding, it would have been even more wonderful if America's children—more than one in five of whom grew up in poverty—could have made such a cheerful claim as well.

5

PEERS OVER PARENTS

Asked of eighteen- to twenty-nine-year-olds in 1990.
In bringing up your children, do you think you will:

Spend the same amount of time with
them as your parents did with you   26%

Spend more time   64%

Spend less time   9%

SOURCE: *TIME* MAGAZINE

QUALITY TIME

In the fifties and sixties, American workers made tremendous gains in productivity and efficiency. These decades also saw huge increases in the numbers of time-saving appliances sold to American families—washing machines, labor-saving kitchen gadgets, vacuum cleaners. Efficient computers and robots for the workplace were on the horizon. We seemed to be becoming so efficient with our lives that there were great concerns about what we would do with all of the resulting leisure time. In 1967, testimony before a Senate subcommittee estimated that by 1985, people would be working twenty-two-hour workweeks, or only twenty-seven weeks a year. They would retire at age thirty-eight. There was a great deal of talk that all this free time would be our downfall (just as it was said of the Roman Empire).

Needless to say, these predictions and fears couldn't have been more in error. From 1973 to 1989, productivity increases stalled, and the average workweek, including commuting, had risen from forty-one to forty-seven hours. Over this two-decade period, workers in the manufacturing sector added the equivalent of an extra month on the job each year. A Harris poll indicates that the amount of leisure time available to Americans shrunk over the same two decades from twenty-six hours a week to just sixteen and a half. While everyone was adversely affected by this trend (except perhaps the elderly, who were retiring at a younger age than ever), Free children experienced the loss in parental leisure time as a loss in *parenting* time.

One common justification for the smaller family sizes that followed the baby boom was that parents could spend more time with each child. However, from the time the first of the Free were born, the amount of interaction between parents and children began a steady, decades-long decline. According to the Family Research Council of Washington, D.C., in the early sixties the average parent had roughly thirty hours of contact with his or her child each week. By the time the last of the Free were young children, in the early eighties, that amount had declined to just seventeen hours. One can imagine how the caliber of work completed on a job would decline if 40 percent of the available work hours were slowly eliminated, yet this much parenting time was taken from children with barely a raised eyebrow. In the hurried atmosphere of the late twentieth century, the Free's parents were simply too busy to devote adequate time to their kids. In a study conducted by social psychologist Lois Hoffman at the University of Michigan, it was found that the average mother spent less than ten minutes each day reading or playing with her preschool children. Mom added another thirteen minutes eating with them, and twenty-one minutes watching television with them.

Lest it appear that women alone are responsible for this neglect, they seem almost overbearing when compared with their male counterparts. A study of American fathers in the early eighties indicates that they spent only *thirty-seven seconds* in *any* kind of verbal interaction with their children during a typical day. The average adolescent in 1986 spent but five minutes alone with his father, and half of that was watching television. All in all, parents spent the same amount of time each day with their teenage children as they did watching the news. Thus, out of that scant seventeen hours of weekly parental contact, nearly all was spent in such repetitive mundane activities as eating, shopping, cleaning, or in the nonactivity of watching television. Parents did acknowledge this diminished interaction by inventing a term for the short amounts of time they could find to spend with their kids—"quality time." The concept that it was sufficient to devote only brief periods of attention to their children, as long as this was time well spent, was a weak justification for not giving children what they really needed, which was "more time."

The Free are quite aware that their childhoods lacked the supervision that was needed and deserved. When *Time* magazine asked "twentysomethings" in 1990 whether they spent more time in their youth being with their parents or watching television, the young adults, by a 45-percent-to-43-percent margin, acknowledged a greater familiarity with the tube. Nickelodeon, the cable-television network aimed at children, asked the youngest of the Free, in 1987, to name the things they wanted more of in their lives. The overwhelming top answer was not more toys, money, or vacations from school, but more time with their families. Well aware of the lack of parental contact, "kids understand that they are being cheated out of childhood," wrote Edward Zigler of Yale University. "There is a sense that adults don't care about them." Hallmark came up with "Have a super day at school" cards in the late eighties, to replace Mom and Dad being there to say the same thing.

THAT'S WHAT FRIENDS ARE FOR

Who picked up the slack? With whom did the Free spend their time? The Free. In 1982, an estimated 7 million six- to twelve-year-olds (about one in four of that age) were "latchkey" children, a term that didn't exist before the Free. The name is derived from the house key that parents would tie around their children's necks with a string. (It's interesting that parents would trust children this young to be home by themselves, but they wouldn't trust them not to misplace the key.) These kids essentially fended for themselves from the time school was out until their parents came home from work, and all day during the summer. An additional half-million *preschool* children were left home alone at least part of the day. Overall, a 1987 Louise Harris poll found that 41 percent of parents left their children on their own at least once a week, in addition to the 25 percent who left them alone every day. Afternoons weren't the only lonely time. The 1988 Census Bureau report, "After-School Care of Children," also reported that a half-million children were without adult supervision *before* school. As the world was changing in ways that demanded *more* supervision of children, not less, a significant number of the Free had no choice but to face these menaces alone.

A number of cities established telephone support lines as a link to the adult world for these children. One such program, KIDLINE, was set up in Tucson, Arizona, in 1984 for kids to call when in need of information, support, or assistance in the absence of any adult at home. When the line was established, it was assumed that most calls would be from kids who found themselves in some type of emergency situation. In a three-month study of the line's usage, though, it was found that the great majority of calls were not for assistance in an urgent matter, but were from children who were simply lonely and wanted to talk to someone.

Typically, older youths in the eighties spent four to five hours a day left to their own devices. This is in addition to the roughly two hours spent alone in front of the TV. The Free depended on each other for much of the support and advice that had traditionally been supplied by parents. Of course, other teenagers don't always provide the best counsel. The term "peer pressure" didn't come into being until the time when the influence of friends began to outstrip that of parents. The adolescent culture of the seventies and eighties went far beyond the evening rendezvous at the malt shop that their parents had popularized in the fifties. The Free's "malt shop" encompassed half the day and provided a complete network of strength, comfort, and guidance, virtually free of adult influence.

A number of films in the early eighties, popular with adolescents, captured this subculture. In *Fast Times at Ridgemont High* (1982), the kids depend on each other for everything from sexual guidance and abortion counseling to finding a job. As Pauline Kael wrote in *The New Yorker* about the film's teens, "They've gained independence from the adults at home. The kids are there to catch each other after the falls, and to console each other—they function as parents for each other." In *Sixteen Candles* (1984), a teenage girl's parents forget her birthday, but she's neither very surprised nor particularly upset about this. Who does she turn to for condolence, and even prefer? Her friends. In *Taps* (1981), military-school boys take up arms to keep their school as they want it; the pleas of their parents go unheard. In *Little Darlings* (1980) and *The Blue Lagoon* (1980), teenagers deal with sexual awakening in settings entirely independent of parental supervision. And as teens fought off monstrous villains in the numerous slasher films of the time, adults were quite scarce—except perhaps *as the slasher himself.* In none of these films is a parent's aid solicited, nor do adults even appear on the screen except in a rare scene for comic effect. These and similar films struck a resonant, familiar chord among the Free. However, unlike in the movies, in real life this dependence on other teenagers in lieu of adult direction didn't always result in a very happy ending.

On November 3, 1981, sixteen-year-old Anthony Jacques Broussard strangled to death his former girlfriend, fourteen-year-old Marcy Conrad, in Milpitas, California. He killed the young girl after raping her, then left her body on a secluded riverbank. While the crime itself was appalling, as is any murder, it was not particularly unusual in those violent times. The unusual, and perhaps more disturbing, aspect of the crime was what ensued in the two days between the murder and the notification of the police.

During that time, Broussard bragged about the crime and showed off the corpse to more than a dozen of his high-school classmates. He loaded fellow students into his pickup truck and drove them into the hills outside of town to view the half-nude body of Marcy. Other young people, hearing about "the body in the hills," drove over on their own to look at the victim. Some viewers placed bets on whether or not the body was in fact a mannequin. One observer dropped a rock on the dead girl's face to see if the corpse was real. It was. Others poked the body with sticks, and one girl snipped a patch off the victim's discarded clothing as a souvenir. One conscientious boy, a friend of the murderer, admitted partially covering the girl's body with leaves and discarded plastic bags because "she was naked and I felt it was the right thing to do." Not one of these teenagers, however, perceived that the right thing to do was to report the murder to the police, their parents, or to any other adult.

Finally, two days after the murder, an eighteen-year-old former student of the local high school saw the body and went to the police. Broussard was captured as he returned to town in his truck with a group of friends who had been checking out the body. He eventually pleaded guilty to first-degree murder and was sentenced to twenty-five years to life in prison. He will first be eligible for parole in 1998. Hollywood came out with its version of the story in 1987 with the film *The River's Edge*.

Why wouldn't these students notify their parents or the police of this heinous crime? It wasn't out of fear. Many students reported that Anthony Jacques Broussard was nobody to be afraid of. They certainly weren't trying to protect a friend. As a sixteen-year-old who knew both the murderer and his victim related, "Jacques wasn't that much of a likable person so that people would want to cover for him." Yet none of these young people saw the need to notify his or her parents of what was done. The thought apparently just never occurred to them. In an era when teenage peers rather than adults defined one's standards of morality, the Milpitas students simply weren't quite sure how to react. So they did nothing.

Turning to friends rather than parents or other adults can have other tragic consequences. Dr. Barry Garfinkel, director of the Division of Child and Adolescent Psychiatry at the University of Minnesota Hospital and Clinic, reported in 1988 that teens turn to their friends even when their problems are quite serious. When teenagers are severely depressed or suicidal, the research indicates that in 75 percent of the cases they turn to their peers for help, not to their parents or other adults. Feeling unable to discuss such matters with parents or other adults has possibly contributed to the skyrocketing suicide rates of the Free.

Early on, "experts" assured parents that leaving their kids alone after school facilitated their becoming more self-reliant and independent. They would learn responsibility and how to budget their own time. These presumptions were largely groundless and served mainly to assuage the concerns of worried parents.

The Free seemed to be more in tune with reality than the experts. A 1981 nationwide survey of teenagers, for instance, asked how the problem of teenage vandalism could be stopped. The top response was that parents need to pay more attention to their children. Recent research agrees with this assessment; relying primarily on peers rather than parents for guidance can result in problems that, while not necessarily as dramatic as the Milpitas incident, are nevertheless dangerous. A 1989 study of five thousand eighth-grade students in San Diego and Los Angeles found a direct correlation between the amount of time the teenagers spent on their own and the incidence of substance abuse. The more hours the students took care of themselves after school, the greater the risk of their using drugs and alcohol. As a whole, latchkey children were *twice* as likely to drink and take drugs as those who were under adult supervision after school. The increased risk held true regardless of the student's gender, race, family income, academic performance, or the number of parents in the household.

Schools undoubtedly suffered from these trends. An upstate New York teacher told author Marie Winn in 1982 that students who are left to fend for themselves "seem to develop a lot of anger... We see a lot of the 'If nobody cares about me then I don't care about anything' sort of attitude among these kids in our classroom." And a 1987 Harris poll indicated that teachers considered leaving children on their own after school to be the single biggest cause of young students' difficulties in the classroom.

With what may have been a desperate attempt for busy parents to reclaim some time with their children, or perhaps a result of these same overworked parents going to bed early to try to catch up on lost sleep, Free children got hooked early on late-night television. Studies done in the early eighties show that, in addition to the hours already spent in front of the tube during the day, 3 million two- to eleven-year-old children were watching television between 11:00 P.M. and 11:30 P.M. on any given night. More than 2 million continued watching until midnight. Another million were still turned in to watch the late show after that. No wonder so many of us share David Letterman's wry sense of humor. Of course, each hour in front of that glowing screen meant an hour less of needed sleep. Elementary-school teachers often complained of children falling asleep in class or not being alert enough to pay attention. Schools simply could not take up as much of the slack left by preoccupied parents as they were being asked to.

BECKY BELL One last, sad incident illustrates how the Free's reliance on friends rather than parents could result in tragedy, and how government policy did not adapt. On a Monday evening in September of 1988, soon after her seventeenth birthday, Becky Bell of Indianapolis, Indiana, was put to bed with an apparent case of the flu. Seeing no improvement during the week, her parents finally took her to the doctor at four o'clock on Friday afternoon. Becky was diagnosed as having pneumonia, and her mother and father rushed her to the hospital and checked her in. Things seemed to be under control, so at 7:30 P.M. Bill and Karen Bell left their daughter and went to have some dinner. When they returned a half hour later, they were informed that Becky had had an "incident" and was fighting for her life in the intensive-care ward. Three hours later, they were notified that their daughter had died.

The next morning, the Bells were informed that Becky's death was due to complications from a botched, unsterile, illegal abortion. Becky died from a situation that was not supposed to happen anymore, as the Supreme Court's *Roe v. Wade* decision fifteen years earlier had affirmed the right of a woman to undergo a legal abortion. In Indiana, however, that right wasn't quite as certain. There, and in thirty-four other states, an unmarried girl under the age of eighteen was required to seek parental consent before undergoing an abortion. Becky, for reasons we'll never know, apparently felt she couldn't turn to her parents for this permission. Perhaps she was afraid her parents wouldn't be sympathetic to her situation. Perhaps she simply loved them too much and didn't want to disappoint them. Whatever the reason, the seventeen-year-old girl felt that she couldn't go to her parents for the needed consent.

Indiana's law, as well as the other states', does offer a substitute—albeit a somewhat weak one—for parental consent. The frightened girl could have gone in front of a judge and asked for a waiver. This option works better on paper than in practice. In the four years the Indiana law had been in place before Becky's death, only a handful of these "judicial bypasses" had been obtained, and not one of them was in Indianapolis.

She did turn to her friends for help. The boy who had gotten her pregnant reportedly told her to "get the hell out of my life." Other friends had heard the same thing as Becky—that the local judge was a strict antiabortionist and didn't grant waivers. They simply were unable to offer much else besides sympathy. It will never be known exactly whom else she did seek to help her out, and who gave her the infection that took her life. If she had been able to confide in her parents, she would still be alive today.

THE HALLOWEEN SADIST

The Free Generation grew up with a strong suspicion that every piece of Halloween candy just might have been tainted by a crazed psychopath. Anything that wasn't wrapped had to be thrown away. Apples had to be sliced up in case a razor blade might have been hidden inside. Everything else had to be carefully scrutinized. While rumors of Halloween candy tampering had existed for decades, they had always seemed to be no more than just another urban myth—

something that may or may not have happened somewhere far away. A few cases in the early seventies appeared to recast the myth into a frightening reality, claiming any child as the next potential victim.

Newspapers reported the death of a five-year-old Detroit boy in 1970 who apparently succumbed after eating heroin that had been hidden in his Halloween candy. In 1974, an eight-year-old boy was reportedly killed after eating a cyanide-laced treat. Incidents like this and other widely reported poisonings, such as the tainted Tylenol pain reliever case that took seven lives, seemed to prove the soundness of parental consternation and were used to curtail or even eliminate trick-or-treating for thousands of kids. A childhood tradition lost its charm and was replaced by yet another fear.

It's notable that during this period, Halloween was gradually transformed from a children's holiday into another reason for adults to party. October thirty-first costume parties for adults, almost unheard of in the fifties and sixties, became ubiquitous a decade later as children sat home watching "It's the Great Pumpkin, Charlie Brown" on TV because trick-or-treating was too unsafe.

Was this fear that had been placed in children's heads even justified? Joel Best, a sociology professor at Fresno State University, conducted a study of Halloween terrorism in 1985. He searched for reports of candy laced with drugs, poisons, pins, or razor blades in newspapers such as the *New York Times*, the *Chicago Tribune*, and the *Los Angeles Times*. Out of seventy-six such stories reported from 1958 to 1984, Best noted, "We couldn't find a single case of any child killed or seriously injured by candy contamination." And what of the deaths of the two boys mentioned above? The five-year-old Detroit boy, it turns out, died not as a result of tainted candy, but from eating some of his uncle's stash of heroin that he had found. The eight-year-old did actually die from cyanide-laced candy. Who poisoned it? His own father. There was simply little or no reason to fear the tradition of trick-or-treating, yet Halloween had been essentially taken from many children. Any fear associated with the holiday shouldn't have come from outside, but from within the home.

THE CHILD-STEALING BOGEYMAN

The 1983 television docudrama *Adam* struck fear into the hearts of parents and children across the country. The movie was based on the true story of six-year-old Adam Walsh of Hollywood, Florida. On July 27, 1981, the young boy and his mother were walking around in a local shopping center, and Adam's mother left him alone for a few minutes. When she returned for him, her little boy was nowhere to be found. A massive search was conducted by both law-enforcement personnel and a grassroots citizens' group, but nobody could find the boy. Finally, two weeks later, Adam's murdered body was spotted in a ditch about a hundred miles from where he first disappeared. His abductor and killer has never been found.

There were other widely reported incidents of horrifying child abductions and slayings. Over a fourteen-month period in 1976 and 1977, Oakland County, Michigan, residents were terrified by a killer who claimed four children as victims. Two boys and two girls were slain after being kidnapped. The boys had been sexually molested. The person who committed these acts was never caught. During 1977 and 1978, the so-called vampire killer, named for the bloody nature of his crimes, shocked the city of Sacramento, California, with a series of gruesome murders. Among the victims was a young boy who was found mutilated. Richard Chase was eventually captured and convicted of the crimes.

Of the twenty-five victims definitely linked to mass murderer Ted Bundy, five were less than eighteen years of age. In another infamous case, row upon row of skeletons and decomposing bodies of young boys were found under the floorboards of John Wayne Gacy's home outside Chicago in 1979. He had sexually molested and murdered the boys over a three-year period. From 1979 to 1981, the nation was horrified by the murders of at least twenty-eight young black children in Atlanta. Wayne Williams was captured and convicted of two of these killings. These cases were very real and very terrifying. Yet even so, they were used to mask, and even rationalize, a much more widespread crime.

In the midst of horrible crimes such as these, a confusing array of estimates arose as to how pervasive this trend in childsnatching actually was. A 1983 U.S. Department of Health and Human Services report, for example, put the number of missing children at one and a half million a year. This figure represented the total number of cases, regardless of the different causes by which the children had disappeared; it made no distinction between cases of kidnappings by strangers, abductions by family members, and other explanations. Nevertheless, this incredible statistic was used by missing-children's groups who, albeit with good intentions, inflated their claims about the magnitude of the problem. Jay Howell, then executive director of the National Center for Missing and Exploited Children, estimated in 1985 that between four and twenty thousand children a year were kidnapped by strangers. Senator Paula Hawkins and others quoted a figure as high as fifty thousand a year. Unsatisfied with even this number, a Chicago television station circulated a pamphlet that began: "Nearly *2 million children* in this country disappear from their homes each year. Many end up raped, forced into prostitution and pornography. Many are never heard from again" (my italics). Two million children a year equals *half* the total number of children born each year.

Yet the FBI's data indicates that the actual problem was considerably smaller. In 1981, for example, the FBI, which would typically assist in a case such as a child kidnapping, investigated a grand total of only thirty-five child snatchings. Subsequent years suggested similar numbers. A total of forty-nine such cases were handled by the bureau in 1982, sixty-seven in 1983, sixty-eight in 1984, and fifty-three in 1985. Either the numbers quoted by the National Center for Missing and Exploited Children were overestimated, or the FBI was neglecting to investigate as many as 399 out of every 400 kidnappings. Possible, to be sure, but not likely.

Regardless of the relatively small numbers of children actually being abducted by strangers, a panic that rivaled the best that Orson Welles could produce was taking hold, and the nation began to mobilize to fight this scourge. All of a sudden, faces of the abducted began to appear everywhere. The National Child Safety Council led a campaign in 1985 that put pictures of missing children on 2.5 billion milk cartons, 20 billion grocery bags, and up to 50 billion pieces of mail. Other photos were placed on cereal boxes, film envelopes, subway cars, utility bills, and vending machines. The Pittsburgh Pirates even flashed these pictures on the DiamondVision screen during home baseball games.

A cottage industry sprung up offering solace to anxious parents (and their children). Supermarkets sponsored photographers to put together ID kits for parents to give to police in case their child did get snatched. A dentist even marketed a device that could be implanted behind a child's tooth for location and identification purposes. Undoubtedly, enormous numbers of Free children were frightened rather than comforted; the message was that abduction loomed at every corner, and, given the numbers being cited, the likelihood of this happening seemed alarmingly high. They were reminded of this potential nightmare every morning as they stared at the milk cartons branded with the faces of young victims.

How many children were located as a result of all this exposure? According to the National Child Safety Council president, their efforts resulted in helping to find a total of eleven children by 1985. Only eleven children, when some authorities were arguing that there were *fifty thousand* abductions by strangers each year? While it is wonderful that these eleven children were located, and no dollar figure could equal the relief that was surely brought to the families involved, the success rate nevertheless seems curiously low—or implies that the abduction estimates were grossly overestimated in the first place.

In a program sponsored by the U.S. Department of Justice, researchers determined that the actual abduction figures were indeed quite a bit lower than oft-quoted estimates. They looked into the nationwide total numbers of "stereotypical kidnappings" of children—that is, an abduction by a nonfamily member meeting any one of five criteria: the child was missing overnight, was killed, was transported over a distance of at least fifty miles, was ransomed, or the kidnapper intended to keep the child permanently. They concluded that there were not twenty thousand or fifty thousand of these cases per year. While the data on earlier years is incomplete, there were only an estimated two to three *hundred* such cases in 1988. Even with these smaller numbers, the researchers didn't exclude those children who had been taken by someone known to them. The number of kidnappings by a stranger was even smaller. When the case ended with the child being murdered, as in the Adam Walsh case, the incidence was lower still. Between 1980 and 1984, the researchers determined, somewhere from a conservatively estimated 52 to a gloomier high estimate of 158 children suffered this fate each year.

What accounts for the gross overestimations of child abductions in the early eighties? Surely there were enough problems at home that adding yet another fear was unwarranted. With the dissolution of the family, shamefully inadequate child care, and children facing the stress of being forced to grow up too quickly, why add another anxiety on top of all this? And why a fabricated one at that? The answer just may be that the phenomenon arose as a result of all these problems that were based closer to home. Because of the pressures of work, rising single-parenthood, and shrinking amounts of time available to spend with their children, parents likely developed additional anxieties about their children's welfare. And with this diminished influence over their children, parents would feel more uncertainty about their abilities to properly protect and care for them. One response then was to project outward the trepidation that lay within. In their book *Missing Children*, Martin Forst and Martha-Elin Blomquist sum up this idea. "Missing children," they write, "became a symbol for grappling with issues that could not be readily articulated or resolved. Moreover, seeing the problem of missing children as a crime control and law enforcement problem gave parents and policymakers false assurance."

By attempting to shift their obligations on to authorities such as police departments, parents could avoid facing many responsibilities that one assumes upon having a child. Moreover, by channeling so much energy into resolving a false crisis such as the child-abduction epidemic, very real ones like child abuse and a lack of parental guidance ended up neglected. Even though a growing number of the Free had to face it alone, the outside world is not as frightening as many of them were led to believe. There are few Halloween sadists or child snatchers. The world at home, however, was for many perhaps much more painful than they would have ever believed was possible.

In contrast to the few hundred "stereotypical kidnappings" of children that occur each year, the Department of Justice researchers estimated that there were over *350,000* incidents of children being abducted by a member of their own family in 1988 alone. These included cases of a child being taken in violation of a custody ruling or the failure to return a child after an approved parental visitation. The more severe cases of an abducted child being transported out of state by a family member, an attempt to prevent the other parent from contacting the child, or intent to permanently keep the child numbered more than 160,000. Thus, in roughly 999 out of a thousand cases of a child being snatched, one need look no further than the immediate family to find the culprit.

LOOK HOMEWARD, ANGEL
Children who stayed at home were not always free from harm either. The American Humane Association has been compiling data on child abuse every year since 1976. In that first year, a little over a half-million cases of abuse or neglect were reported, already a staggering figure. By 1982, the number had risen to an estimated 1 million cases. That number had *again* doubled by 1985, to total *2 million*. In one decade, the number of children victimized in what former Health and Human Services Secretary Louis Sullivan called our national tragedy had grown by 300 percent. Each year, about forty thousand of these children were injured badly enough by their parents or primary caregiver to require hospitalization. Unfortunately, these figures don't appear to be grossly overestimated, as was the case with child snatching. In fact, since these estimates are based only on *reported* cases of abuse, the actual numbers are likely much higher.

Author Neil Postman has hypothesized that because childhood innocence was no longer seen as a positive quality, and children were being forced to grow up more quickly, abusing them no longer seemed so appalling. Children "are beaten because they are not perceived as children," he claimed, in his 1982 book *The Disappearance of Childhood*. Children had become miniature adults, not innocents in need of protection. This theory holds up in regard to the most extreme form of abuse, homicide. During the seventies, the age group that felt the largest-percentage increase in homicide were those between one and four years old. While great strides had been made during the forties and fifties in combating childhood diseases, murder had taken up much of the slack. By 1980, it had become a greater cause of childhood mortality for the Free than any illness.

While the murder of young Adam Walsh got much attention in the press and around the dinner table, the fact is that only one in ten murder victims under the age of eighteen was killed by a stranger. By contrast, in 1983 mothers were responsible for 13 percent of such homicides, and fathers another 10 percent. Other family members and acquaintances accounted for an additional 44 percent. Thus, the great majority of homicides committed against children were committed by the victim's parent, other relative, or family acquaintance. In fact, the younger the murder victim, the more likely the crime was committed by his natural parents. Family values Free style.

6

A GROWING PESSIMISM

Number of drunk-driving arrests nationwide
for persons aged 10 and under:

1971—18

1980—166

SOURCE: FBI, UNIFIED CRIME REPORTS

THE ADULT CHILD

David Elkind, in his 1984 book *All Grown Up and No Place to Go,* offered a sad portrait of the Free Generation raised amid the rapid pace and high stress of modern society. "They have had a premature adulthood thrust upon them," he wrote. "Teenagers now are expected to confront life and its challenges with the maturity once expected only of the middle-aged, without any time for preparation." As he had done in his 1981 bestseller *The Hurried Child,* Elkind presented compelling evidence that while the pace of life had increased for everyone, America's young people were paying a particularly high price as they were rushed into roles that inexperienced minds often have trouble managing. Even schools, traditionally a haven from society's ills, ceased to provide refuge as theft, violence, and substance abuse became as widespread in the high schools as they were on the streets. It was estimated in the eighties that 135,000 children were bringing guns and a million bringing knives to school *each day.* In school, childhood innocence truly could prove perilous. As one Bronx junior-high-school teacher put it, "The kid who demonstrates fear is raw meat."

Besides the possibility of being shot in school, one very adult concern that captivated the Free was the nuclear threat. Although political developments in recent years seem to have reduced the risk of nuclear holocaust, during the eighties the concept became almost an obsession for the Free. A national survey of more than forty thousand teenagers in 1982 ranked this as the number-one concern of teenage boys and number two among girls, overshadowed for girls only by the fear of a parent's death. In that year, 35 percent of male high-school seniors stated that they worried about nuclear war often, more than four times the percentage responding so during similar polls in the seventies. The new realizations that such a war would likely bring about a cataclysmic "nuclear winter"—and was therefore unwinnable and inevitably fatal—had added a new dimension to the threat. When Pamela Douglas, a teacher of screenwriting at UCLA and USC, assigned her sixty students to write a story for class, a full 20 percent of the plots involved a central character who is among the last surviving human beings after a nuclear war. Brown University students voted in October of 1984 to stock poison tablets in the school infirmary, so that in the event of a nuclear catastrophe they could commit suicide rather than perish from the fallout.

When essayist Lewis Thomas contemplated the imminence of nuclear disaster that had captured the fascination of the Free, he observed that the idea was "bad enough for people in my generation. We can put up with it, I suppose.... We are moving along anyway." However, he pondered, "How do the young stand it? How do they keep their sanity?" Writer David Leavitt responded to this question by noting "we do not go crazy, because for us the thought of a world with no future—so terrifying to Dr. Thomas—is completely familiar; is taken for granted; is nothing new." Nineteen-year-old Shellie Wilburn told the *Washington Post* that the expectation of impending war made long-range personal goals rather pointless. "I'd like to find the right guy before it all ends," she shared with the reporter.

When a war came along that primarily included the Free as its soldiers, the Persian Gulf War, they proved more perceptive of the dangers of using nuclear weapons than their elders. While World War II nostalgics like radio announcer Paul Harvey were urging the immediate use of tactical nuclear weapons on Iraq, a Gallup poll showed that those aged eighteen to twenty-nine were the most likely to oppose such an idea. The younger generation preferred less extreme measures of solving military conflicts.

Slightly less cataclysmic expectations became fixtures in the minds of America's youth as well. With the rise in gun violence on our streets, a 1993 Gallup poll found that one Free teenager in three believed he or she would be shot to death before reaching old age. The future didn't seem to hold enough promise to forgo more immediate gratification for a growing number of young people. Seeing their families disintegrate, more and more of their peers slip into poverty or fall victim to violence, a dismal economic future, and (at the extreme) the perceived likelihood of nuclear war, many Free youths felt a sense of pessimism that often overshadowed hopes for the future.

For example, Dr. Gabe Mirkin, author of *The Sportsmedicine Book*, posed an interesting question in 1981 to one hundred young track-and-field athletes about their thirst for renown: If there were a drug available that would make them an Olympic champion but would kill them a year later, would they take it? To his disbelief, more than half of the athletes answered that yes, they would readily make this Faustian bargain, even given the consequence of certain death. Incredulous that Mirkin's survey could actually represent any sort of pervasive attitude among young athletes, Bob Goldman polled weight lifters and track-and-field athletes on whether or not they would take a drug that would enable them to win every competition for the next five years but would kill them at the end of that period. Goldman reported that 52 percent responded that they would take such a drug; they were indeed willing to give their lives for the short-lived thrill of victory. Like Camus's Dr. Rieux musing about his existential reality when faced with the expanding menace of the plague, the Free seemed to develop a deep anomie, with the disturbing vision of a grim future perhaps serving as the catalyst. In a number of ways, consideration for future concerns gave way to more immediate indulgences, sometimes with unfortunate or even tragic results.

TOO FAT, TOO THIN

The affliction known as anorexia nervosa was, until the 1970s, exceedingly rare. During the sixties, for example, the University of Wisconsin Hospital reports that typically one anorexic a year would be admitted; in 1982 alone over seventy such patients were admitted to this one institution. This horrifying disease in which young women (and, much less often, men) intentionally starve themselves, sometimes to death, reached what many called epidemic proportions, afflicting as many as one young woman in twenty according to a 1987 House Select Committee. A related disorder, bulimia, known in the teen argot as "binge and purge," has been estimated to afflict an even higher number. By 1985 the problems were so widespread that the country's first residential facility designed exclusively for the treatment of eating disorders, the Renfrew Center, was opened in Philadelphia.

While experts argue about the exact causes of both anorexia and bulimia, what they do seem to agree on is that the disorders depend on the individuals' biological and psychological predispositions to the diseases, their family situations, and the social climate. In the case of anorexia, it is also generally agreed that this self-induced ailment indicates a low self-image brought about by one or more of the above roots of the disease. Susie Orbach, author of the book *Hunger Strike*, suggests that "anorexia is an attempted solution to being in a world from which at the most profound level one feels excluded, and into which one feels deeply unentitled to enter." Simply put, anorexic girls do not feel good about themselves, and powerless to change.

This manifestation of self-doubt might not be so inconsistent with the hurried, often neglected childhood that confronted so many of the Free. Joan Jacobs Brumberg wrote in her 1988 Book *Fasting Girls* that

> "the 'anorectic generations,' particularly those born since 1960, have been subject to a sense of insecurities that make hererosexuality an anxious rather than a pleasant prospect. Family insecurity, reflected in the frequency of divorce, and changing sex and gender roles became facts of life for this group in their childhood."

Lack of guidance and support made adolescence a very confusing time for many girls, and starving themselves may have been a desperate stab at gaining some measure of control.

In the case of bulimia, while the roots of the disease likely have some similarities to anorexia, Rachel Kranz and Dr. Michael Maloney, authors of the 1991 book *Straight Talk About Eating Disorders*, add that

> often the girl who becomes bulimic reports that she didn't get sufficient care when she was a child. . . . [She] may have been given the message that her parents were too busy, frightened, or insecure to help her with her problems, so that she had to learn early to rely on herself.

Laurel Mellin, director of a center for eating disorders in San Francisco, believes that the phenomenon is intimately linked to problems in the adolescent's family. "Mother's increasing presence in the workplace, father's failure in picking up the residual 50 percent of parenting . . . and marital instability" all contribute to a situation in which children are denied the necessary nurturing and guidance. The stress that results from this deprivation can manifest itself in a variety of ways, including eating and weight problems. The number of bulimia victims among the Free may have reached a certain critical point. A 1981 study of college women showed that a woman who purges almost always knows another who does the same. And a woman who does not engage in such behavior rarely knows anyone else who does. The more who already purge, the more who join the crowd.

One note of hope: Although still a serious, familiar problem, recent studies indicate that the affliction rate of anorexia may have begun a downward turn in recent years. History just may record this terrifying malady as "our" disease.

Paradoxically, given the rise in anorexia cases, Free children also suffered from obesity at a much higher rate than the previous generation. A study done in the mid-eighties indicated that more than one-fourth of children aged six to eleven were defined as obese, up by 50 percent from twenty-five years earlier. The American Academy of Pediatrics called overweight children the single most important health issue facing pediatricians. While there may not be a direct correlation, the fact that an A. C. Nielson survey showed that kids of that age spent twenty-two hours watching television each week may help to explain such an increase during an era when American adults were jogging and hitting the gym in record numbers. Many were apparently unaware of their children's distress even when it was exhibited in such physically unhealthy ways.

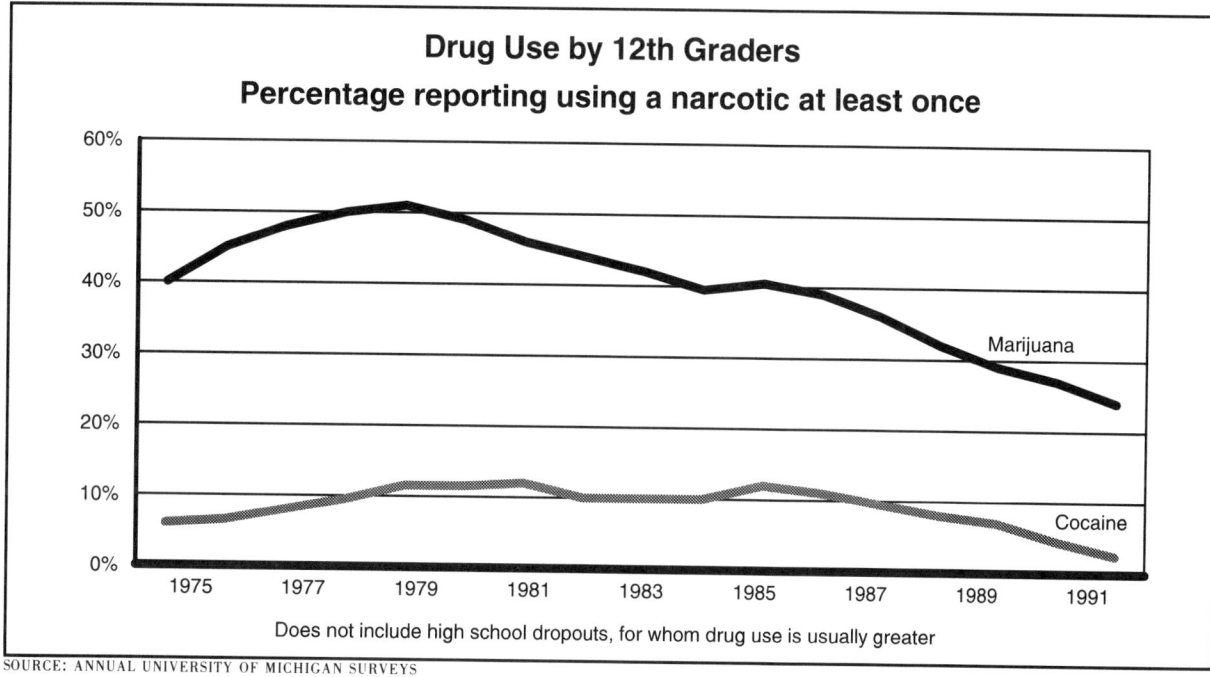

Drug Use by 12th Graders
Percentage reporting using a narcotic at least once

[Chart showing Marijuana use declining from about 40% in 1975, peaking around 50% in 1979, then declining to about 22% by 1991; Cocaine use staying around 6-11% from 1975 to 1987, then declining to near 0% by 1991]

Does not include high school dropouts, for whom drug use is usually greater

SOURCE: ANNUAL UNIVERSITY OF MICHIGAN SURVEYS

WAY BEYOND CANDY CIGARETTES

Taking drugs was one destructive act that trickled down from the young adults of the sixties to the children of the seventies and eighties. Whereas in 1962 only 4 percent of the entire population had ever taken an illegal drug, a study conducted by the National Institute on Drug Abuse two decades later showed that 64 percent of the Free had tried an illegal drug before finishing high school. More than half of high-school seniors had tried marijuana, and 16 percent had taken LSD. The Department of Health, Education and Welfare determined in 1978 that one in nine high-school seniors—the first wave of the Free—was smoking marijuana *daily*. Cocaine, which rose in popularity throughout the Boomer teen years, continued upward with the Free with use among teenagers peaking in the mid-eighties.

Even alcohol, long a staple of youth insubordination, saw a dramatic rise in popularity from the Boomers to the Free. In 1966, 19 percent of high-school students reported having been drunk at least once. The proportion had more than tripled by the mid-eighties, and a survey of junior-high-school students showed that 65 percent of *thirteen-year-olds* had drunk alcohol at least once that year. A survey conducted by the *Weekly Reader* student publication in 1987 even found that more than a third of all fourth-graders had been pressured to try alcohol.

Although alcohol has long been synonymous with college life, the Free have upheld this tradition to new extremes. A 1994 Columbia University report found that while nearly all students drink to some extent, the number who drink specifically to get drunk has grown tremendously. Since 1977, the percentage who drink just to get drunk tripled among women, to 35 percent, and doubled among men, to 40 percent. While drug use has dropped in recent years, these high drinking rates indicate that this generation is not about to give up all its mind-altering substances.

The year 1982 saw drug use by high schoolers peak, despite the common belief that there were further increases in the eighties. Throughout the remainder of the decade and beyond, there has actually been a steady decline. In fact, in 1991 fewer than half of high-school seniors reported having tried an illegal drug at least once, the first time since 1975 that such a low percentage reported so. Even use of cocaine, the "drug of the eighties," dropped nearly half during the decade separating the oldest and the youngest of the Free. In addition, marijuana use was cut by a third. Alcohol, however, has shown no decline in popularity, with use remaining high throughout the decade. The increased drug use among the Free (particularly with the first half of the generation) and higher drinking rates among ever-younger children might not seem so surprising given some other aspects of their youth. While these activities did filter down from young adult Boomers to the Free children, the younger set wasn't necessarily simply imitating their older brothers and sisters. Forced to accept more responsibilities than previous generations of youths and given the mandate for making more of their decisions with less help from their parents, many children of the seventies and eighties simply assumed some of the adult prerogatives that went along with their adult obligations. Just as many adults seek relief from the stresses of life in drugs or alcohol, so did a growing number of the Free. They were just compelled to make these choices at a much younger age.

BABIES HAVING BABIES

As adults greatly curbed their rates of having babies in the seventies and eighties, kids began to pick up the slack. By 1993, this problem had become so familiar that when *Los Angeles Times* reporters looked into the teenage pregnancy situation in their city, they were concerned, but not particularly surprised, by the high rate of sexual activity and low rate of contraceptive use. They were startled at one specific development, however. "No longer can teen births be written off as the result of 'unintended pregnancies,'" they determined. "Increasing numbers of girls, some as young as thirteen, say they are having babies because they *want* to." As one young, pregnant girl told a reporter, "I wanted somebody to love. Why is that so hard to understand?" Confronted with this fact, Gayle Wilson Nathanson, executive director of the Youth and Family Center of Inglewood, California, expressed her disbelief at the ground lost during the last two decades. "If anyone had told me twenty years ago that we would be at this point today," she explained, "I would have said it was not possible—*not possible*."

As with the drug situation (the other great social movement originating in the sixties), the Free certainly lived the sexual revolution along with the rest of the country. They were just younger than everyone else while doing so. Whereas only 26 percent of women in 1971 reported having had sex at least once before the age of seventeen, just over a decade later, 48 percent could make that claim. This proportion was nearly as high as that of boys, of whom 55 percent lost their virginity by their seventeenth birthday.

One problem with children's involvement in the sexual revolution is that they were much less likely to use contraception than their older counterparts. A 1979 survey, for example, showed that 25 percent of sexually experienced teenagers never used any method of contraception. And only a third used it consistently. The rest reported using it sometimes or most of the time. Not surprisingly, young girls also showed a meteoric rise in the number of pregnancies. In 1978 alone there were more than 1.1 million teenage pregnancies, and a decade later the Alan Guttmacher Institute estimated that 44 percent of all Free girls nationwide experienced a pregnancy before leaving their teenage years, including an astounding 63 percent of black girls. In any given year during the eighties, more than one teenage girl in ten became pregnant.

What many have pointed out is that the much-hyped "epidemic" of births to teenage mothers was not an epidemic at all. The rate of births to teenage mothers dropped steadily from a peak in 1957, when there were ninety-seven births for every thousand women aged fifteen to nineteen, so that by 1985 the

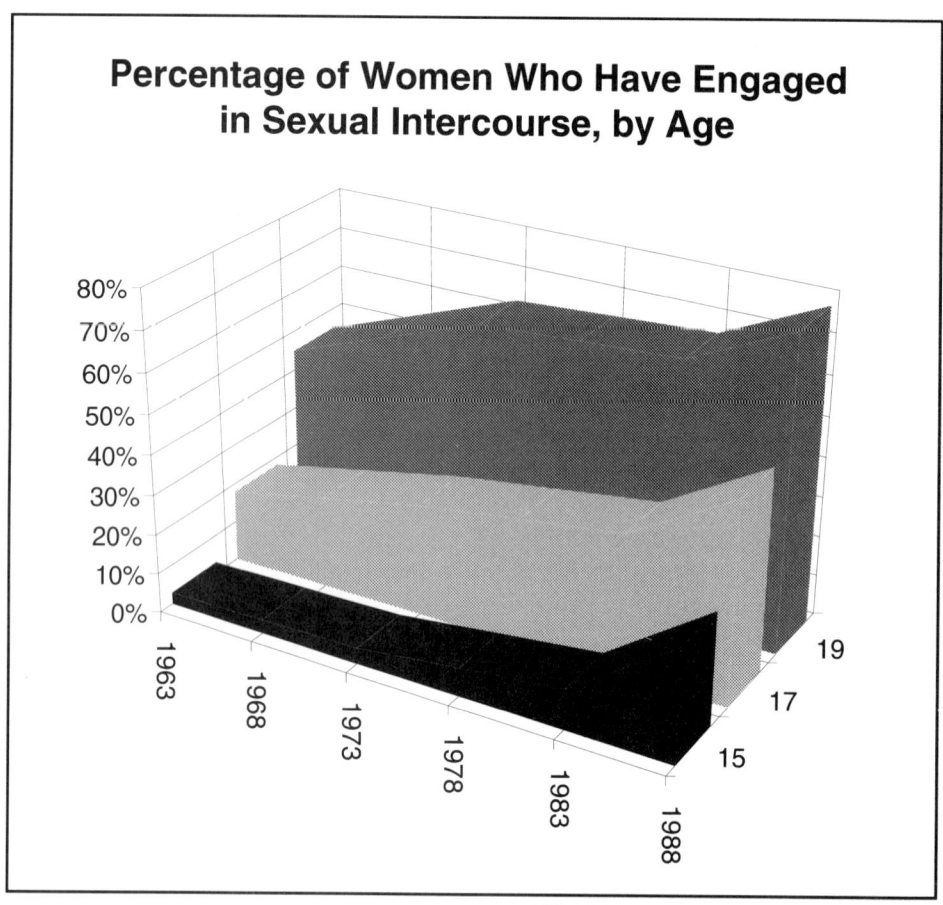

Percentage of Women Who Have Engaged in Sexual Intercourse, by Age

SOURCE: NATIONAL CENTER FOR HEALTH STATISTICS

rate had been cut nearly in half.[1] Of course, a major factor contributing to the overall drop in births, given the rise in pregnancies, is the availability of abortion after the 1973 Supreme Court ruling of *Roe v. Wade*.

The ratio of abortions to births is higher for teenagers than for the rest of the population. In 1979, for example, there were 1.2 abortions for every live birth to a teenage mother, more than twice the rate for older women. And for very young girls, those under fifteen, the ratio was higher yet. Over a half-million teenage girls each year terminated their pregnancies through abortion during the eighties.

Despite the overall decline in teen birth rates, there was nevertheless an

---

[1] As with so many other areas of society in the late eighties, however, the teenage birth rate also took a turn for the worse, with 1989 seeing a 19 percent higher rate than was seen in 1986.

accompanying explosion in the number of births to *unmarried* teenagers. While the typical teen mother in the fifties and sixties was a married eighteen- or nineteen-year-old, by the eighties she was more likely to be an unmarried sixteen- or seventeen-year-old. The proportion of teen births to mothers who were not married escalated from only one in seven in 1960 to 56 percent of such births by 1984. Only 87,000 babies were born to unwed teens in 1960, but twenty years later more than a quarter-million babies were coming into the world each year by an unmarried teenage mother.

The roots of the rise in sexual activity by unmarried teenagers likely lie a little deeper than merely mirroring the actions of adults around them. As Dr. Lillian Rubin, a sociologist at the University of California at Berkeley, observes, unlike earlier generations, teenagers in the eighties had "a sense that they alone call the shots on their sexual behavior." Pressure and advice of peers on this matter, as well as in most other areas, usurped the influence that traditionally came from parents. Of course, the fact that working or missing parents left a lot of houses empty for much of the day made it that much easier to make a quick, clandestine rendezvous. Teenagers who begin having sex at a young age and without contraception generally tend to come from backgrounds that have been lax in providing parental attention, circumstances that fit a growing number of the Free. "They're little kids with grown-up problems," offers Kim Cox, health director at a San Francisco high school. Many of them are moved to having sex not by the love or compassion or other urges that make sense to adults, but by a craving for intimacy that has gone unfulfilled by their families. "Sex," says Cox, "is an easy way to get it."

An often volatile debate arose during the eighties over the issue of making contraception more widely available to teens. While Surgeon General C. Everett Koop called for wide-scale distribution of condoms by the schools, others such as Secretary of Education William Bennett argued for more emphasis on teaching the benefits of abstinence. The Reagan administration even flirted briefly with the idea of a "squeal law" under which family-planning clinics would be forced to notify the parents of minors who sought birth-control services. Once again, as society pushed teenagers toward one norm of behavior, the government was determined to drive them toward another—or make them pay the penalty.

One of the lesser reported elements of the rise in teenage pregnancies is the fact that most of the *fathers* of the babies are not teenagers at all. In California, for example, only 28 percent of the fathers of teenage girls who gave birth in 1985 were under the age of twenty. In San Diego County, adult men fathered 85 percent of the babies born to girls under age seventeen. As Judy Kirsten, who headed a program for pregnant minors in San Diego, noted, "This used to be called statutory rape and was legally prosecuted. It is not being prosecuted anymore." Actually, it is still called statutory rape and it is still a crime. But Kirsten is correct in stating that it is no longer prosecuted. "The courts are too jammed with other things," she added, "the girls are not good witnesses, or they fear that the father will retaliate against them."

The final consequence of the increase in teenage sexual activity among the Free was a corresponding rise in the number of young people contracting sexually transmitted diseases (STDs). Two and a half million adolescents a year contracted some form of STD during the eighties. The Alan Guttmacher Institute estimates that of the 12 million new STD infections that strike Americans each year, 8 million of the affected are under the age of twenty-five. In the case of the most formidable of such diseases, AIDS, by the late eighties those aged twenty to twenty-nine accounted for 21 percent of the individuals diagnosed with the virus. But given the latency period of HIV, this means that these young people were likely infected when they were still teenagers.

In fact, despite a decade of AIDS awareness and education, a recent San Francisco study of young gay men found that a startling percentage were still engaging in risky sexual practices. Even as the AIDS rate has slowed among older gay males, it is increasing among the Free. Alarmingly, the researchers discovered that the younger group is taking *even more* risks than the older men did when they were the same age. As one nineteen-year-old explained in the *Los Angeles Times*, the risky behavior isn't always bred from ignorance. "I knew, and then I went out and did everything."

Even with less threatening, but nevertheless still dangerous, STDs, teenagers have seen untoward increases in infection rates. The incidence of gonorrhea, for example, tripled among fifteen- to nineteen-year-olds from 1960 to 1988, and quadrupled for those aged ten to fourteen during the same period. The Centers for Disease Control found that in 1991, teenage boys were infected with this disease at a rate six times as high, and teenage girls *twenty-two times* as high, as for adults over age thirty.

Just as adults occasionally have to suffer the consequences of engaging in risky sexual behavior, the Free discovered in their teenage years that they were not immune either. But while these consequences can cut equally sharp in cases such as AIDS, in other areas—pregnancy, for example—a blessed event for an adult can be a most unwelcome one for those who aren't quite yet equipped to take on such responsibility.

Given the escalating rates of teenage STD infections, unplanned pregnancies, drug use, and other social and emotional problems, a commission was formed in 1990 to assess the overall health situation facing our young people. Comprised of medical, health, and business leaders, the council formed by the National Association of State Boards of Education and the American Medical

Association came to a sobering conclusion: "Never before has one generation of American teenagers been less healthy, less cared for, or less prepared for life than their parents were at the same age." Yet another ignoble honor. The Free were not completely unaware of the situation. To cope with the gloomy future they anticipated, *carpe diem* had become the motto for a great many young people.

THRILL SEEKERS

The combination of diminished parental supervision and a fatalistic view of the future led the Free to engage in innovative new activities. While previous generations had taken their share of risks—drag racing and various forms of fraternity hazing come to mind—the youth of the eighties scoffed at these comparatively mild activities while taking the youthful penchant for risk to new extremes.

In March 1990, an eighteen-year-old freshman at the University of Massachusetts, Joel Mangion, was playing a game known at the school as "elevator surfing." The idea of this activity is to ride up and down the dormitory elevator shafts on top of the car. While playing this game, Joel lost his footing and plunged eight stories to his death. Elevator surfing was popular in the housing projects of New York City as well, where the kids also had a variation dubbed "helicopter," in which youngsters snuck into the pit at the bottom of an elevator shaft and rode beneath the car holding on to the electric cable that connects underneath it.

In November 1989, apparently on a dare, twelve-year-old Walter McMillan, a member of a group that called themselves the Little Tough Guys, attempted to somersault from a beam on the twenty-sixth floor of an elevator shaft onto an approaching car. Tough and little though he was, Walter got caught between the beam and the elevator car. His legs were crushed, and he died a few hours later as a result of internal injuries. Far from being an isolated incident, Walter's death was one of about forty injuries suffered during elevator surfing in 1989. Nearly two hundred people were arrested in New York City for engaging in the activity that year. Officer Herbert A. Sellers of New York offered an explanation for why a young boy would do something so dangerous: "These kids don't have enough areas to play or enough creative things to do."

There was another deadly game popular in New York City in the late eighties. The activity, called "tracking," is a perilous version of the age-old game of chicken. Youths tried to run along the tracks from one subway station to the next, and if a train approached, they would stand their ground and wave at the engineer, finally jumping to safety at the last second. On January 9, 1991, fourteen-year-old Jean Guerrier was "tracking" with some friends when the M train came screaming into the station. While trying to jump to safety, Jean slipped on the track and was struck by the train and killed. Transit officials couldn't say exactly when this game rose to popularity, but during visits to schools in 1991 they were stunned at the number of students who claimed to have played it. Most of the youths reported having learned of the game in sixth grade, when they were eleven years old.

Like the football hero of a movie called *The Program,* a number of teenagers in late 1993 discovered a dangerous new way to test their manhood. Attempting to prove they possessed nerves of steel, the idea was to lie in the middle of a busy street and let the cars whiz by them on both sides. Unlike in the film, however, this test of courage often proved to be as deadly as it was daring. In a single week, amid reports of scores of teenagers performing the stunt, two young men were struck and killed by cars and two others were critically injured. As psychiatrist Dr. Robert Gould observed about the phenomenon, "Kids will vie with each other for who can be most like the movie hero. Only in this case, the bravest may be the deadest."

The games haven't all been this lethal, but could be destructive in other ways. On June 13, 1989, callers to the Palm Beach County Probation Department in Delray Beach, Florida, were surprised to find themselves speaking not with a solemn-toned officer, but rather with a phone-sex worker named "Tina" in New York State. Probation officers hadn't brought the woman into their office as a joke. Somehow, *every* call to the probation department near Miami was being mysteriously routed to another part of the country, at no additional charge to the caller, to a pornographic-sex hotline!

While this is indeed a clever prank, the engineers at Southern Bell found no humor at all in the fact that someone had penetrated their computer security and reprogrammed the system. On the heels of this dangerous antic, no fewer than forty-two telephone company employees, dubbed the "Intrusion Task Force," were put on an around-the-clock assignment scrutinizing records and monitoring the computers for clues to the electronic incursion. A month later, the investigators were able to trace the responsibility of the "Tina" gag to a sixteen-year-old who went under the computer-hacker handle of Fry Guy and lived thousands of miles away in Indiana.

Fry Guy had earned his appellation by earlier breaking into the mainframe computers run by the McDonald's Corporation and programming in handsome raises for some of his burger-slinging buddies. He had later expanded his range of computer crime to include scamming long-distance access codes and obtaining cash advances on other people's credit cards. He finally met his match with the technicians at Ma Bell.

Fry Guy wasn't the only practitioner of hacker crime. On November 2,

1988, some six thousand computers linked by the Internet system were crippled by a little piece of rabbitlike reproducing code implanted by Cornell graduate student Robert Morris. Even though Morris's "worm" was actually a programming bug that got out of hand, thousands of hours of scientific research were lost due to his antics. And in 1990, three Atlanta teenagers calling themselves the Legion of Doom were sentenced to prison terms of fourteen to twenty-one months for a variety of illegal computer violations.

It's difficult to say how many others were wreaking havoc with their hacking, but it's likely an impressive number. The Southern Bell inquiry alone turned up a startling number of system intrusions. Company databases had been manipulated; phone numbers had been created with no name associated (and therefore nobody to bill); a diagnostic feature had been tampered with so that hackers could use it to listen in on any call that was routed through the system's switches. While all of the young hackers arrested were clearly intelligent and creative, they chose to use their skills not to improve themselves or their communities, but to engage in ever more injurious acts. Although none of their actions amounted to anything as serious as the nuclear catastrophe almost occasioned by the teenager's electronic mischief in the 1983 film *War Games,* and on the surface they seem not to have caused great harm at all, they actually cost the injured parties thousands or even millions of dollars in system redesigns and new security measures. For the most part, hackers engaged in such destructive activities just for the thrill of it.

The impetuous behavior of the Free is one characteristic that hasn't gone unnoticed by older adults. When a Gallup poll asked Americans who was more reckless, the young people of today or the Boomers, by an overwhelming five-to-one margin the respondents gave the Free the edge. After studying adolescent deaths, Dr. Mimi Mahon has observed that among today's teenagers, "There's no such thing as a reasonable or realistic fear for them." Finding alternatives to such behavior has been slow, but at least people seem to recognize the situation. It's commonly believed that teenagers generally tend toward riskier behavior because of a sense of invulnerability or immunity to risk, a belief that one sheds through experience and maturity. But what accounts for the sharp increase in such death-defying activities as lying in the middle of a highway or "elevator surfing" among the Free?

One recent study of 199 youths aged 12 to 18 and their parents may shatter the teen-invulnerability theory. When the teenagers and their parents were asked to evaluate the riskiness of a variety of activities, the youths did not see themselves as unusually invincible; they assessed the risks similarly to the adults. Both the older and younger generations shared the same biases, with individuals tending to see themselves as being less susceptible than others to certain hazards such as getting mugged, becoming an alcoholic, or getting in an auto accident. Certainly teens are not perfect at judging risks, but apparently they are no worse at it than their parents. A sense of invulnerability or immortality doesn't necessarily go hand in hand with adolescence, and this simple explanation just can't explain the increase in dangerous and destructive behaviors of this generation. There must be some other factor involved.

It's possible that the Free have been a bit more reckless and self-destructive than previous youths not as a result of naïveté, but because of having to make more decisions about their behavior with less guidance from their increasingly unavailable parents. In addition, there also seems to be simply less concern—as opposed to more ignorance—by the younger generation about the consequences of certain activities. With the increase in at least one particularly destructive activity—suicide—it's clear that something much deeper than a simple sense of invincibility was at work.

THE ULTIMATE SELF-DESTRUCTIVE ACT

Bergenfield, New Jersey, is a blue-collar community set amid the affluent suburbs of New York City that lie a few miles from the George Washington Bridge. The town was not greatly distinguishable from any number of working-class areas that are scattered across the country—until a tragic event in March 1987. And even then, the town wasn't as different as many would like to believe. On that spring day, seventeen-year-old Cheryl Burress broke off a planned date. Then she and her sixteen-year-old sister proceeded to telephone perhaps thirty friends, one after another; a staggering amount of time was spent on the phone, even for teenage girls. Later that night, Thomas Olton, eighteen, and Thomas Rizzo, nineteen, picked up the sisters, and the four young people drove off.

At some point, the youths had gotten together and laid out a plan to end their lives. The only details known for certain are that the teenagers bought three dollars' worth of gasoline at three A.M. the night they drove away in Olton's 1977 Camaro, and then turned in to one of the garages at the gloomy Foster Village garden apartment complex. They sat together in the closed garage with the car engine rumbling and took turns writing notes on a brown paper bag until they drifed out of consciousness and died.

All four of the teens were estranged, in one way or another, from families that were scarred by a history of divorce and violence. Both boys had been through treatment for drug or alcohol abuse. The two sisters were having difficulties adjusting to their mother's new husband and the kids that he had brought with him into the marriage.

The following night, in Alsip, Illinois, Nancy Grannan, nineteen years old,

Suicide Rate of White Males, by Age

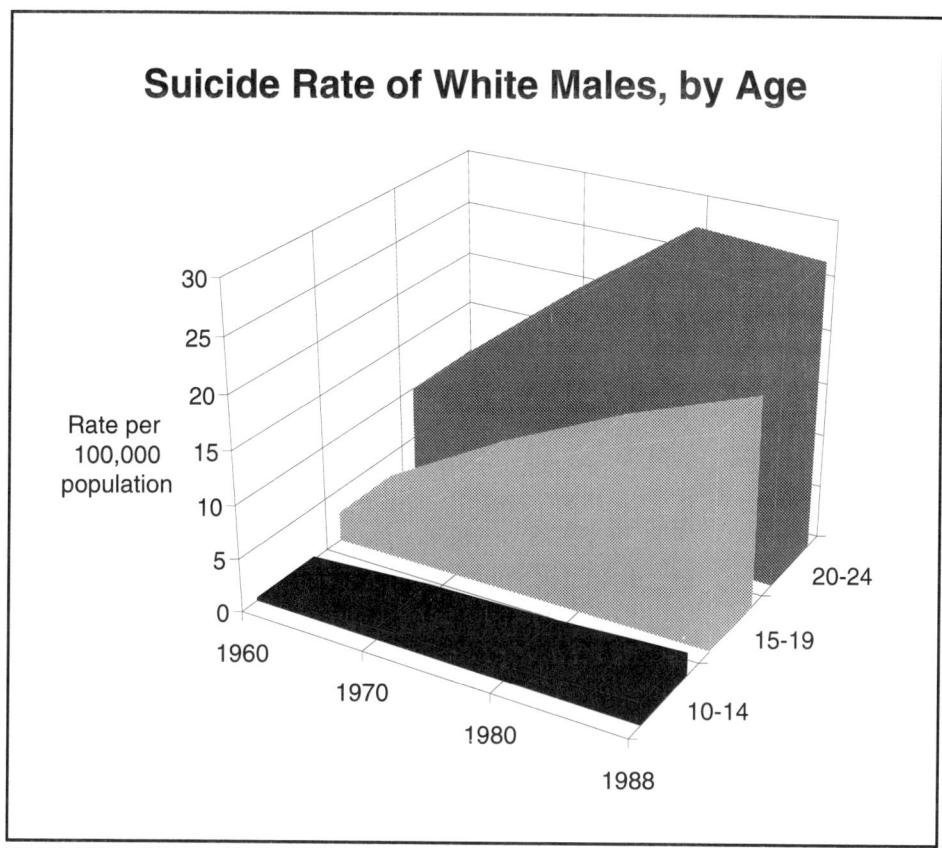

Rate per 100,000 population

SOURCE: 1992 STATISTICAL ABSTRACT OF THE UNITED STATES

and her friend Karen Logan, seventeen, likely saw the news coverage of the Bergenfield tragedy. For a number of days before this, the two girls had been telling friends of a planned "surprise." After saying good-bye to Nancy's boyfriend, they got into her Monte Carlo, parked in her parents' garage, and started the engine. They were found with a total of eleven notes. Karen was clutching a rose and a stuffed walrus; Nancy held her album of wedding photos, a reminder of her failed marriage. And these six teenagers were but a fraction of the roughly thirty who killed themselves during every forty-eight-hour period of the Free teenage years.

Suicide among the Free reached proportions that were unheard of in earlier generations. By 1988, the rate at which young people were killing themselves was double that of 1970 and triple the 1960 rate, becoming the second leading cause of death for the fifteen- to twenty-four-year-old age group. During the two decades, the percentage of younger children killing themselves increased at an even faster pace, with the rate for ten- to fourteen-year-olds more than doubling just from 1980 to 1985. All together, by the eighties, five thousand teenagers a year were committing suicide, and an estimated one hundred times that many made an unsuccessful attempt to do so. According to the CDC Youth Risk Behavior Survey, during one twelve-month period alone over a quarter-million high-school students made at least one suicide attempt that required medical attention.

This is not a phenomenon that is mirrored in the nation as a whole, for over the last twenty years, the suicide rates for all other age groups have remained steady or declined. While historically, the incidence of suicide has gone up steadily with each older age group, by 1988, a twenty- to twenty-four-year-old male was more likely to take his own life than a man of any other age, except for the elderly. More young Americans killed themselves during the decade of the eighties than were killed in our ten-year involvement in Vietnam. The adolescent term "doing it," long a teen colloquialism for having premarital sex, had mutated to mean killing oneself.

Stories of the epidemic sweeping certain areas became frequent in the press. During a seventeen-month period ending in 1980, a cluster of wealthy suburbs north of Chicago saw twenty-eight teenagers take their own lives, prompting newspapers to dub the area "the suicide belt." One high school in the Dallas suburb of Plano saw so many of its students commit suicide that its football rival, in a morose display of humor, chanted "kill them before they kill themselves" during a pre-game rally. A single Washington, D.C., youth home saw eight of its children attempt suicide in the first five months of 1986.

Many people were unsympathetic to this phenomenon; still others were outright callous. Patricia Quann, the director of the D.C. Receiving Home for Children youth agency, discounted the excessive number of suicide attempts at the above-mentioned youth home as mere "suicide gestures" by which the children were only calling attention to themselves and not really in danger. Commenting to the *Washington Post* on one girl's attempt to hang herself with a sheet, Quann remarked, "Hanging from the door—that's not a particularly good way to do it." To a *Newsweek* reporter, Bergenfield's police chief described the four teenagers who died in the suicide pact as basic "pain-in-the-ass-type kids." They were just a bunch of troubled losers, hanging out aimlessly, doing little but drinking and smoking dope and "going nowhere fast." In other words, no one would miss them.

What could cause one out of every three adolescents to report that they had "seriously considered" seeking what's been called the "ultimate numbness"? Not surprisingly, depression has been cited as a factor in 80 percent of suicides.

In a 1988 interview, the head of the Phi Delta Kappa Task Force on Adolescent Suicide, Barry Garfinkel, estimated that between 6 and 8 percent of junior- and senior-high-school students were "severely and profoundly" depressed at any given point in time, a great increase over previous decades. He also observed that "family breakdown is associated with higher rates of suicide among young people," a finding that was corroborated by a number of other studies. A 1988 study of 752 families by researchers at the New York Psychiatric Institute, for example, found that young people who attempted suicide didn't differ significantly from those who didn't in terms of age, income, or religion. What *did* distinguish them was that they were more likely "to live in nonintact family settings" and to have minimal contact with their fathers.

The escalating suicide rates of this young generation were briefly thrust into the spotlight with the 1994 death of singer Kurt Cobain. While legions of young fans swarmed to Seattle to mourn his suicide, older Americans struggled to understand how this young man could take his own life at a zenith in his career that most can only dream of. His suicide served as a dark reminder of how alienated many of the Free are, but his life and death were also a heartbreaking illustration of just how much more tension and anxiety have accompanied growing up in recent, turbulent decades.

7

NEW EXTREMES OF DISCIPLINE

Amount spent on residential
treatment centers for
emotionally disturbed children:

1969—$123,000,000

1990—$1,969,000,000

SOURCE: U.S. DEPARTMENT OF HEALTH AND HUMAN SERVICES

BRAVE NEW WORLD   Sounding like a passage out of George Orwell's ominous novel *1984*, although he predated the British author's foreboding society fifteen years, President Richard Nixon made a foreboding request to his Secretary of Health, Education and Welfare in December of 1969. The request was attached to a memo from Arnold A. Hutschnecker, a New York physician. The doctor was proposing that "the Government should have mass testing done on all six- to eight-year-old children . . . to detect [those] who have violent and homicidal tendencies." Nixon was requesting the secretary's opinion "as to the advisability of setting up pilot projects embodying some of these approaches." Hutschnecker maintained that studies indicated "future delinquent tendencies" could be predicted in *nine out of ten cases* in children of this age. He was proposing that the government try to correct these "tendencies" before they manifest themselves in actual committed crimes.

This was not an isolated proposal. James Allen, then Assistant Secretary for Education, spoke before the annual convention of the National School Boards Association a few months later and proposed that every child, at the age of two and a half, be brought to "a Central Diagnostic Center" to determine as much information about the child's background as possible, including an "educational diagnosis, a medical diagnosis, and home visits by a trained professional." The idea was to ascertain, *by age two and a half*, the child's "general potential as an individual," and to create "a detailed prescription for the child and, if necessary, for his home and family as well." On the surface, who could find fault with Allen's suggestion? He merely wanted to diagnose and remedy any "deficiencies." Nobody was being punished. Call it defective gene scrubbing.

Within three years, a number of school systems across the nation embraced the concepts of Hutschnecker and Allen with a variety of new programs. San Francisco's Unified School District used Allen's speech as the basis for a recommendation to test and "treat" where necessary all children beginning at the age of three. Schools in Southern California established projects to identify "predelinquents." In Baltimore, schools were looking for "maladaptive tendencies." The wave of special-education laws passed by some thirty states in the early seventies mandated screening not only for bad vision, teeth, and hearing, but in many cases for "Oedipal conflicts," "ego disturbances," "social behavior" problems, and a host of other psychological abnormalities. Of course, any detected problems must also be "remedied." Although the times embodied a general rebellion against "the system," where as many as 4 million children were concerned, "the system" was about to embark on yet another ill-conceived grand experiment.

BIRTH OF A DISEASE

By the early seventies, a new "epidemic" had sprung up and was sweeping the country. It wasn't swine flu or herpes; it didn't even earn a single cover story in *Time, Newsweek,* or *Life.* And yet it purportedly afflicted as many as 40 percent of all children in the United States. The "disease" was MBD, minimal brain dysfunction. It was the supposed biological basis for a vast assortment of disorders that were classified at the time by the general term "learning disabilities" (LD). MBD's victims were, according to the 1966 report issued by a task force organized by the Public Health Service, "children of near average, average, or above average general intelligence with certain learning or behavioral disabilities ranging from mild to severe." With this sort of nebulous language typifying the way the "disease" was discussed, the task force went on to identify *ninety-nine symptoms* to assist doctors and teachers in detecting this disorder in children who otherwise appeared normal. These symptoms included both hyperactivity and hypoactivity, as well as other indications as varied as being "sweet and even tempered, cooperative and friendly"; "easy acceptance of others alternating with withdrawal and shyness"; being "overly gullible and easily led"; being "socially bold and aggressive"; and having "excessive need to touch, cling, and hold on to others."

The so-called epidemic was spreading quickly. A 1971 Department of Health, Education and Welfare report speculated that 3 percent of the school-age population suffered from moderate to severe hyperactivity, the most common

MBD diagnosis. By 1974, the numbers had already risen to an estimated 15 percent. This "disease," if left untreated, could result in any number of catastrophic outcomes.

Nancy Ramos, who, in the mid-seventies, headed the California Association for Neurologically Handicapped Children, a support group for the parents of children smitten by this disease, noted that a sizable percentage of MBD children come from single-parent homes. "But it's not the broken marriage that causes the LD," she asserted, "it's the learning-disabled child that broke up the marriage in the first place." Psychiatrist Camilla Anderson, speaking before fifteen hundred suburban parents and teachers in a conference on learning disabilities, contended that MBD was the cause of everything from bad financial planning to violent crimes and slums, even unconventional sexual positions. She elaborated on these views in her 1972 book *Society Pays: The High Costs of Minimal Brain Damage in America*. Unconventional sexual positions? This pestilence had to be stopped.

SOMA HOLIDAY

Ms. Anderson's recommendation to sterilize all MBD victims, to supposedly break the genetic link that perpetuates this horrible malady, fortunately went unheeded. But the treatment of choice was something only slightly less dramatic—mood-altering drugs. Although tranquilizers as strong as Thorazine, a powerful sedative, were prescribed to alleviate problems in the classroom, the drugs of choice were Ritalin, an amphetamine made by Ciba-Geigy, and related medications such as Dexedrine and Cylert. Although Ritalin acts as a stimulant in adults, for reasons not completely known it functions as a sedative in children. By the mid-seventies, it had become a veritable cash cow for the company. One hundred and fifty thousand children were put on Ritalin in 1970. The number climbed to almost half a million by 1974, then jumped to 1.8 million by 1977. And these figures only represent new prescriptions. Authors Richard Hughes and Robert Brewin estimate that all in all, between 3 and 4 million children, the vast majority boys, were chemically treated for MBD during the seventies. The drugs were recommended for children as young as eleven months old.

The growing popularity of these drugs can be partly attributed to aggressive promotional campaigns by Ciba-Geigy and other pharmaceutical companies. Ciba actively promoted Ritalin, not only to physicians, but also to educators, PTAs, and the media. They distributed one flyer titled "The MBD Child: A Guide for Parents," as well as the ninety-six-page "Physician's Handbook: Screening for MBD." Their descriptions of MBD's symptoms were as vague and all-encompassing as those of the Public Health Service task force, and, predictably, Ritalin always held the cure. Not only was it the answer for the classroom disorder induced by MBD students; it was a virtual panacea. The National Easter Seal Society heralded the benefits of chemical therapy, claiming these drugs "can turn a non-achieving, hyperactive child into an interested, alert, cooperative student within twenty minutes!"

To make the learning-disability diagnosis more palatable to the parents of the Free, stories were widely circulated in drug-company literature and the mainstream media that romanticized MBD. In magazines as diverse as *Psychology Today* and *People*, in television specials on LD, and in advertisements, LD was designated "the affliction of geniuses." Self-titled experts on the topic "proved" that great men such as Albert Einstein and Thomas Edison suffered from this disorder. If only they had had access to the treatments available today, went the idea, who knows how much more they might have given us. The diagnosis was marketed as a twisted sort of status symbol. Your LD child, went the underlying presumption, is just like these men, but if untreated he can never reach his potential. Interestingly, no explanation was ever given as to how Einstein and Edison avoided the inevitable tragic downfall, nor did it seem to occur to anyone that the last thing one would want to do would be to "treat" a future Einstein.

James Bosco, a professor of education at Western Michigan University, speculated in a 1974 paper, "Teaching with Drugs," on the "awesome potential" for using chemical treatments to teach and aid learning. "Future teachers will be trained in a school which is an amalgam of contemporary schools of education, medicine, and pharmacy," he predicted. "A considerable portion of the teacher's training will be devoted to understanding physiology and psychopharmacology, which will equip the teacher to use substances which affect learning and learning-related behaviors." He foresaw these teacher-healers handing out pills to students for everything from problems paying attention to difficulties in learning math. Presumably teachers would no longer have to spend time simply teaching these things.

IS THERE A DOCTOR IN THE CLASSROOM?

While physicians wrote in prescriptions for Ritalin and the other drugs, the initial diagnoses were typically made by elementary-school teachers, not generally recognized for their expertise in the field of medicine. Once teachers witnessed the calming effects of drug treatment on boisterous children in their classes, many quickly saw it as the answer to their prayers. One Long Island pediatrician explained in the 1979 book *The Tranquilizing of America*, that "schoolteachers are very impressed with drug therapy because here we have a kid who is climbing the walls and now suddenly he's sitting down so they can work with him." They quickly learned to rationalize these decisions. If kids weren't learning, related the physician, "it wasn't the teacher's fault. It was this hyperactivity." Teachers in some school districts were given wide authority to interpret a student's medical needs.

This latitude could result in devastating effects on parents and their children. In their 1975 book *The Myth of the Hyperactive Child*, Peter Schrag and Diane Divoky related the experience of a family in Little Rock, Arkansas, whose children had been ordered to be placed on medication by their teachers, but who refused to comply with the order. "We received almost daily notes from the children's teachers and calls from the school. We were told that our children had completely quit trying and were failing every subject. We knew what they were trying to accomplish by this because we knew parents in the neighborhood that submitted . . . because they couldn't take the pressure. Believe me, it wasn't a pretty sight to see little children's personalities changed with the use of drugs." Their horror climaxed when they were given a call by the school principal, who threatened "taking it out of our hands. . . . The school officials were contemplating using our children in a trial court case to see if children could be put [on medication] without the parents' consent." The family moved to another state. But the situation in some other states was no less dire. Dr. Nancy Durant, a New Jersey child psychiatrist, observed that "we have kids who are put out of school . . . and we are told that they cannot return until they are on medication and have been on it for ten days."

Even when specialists were called in to verify a teacher's diagnosis, in too many cases the tests carried out to assess the legitimacy of the decision were interpreted not objectively, but so as to automatically support the teacher. One Fordham University sociologist explained in a 1978 interview that when these tests were performed, "very often the tests are inexact and the children are wrongly diagnosed, and the pressure is on to keep them quiet and drugs are prescribed." With most objections to the drug thus ignored, Ritalin became so prevalent in the mid-seventies that it was referred to as "the smart pill" in playground talk.

THE LIVING DEAD   If the calming effect that Ritalin and similar drugs had on students—the effect that so delighted teachers—was genuinely beneficial and facilitated learning, then perhaps all this would be making too much of a small thing. That would be an arguable defense if not for one fact—calming children down is the *only* "constructive" effect that these drugs produce.

The acceptance of drugging children had become so widespread that this prevalence alone was often used to justify perpetuating the practice. In their 1977 book *The Hyperactive Child in the Classroom*, Frank P. Alabiso and James C. Hansen asserted that "the best testament to the effectiveness of chemotherapy is the frequency with which drugs are used in the treatment of hyperactive children." What the rampant use of psychoactive drugs on children did was mask the fact that the entire practice was to a great extent nothing but a house of cards.

Even the original 1966 Public Health Service task force acknowledged the "purist point of view" that MBD is "in most instances an unproven presumptive diagnosis." However, they were not averse to rejecting this conclusion in favor of the more "pragmatic case" that they ultimately supported. Schrag and Divoky note that "of the 756 reports on the psychotropic medication of children published between 1937 and March 1971, only a handful reflected controlled studies using the direct measurement of behavior to indicate drug effects; in more than half of those studies, no significant difference was found between drug and placebo effect." They add that "the only study that included 'normal' children showed that they responded in exactly the same way as those said to be hyperactive."

Noted child psychiatrist Dr. Gerald Coles reviewed every study conducted from 1940 to the mid-seventies that specifically addressed the influence of stimulant drugs on learning disabilities, which were the alleged reason for prescribing any such medication. Of the total of seventeen studies, which he notes had almost all "been poorly designed and controlled," the results were, even so, convergent. "Stimulant drugs have little, if any, impact on . . . long-term academic outcome." Their major effect seemed to be an "improvement in classroom manageability." A representative study published in the *American Journal of Orthopsychiatry* in 1976 found that after a group of elementary-school students were put on Ritalin, their teachers associated their new tranquillity with increased achievement. However, objective measures showed no positive effect on learning ability or perceptual skills. Furthermore, the kids were judged to be less energetic and less emotionally expressive.

Perhaps the most astonishing study of the effects of Ritalin was conducted at the Montreal Children's Hospital by Dr. Gabrielle Weiss. This controlled five-year study was even underwritten with a grant from Ciba-Geigy, lending one to suspect that the conclusions might be skewed in favor of the company. Yet Dr. Weiss concluded that the drug "did not significantly affect [the children's] outcome after five years of treatment." In testing two groups of children, all diagnosed as hyperactive, one group was given Ritalin and the other given nothing (a third was given Thorazine). There were essentially no differences between the medicated and nonmedicated children in emotional adjustment, delinquency, mother-child relationship, or academic performance. When was this study completed? Nineteen seventy-two. Perhaps 4 million Ritalin prescriptions would be needlessly written in the ensuing decade. Dr. Coles, along with many others, concluded that "after decades of research, it has still not been demonstrated that disabling neurological dysfunctions exist in more than a minuscule number of these children." Even a recent study that suggests that there may be a physical link between hyperactivity and the brain's ability to metabolize glucose recognized that there was "no significant difference . . . between patients with hyperactivity who had current learning deficits and those who did not."

The MBD diagnosis had become so abused that in 1979 the FDA finally ordered it eliminated as a diagnostic term. Ciba-Geigy stopped advertising Ritalin as a cure. MBD was removed from the 1980 edition of the *Diagnostic and Statistical Manual of Mental Disorders* because of its ambiguous definition. The use of psychoactive drugs on kids dropped off considerably.

Thus, for all intents and purposes, between 3 and 4 million Free children were given sedatives simply to make them more compliant in the classroom, or because their behavior was outside of some ideal that a particular adult desired. Drugging children had become, to use Schrag and Divoky's phrase, "the 'enlightened' answer to spanking."

SHORT AND SWEET

None of this would merit a significant place in any history of the Free if it were not for the fact that Ritalin and similar drugs that were prescribed to so many children were known to have possibly severe side effects. One mother relates how her five-year-old son was affected when placed on Ritalin in the mid-seventies. He "had a loss of appetite and insomnia. . . . The drug made him so nervous that he kept picking on his nails and cuticles. His skin was torn to his knuckles." She finally refused to give the drug to him anymore. During withdrawal he "went through periods of depression, anxiety, sleeplessness. Then he would sleep all day. . . . He was extremely unhappy and had pains in his stomach." Her son's reaction was not uncommon. Other adverse reactions include skin rash, nausea, dizziness, headache, blood-pressure and pulse changes, cardiac arrhythmia, and a host of other symptoms. Perhaps the most serious side effect is stunted growth, one of the reasons why Ritalin had been banned in Sweden and Japan by the mid-seventies.

What may have been overlooked due to careless MBD diagnoses and an overreliance on drugging were real academic difficulties. Dr. Gerald Coles cites as an example a series of studies carried out from the fifties to the seventies that dealt with a familiar problem young children have, reversing letters. Many kids confuse "b" and "d" or "p" and "q," a predicament that often brought the hasty determination of dyslexia, a commonly diagnosed form of LD, and subsequent medication. Coles relates that "the studies showed that the discrimination necessary to avoid reversals was a 'learned cognitive skill'—in other words, an ability children needed to be taught." No pill can teach a child skills such as this. For treatment of alleged hyperactivity, other studies showed that a simple change in the child's diet could bring about great improvements in calming him down. Giving a kid a pill was simply easier than devising a truly effective strategy to alleviate any academic difficulties.

Perhaps even more dangerous than the physical side effects of drugging so many children in this manner were the psychological implications. To tell a child that he must take a pill in order to change his behavior sets a worrisome precedent. Writers Lori and Bill Granger, whose own son was misdiagnosed with a learning disability in 1982, wrote in their 1986 book *The Magic Feather: The Truth About "Special Education"* that "some kids even learn to ask for their pills to control themselves—having absorbed the idea that they are not personally able to take responsibility for their emotions or their performance in class." Dr. Mark Stewart, a child psychiatrist, commented that when a child has been on such drugs for many years, not an uncommon scenario, problems await him further on down the road. "The drugs hid the child's real personality," he noted, "often leading to a postpuberty identity crisis. By the time the child reaches puberty he is a child who does not know what his undrugged personality is." Schrag and Divoky wrote that "an entire generation is slowly being conditioned to distrust its own instincts, to regard its deviation from the narrowing standards of approved norms as sickness." We can be thankful these enlightened treatments weren't around in Edison's or Einstein's day. We may have never developed light bulbs (or nuclear weapons).

Possibly the most damaging consequence of chemical treatment of kids is an early reliance upon drugs to achieve a desired disposition. As far back as 1971, a blue-ribbon panel assembled in Washington to study the repercussions of using psychoactive drugs on children noted this problem. The panel acknowledged the "insidious fear of establishing early in life a predisposition to use drugs, whether legal or illegal, to induce a desired but not necessary mood or behavioral change." These fears may have been well founded. One study that tracked a group of 103 boys who were diagnosed as hyperactive in the mid-seventies found that by their early twenties, four times as many of these young men were abusing drugs as those in a control group from similar backgrounds. Habits learned early are hard to break.

I WAS BAD BECAUSE YOU FORGOT TO GIVE ME MY PILL

MOTHER'S LITTLE HELPER

How did this practice of drugging children become so widespread in the face of so much evidence that essentially revealed the futility and even inherent dangers involved? A combination of medical findings and misdirected sociological beliefs resulted in the shameful phenomenon. In the late sixties, there were a number of medical breakthroughs in neurology that presented hard evidence that a tiny percentage of the population did suffer from actual brain damage or other neurological problems. The scientists involved in this research perhaps had no idea of the way in which their findings would be used.

Some have speculated that the new special-education terminologies of the early seventies evolved mainly to placate the expanding middle class. One author explains that terms like MBD and LD "extricated parents from 'blame,' as, for example, the classification 'emotionally disturbed' would not have done; second, the term[s] did not carry the stigma of 'mildly retarded.' " Parents were relieved that their childrens' "problems" were not their "fault" at all. In fact, they were not the teacher's fault either, or anyone else's. It's just a simple birth defect. The irony is that the original definition of MBD itself precludes any actual determined physical basis. Its "precise cause is not known," asserted the Ciba-Geigy literature. Nonetheless, these new designations appeased a lot of parents and teachers.

In the seventies, the adult method of choice to alter one's emotions was certainly prescription drugs. After all, more than 4 *billion* Valium and Librium were swallowed in 1977 alone to relieve "anxiety attacks." With so many parents relying on pills to rid themselves of unpleasant feelings, why would they not imagine the same relief being available for their children? What is the most upsetting is that this widespread chemical intervention was actually seen as a legitimate method of controlling small children whose only crime was to annoy a teacher, exhibit a little excess energy, or fail to live up to some adult's expectation of behavior.

WE JUST DON'T WANT YOU TO HURT YOURSELF

Once the FDA banned the MBD diagnosis, another development rose up to take its place. In 1979, the United States Supreme Court issued a little-publicized yet pivotal decision regarding a citizen's right to due-process protections under the law. The decision didn't apply to everyone. In fact, it affected only one group—the Free Generation—while it greatly empowered their parents and others who might presumably be working on behalf of a child's "best interests." In the case, *Parham v. J.R.*, the Court determined that states do not have to adopt measures to regulate the confinement of juveniles in psychiatric facilities deeming that "parental discretion, reinforced by the judgment of admitting staff that inpatient treatment was medically necessary, was adequate to protect minors' constitutional interests." Legal protections that apply to adults in attempts to commit them to psychiatric hospitals no longer pertained to minors.

In dissenting, Justice William Brennan noted that when a parent takes the extreme measure of institutionalizing his child, it is likely to indicate family turmoil and isn't necessarily related to problems centered in the child. A stressed parent could very well be grasping at the easiest, most convenient means of getting rid of an irritating teenager for a while, regardless of what would be best for the child. Lois Weithorn, a psychologist and lawyer, has called the *Parham* decision "unbridled discretion for parents." We've already seen what some adults working "in the best interests of the child" were capable of. This is one group of people to whom one didn't want to give "unbridled discretion."

Not surprisingly, institutionalizing children spread like a flu epidemic after this ruling. In 1971, a child being confined in a private psychiatric hospital was almost unheard of; there were only 6,500 minors nationwide in such facilities that year. By the end of the decade, when *Parham* was handed down, the number had already doubled. Then from 1980 to 1986 alone, adolescent admissions to "junior psycho wards" shot up 350 percent to nearly 50,000. The trend continued upward, and by the end of the decade of the eighties, the figure had reached nearly 200,000. Thus from the time the last of the Boomers hit his teenage years to the time the last of the Free did, the chances of being institutionalized as a minor increased by a factor of thirty. As the decade of the nineties began, there were more children and adolescents sitting in mental hospitals nationwide than there were people living in soon-to-be President Bill Clinton's hometown of Little Rock, Arkansas.

These young people were being admitted for a variety of new afflictions. Whereas the few patients of previous decades had been committed for problems such as suicide attempts or debilitating drug addictions—circumstances that may very well warrant such a drastic measure—many were now being placed under psychiatric care for treatment of nebulous conditions like "conduct disorder" or "adolescent adjustment disorder" as well. In many cases, children were confined for the crimes of truancy, arguing with parents, or "promiscuity." According to data compiled in the mid-eighties by the House Select Committee on Children, Youth and Families, in 40 percent of cases of adolescent psychiatric confinement the action was found later to be "unnecessary." A recent University of Michigan study came to even more distressing conclusions. The researchers determined that 70 percent of such admissions were not only unnecessary, but were "inappropriate and potentially harmful" to the children involved, and that most of the children studied had been hospitalized for relatively minor personality disorders or nonaddictive drug use.

Troubled teens had become big business. Between 1969 and 1982, private ownership of the hospital facilities that treat them grew by 150 percent and continued upward throughout the next decade. By 1986, 85 percent of the facilities were under franchise ownership. Several major hospital chains were growing by 20 percent a year. How was such incredible growth achieved? Savvy marketing. Mellow advertisements extolling the miracles that the facilities can perform for your problem child became commonplace on television and radio. In addition, hospital employees were sometimes paid bonuses for bringing in new business. The *Chicago Tribune* reported a contest held by the Charter Medical Corporation, which managed a number of psychiatric facilities, with the winner determined from the number of admissions and referrals generated by its employees. The grand prize was an eight-day cruise for two in the Caribbean. A great way to boost admissions, but who was looking out for the patients' best interests?

A few other trends were responsible for the rise in teenage admissions. For one thing, more and more parents had sought therapy or psychiatric help for themselves, and could thus be quick to seek the same treatment for their children at the signs of any emotional difficulties, even those that simply go hand in hand with adolescence. Additionally, health-insurance providers increasingly were willing to pay for psychiatric hospitalization, but not for outpatient treatment. In fact, by 1986, thirteen states had mandated that insurance plans provide such coverage, and more states were to follow. As Dr. Ira Lourie, director of the Child and Adolescent Service System of the National Institute of Mental Health told *Newsweek*, "There are a lot of options available—but often kids end up in hospitals because that is what insurance will pay for." The length of a patient's stay often corresponded to the extent of his insurance coverage.

Finally, the same social developments that contributed to so many other problems the Free experienced were a factor in teen institutionalization as well. Sylvia Ann Hewlett, author of the 1991 book *When the Bough Breaks: The Cost of Neglecting Our Children,* found that "divorce and single parenthood seem to trigger a large proportion of these psychiatric admissions." In fact, more than 80 percent of children confined to in-house psychiatric facilities are from families in which the biological parents no longer live together. No one can say if the splintered family caused the child to need such help or was merely the impetus for the parent to feel the need to send the child away, but two USC sociologists, authors of the 1986 study "Mental Health: The Hidden System of Adolescent Social Control," related a sad concession about the options available to many teenagers: "Hospitals may be the most humane alternative for many children, particularly those with chaotic family situations."

The Free learned to dread the words that terrified the narrator of Los Angeles rock group Suicidal Tendencies' 1983 classic, "Institutionalized." Lying in introspective contemplation in his room, and wanting only to drink a Pepsi, the boy is confronted by his parents, who say, "We're afraid you're gonna hurt yourself, so we decided that it would be in your best interests if we could put you some place where you could get the help that you need."

8

HOME AWAY FROM HOME

Number of eighteen- to twenty-nine-year-old state prison inmates nationwide:

1970—90,934

1991—323,798

SOURCE: U.S. DEPARTMENT OF JUSTICE

RUNNING TO STAND STILL

Increasingly during the seventies and eighties, teenagers discovered one method of avoiding being sedated, incarcerated, or otherwise troubled by their own families: They ran away from home. The runaway has long been an American icon—the embodiment of the sort of romantic adventurer for which many of our forefathers stood. Huckleberry Finn took off and paddled his way down the Mississippi, along the way growing from a boy into a man and learning how to love and respect others who might be different. Horatio Alger–type stories of young boys and girls running away to find fame with the circus have long been commonplace in American juvenile fiction. Even the flower children of the sixties ran away in search of lifestyles and environments that they considered aesthetically and morally superior to the supposedly stale existences of their parents. For the Free, however, who fled home in unprecedented numbers, there was no romance behind their actions, and rarely did a fairy-tale ending conclude their flight. For unlike previous generations of runaways, children who set off on their own in the eighties and nineties were likely not running to find an ideal, but were desperately fleeing to *escape* an unbearable situation at home.

The actual number of runaways is impossible to derive, as the definition of what constitutes running away is debatable and, furthermore, many incidents go unreported. But most estimates put the figure at between 1 million and 1.5 million youths a year who remained away from home at least one night during the eighties. This was roughly double the number of 1970. Since the actual number of teenagers in the population declined during this period, these figures are even more remarkable. Even the most serious type of case, the cross-country wayfarer who shows up helpless at places like New York's Port Authority bus terminal, likely amounted to hundreds of thousands per year. Los Angeles officials estimated that roughly ten thousand runaways came to the streets of Hollywood during any given year. For these children, to choose the unknown dangers of big-city streets over living at home indicates a tragic desperation.

An even more alarming situation than the rise in runaways was the extraordinary number of children who didn't leave home on their own, but were thrown out of the house by their parents—a phenomenon that was almost unheard of a few decades earlier. "Discarded children," "pushouts," or "throwaways" numbered over 125,000 a year, according to one 1988 study. These kids were abandoned or told to leave home for offenses such as misbehaving, getting pregnant, or even eating too much. Adding to that group the youths who have been placed in foster homes, detention centers, and mental-health facilities, a 1989 House committee put the total number of throwaways at that time at nearly 500,000 and rising. Representative Thomas Bliley, Jr., commented that this enormous problem reflects "the devaluation of human life" in our society. Adding to the tragedy of the "pushouts" is that they often don't show up in statistics for runaway or missing children, because no one back home is looking for them.

The roots of this mushrooming problem lie in the declining regard for children's concerns during these years. The House panel, for example, cited the growing problems of "alcohol and drug abuse . . . the devastating trend since 1970 toward family dissolution," and the lack of funds available to help those at risk. Of those who left on their own, the vast majority were victims of physical or sexual abuse who saw no other way to escape the horror of their home life.

The life they find on the road, though, is usually a far cry from the adventures of Huck Finn or a happy-go-lucky circus performer. New York City Police interviewed 168 runaway youths in a 1986 program called Operation Outreach and found the options available to the children to be limited and generally unhealthy. About one in five panhandled as a means of survival, and twice that number became involved in prostitution. Researcher Dotsin Rader studied runaways on the streets and found that selling their body was the fate awaiting a large percentage of the kids. "Runaways in the streets for more than a month usually end up as prostitutes because they have no other way to make do. They will remain in it, on average, for at least three years," he found. The consequences faced by these children are as serious as those of any prostitute; a major cause of death among boys who are engaged in prostitution is rectal hemorrhage. And of course, the specter of AIDS that looms over everyone is especially threatening to these kids. Paradoxically, however, a *Newsweek* reporter found in 1988 that this isn't as much of a concern as one would think. "AIDS is not a dominant fear on the streets. Hour to hour, there is enough else to be afraid about." As one young runaway told the reporter, "You learn to survive. But you also learn not to care if you don't." Unfortunately, many don't survive. An estimated five thousand kids a year were buried in unmarked graves during the eighties, unidentified and unmourned.

Faced with a growing number of families failing to provide an environment stable enough to keep their kids from fleeing, America was slow to offer alternatives to this situation. Programs for foster children, for example, generally received only a small fraction of their authorized funds, and youth shelters remained woefully understaffed and underfinanced. Instead, the response to this disturbing situation was a tendency toward building more jails and institutions for youths rather than putting the resources into programs that prevent the need for such extreme and harmful measures in the first place. As in so many other areas in the last two decades, the course of action had been to ignore the problem until it was too late.

THE CRIME ROLLER COASTER

The criminal record of the Free is an enigma. It is a two-part story. The first wave of the Free reversed the juvenile crime trend that had been rising since World War II. But then, in the mid-eighties, the decline was abruptly halted as the crime rate again began zooming upward. By the dawn of the nineties, young adults and children were committing violent crimes at a rate unprecedented in U.S. history, and we were incarcerating our population at a rate higher than that of any nation on earth. Only South Africa even came close.

In the late seventies and early eighties, the youth that had proven to be so compliant in other areas of life were increasingly so in their respect for the law as well. Juvenile arrests were on the decline, both in real numbers and as a percentage of the population, and there was talk that the crime boom that accompanied the baby boom might at last be over. In California, for example, from 1975 to 1985 there was a 36 percent decline in the share of the juvenile population arrested. And the declining arrest rate of youths didn't simply mirror the trend of the adult population; the overall adult crime rate increased in the state over the same period.

The youth crime rate was dropping so steadily that police and school authorities began to conceive of ever more creative ways of ensnaring young criminals. Police forces across the country began planting "moles" in high schools to buy drugs from students, and narcotics-sniffing dogs were brought in to check out lockers.

Male Homicide Arrests by Age, 1970 - 1991

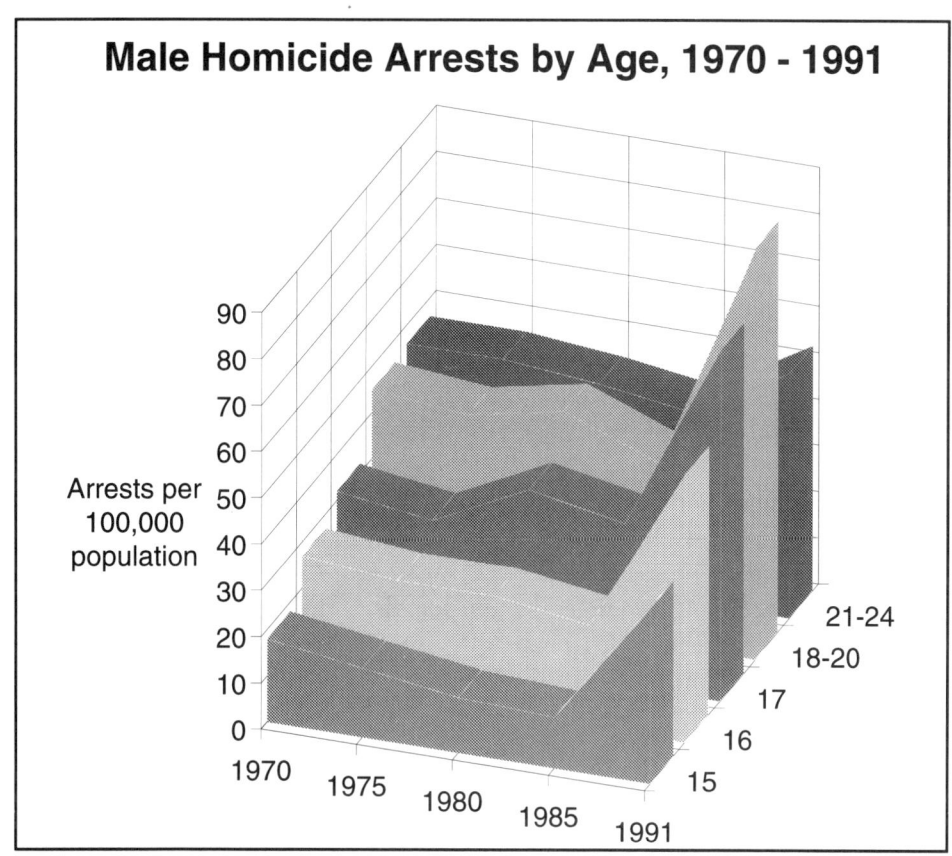

SOURCE: NORTHEASTERN UNIVERSITY, NATIONAL CRIME ANALYSIS PROGRAM

Despite such police initiatives, the number of juveniles arrested nationwide dropped considerably from the seventies to the eighties. However, the number of those arrested who were subsequently *imprisoned* skyrocketed. A Free teenager arrested for a crime was *three to four times* more likely to be incarcerated than his Boomer counterpart of a decade earlier. And he was also much more likely to be locked up for committing a nonviolent crime. During hearings on juvenile delinquency in 1973, it was estimated that on any given day, there were almost eight thousand young people held in prisons in the United States. Despite the ensuing drop in juvenile crime, fifteen years later, California *alone* could claim this many teenage inmates. In 1990 the nation was shocked to discover that one young black man in four was either in prison, on probation, or on parole—more than were enrolled in college. Just as they were overrepresented in hospitals and mental institutions, Free youths were overrepresented in prisons as well.

In the mid-eighties, however, the juvenile crime rate began to match the skyrocketing incarceration rate. From 1985 to 1991, the rate of homicide arrests for teenagers and young adults more than doubled. And, surprisingly, the greatest increase in the overall crime rate was seen by teenage girls, with the number arrested for all violent crimes soaring by 62 percent in a decade. With this reversal the Free stood alone, for the arrest rates of older adults dropped during this interval. After more than a decade of steadily dropping juvenile crime rates, now, largely fueled by the drug wars in urban areas and the growing availability and increased firepower of guns, the Free exploded in violence that was unparalleled in American history.

Free-style crime tended to be more random, senseless, and savage than it had been for previous generations. In 1989 the nation listened in horror to the news reports and trial proceedings of a gang of youths in New York City who brutally beat, knifed, and raped a twenty-eight-year-old woman who was jogging in Central Park. They had been "wilding," or committing random mayhem because "it was fun," as one of the accused teenagers told the Manhattan district attorney. In a six-month period in 1989 and 1990, four Chicago youths were murdered by fellow teenagers for their waist-length warm-up jackets that bore the insignia of their favorite professional athletic team. The value of the jackets was between $90 and $200. Three 1988 New York City prep-school graduates, looking to fund the repairs for a car they had damaged, set out on a shooting and robbery spree that resulted in one of them being gunned down by a police officer and the other two facing robbery and attempted murder charges. The mayhem transcended all geographical and economic borders, but had one indelible characteristic: the youth of the brutal perpetrators.

ADULT CRIMES, ADULT PENALTIES, CHILD CRIMINALS

Such heinous crimes deserve harsh sentences, and, in a reversal of precedent, that is what they got. Unlike in the seventies, when Boomer youths were entitled to sealed court records and relatively light sentences, the Free juvenile offenders of the eighties were dealt with more severely, and increasingly tried as adults.

In March of 1989, weeks shy of his tenth birthday, Cameron Kocher of Kunkletown, Pennsylvania, was left at home by himself while his parents were at work. He found the key to his father's gun cabinet, opened it, pulled out a high-powered .35-caliber Marlin rifle, and pointed it out a second-story window. Setting seven-year-old Jessica Ann Carr in the sights as she raced across a nearby field on a snowmobile, he pulled the trigger. Jessica had bragged a few hours earlier that she could beat Cameron at video games. The bullet tore through the little girl's back, shattered her spine and burst out her chest. She died two hours later. Rather than indicting his parents for the negligence of leaving their guns so accessible, the courts charged Cameron with criminal homicide, which, in Pennsylvania, mandated that the defendant stand trial as an adult regardless of age.

In New York, Florida, New Jersey, and other states, laws were changed so that children between the ages of thirteen and fifteen could now be tried in adult courts and sentenced to long prison terms. A commission formed by the attorney general in California recommended sending juveniles convicted of murder to prison rather than to California Youth Authority facilities. Laws that protect the privacy of arrested juveniles were eliminated, clearing the way for newspapers to report on the court proceedings. Nationwide, a total of 61,253 children were referred to adult criminal courts in 1987 alone.

The tough-on-crime eighties came just in time for the Free to take over the population of the prison system. While the average sentence of a young person convicted of any crime in 1975 was just under forty months, in 1991, a criminal could expect a sentence of fifty-seven months. For drug violations, the fastest-growing area of crime, the average prison sentence nearly *doubled* from the seventies to the nineties. The pinnacle of the sentencing furor came when eighteen-year-old Ronald Harmelin was ordered in 1986 to a Michigan prison for life, with no possibility of parole, for possession of cocaine—his first offense. Harmelin joined sixty other first offenders in Michigan serving life terms for nonviolent drug violations. The Supreme Court later ruled that this punishment was not unduly severe. With such sentencing guidelines, prison became so commonplace in the inner cities that some, like Barry Krisberg, executive director of the National Council on Crime and Delinquency, argued that the seeming inevitability of jail time had voided the deterrent factor of prison. "Years ago, the story that someone had gone to prison was almost big news," Krisberg told the *New York Times* in 1992. "Now it's ordinary. Some young men have said to me, going to prison in their community is like going to the army was for my generation. You spend a couple of years in the army, we spend a couple of years in prison."

Children were not spared the most severe sentence of all. Ronald Ward earned the title of America's youngest death-row prisoner in 1985 when an Arkansas jury sentenced him to die by lethal injection for the murders of two elderly women and a twelve-year-old boy. Ronald was fifteen years old. Wayne Thompson of Oklahoma was also fifteen when he and three others murdered his sister's former husband following a heated argument. He, too, was sentenced to death by lethal injection. Terry Roach was all of seventeen when he and two friends murdered a young man and his girlfriend. He pleaded guilty in a nonjury trial and was sentenced to die in the electric chair.

Nor were girls spared in the state's tenacious quest to make young criminals pay for their offenses. Paula Cooper became the youngest female on death row in memory when she was sentenced to die for the 1985 robbery and murder of a seventy-eight-year-old Bible-school teacher in Gary, Indiana. Paula was fifteen. Her case became a cause célèbre in Europe, eliciting more than 2 million petition signatures in Spain, Germany, France, and Italy urging leniency because of Paula's childhood of severe abuse by her parents, neither of whom even came to the courtroom to hear their daughter's sentence. Pope John Paul II even attempted to intervene on her behalf.

In his 1981 book *The Kid Business*, author Ronald Taylor described the mood toward harsher penalties for young offenders: "It was uncanny. The thirst for retribution, the self-indulgent mood that demanded severe punishment for youngsters . . . rather than spending the time and resources before the murder at least to attempt to help such children, was disconcerting." In 1986 there were thirty-one prisoners on death row for crimes committed as juveniles. Amnesty International found that only eight individuals were executed worldwide for juvenile crimes between 1978 and 1988. Three out of those eight youths were executed in the United States. The only other countries that had executed juveniles were Pakistan, Rwanda, and Bangladesh.

In 1988, the Supreme Court barred executions of those who were under sixteen at the time of their crime. Ronald Ward thus had his sentence modified to life imprisonment without possibility of parole. Wayne Thompson's sentence was also changed to life. Paula Cooper's was reduced to thirty years to life. Terry Roach, however, didn't make the cut. "Won't nobody have to drag me in there," he remarked to a reporter as his date with the chair drew near. And nobody did. As he sat strapped in the electric chair, he struggled through a brief statement, having barely learned to read. "To the families of the victims, my heart is still with you in your sorrow. May you forgive me just as I know the Lord has done." He added, "I pray that my fate will someday save another kid from the wrong side of the tracks." He died nine minutes later, after absorbing jolts of as much as 2,300 volts of electricity. Outside the prison compound, a mob had gathered. They weren't the standard anti–death-penalty protesters who tended to demonstrate at the sites where capital punishment was being administered; they had come to cheer the execution of a mentally impaired criminal for a crime he had committed before he was even old enough to vote.

EYE FOR AN EYE Perhaps suprisingly, the Free are America's staunchest supporters of capital punishment. A 1987 Gallup poll showed that 83 percent of those aged eighteen to twenty-nine favored the death penalty for persons convicted of murder—the highest share of any age group. Recent college surveys show twice the support for capital punishment as Boomer college students had indicated, as well as a significantly higher portion of students who believe there is too much concern for the rights of criminals. Just as one segment of the young was committing crimes at record rates, the larger segment was also demanding retribution for a criminal's offenses.

One explanation of the heavy Free support for tough punishment of criminals is that they are also the most likely to be the *victims* of crime. The rate of crimes committed against the Free has mirrored the down-and-up rate of crime committed by the Free. From the mid-seventies to the mid-eighties, for example, homicide victimization rates for fifteen- to nineteen-year-olds fell by 4 percent to 7 percent each year. But then they zoomed upward. In urban centers in 1989, there were nearly twenty-eight firearm homicide deaths annually for every hundred thousand teenagers. Black male teens were being murdered at five times this already astounding rate. Although the homicide rates in suburban and rural areas were much lower, the eighties saw a 61-percent rise in the rate of kids being shot, making gunshot wounds the leading cause of death for boys in this age group.

According to the Department of Education, by the late eighties, 81 percent of the victims of all violent crime were aged 19 or younger. For all teenagers, male and female, vehicle accidents were the leading cause of death, followed by homicide, with suicide in third place. If a member of the Free died during the teenage or young adult years, in *four out of five* cases it was a violent death.

In the aftermath of two youths being shot to death by police and another being killed after crashing a stolen car, Edna Williams of Newark, New Jersey, explained to a *New York Times* reporter, "I can't let go because children are still being killed. Whether they're killing themselves or putting police in jeopardy and getting shot, they're dying." The Free likely support a tough-on-crime stance not out of a blind thirst for retribution but because, like Ms. Williams, they're simply tired of living amid so much violence.

9

WHAT A DIFFERENCE TWENTY YEARS MAKES

Fordham University Index of Social Well-Being in the U.S.*
(Scale 0 to 100)

1970 level—75

1991 level—36

SOURCE: *NEW YORK TIMES* 5 OCTOBER 1992:16.

POP-CULTURE ICONS THEN AND NOW

The childhood and teenage experiences of the Boomers and the Free Generation are pointedly different. From the fifties and sixties to the seventies and eighties, the country underwent monumental transformations in the political and social arenas. The forces that shaped these two markedly different generations are illustrated below, in a comparison of the popular culture and media influences to which we were both exposed. It would be an understatement to say that things have degenerated in some areas. If it's true that we're products of our environment, this list might help explain a few things.

---

*The index combines measurements of sixteen social problems including unemployment, poverty, suicide, and child abuse.

	BOOMER YOUTH	**FREE YOUTH**
Sex-Related Anxiety	Crabs	AIDS
Influential Crossover Religious Man	Rev. Martin Luther King	Rev. Donald Wildmon
Hot Sports Car	Ford Mustang	Delorean
Pop Music Superstar	Michael Jackson (child prodigy)	Michael Jackson (reconstructed, reclusive enigma)
World Boxing Champ	Muhammad Ali	Leon Spinks
Rock Megastar Group	The Beatles	The Bee Gees
U.S. President	John F. Kennedy	Gerald R. Ford
Dastardly Movie Villain	Norman Bates	Freddy Krueger
Street Gang Movie	*West Side Story*	*Colors*
Teen Angst Novel	*The Catcher in the Rye*	*Less Than Zero*
Music Innovation	Rock and Roll	Disco
Popular Bubble Gum Cards	Baseball Cards	"Garbage Pail Kids" Cards
Anxiety of Youth Film	*The Graduate*	*The Breakfast Club*
Campaign Buzz Words	I Like Ike	Read My Lips
Dance Craze	The Twist	Slam Dancing
Vice Presidential Achievement	Richard Nixon's Kitchen Debate with Khrushchev	Dan Quayle's Spelling Lesson
Popular Street Drug	Pot	Crack

	BOOMER YOUTH	**FREE YOUTH**
Childhood Military Memory	World War II	Vietnam
Foreign Affairs Antagonist From a Puny Nation	Fidel Castro	Ayatollah Khomeini
Teen Music Sensation	Buddy Holly	Marky Mark
Child Care Development	Dr. Spock's *Baby and Child Care*	*Toughlove*
NASA News	Apollo 11 Moon Landing	Space Shuttle Challenger Explosion
Education Trend	New Math	No Math
Marilyn Monroe Wannabe	Marilyn Monroe	Madonna
TV Holy Person	Billy Graham	Jimmy Swaggart
Animated Superhero	Superman	Teenage Mutant Ninja Turtles
Teen Coming-of-Age Movie	*American Graffiti*	*Revenge of the Nerds*
Amorphous Childhood Toy	Silly Putty	Slime
Civil Rights Icon	Medgar Evers	Rev. Al Sharpton
Television Talent Showcase	"The Ed Sullivan Show"	"The Gong Show"
Boxing and War Film Tough Guy	John Wayne	Sylvester Stallone
Economy Car	Volkswagen Beetle	Ford Pinto

Part Two

THE BLACKBOARD JUNGLE

10

SCHOOLS WITHOUT WALLS

Percentage of Americans aged eighteen to twenty-four who properly identified the following on an unlabeled world map:

Britain	32%
Japan	35%
France	37%
Italy	57%
Mexico	74%
Canada	78%
U.S.	82%

SOURCE: 1988 GALLUP SURVEY CITED IN *U.S. NEWS & WORLD REPORT*

TEACH YOUR CHILDREN WRONG

Comedian Steve Martin performed a routine on his 1978 comedy album *A Wild and Crazy Guy* about a joke that parents could play on their child. The idea was that from the time the child is an infant, you "talk wrong" around him. Speak nothing but gibberish around the child, so that he learns a bizarre sort of nonsensical language. Martin joked that on the child's first day of school, he'll raise his hand and say something like, "May I mambo dogface to the banana patch?" And everyone will have a good laugh.

Who could have guessed this comedy sketch would prove a sort of prophecy? Only the joke wouldn't be played by mischievous parents; it would be played by the schools. As the technological advances in the world were demanding a greater quality of education than ever before, the educational system, slipping in the wrong direction, was performing a monumental disservice. The children and parents who had entrusted the schools to prepare the next generation for the future would prove to have been inexcusably betrayed.

The extent of the joke was first revealed in the National Commission on Excellence in Education's 1983 report, *A Nation at Risk*. In the report, issued as the very first of the Free were just graduating from college, the commission noted that because of the deficient education imparted by our schools, the Free were likely to set a dangerous precedent. "For the first time in the history of our country," reads the report, "the educational skills of one generation will not surpass, will not equal, will not even approach, those of their parents." The causes of this crisis are widespread, encompassing vast changes in school curricula, organization of school structure, political developments, and the general attitudes of society. The grand experiments in education performed on the Free just may be the most outlandish and the most damaging of all those that society has attempted in recent decades.

Public education in America has long been considered "the great equalizer," providing a level playing field for each child and enabling anyone, from the poorest to the most wealthy, an opportunity to realize his potential. To this generation, however, it has functioned in the role of "the great polarizer." For those who were fortunate enough to have good guidance from parents or other adults to compensate for the lack of guidance provided by the schools, the education experiments allowed for a solid, comprehensive learning experience. For the rest, unfortunately a much larger group, the result is a "nation at risk."

DOWN WITH THE TEACHER, UP WITH THE BUREAUCRAT

The radical reforms the schools underwent in the late sixties were another result of the general disdain for "the system" that prevailed during that time. As one teacher explained, "Traditional became synonymous with bad and innovative synonymous with good. So the way we used to do it was wrong and the new way was at least worth trying." What was demanded was that "old" values such as structured learning and professionalism be cast aside in favor of nourishing the natural, spontaneous inner spirit of children. John Holt wrote in his best-selling 1964 book *How Children Fail* that "schools should be a place where children learn what they most want to know, instead of what we think they ought to know." Thus the experiment began.

As the direct link between "the system" and the child, teachers bore the brunt of the condemnation. A number of widely read books attested to the inadequacy and even the threat that our teachers pose. "Teachers' questions," wrote Holt, "like their tests, are *traps*." He described a ten-year-old girl who was having trouble in math. "If she had simply been allowed to live and grow in her own way, the chances are good that in a world full of numbers she would have learned more about numbers than she ever learned in school." Her mind had been filled with "junk—untrue 'facts,' meaningless and garbled rules." Holt summed up his premise by tersely stating, "To a very great degree, school is a place where children learn to be stupid."

Ivan Illich, in an enormously successful 1970 book, went even further. As his title suggests, he advocated completely *Deschooling Society*. "Teachers," wrote Illich, "more often than not, obstruct such learning of subject matters as goes on in school. . . . Children learn most of what teachers *pretend to teach them* from peer groups, from comics, from chance observations, and above all from mere participation in the ritual of school" (my italics). In summation, Illich asserted, "School leads many to a kind of spiritual suicide." Teachers who read Holt, Illich, and others such as A. S. Neill could only conclude that they were entirely without virtue, that not only were their efforts failing to help their students, but they were actually inflicting irreparable damage. In fact, the sentiment wasn't only that teachers have failed to teach, but that *teachers must learn from their students.*

Schools, in concert with outside forces, put the new anti-teacher sentiment into practice using the traditional methods—cutting their pay and diluting their authority in the classroom. While teachers have long been underpaid, this custom had largely been reversed during the "pursuit of excellence" in the fifties and sixties, when teacher pay nearly doubled in real dollars over the two-decade period. With the revelation that teachers alone are responsible for every school-related problem, however, their salaries predictably took as severe a hit as did their status in society. Teachers saw a decade-long salary decline during the seventies. Moonlighting became commonplace as a means to try to stay even. What's more, the average beginning salaries of teachers declined even more steeply, keeping many talented college graduates from pursuing a career in education at all.

Since teachers were now deemed too incompetent to develop the classroom curriculum, others were brought in to take over the job. Between 1960 and 1984, the number of educational professionals such as curriculum specialists and instructional supervisors increased by an astounding 500 percent—nearly ten times the growth rate of classroom instructors. Funds were deliberately diverted from teachers to administrators. During New York City's 1976 budget crisis, fourteen thousand teachers were let go, but the jobs of the city's thousands of administrators and bureaucrats were sacrosanct. Chicago's Board of Education moved into its new headquarters—dubbed "Pershing Gardens"—a converted warehouse featuring piped-in music and a panoramic view of the city from its fifth-floor cafeteria, and a price tag of $22 million. At the same time, then Secretary of Education William Bennett proclaimed the city's schools "the worst in the nation."

Adding even further to teachers' growing reputation of inadequacy was that, too often, the reforms implemented by these new administrators were stale, prepackaged programs thrust upon teachers with little opportunity for feedback.

One popular program, called "DISTAR," used in schools across the country, went so far as to inform teachers exactly which words they should use in the classroom, and even when they should smile! Principals ordered mandatory exam review days, special no-homework periods, and designated testing days for all subjects. Whether or not these policies accommodated the teacher didn't seem to have much bearing. Teachers in the seventies and eighties couldn't win. On one hand, critics such as those calling for "deschooling society" were blaming them for society's ailments; on the other, their own administrators weren't even allowing them to use the techniques and experience that they felt were necessary for good teaching.

THE DECLINE OF THE TEACHER

The drop in esteem for teachers spread beyond callous administrators. From 1969 to 1982, the number of parents who said they would like to have their children become teachers in the public schools dropped from 75 to 46 percent. As for the Free, while nearly one in five 1970 college freshmen said they wanted to teach in elementary or secondary school, in 1982 only one in *twenty* expressed the same ambition. And only 2 percent of the freshmen expressed the desire to teach at the high-school level.

The Free's teachers were certainly not so out of touch as to fail to perceive these opinions. When a 1989 nationwide Gallup poll asked teachers what their greatest sources of job-related stress were, the top answer was a lack of parental support and interest. Indifference by parents caused teachers more anxiety than disciplinary problems, drug use among students, and even low salaries.

If a member of the Free Generation wishes to express appreciation, or disaffection, to a former teacher, it's likely that the teacher is no longer in the classroom. In 1981, a full third of high-school teachers polled said that they would not go into teaching again given the option—three times as many as had indicated so a decade earlier. And these forewarnings were not idle threats. A national sample of teachers who began their careers between 1976 and 1985 showed that nearly half of those who had taught for at least one year were no longer teaching in 1986.

Adding further to the teacher-quality problem is that the last few decades have seen primarily lower-achieving students entering the teaching profession in the first place. In 1973, college students planning to major in education had scored fifty-nine points lower than the national average on the Scholastic Aptitude Test, which was cause enough for alarm. But by 1982, future teachers were scoring eighty-two points lower than an average that had itself fallen. Eric A.

Hanushek of the University of Rochester reviewed 130 studies of factors that affect student achievement in school. He concluded that the only reasonably consistent finding wasn't related to the size of a school's budget or the student-teacher ratio. Rather, students' educational attainments increased with the intelligence of the teacher. With teacher aptitude such an important factor in a child's education, the result of our best candidates eschewing the teaching profession was to put at risk the education of an entire generation.

THE END OF THE FUNDING PARTY

American Grading of the Public Schools

	A	B	C	D	F
1974	18%	30%	21%	6%	5%
1981	9%	27%	34%	13%	7%

SOURCE: ANNUAL GALLUP SURVEYS

Americans didn't put much faith in the Free's schools, and they demonstrated their disfavor with a tightening of the proverbial purse strings. A longtime teacher spoke in 1983 to Ernest Boyer, who was conducting a study of America's high schools, about "the good old days" of the 1950s. "We couldn't have had a more supportive community. We never had a bond issue that was voted down. Anything the school wanted we would get." A 1955 Gallup poll found that two thirds of Americans were willing to pay extra taxes for the schools, particularly to raise teachers' salaries. But in 1980, only 30 percent were willing to make this sacrifice for the schools. Only four dollars in ten that were requested by school boards were given the green light by voters in the seventies. As the Boomer children became adults having fewer children of their own, there was simply a smaller share of Americans who had a direct stake in the quality of our schools. Then 1978 saw a "taxpayer revolt," and the schools were the greatest casualties of the war. The "revolution" that was centered in the universities in the sixties was replaced by a revolution *against* the schools a decade later.

Long a bellwether of social trends, California voters struck a blow against the Free Generation that would have immediate implications and would haunt them from then on. In 1978 Californians voted by a two-to-one margin for Proposition 13, which slashed property taxes—the primary source of school funding at that time—by more than half.[1] Following California's lead, thirty-seven other states adopted property tax cuts of their own over the next two years.

---

[1] Proposition 13 contained other clauses that would unfairly disadvantage the Free later (see chapter thirteen).

Prop 13 precipitated drastic cuts the very first year after its adoption. One hundred and five million dollars was cut from California's summer-school programs, all but eliminating them; $1.5 million was cut from proposed purchases of new library books; state support was eliminated from a science program in San Francisco's schools; inflation adjustments for child-care programs were cut. And this was only the beginning. California had the benefit of huge budget surpluses to cushion the blow that first year. Subsequent years saw substantially steeper reductions as the entire school funding system had to be revamped.

School financing ran into similar obstacles across the nation. In fact, from 1965 to 1980, reversing a steady ascent, the proportion of public expenditures earmarked for education fell by more than 20 percent.[2]

The Free observed one obvious consequence of the funding shortfall as *decay* became the word most synonymous with school buildings. With fewer dollars available, classroom projects simply had to take priority over fixing crumbling walls and ceilings, graffiti, peeling paint, broken windows, and other "nonessentials." A 1983 survey of 100 school districts in thirty-four states showed that 71 percent of the schools inspected were in need of roof repairs or replacement. Twenty-seven percent needed their heating or air-conditioning equipment repaired or replaced. One in five of the buildings even failed legislated fire and safety standards. It was estimated that $25 billion of repairs were needed in the nation's schools overall, an amount nearly twice the *total* federal funding for primary and secondary education that year. Apparently, most of the shiny new buildings that were built during the fifties hadn't been touched since. The psychological effects alone of sitting in a deteriorating classroom are enough to convince a student that school is unimportant and that society has higher priorities. In this way, at least the message was consistent.

SCHOOL DECONSTRUCTION

Educators decided to make the Free guinea pigs for a number of ill-conceived experiments in the organization of the school. Led by authors such as Illich and Neill as well as others like Jonathan Kozol and James Herndon, a movement swept the country attacking the "oppressiveness" and "conformity" of the traditional school. In its place was the call for encouraging spontaneity, compassion, sensitivity, and self-expression, rather than competition for grades and

---

[2] By 1990, after historically leading the world in educational funding, the U.S. lagged behind most other industrial nations in the proportion of GNP devoted to primary and secondary education.

test scores. This debate was not limited to scholars and theorists but was put into action in school districts across the country. Classroom walls were literally torn down, creating "schools without walls"; "free" and "open" schools were established. Alternative schools, mini-schools, "optimal" programs, internships, apprentice and action learning, and independent study—terms as nebulous as the programs themselves—were all put in place at the expense of conventional schooling. Harvard educator Diane Ravitch noted in her 1985 book *The Schools We Deserve,* "The idea was no longer to 'educate' the child in the traditional sense of filling him up with knowledge, but to free him from his dependence on teachers, schools, and books."

The experiments were not limited to a few individual school districts scattered in rare progressive towns. At least five major national studies published in the early seventies advocated measures even beyond the radical reforms already being undertaken. The reports, compiled by influential groups such as the National Association of Secondary School Principals (NASSP), dealt with different areas of education, but all came to some similar conclusions. Recommendations included lowering the age for compulsory school attendance; increasing program options and alternatives, especially in nonschool settings; more work options in place of formal schooling; and shortening the school day. "Why should schools continue such 'purely custodial functions' as keeping unmotivated fourteen-year-olds in school who don't want to be there?" asked one commission. This panel also urged expanding the use of television in the classroom (apparently feeling that four hours of staring at a TV each day were not enough). The National Panel on High Schools and Adolescent Education suggested reducing the academic day to *two to four hours*—to remove "nonacademic fat." All of these reports proposed moving a substantial portion of the educational process outside of the classroom, usually through work opportunities (who needs trigonometry when one can learn to make change as a cashier?). As ludicrous as these recommendations may appear today, schools then took them quite seriously.

The early eighties, as evidenced by *A Nation at Risk,* saw a growing awareness of just how out of hand our schools had become. A group of business executives in California calling themselves the California Roundtable was among the first to conduct a comprehensive inquiry into the quality of schools. In 1982, it published its study, finding that a good number of the outlandish recommendations of the reports issued a decade earlier had indeed been followed. They found that both the school day and the school year had grown shorter, and also that high-school seniors often received credit for work experience that was unrelated to their studies. Not surprisingly, with the shorter school day, it wasn't the "nonacademic fat" that was trimmed; it was the academic requirements.

Across the country, attendance policies had been either relaxed or eliminated in the name of freedom and an "unrestricted" educational experience. The vast majority of high schools established special smoking areas for students, sanctioning a documented health risk in the process. For the most part, students were given carte blanche to call their own shots. With this abrogation of school authority and guidance, students weren't given just the *option* of making their own choices—choices they were often ill equipped to make on their own—they were given a *mandate* to do so.

THE FEEL-GOOD SCHOOL

The dominant theme of the scant academic planning that did exist in the seventies and eighties was that the "self-esteem" of the student was as important—or even more so—than any particular academic goals. If a child felt good about himself, so the reasoning went, whether or not he had attained any particular educational goal, he would feel the flush of self-worth and enter the world a confident, well-adjusted young person. As one Los Angeles middle-school teacher explained, "The most important job in junior high is not subject matter, but morale."

One consequence of this concept was that grades for the Free simply lost much of their significance. In a study conducted by the NASSP in the early eighties, the researchers found that teachers often made little association between classwork and grades. One teacher explained to the NASSP researchers that "it's very unfair if a child comes and really puts forth an effort and is doing his very best and is there every day trying, and yet you defeat him with an F." She continued, "I'm going to do what I can to enhance his self-image and to make him think that the world is good. I'm not going to give him F's just because he's not capable of doing what the average student in the room is doing." Before public outcry nixed the idea, San Diego's schools attempted to completely eliminate the handing out of failing grades no matter how poor a student's work was. As Arthur Powell, author of the NASSP report, discovered, "failure comes from not attending or not behaving. Performance is remarkably irrelevant."

Although the Free's grades were superior to those of their predecessors, SAT scores would prove that the Free had not simply gotten much smarter. Adults had so bought into the anti-academic sentiments espoused by educators that by the eighties a number of surveys showed that the parents of the Free didn't even consider academic work to be the primary purpose of schools. They gave greater importance to the social and personal skills acquired.

Ambitious academic programs were instituted solely in the name of raising self-esteem. Berkeley, California, instituted a series of experimental minischools in 1971 that emphasized ethnicity, under the assumption that minorities' acade-

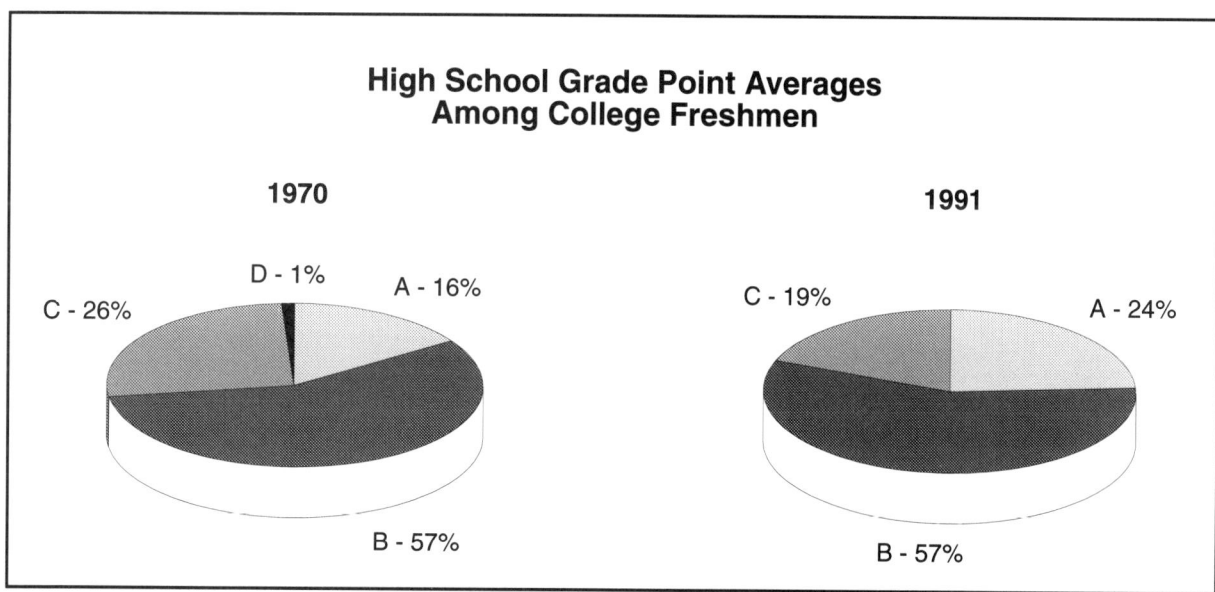

High School Grade Point Averages Among College Freshmen

1970: D - 1%, A - 16%, C - 26%, B - 57%

1991: C - 19%, A - 24%, B - 57%

SOURCE: THE HIGHER EDUCATION RESEARCH INSTITUTE, UCLA

mic difficulties were mainly due to low self-esteem originating in mainstream America's cultural imperialism. In these new places, blacks would study blackness and Hispanics chicanismo. The pride thus instilled would allow the confident students to overcome any difficulties. A few years and millions of dollars later, test scores proved the program to be an academic fiasco. The federal government shut down the two principal schools, Black House and Casa de la Raza.

The most extreme program developed for the cause of raising self-esteem was that ordered by a federal judge in 1974. In a ruling handed down in Ann Arbor, Michigan, the city's English teachers were ordered to take classes in "Black English" so that they could instruct their students in the jargon spoken in inner-city ghettos. The rationale for this was that students had a right to "their own patterns and varieties of language—the dialect of their nurture or whatever dialect in which they find their own style." Besides, explained a group of professional educators, there exists no "correct" or "incorrect" language. "The claim that any one dialect is unacceptable amounts to an attempt of one social group to exert its dominance over another," read their proclamation. A teacher speaking correctly is essentially repressing his students. It's interesting, and surprising, that no movement evolved to teach in Valley-girlese or Santa Cruz surfer lingo—two dialects that are as distinctive and grammatically incorrect as any spoken in our inner cities. Just as well—the Ann Arbor mandate was dropped after only a few years, as it was found to be ineffectual in improving the education of black students.

One paradox of stressing self-esteem over academics came to light in an international math test given to thirteen-year-olds in 1988. American students were dead last among the nations who took the test, yet they led the pack in considering themselves "good at mathematics." Korean children, only 23 percent of whom judged themselves good math students, also happened to be the highest-scoring students. The Free may have developed some of that high self-esteem — perhaps arrogance is a more appropriate term—in school. Unfortunately, what they needed to learn may have been a little humility, and a lot more math.

SPONTANEOUS EDUCATION

A further development rooted in the deschooling movement was the near abolition of homework. When A. S. Neill was asked about homework in the 1960's book *Summerhill*, he replied, "The homework habit is disgraceful. Children loathe homework, and that is enough to condemn it." Schools took such advice to heart. A 1979 survey by the California Department of Education found that a third of all sixth-grade pupils never did any homework whatsoever. Even among high-school students, one in four didn't receive a single writing assignment over the six-week period studied. In a decade, the average amount of time high schoolers devoted to homework was cut *in half.*

The disappearance of homework became a troubling downward spiral of cause and effect. A math teacher explained his position to the NASSP researchers: "The big problem for these kids is getting to the school in the morning, bringing their books, and being polite. Adding required homework would be too much." Another teacher complained to the *Lost Angeles Times* that "if I give a ten-page paper in sociology, I get a three-page paper." So how did he respond to this trend? "I abandoned requiring a lot of outside work," he said. "I caved in to the pressure." In one college-prep English course, a new school policy mandated that the four novels assigned during the year be read during class. Rather than bringing *The Scarlet Letter, The Red Badge of Courage, Huckleberry Finn,* and *The Great Gatsby* home to read, the students would simply sit in silence and read them during the daily class period. The reason for this? Parents had complained that assigning the books to be read at home was excessive homework. The teacher of this class didn't seem to have a problem with the policy either. "I like this," he explained. "We give them a week to read the book in the class and I'll give them a paper to do and they will have read it." For the Free, the "home" element was eliminated from homework, and the students would pay dearly in the end.

GET OUT WHILE YOU CAN

With the decline of the public schools, the parents of the Free began to take matters into their own hands. Rather than using their voice to demand improvements in the school systems, though, they increasingly turned to private schools. From 1970 to 1977 alone, enrollments in nonsectarian private schools grew by 60 percent. And this increase came during a period when the school-age population dropped by 3.9 million students. In Boston, a city that was ravaged by disorder in the schools for the greater part of the seventies, an estimated nine out of ten parents who could afford it sent their kids to parochial or private school. Especially telling is that nearly half of Chicago's public-school teachers in the eighties sent their own kids to private schools.

A 1982 report by sociologist James Coleman established that parents who pulled their kids out of the public-school system made the right choice. Coleman found that private high schools produced higher-achieving students than did public schools, even when the students' backgrounds were similar. He determined that the reason for the higher achievement was that private schools "create higher rates of engagement in academic activities ... school attendance is better, students do more homework, and students generally take more rigorous subjects." The private schools also had a more stringent disciplinary climate and stricter graduation requirements. Perhaps the most notable conclusion in Coleman's report is that, despite the public-school emphasis on "feeling good" and the private-school emphasis on academic achievement, students in Catholic and private schools actually exhibited *higher* self-esteem than did those in the public schools. Apparently the high-paid public-school administrators had gotten this cause-and-effect relationship backward.

FALLOUT FROM THE "MOVEMENT"

Even more unstructured and aimless than the organization of the public schools was the curriculum that the Free were expected to study. What former California Superintendent of Schools Bill Honig has termed "curricular anarchy" traced its origins directly to the university student protests of the late sixties. Universities dramatically lowered their academic requirements, and in turn relaxed their admissions requirements. Requisite courses had been so thoroughly eliminated by the early eighties that half of our colleges had *no* specific course requirements for their incoming freshmen to have completed, and at least a third accepted essentially everyone who applied. Only one college in four even considered a student's high-school courses in making a decision for or against admission. Even worse, as the colleges reduced their admissions requirements, the high schools reduced their graduation requirements.

SCHOOLS WITHOUT WALLS 115

Of course, this development also harkened back to the carefree schools envisioned in the popular "deschooling" books of the sixties. Influential educators and writers disparaged the idea that there should be specific educational goals to strive toward. Following the lead of the universities, required classes were eliminated as many argued that it was unfair to make any student take a class he or she didn't want to take. It was claimed that no particular class was more worthwhile than any other, so students should be able to take whatever they wanted. Rather than course requirements serving as the starting point in defining a good curriculum, it was determined that the requirements themselves were unnecessary and even potentially harmful.

MAJORING IN "OTHER"

The high-school course load of the Free could be considered eclectic, to say the least. The 1982 California Roundtable study noted a "disturbing decline in academic course enrollments statewide, linked with a marked increase in non-academic electives." To verify such findings, the U.S. Department of Education studied transcripts from more than six thousand high-school students covering the years 1964 to 1980, and found "a systematic devaluation of academic" courses taken over the fifteen-year period.

The DOE study also found that some courses had seen remarkable increases in popularity over this time. The top-ten growth areas were:

> Physical education
> Music performance
> Remedial English
> Driver education
> Cooperative education
> Health education
> Distributive education
> General shop
> Training for marriage/adulthood
> Vocational home economics

Not a whole lot of reading, writing, or arithmetic on the list, with the exception of remedial English, which attempts to make up for what should have been learned earlier. Another study by the NASSP found that the greatest rise in state educational requirements was in "Other"—that is, electives that don't fit into any academic category. The authors of *A Nation at Risk* were amazed to find that "time spent learning to cook and drive counts as much toward a high school diploma as time spent studying math, English, chemistry, U.S. history, or biology." You give fourteen-year-olds a smorgasbord from which to select their classes, and a lot of them are going to fill up on junk food.

The watered-down curriculum has had consequences. A 1988 Gallup survey of Americans aged eighteen to twenty-four, the eldest of the Free, generated endless catcalls in the media as it revealed how little young adults knew about geography. More than half of this group failed to identify Central America on an unlabeled map of the world. Seventy percent were unable to correctly place Britain. And one in five couldn't even find the United States! What wasn't published along with the Gallup findings was the fact that many American schools no longer teach geography at all. The percentage of students who took pure geography courses fell by 75 percent between 1960 and 1980. Only one in twenty of the Free took such a course. One reason? Because they didn't have to. Even in 1988, five years after we were declared a "nation at risk," only four states required a geography course for graduation from high school.

The biggest laugh to be had at the Free's expense came in the late eighties, as many of them were just finishing their schooling. The new educational authorities, like E. D. Hirsch, author of *Cultural Literacy,* and Allan Bloom, author of *The Closing of the American Mind,* were now saying that yes, there is a certain indispensable body of knowledge that every person should have learned. However, through largely no fault of their own, the Free hadn't learned it.

Former Assistant Education Secretary Chester Finn has summed up the results that schools can expect from their students: "Most young people learn pretty much what they are obliged to learn by parents and teachers—and in matters academic, not a great deal more." High-school seniors surveyed in the eighties reported that while their own study habits were certainly lacking, they essentially did achieve the minimum required. But the students weren't averse to higher standards; the seniors favored *more* emphasis on academic subjects, and they criticized poor teaching as having interfered with their education. In fact, the percentage wishing for more stress on academics grew by 50 percent from 1972 to 1980. And, most astonishing to those who have felt we must coddle minority students to raise their self-esteem, 66 percent of black children said that school was not challenging enough for them.

When Jane Norman and Myron Harris interviewed teenagers on a number of subjects in 1981, they asked them to identify those traits that "make a teacher good." The top three responses were that the teacher grades fairly, knows his subject, and is enthusiastic about the subject he teaches. The three responses given the least weight: that the teacher likes kids, gives little or no homework,

IF ONLY THEY HAD ASKED THE STUDENTS

and can maintain classroom discipline. In other words, the students thought a good teacher was one that knew and taught the subject well. The students wanted to learn, not be entertained.

EVERYBODY IS ABOVE AVERAGE

With the growing awareness in the eighties that maybe the great educational experiments had indeed gone a bit awry, cries for change began to sound. The first reaction by the schools wasn't to actually modify the curriculum or take other actions to insure that our students learn more effectively, but to mandate minimum competency tests to supposedly prevent unqualified high-school seniors from obtaining a diploma. The number of states that required the exams grew to thirty-eight in just a few years. The one notable characteristic of the minimum competency tests that were instituted was a literal definition of the term "minimum competency." One test, for example, included the following questions intended to test reading comprehension:

EMERGENCY INFORMATION

Fire:	555-2115	Your fire department's number
Police:	555-1155	Your police department's number
Doctor:	555-0734	Your doctor's number
Ambulance:	555-1157	Ambulance number
F.B.I.:		Federal Bureau of Investigation: Dial 555-9110
Coast Guard:		Search and Rescue Emergencies: Call 555-9822
Highway Patrol:		To report emergencies, call OPERATOR: Ask for 555-2000
Secret Service:		U.S. Secret Service: Dial 555-4830 or in any emergency, dial the operator

You would dial 555-1155 to reach:
- A. the fire department
- B. the police
- C. an ambulance
- D. a doctor

Bonnie has the flu, and her father wants to take her to the doctor for a shot. What number should he call?
- A. 555-0734
- B. 555-1155
- C. 555-2115
- D. 555-1157

Here is a sample mathematics problem from another minimum-competency test:

> Mr. Levi is an hourly employee who receives $5 per hour. He receives time-and-a-half for any time over 8 hours on any given day. The following is his time card for last week.
>
> | Monday | Tuesday | Wednesday | Thursday | Friday |
> |--------|---------|-----------|----------|--------|
> | 8 hours | 8 hours | 8 hours | 9 hours | 9 hours |
>
> How many hours overtime did he work last week?
> A. 1 hour
> B. 1.5 hour
> C. 2 hours
> D. 2.5 hours

Correctly answering these questions might have indicated an acceptable minimum level of academic achievement for a fourth-grader, but certainly not the high-school seniors who were administered such tests. With the approach the schools chose to take—that is, testing at the end of schooling rather than making improvements during the school years—it's not surprising that the exams would be undemanding. To administer exams that truly required an adequate level of knowledge would most likely result in significant percentages of students failing the exams. Thus, the schools would be forced to admit that they had been woefully inadequate in educating many students. Offering such questions as those above at least allowed them to maintain a pretense of providing a decent education for a while.

There were other instances in the testing frenzy of the eighties in which schools proved that they were not so dedicated to actually educating students, but were quite dedicated in making the public *think* that students were being well educated. In April 1987, sixteen schools were found to have cheated on the California Assessment Program test given to the state's sixth-graders. The cheaters were identified by checking test booklets for unusually high numbers of erase marks and then looking to see how many of the erased items were then marked correctly. The cheating could only have occurred by teachers prompting their students, or by the teachers themselves making the corrections. Also in 1987, all fifty states reported above-average scores on national standardized achievement tests. Either school administrators were lying, or they were simply as poor in mathematics as the students whom they were supposed to be teaching.

Scholastic Aptitude Test Scores
1967 - 1993

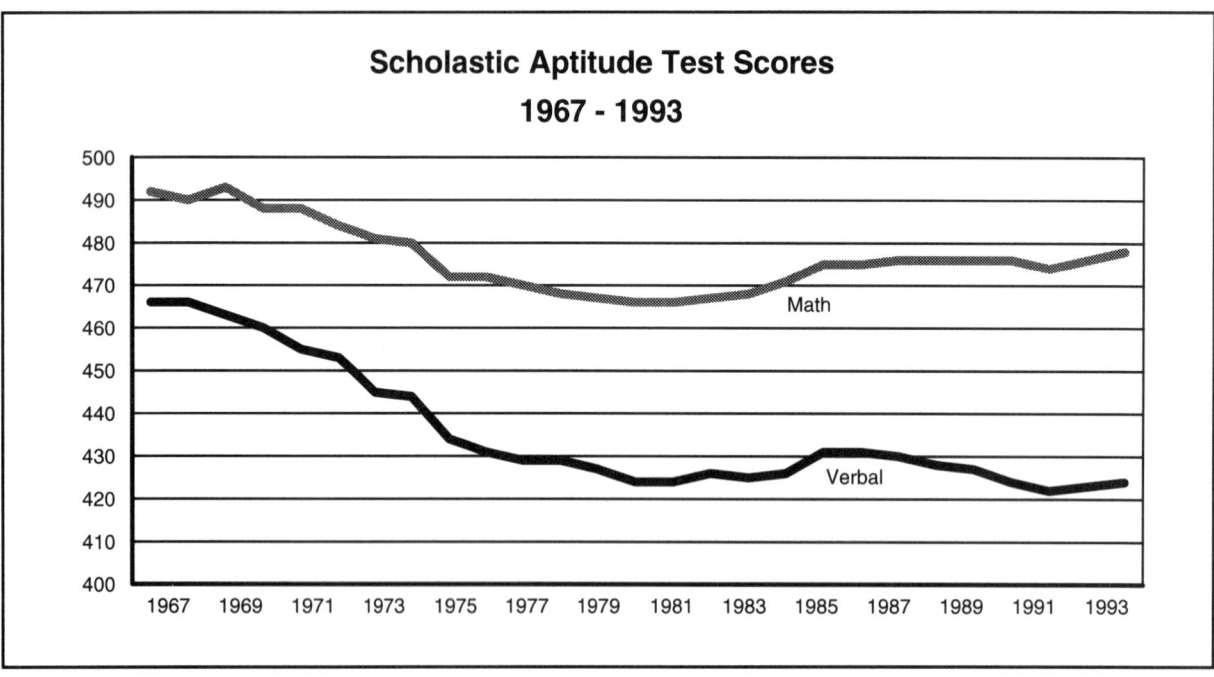

[Line graph showing SAT Math scores declining from ~492 in 1967 to a low around 1980, then rising to ~478 in 1993; and SAT Verbal scores declining from ~466 in 1967 to ~424 in 1993.]

SOURCE: U.S. DEPARTMENT OF EDUCATION

RESULTS OF THE EXPERIMENT

A great deal has been written about the three-decade plunge in SAT scores. What caused it? How can we reverse it? Does it really even matter? The first reaction to the drop was that the increased diversity among the test takers—more minorities, women, and low-income students—was the likely cause. Unfortunately for this simple explanation, the mix of students taking the SAT has remained essentially stable since 1970. Furthermore, the number and proportion of high-scoring students has fallen even more precipitously. The decrease in high scorers is certainly unrelated to the overall composition of test takers.

Answering other claims that the SAT itself was an inaccurate and incomplete gauge of student achievement, researchers Annegret Harnischfeger and David E. Wiley analyzed other standardized tests, including the American College Test (ACT), the Iowa testing program (used throughout Iowa and in other states), and the Minnesota Scholastic Aptitude Test (administered to nearly all high-school juniors in the state). Studying these exams from the sixties and seventies, they found a pattern of decline consistent with the SAT drop. What Harnischfeger and Wiley also discovered was that the higher grade levels showed steeper declines than lower grades, indicating that students weren't necessarily coming to school less equipped than were previous generations; *they were falling further behind the more they moved through the school system.* While the two researchers were careful to allow a variety of contributing causes for the overall drop, they nonetheless concluded that substantial enrollment declines in traditional subjects "parallel closely the test score decline pattern."

A survey released in the late eighties showed that 8 percent of seventeen-year-old white children were functionally illiterate in the U.S. as well as an astonishing forty-two percent of black children of the same age. William Brock, Ronald Reagan's Secretary of Labor, estimated that 700,000 high-school graduates "get diplomas each year and cannot read them." The consequences of the poor education the Free Generation received reaches beyond U.S. borders. When the first International Mathematics Study was conducted in the early sixties, American educators were proud to find that the strongest 5 percent of our students were as proficient as the upper 5 percent of students anywhere in the world. When the second such test was given in 1981, the results showed a sad development. The highest-scoring 5 percent of the new generation were now in the bottom fourth of the international sample. In the 1988 international Gallup survey on young people's knowledge of geography, American eighteen- to twenty-four-year-olds scored dead last, behind those of Britain, France, Italy, Canada, West Germany, Sweden, and Mexico. In our global economy, it's not hard to see how our poor schools have put not only a generation at risk, but our entire nation.

Paradoxically, there is one group that has profited from our appalling schools—the schools themselves. As the lower grades fail to educate the young, additional jobs are needed at the high-school level to try to correct this. As the high schools fail, the colleges in turn are provided with additional opportunities. The 1982 California Roundtable report noted that half the students entering the state university and college system were enrolled in remedial courses in English and math, classes that probably wouldn't be offered at all had the high schools done their job. In a painful example of a self-sustaining bureaucracy that benefits by its own ineptitude, the school system requires ever-increasing funding at the expense of the rest of society.[3]

What may be the greatest irony of the school decline was pointed out in the conclusions to the National Association of Secondary School Principals' 1985 report. Noting the dismal job market the Free face (which is covered in detail in chapter twelve), the researchers make an association among the decline in achievement, the classroom policies devoted to placating students, and future economic prospects: "Perhaps high schools teach students what they most need to know: how to endure boredom without protest." In a perverse way, maybe our schools have given the Free exactly what they need—limited knowledge to go along with limited expectations.

---

[3] Arguably the biggest loser given the educational deficiencies is the business community which is now spending over $50 billion annually training underskilled workers.

11

COLLEGE

Total number of humor magazines published on
American college campuses:

1970—45
1986—19

Total number of conservative newspapers published on
American college campuses:

1979—1
1992—70

SOURCE: 1986 DIRECTORY OF THE COLLEGE STUDENT PRESS IN AMERICA *CHANGE* JANUARY/FEBRUARY 1993

THE $100,000 EDUCATION

Before the Boomers reached college age, higher education had never been an available option for the majority of young adults. As recently as 1960, only 18 percent of U.S. public-school students were graduating from college. But by 1974, despite their large numbers, 60 percent of Boomer high-school graduates were able to continue their education at the college level. In fact, more than 44 percent of all Boomers had completed at least four years of college by 1980. The drive for universal access to higher education seemed to be firmly entrenched in the American psyche, and ambitious programs like California's 1960 Master Plan for higher education, along with new student loan and grant programs, were transforming the vision of college education for all into a reality. But then two decades later a strange thing happened; opportunity was reversing itself.

The most obvious manner by which the Golden Door was being closed was with skyrocketing tuition. The average cost of attending a private college for the 1977–78 school year was just $5,000, including room, board, and tuition. In real terms, schools had been dropping their costs throughout the decade of the sev-

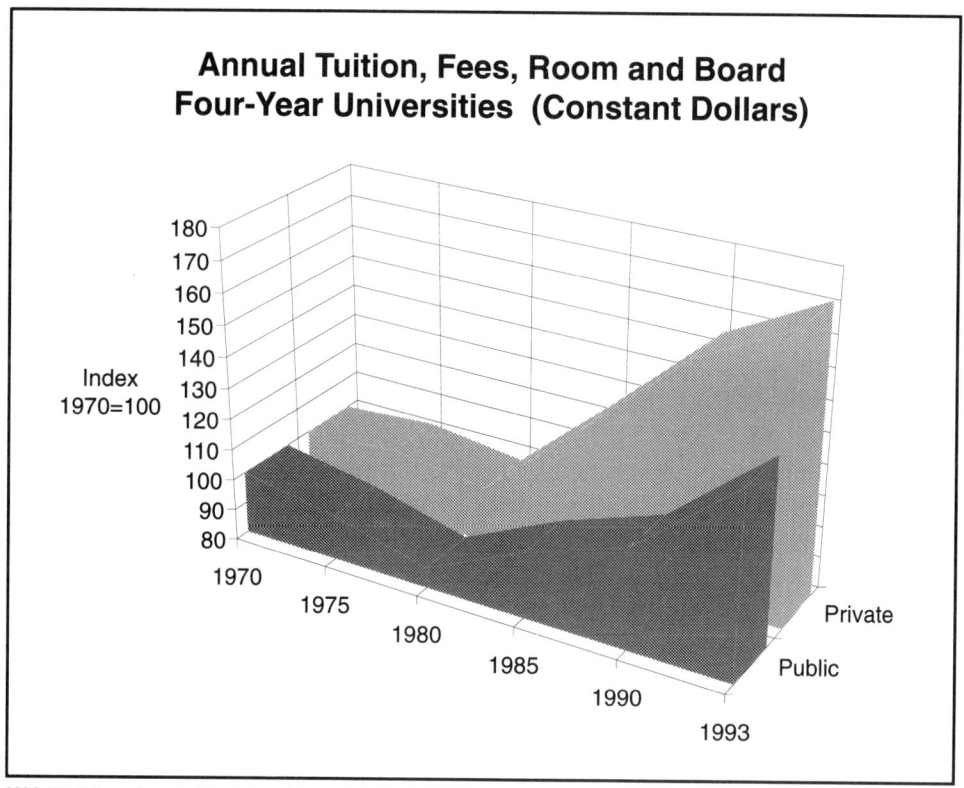

**Annual Tuition, Fees, Room and Board
Four-Year Universities (Constant Dollars)**

SOURCE: U.S. NATIONAL CENTER FOR EDUCATION STATISTICS

enties. This effort, combined with the new aid programs, made higher education a true bargain. But this trend swung dramatically in the opposite direction around this time, and the 1992–93 academic year saw that the annual cost had risen to $18,000. Adjusted for inflation, the price tag for attending a private university rose more than 70 percent during this decade and a half, with the public schools seeing an increase in the financial burden of more than half with no relief in sight. Top schools such as Stanford and Harvard were setting students back a cool $25,000—almost double the cost of twenty years earlier in constant dollars.

As the Free entered college, soaring costs had drastically changed the way many schools look at their prospective students. Wesleyan University made the ability to pay a criterion for admission, while the Ivy League universities found themselves enmeshed in the scandal of fixing the amounts of aid made available to low-income prospects so that no single school would have to absorb too many financially needy students. According to one research firm, a top Boomer student in 1972 from a low-income family was just as likely to attend college as his "medium-ability" classmate from a high-income family. A decade later, however, 89 percent of wealthy, "medium-ability" students enrolled in college, but only 70 percent of his high-achieving but poor cohorts did so. Skyrocketing costs were transforming higher education back from a universal dream to an elite privilege.

THE SIX-YEAR UNDERGRADUATE

Stanford University president Gerhard Caspar recently called for a rethinking of the concept of the four-year college education, advocating more flexibility to match increasingly diverse offerings of programs. What he and others who are considering such a review are finally acknowledging is that the four-year bachelor's degree has been disappearing for the past two decades. By 1990, the average college undergraduate was taking more than six years to earn a degree; fewer than half graduated after the traditional four years of study. So the average college career actually costs even 50 percent more than many of the sky-high figures imply—and, of course, paying one's way is a major reason for the extra semesters.

Graduate students could expect an even longer haul. By the nineties, earning a Ph.D. had become such a prolonged process that the average candidate could expect to spend ten and a half years *after* graduating from college obtaining his doctorate. Female graduate students now average two years beyond that, and the typical black Ph.D. candidate spends nearly fifteen years working toward the degree. In the 1978 film *Animal House*, John Belushi got a good laugh by complaining, "Seven years of college gone to hell!" If he were a college student in the 1980s or early 1990s, he would have been completing his studies in only slightly longer than average time, and nobody would get the joke.

Because of the high costs of college and the longer amounts of time often needed to graduate, and arguably exacerbated by the poor academic preparation given students during the elementary- and high-school years, the Free will likely be the first generation of Americans to be less educated than the previous, despite the increased economic necessity of obtaining a college degree. In fact, a federal study by the Department of Education tracking twenty-five thousand students in three different years has found a dramatic decline. Looking into all degrees, including two-year and vocational programs, the study showed that nearly half of the Boomer high-school class of 1972 had earned some kind of diploma after four years, but fewer than one in five of their counterparts a decade later had done so. After seven years of schooling, the discrepancy had closed a little, but the Free were still obtaining their degrees at only slightly higher than half the rate that Boomers had. While lowered college admissions standards have enabled a greater proportion of the Free to *begin* college than ever before, enormous numbers have either chosen, or been forced, to abandon their educations.

As with so many other social developments experienced by the Free, minorities are the greatest casualties of this trend. The percentage of middle-income black men continuing on to college, for example, was cut nearly in half from 1975 to 1986. Keeping those who did go to college from leaving school has proven difficult as well. The rate of dropping out or otherwise failing to complete their college studies after six years for the shrinking pool of black and Latino college enrollees was a staggering 74 percent for the high-school class of 1980. While financial concerns certainly contribute to the problem, a greater factor is likely that our elementary and high schools are simply failing minorities. Unless this trend is reversed, the educational gains that minorities made beginning in the fifties will have largely been erased.

"Never has a higher education been more important as a means to a better job," concluded the authors of a 1988 article in *Forbes* magazine. They added, "yet never has it cost more." The Free found themselves in the midst of a Catch-22: The economy had become polarized, with quality jobs requiring a college education at one extreme, and dead-end, low-paying service jobs at the other, and the rising costs of obtaining that critical education put it out of reach for a growing number. The wage gap between those with college degrees and those without narrowed during the Boomers' college years, fueled perhaps by a glut of degreed workers. But during the eighties, the trend headed sharply in the other direction. *Time* magazine calculated in 1990 that a member of the Free Generation with a college degree could expect lifetime earnings that total four times as much as those of someone without one. With the disappearance of high-paying, unskilled jobs, a college education is as much about survival as anything else. You no longer go to college just to learn. You go to college because you have to.

COLLEGE OR BUST

Incredibly, the Reagan administration used the widening wage gap as justification for *cutting* federal aid programs for education. "The college graduate will earn $640,000 more than the high-school graduate over his lifetime," explained education secretary William Bennett in a 1986 speech. "It is only sensible—and only fair—that that beneficiary pay the cost rather than the taxpayers." The logic of this argument falters with the consideration that escalating costs have made it impossible for a growing number to remain in college in the first place, and the fact that no university will accept an IOU for tuition with future earnings as collateral. Furthermore, the extra taxes alone that would be added to the treasury on the $640,000 Bennett claims would be earned would far surpass the amount of aid offered.

There is another phenomenon that explains most of the growing wage gap and poses an additional argument against Bennett's reasoning. The widening difference between the earnings of those with a university education and those without is due not to the fact that salaries of college graduates have increased markedly in the last dozen years (in fact, they have been flat), but rather to the fact that wages of high-school graduates have declined sharply. Rather than bidding up salaries of college graduates, employers have been bidding down the wages of everyone else. Despite all this, student aid was cut severely for the Free, and only time will tell what consequences this will have.

COLLEGE AND BUST

In the commendable campaign to allow as many students as possible to attend college in the sixties and seventies, a variety of student-aid programs were established, ranging from the National Defense Student Loans to the Basic Educational Opportunity Grants (which were later renamed Pell Grants). These programs were widespread and generous; as recently as the late seventies, a Pell Grant, awarded to the neediest students, paid for 50 percent of a recipient's college costs. Support for students at the state level also rose continuously during the sixties and seventies. Even as tuitions headed skyward, though, student aid began to dry up just as the last of the Boomers were leaving college and the first of the Free were enrolling.

Student aid was high on the Reagan hit list when he went to war against social spending. The first program to go was the $2 billion paid through Social Security to the children of deceased, retired, or disabled workers—a program that put thousands of Boomers through school. And while college tuitions rose by 50 percent during the eighties, Pell Grant increases were nowhere near as high, so that by 1990, they were covering less than a third of a recipient's needs. Certainly this has been a major factor in the declining enrollments of the top students who just happen to come from low-income families. Affecting many more middle-class students, assistance that used to come in the form of grants now came as loans, and support at the state level began a long decline. The overall picture showed that in just two years, from 1981 to 1983, federal subsidies for students fell by 20 percent, a total of $4 billion.

These cutbacks resulted in a number of repercussions, not the least of which is the tumbling college completion rates. And with outside aid slashed, the schools themselves were forced to take on a higher proportion of financial assistance, ultimately raising tuition rates for everyone. In another instance of twisted logic, the education secretary claimed that the availability, not the reduction, of federal aid was the cause of tuition increases. Apparently envisioning trustees siphoning off millions of excess dollars for themselves, he asserted, "Colleges raise costs because they can."

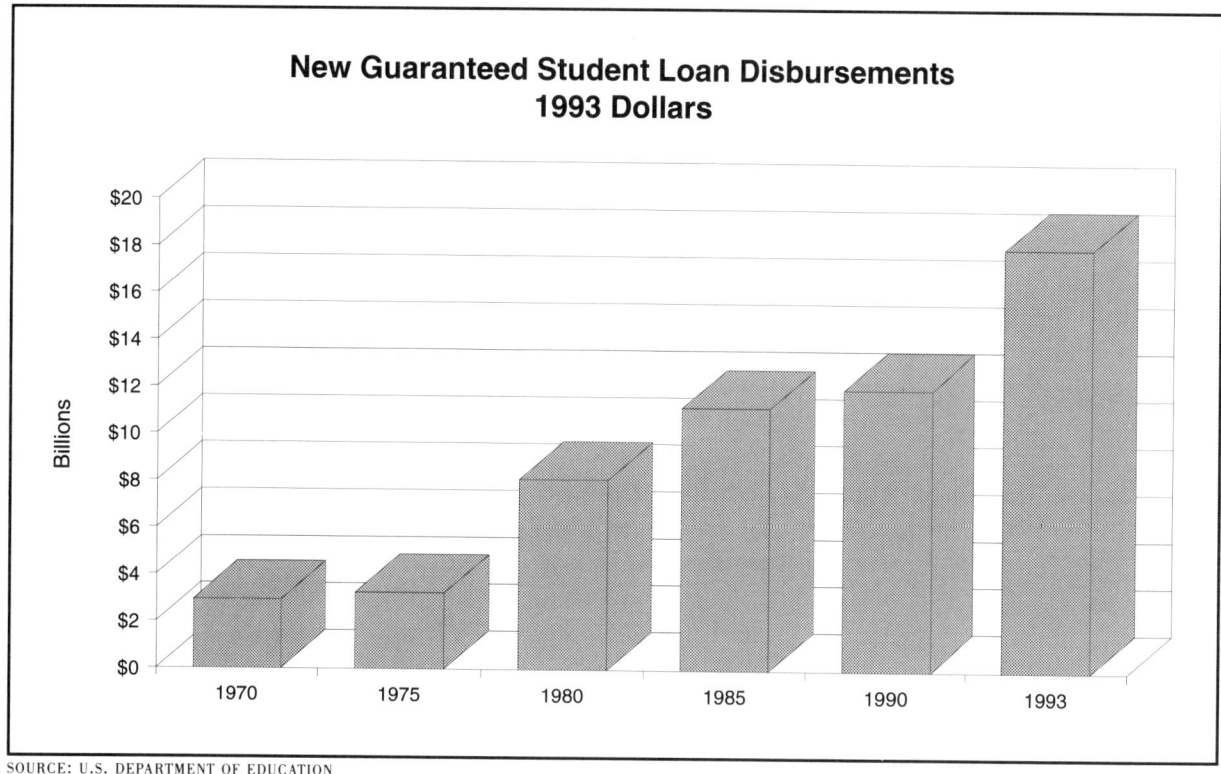

**New Guaranteed Student Loan Disbursements
1993 Dollars**

SOURCE: U.S. DEPARTMENT OF EDUCATION

The other consequence of the cuts in aid coupled with the rising costs is that the Free were compelled to take on enormous amounts of debt to finance their college careers. A 1986 study by the Joint Economic Committee of Congress noted with alarm that students were borrowing more than $10 billion a year, a 300 percent increase over the previous decade. A recent graduate of a four-year undergraduate program could expect to be burdened with $9,000 in debt. "I myself have taken out $18,000 in loans for 5½ years of school," Stephanie Bloomingdale of the U.S. Student Association told *The San Francisco Chronicle*, "and I don't know how I'm going to pay that back." All in all, the new, often overwhelming financial pressures of seeking a higher education, combined with the greater necessity of obtaining the degree, made the college experience a wearisome, Sisyphean ordeal for many.

GET A JOB

Goals of College Freshman

	1970	1989
To be very well off financially:	39%	75%
To make more money by attending college:	50	72
To develop a meaningful philosophy of life:	80	41

SOURCE: *AMERICAN DEMOGRAPHICS* APRIL 1990 AND JANUARY 1991

The Free entered college a more pragmatic, pre-professional, and politically conservative group than those who preceded them. On topics such as drugs, the death penalty, and the rights of criminals, Free students indicated a dramatic shift to the right. Even concern for issues like environmental problems and racial strife hit lows on campuses in the eighties. In no area, however, did the Free demonstrate a greater change in ideals from Boomers than in the motivation for attending college at all. With great debts burdening them and facing a shrinking job market, college became a career move. In fact, when incoming freshmen were asked to state "important reasons for going to college" on a survey in the mid-eighties, the top three responses were "to have a more satisfying career," "to prepare for a specific career," and "to get a better job." Posters showing a well-heeled man perched on the hood of a Rolls-Royce declaring POVERTY SUCKS were as commonplace on dorm-room walls as Farrah Fawcett posters had been a decade earlier. Students could be seen walking around wearing T-shirts espousing the higher education maxim of WORK, STUDY, GET RICH. The areas of study that students chose showed that they were serious about these intentions and were not going to be swayed into "more meaningful" fields.

Degrees in Selected Fields as a Percentage of all Degrees

	1968	1984
Biological Sciences	5%	4%
Business	13	24
Education	21	10
Foreign Languages	3	1
Physical Sciences	3	2
Social Sciences	19	10

SOURCE: U.S. DEPARTMENT OF EDUCATION,
NATIONAL CENTER FOR EDUCATION STATISTICS

The Free chose money over metaphysics during their college years. A 1986 nationwide poll showed that four out of five college students believed that choosing a low-paying field that you happen to like is, plain and simple, "a mistake." Enrollment in economics courses at Harvard tripled in a decade. Fully 40 percent of the 1986 Yale graduating class applied to a single company, the investment-banking firm First Boston. Yet the pursuit of a decent job was not the thoughtless display of greed that critics have deemed it. On the contrary, most students would have preferred to avoid the stress that goes along with worrying about future employment, but they knew that to do so would mean to lose out.

Two Stanford University researchers looked into the phenomenon of students following more career-oriented majors in the eighties and came up with some conclusions that the Free had seemed to infer on their own. Herant A. Katchadourian and John Boli followed the college experience of a number of students during their years at Stanford looking to distinguish "intellectuals" from "careerists." Intellectuals were defined as those who were enrolled in college in order to learn to "think critically," to develop "ethical and moral values," or to develop "artistic and aesthetic taste and judgment." They studied subjects that they found interesting and intellectually challenging and were seeking careers that offered creativity and originality.

Careerists, on the other hand, were in school to acquire "marketable skills" and for "future financial security." They followed a course of study as preparation for graduate school or one that would be useful for their intended career. Careerists were looking for jobs that offered status, prestige, or high income. What the researchers' 1985 report indicated was a direct link between a student's family finances and his propensity toward careerism or intellectualism. Those coming from low-income families were three times as likely to follow a career-oriented path as an intellectual one. Likewise, students from families earning more than $100,000 were 30 percent more likely to be an intellectual than a careerist. In other words, students tend to pursue job-related majors when they feel they have to.

In the sixties and seventies, millions of Boomers pursued new, eclectic majors simply because they could afford to. The economy was in the midst of a three-decade boom, jobs were plentiful, and students were graduating from college free from the burden of student loan debt. Why not study what you want rather than what you "should"? The Free could not afford such a luxury. They entered college when the only large firms that were hiring in significant numbers were in the financial sector. Companies weren't even looking at liberal-arts majors unless they had a substantial business or technical background to supplement their studies. One indication of this environment came to light in 1990 when a group of students at UC-Berkeley applied for a VISA card that had been promoted on campus with the pitch "no previous credit history required." All had their applications rejected simply because they were humanities majors. The *Los Angeles Times* reported that in rejecting the applications, "the bank's rationale is that these students are less likely to repay debts because they will not land the high-paying jobs that go to business or engineering graduates." If the Free were materialistic in their studies, it was largely because they saw no alternative. They did what they needed to survive in an economy that worshiped Donald Trump and Michael Milken and largely ignored its poets and teachers.

THE HIGH-SCHOOLIZATION OF THE UNIVERSITY

Likely as a result of both inadequate high schools and open-door, undemanding admissions policies, colleges began to see a rising proportion of students coming to the hallowed halls unprepared for the higher level of work. Highlighted by the rising college dropout rate, this problem forced other changes in the university as well. A 1984 survey of college faculty showed that more than half of the respondents agreed with the statement "The academic ability of the undergraduates at my institution is 'fair or poor,' " and a whopping 83 percent thought that "teaching would be a lot easier here if students were better prepared before they were admitted." The faculty members weren't being facetious; nearly half the Free who attended college flunked at least one course. Even Ivy League and other top institutions began to see increasing enrollments in remedial courses designed to bring students up to the minimum level necessary to continue on with college-level courses. Education researcher Helen S. Astin wrote in *Educational Record* that at UCLA, for example, "Though we admit only the top 12 percent of graduating high school seniors, half of all our new freshmen are placed in noncredit remedial math and English courses. The reality of working with underprepared students must confront everyone."

The other academic problem seen on campuses across the country was a hard-to-pinpoint, general drop in student enthusiasm toward school. Likely the culmination of a number of trends—the drudgery of financing the ever more expensive tuition, the necessity of going to college for decent job prospects rather than the quest for learning, spending increased classroom time simply catching up on what the high schools failed to teach (not to mention their childhood exposure to anti-school sentiments)—students increasingly showed signs of simply going through the motions toward the degree. A 1984 survey showed that more than half of college students spent fewer than two hours a week in the school library, with one fourth reporting never using the library at all. Four of the top-ten best-selling books at university bookstores in 1989 were comic books, and 80 percent of students never bought *any* books outside of their class texts. UCLA's annual nationwide survey of incoming freshmen that year showed that only 10 percent did any reading for courses beyond the minimum demanded by the teacher, the lowest level since the surveys were begun. The same survey also indicated that record low numbers of students studied with others or engaged in such activities as visiting art galleries and museums. Students seemed to care more about surviving their classes than relishing the academic experience.

Cheating became commonplace; a 1983 Indiana University survey revealed that fully one student in three admitted to looking at another's test during an exam. A later survey reported in the *Boston Globe* found that 50 percent of college students nationwide admitted to cheating at some point in their university careers. In the spring of 1991, seventy-three students in an introductory computer-science course were disciplined for taking part in the largest cheating scandal in the history of the prestigious Massachusetts Institute of Technology. Professors reported students coming to their offices and virtually demanding an A for the class. Perhaps an indication of the general cynicism held by the Free, the perceived connection between hard work and good grades faded. Students seemed to simply want to get college over with while enduring the least amount of pain possible. Actually learning was a secondary issue.

ANXIETY U.

During the Free college years, campus counseling centers went from a previously available but seldom-used service to a visible indicator of a burgeoning underlying atmosphere of stress among students. Dr. Barbara McGowan, head of the psychological counseling department at UCLA, complained that her agency's resources were becoming strained by a 10-percent increase in their caseload each year during the eighties. At the University of Maryland, an estimated 11 to 18 percent of students sought counseling in any given year, and nationally, one student in four sought help at some point during their college career. Dr. Samual Klagsburn, a New York psychiatrist, established a private psychiatric hospital called Four Winds exclusively for college students who had undergone emotional difficulties. In a *New York Times* article, he noted that today's students are subject to stresses not experienced by previous generations.

With working longer hours, going deeper and deeper into debt, and worrying about the inevitable annual tuition hikes and shrinking job market, the college experience for the Free was very different from that of their parents. Four years of exploring and growing had, for many, become six years of feeling hurried, pressured, and anxious.

THE "MOVEMENT" AND THE CURRICULUM

The academic legacy left to the Free was a result of the battle cry of students in the late sixties and early seventies for more "relevant" courses. As historian Christopher Lasch observed in his 1978 best-seller *The Culture of Narcissus*, this crusade essentially "embodied a militant anti-intellectualism" with its primary objective as simply lightening the workload of the students under the guise of "high pedagogical principle." As with many other outlandish demands of student protesters of the time, universities obligingly disposed of the traditional curriculum even though no one had actually proved that it was not "relevant" in the first place. The result was what a Carnegie Foundation report called a "disaster area." In response to the student outcry, course requirements were greatly reduced or even eliminated; the number of elective courses rose; more student-demanded courses were added. For the most part, the general sense was that college students should be able to study whatever they please, and nothing else, and then be given a degree after accumulating the necessary number of units.

As the Free moved into the greatly transformed universities, they encountered an academic situation not tremendously different from the disorder of their high schools. In the areas of study that were declining in popularity, the accompanying drop in general education requirements engendered a profusion of new courses intended to retain and attract students. University of Illinois professor George Douglas related in his 1992 book *Education Without Impact* how his school's philosophy department dealt with this predicament. As students turned away from the humanities toward the professional majors, departments such as philosophy were threatened by dropping enrollments. "How did they solve the problem?" Douglas asks. "The department inaugurated a number of . . . 'blue baby' courses—with names like Philosophy and Sex, or Philosophy and the Urban Crisis, or Philosophy and Cinema"—in effect duping undergraduates into their department with less complex subjects, in the hope that a few would opt to stay. In similar cases, Duke's English department added courses with titles like Melodrama and Soap Opera, and Narcotics and Narrative. Temple University's American Studies department has offered a course since 1978 entitled Unidentified Flying Objects in American Society, in which the professor teaches from his book, *Secret Life: Firsthand Accounts of UFO Abductions*. Students are taught about space aliens who communicate telepathically and steal sperm and eggs from hapless human victims, and how the government has conspired to keep this knowledge a secret.

In order to lure students, such classes were offered under course titles that could be quite deceiving and give little insight to actual course content. When Pete Schaub, a University of Washington at Seattle business major, enrolled in

Introduction to Women's Studies in 1988, he expected to learn about "the history of women and the contributions they have made." What the teachers instead informed the class on the first day was that "the traditional American family represents a dysfunctional family unit." Students who argued this point were drowned out with chants of "Denial, denial," by teaching assistants hired by the course's two professors. A few classes later, guest speakers addressed the class about masturbation. "They said you don't need a man," said Schaub. "They proceeded to show how to masturbate with a feather duster, and they had dildos right there." This was Introduction to Women's Studies. One can only imagine what went on in the upper-division courses. In one lecture, one of the professors asserted that U.S. statistics showed that lesbians do a better job of raising children than do married couples. Schaub wanted to know the source of this information. "I asked after class," he told the *New York Times*. But the teacher "wouldn't hear of it. She said: 'Why are you challenging me? Get away from me. Just leave me alone.'" The next day, Schaub showed up for class to learn that he had been banned from the classroom. The teacher had two campus police officers waiting in the hall to escort him away. Schaub was advised by an associate dean to drop the course.

What enabled nonacademic or pseudoacademic classes to survive and flourish is that while more substantive classes were dropped from the list of requirements, their replacements were allowed to fulfill the cafeteria-style curriculum requirements that most schools retained. Duke's Melodrama and Soap Opera offering, for example, helps to fulfill the school's "Arts and Literature" requirement. Temple's UFO course relieves American Studies students of taking other classes such as Social Literature in the United States, or Courtroom in the American Society. Even Washington's study of masturbatory techniques fulfills the school's requirement titled "History, Philosophy, Civilization." Paradoxically, by taking this class, students can avoid taking courses in history, philosophy, and geography.

While some universities have long offered courses known as "Rocks for Jocks" or "Science for Giants," by the late seventies, nearly every college offered a number of courses like the University of California at Davis's Social and Psychological Aspects of Clothing, providing enlightenment on the "social and cognitive factors influencing management and perception of personal appearance in everyday life."

Not surprisingly, with the increase in less challenging courses, the Free experienced a great deal of grade inflation over previous students, just as they had in high school. Economists Richard Sabot and John Wakeman-Linn of Williams College studied the grades imparted at their university. From 1963 to 1986, they found that the percentage of students receiving a grade in English higher than a

B-plus had nearly tripled. Correspondingly, the proportion of students awarded grades of C or lower fell by 75 percent.

Intrigued by their findings, the two examined eight other top colleges and discovered that grade inflation was widespread at seven of them. In the fields studied, more than three-fourths of the students had at least a B average. Nearly *half* of the Williams College class of 1993 graduated with honors. Previously considered average, a grade of C now was given to those who were at the bottom of the heap. Only by not showing up for class at all did any of the Free usually receive a failing grade.

Just as the decline of the high schools is indicated by the steady drop in SAT scores, so can the results of the university experiments with the curriculum be measured by the less publicized Graduate Record Exam (GRE) scores, which college graduates take when applying to postgraduate programs. Predictably, the most extreme declines were in those disciplines that saw the greatest proliferation of "fuzzy" courses. The test scores in English literature, history, and political science all saw significant decreases from 1965 to 1992. The education, psychology, and GRE verbal exam marks also fell during this period. By contrast, whether due to the integrity of the department faculties or because the disciplines themselves allow less latitude for political manipulation, the areas of study that resisted the tendency toward watered-down courses didn't see such steep declines.

What's even more disturbing about the precipitous drop in GRE scores in the afflicted areas is that, while nearly everybody takes the SAT, in general only the cream of the crop go on to graduate study. These students are the ones who will be teaching at and running the schools of the future. As the universities provide an increasingly inadequate education to even the top students, the seeds of a long, downward spiral are sewn.

Attempting to gauge the achievements of the average college student, the National Endowment for the Humanities gave a multiple-choice test to college seniors at universities across the country in 1989, and found some embarrassing results. Only 58 percent of the seniors could place the Civil War in the correct half-century, and 60 percent couldn't identify who was president at the time of the Korean War. One student in four didn't even know that Columbus first landed in the Western Hemisphere prior to the year 1500. These were students on the verge of receiving a college degree. One could only wonder about the academic deficiencies of the 75 percent of young adults who hadn't advanced this far in their schooling.

The lowered academic requirements of universities, the corresponding grade inflation, and reports such as the NEH exam prompted some serious

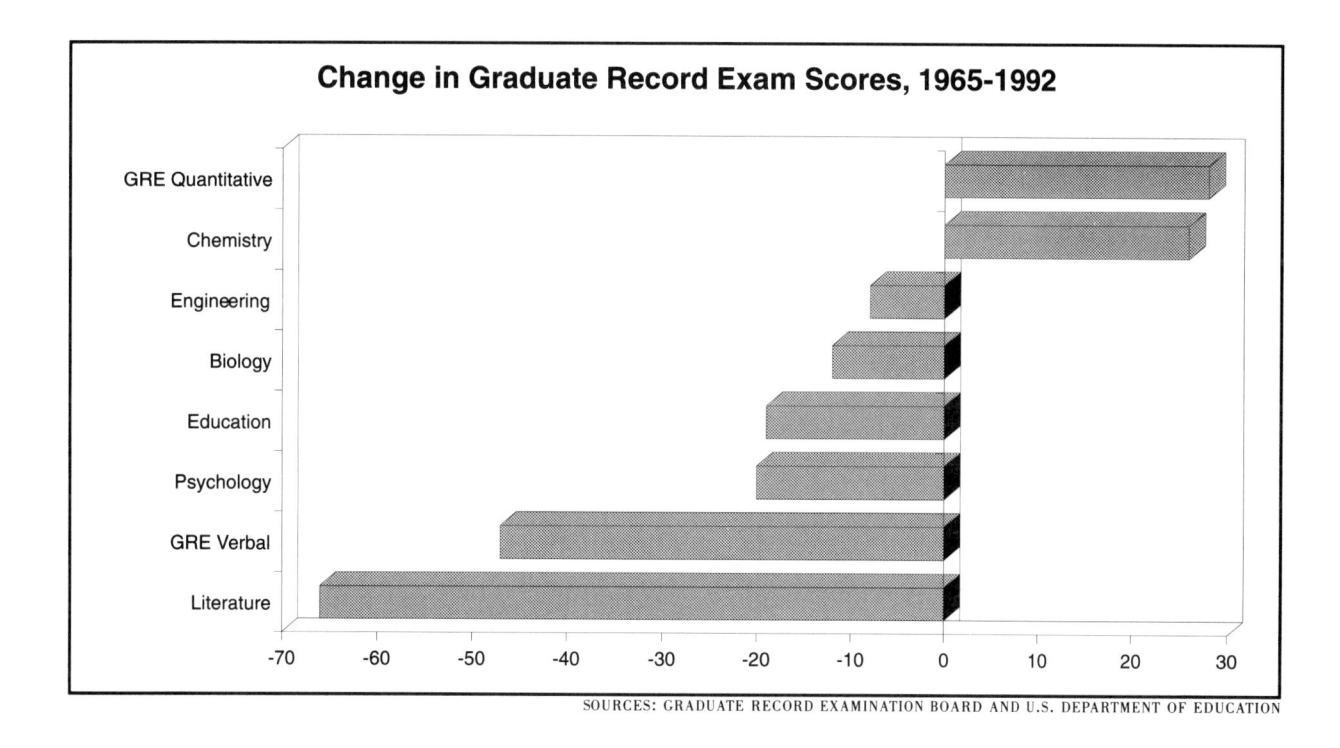

Change in Graduate Record Exam Scores, 1965-1992

GRE Quantitative	~30
Chemistry	~27
Engineering	~-5
Biology	~-12
Education	~-18
Psychology	~-20
GRE Verbal	~-47
Literature	~-65

SOURCES: GRADUATE RECORD EXAMINATION BOARD AND U.S. DEPARTMENT OF EDUCATION

charges about the educational accomplishments of the Free. The Carnegie Foundation completed a study of American higher education in 1987 and concluded that "many of the nation's colleges are more successful in credentialling than in providing a quality education for their students." Allan Bloom's runaway bestseller of the same year asserted that the universities were largely responsible for, in the words of the book's title, "The Closing of the American Mind." Nabeel Alsalam of the National Center for Education Statistics observed that "for quite a few people, college seems to be a place to learn what they should have learned in high school." Businesses certainly are aware of the changes in our universities' standards. With grade inflation and lightened graduation requirements, it has become that much more difficult to ascertain exactly how capable a graduating student may be. Consequently, when many companies recruit employees, they are choosing simply to ignore the large state schools in favor of the selective, private universities where there is less uncertainty about hiring an unqualified person. Even though it is important to bring as many young people as possible to our campuses, it is perhaps more critical that we improve the *quality* of the degrees awarded.

THE ABSENT PROFESSOR

One would hope that universities were using the increased revenue that resulted from higher tuition to maintain the quality of their faculties. But who taught the Free during their university days? To a large extent, the Free themselves. Graduate teaching assistants, long a source of classroom instruction in American universities, but previously limited to senior graduate students on the verge of completing their Ph.D.s, became omnipresent in the lecture halls for this generation.

At Ohio State University, for example, by the late eighties a full 39 percent of all classes attended by its forty thousand students were taught by student teachers. Even those at the nation's most elite—and expensive—universities witnessed this growing phenomenon. At Yale, one fourth of the classroom teachers were graduate teaching assistants. And every single freshman English section at Stanford was taught by a graduate student who was likely only a few years older than those he or she was teaching.

This overreliance on student teaching assistants sometimes had devastating consequences. When 2,200 student teachers at the University of Massachusetts went on strike for higher wages in 1991, nearly 60 percent of undergraduate classes were canceled. During a strike a year later at Berkeley by graduate TAs seeking union recognition, the school was all but shut down during the weeks leading up to final exams. Evidence of the priorities of the nation's universities toward its undergraduates could be seen at America's oldest college, Harvard. Annually, the school offers the Levenson Award for Outstanding Teaching, given on the basis of classroom instruction rather than outside achievements. In both 1986 and 1987, the professors who won this prize were nonetheless denied tenure and fired. Their acknowledged expertise in the classroom wasn't enough to warrant keeping them on staff.

With some basis in the lamentable educational background with which many of the Free entered college, many professors seemed to have grown disillusioned with their students. We've seen that more than half of the nation's university faculty considered their students unprepared for college work, and some spoke in even stronger terms. Professor Allan Bloom complained that "university officials have had somehow to deal with the undeniable fact that the students who enter are uncivilized." Wendy Kaminer of Radcliffe wrote about teaching college freshmen: "I quickly discovered that my students were interested only in issues that were dramatized. . . . Raised on 'Donahue' and docudramas, they found mere discussions of ideas 'too dry and academic.' You can't even be academic in academia anymore." And Robert Bellah, professor of sociology at Berkeley, flatly asserted, "A third of my students are illiterate. By that I mean they are unable to understand a complex sentence, or write one that makes much sense." While such attitudes may not necessarily have been unfounded, our universities' dwindling attention toward classroom instruction certainly was providing too little assistance toward improving the situation.

IN LOCO PARENTIS REVISITED

When they were in college, Boomers all but eliminated the concept of a required code of behavior for students. Matters such as drugs, sex, and drinking were adult concerns, went the rationale, and students, as adults, should have the right to make such choices for themselves. Unfortunately, this is the one advancement that many schools decided to reverse upon the Free's enrollment in college.

The idea of *in loco parentis,* or substitute parent, surfaced in some invidious ways. Whereas Boomers as students had been beneficiaries of the free-speech movement, Boomers as professors have often been instigators of the *less*-speech movement. The result of *this* revolution would be great limitations on students' freedom to express their opinions, and it wouldn't be kindled by student desires, as was the case in the sixties. Rather, it would be imposed on them by their instructors. As Middlebury College professor Jay Parini wrote in the *Chronicle of Higher Education* in 1988, "After the Vietnam War, a lot of us didn't just crawl back into our literary cubicles; we stepped into academic positions. With the war over, our visibility was lost and it seemed for a while—to the unobservant—that we had disappeared. Now we have tenure, and the work of reshaping the universities has begun in earnest." Clark Kerr, former chancellor of the University of California system, noted the danger of any exploitation of the university for political purposes in his 1991 book *The Great Transformation in Higher Education 1960–1980.* "The presence of the university carrying out its normal functions changes society fundamentally," he explains, "but the attempted manipulation of the university, for the sake of specific political reforms, changes the university for the worse more than it changes society for the better." At the same time the United States Supreme Court was giving America, particularly those on the far right, a lesson in constitutional rights with its ruling that burning the U.S. flag—an act that a great many find offensive—is a legally protected form of expression guaranteed by the First Amendment, universities were attempting to impose disturbing limits on what their own students could say or do.

The University of Michigan, site of the self-important 1962 Port Huron Statement, instituted the eighties' version of a reform-the-world manifesto with its policy on "Discrimination and Discriminatory Harassment." This statement ordained as punishable offenses "any behavior, verbal or physical, that stigmatizes or victimizes an individual on the basis of race, ethnicity, religion, sex, sexual orientation, creed, national origin, ancestry, age, marital status," or—lest anyone question which generation is behind such prohibitions—"Vietnam-era veteran status."

In the fall of 1989, at the behest of an anonymous instructor who sued the university, District Judge Avern Cohn ruled as unconstitutional the entire Michigan policy, stating that "the public expression of ideas may not be prohibited merely because the ideas are themselves offensive to some of their hearers." At this setback, the university drew new speech guidelines that would fall within court-mandated standards. As writer Dinesh D'Souza commented, "a university that was once dedicated to maximum freedom of mind and conscience" was now struggling to find the minimum amount of freedom it would have to insure to remain within the law.

The University of California at Berkeley, the University of Connecticut, the University of Wisconsin, and over two hundred other schools followed Michigan's lead with their own versions of limiting free speech in the name of "sensitivity." At Emory, the policy prohibiting sexual harassment by students, faculty, and staff was expanded to include "all kinds of discriminatory harassment—by race, color, national origin, religion, sex, sexual orientation, age, handicap or veteran's status." (At least Emory included veterans of *all* wars under the umbrella of protection.) The University of Connecticut warned of penalties ranging from reprimand to expulsion for offenses ranging from "inconsiderate jokes" to "misdirected laughter" to "conspicuous exclusion from conversation." Tufts created three levels of "allowable speech," with corresponding "speech zones." Freedom of speech was protected in public areas and campus publications; derogatory or demeaning speech could be restricted in classrooms, libraries, and dining halls; in dormitories the right of free speech simply no longer existed, and no conversations deemed insensitive would be tolerated. Protesting students lampooned the ruling using tape and chalk to divide the campus into the "free speech zone," the "limited speech zone," and the "twilight zone" while posting warnings to students that they might be entering areas where their constitutional rights were no longer valid.

Whereas conservative boards of trustees once enforced university limitations on voices of the far left, it was now mainly left-leaning faculties that limited the voices that ran counter to their own ideology. It should be noted that just as it was only a distinct minority of vocal students who brought about the campus unrest of the sixties, so was it but an outspoken minority who brought about these radical and intolerant reforms in the eighties. At Michigan and Berkeley, for example, about three quarters of the faculty abstained from voting on the measures described above.

A whole new set of colloquialisms were coined for the new proscriptions. Smith College staff members warned their students to refrain from *lookism,* judging people by their physical attractiveness. Or there was *ableism,* the Smith umbrella term for prejudice against those who are *differently abled, physically challenged,* or just plain handicapped. Connecticut's "misdirected laughter" violators were guilty of *laughism.* The creation of new "isms" was limited only by the imaginations of those who drafted the speech policies.

Once the mandates were put into place at many universities, it quickly became apparent that the threats of disciplinary action for violators were to be taken seriously. An Occidental College student was suspended for the 1991 school year for calling a female student a "four-letter word" when she refused to open the locked door to the dormitory where a friend lived. A student peer review board found him in violation of the policy banning "verbal abuse." In 1986, a Yale sophomore circulated a satirical flier promoting the school's "Bestiality Awareness Days" during Yale's annual "Gay and Lesbian Awareness Days." The university's executive committee found him in violation of the school's harassment policy and sentenced him to two years' probation. At the urging of Yale president Benno C. Schmidt, a First Amendment specialist, the student appealed the verdict and won.

In 1992, UCLA fraternity Theta Xi was suspended from its national organization and subjected to a university investigation for a book of drinking songs that included verses advocating sexual violence. Even though the fraternity's chapter president maintained that the songbook had been withdrawn more than a year earlier because some members found some of its contents offensive, an old copy was found in a Westwood apartment and subsequently published in the campus feminist magazine, *Together,* prompting the investigation.

Similar actions were taken across the country. A Brown University student was expelled for shouting racial slurs. The University of Connecticut attempted to kick a student out of campus housing for a similar offense. Stanford ejected a student from a dormitory for yelling anti-homosexual epithets at a member of the house staff. The University of Pennsylvania shut down a fraternity house for a year because of a party at which two black strippers performed. The action wasn't taken because of the pornographic aspects, but for the alleged racism inherent in the choice of the strippers. A Michigan student was reprimanded and required to take a sensitivity seminar for writing an offensive limerick for a class assignment.

Just as the campus chaos of the sixties failed to better society, but succeeded in tarnishing the academic rigor at many universities, the repressive behavioral codes of the eighties left campuses a little less tolerant than they once had been. With all of the other newly added pressures of college life in the eighties and nineties, the last thing students needed was to be wary of even expressing their opinions lest some faculty member deem them "insensitive." But as many found out the hard way, this was yet one more hurdle placed in their way as they just tried to get an education.

Part Three

THE IMPOVERISHED GENERATION

12

WORKING MORE FOR LESS

Number of personal bankruptcies filed nationwide:

1972—182,869

1992—899,840

SOURCE: ADMINISTRATIVE OFFICE OF THE U.S. COURTS

In the mid-1970s, a series of blue-ribbon commissions, including the President's Scientific Advisory Committee, concerned by what was perceived as "increasing social deviance and lack of motivation" among the young, recommended increased adolescent employment as a means of correcting this depravity and apathy. With one typical admonition, sociologist James Coleman warned that the young were becoming expert consumers without developing any knowledge of how to produce, or about the connection between work, income, and consumption.

Widespread employment would be a virtual panacea, it was believed, cultivating personal and social responsibility, as well as providing a financial boost to a drifting economy. As Cornell University's Urie Bronfenbrenner, one of those who suggested such measures, later stated in the introduction to the 1986 book *When Teenagers Work*, "Rarely have the recommendations of social scientists been so rapidly and fully transformed into reality." But he was compelled to add, "And rarely have the consequences of a recommended reality proved so contrary to the original scientific predictions." A principal reason for Bronfenbrenner's about-face is that the economy has undergone some enormous transformations in recent years. Widespread teenage employment in the eighties was a far cry from the weekend jobs of the fifties at the hardware store or soda fountain under the watchful guidance of a firm but supportive boss.

The first paradox of the rise in teenage employment was that, to a large degree, those who it might be said most needed a job were the least likely to have

CHILD LABOR

one. Whereas in earlier generations young people who worked generally did so because they had to, and those who didn't have to work didn't, this trend was turned on its head for the Free. Several studies in the early eighties showed that the lowest rates of employment were among children from the lowest income levels—children who could have used a few dollars for necessities that their families were unable to provide. Conversely, the highest rates were among those who came from families in the higher income levels, teenagers who were essentially working not to build character or learn responsibility—or even to save money for college—but merely to have more spending money. The result was an even more pronounced polarization between haves and have-nots in the schools and other places frequented by teenagers.

The great majority of working adolescents essentially had free rein to spend their incomes however they wished with little or no supervision by their parents, and only a tiny percentage saved anything for future needs. The money they did spend was an unprecedented amount, nearly $50 billion in 1985, a third more per capita adjusted for inflation than teenagers had at their disposal only ten years earlier. While the market for adolescent dollars had been created decades before, with the introduction of items like Hula Hoops and 45 rpm records, eighties teenagers had tastes that were quite a bit more extravagant, leaning more in the direction of compact disks and stereos to play them on, electronic games, and designer clothes. Stretch limousines parked in front of the high school on prom night became a familiar sight. Money was available to so many working young people that professor of child study David Elkind warned in a 1987 *Parents* magazine article that "it may lead teens, unencumbered by adult responsibilities, to engage in a level of consumption that is inconsistent with the obligations that they will face in the coming years." He had forecast what many young adults experienced a few years later—they had more spending money in high school than they did as adults.

The proportion of teenagers who worked was 50 percent higher in 1980 than it had been twenty years earlier. Somewhere between two thirds and three fourths of those of high-school age were employed during the eighties. In the western part of the country, 80 percent of high-school seniors held a job of some kind. With slight variations during economic ups and downs, the level would stay that high from the first wave to the last of the Free. And the hours worked were considerably more than an afternoon here and there. In a 1981 survey titled "High School and Beyond," researchers found that the average high-school sophomore boy with a job put in 15 hours of work each week, and the average girl put in 10.5 hours. By senior year, both boys and girls had added another six to seven hours per week. Thus, on top of going to school, the *average* employed senior was spending time at work equal to an adult part-time job. In addition, about one student in ten worked 35 hours or more each week, the equivalent of a full-time job. This amount of work brought in $200 a month on average, with incomes of $500 a month not uncommon. But only one in twenty contributed any portion of this toward the support of their families. It was theirs to spend as they wished.

On the surface it seems hard to find fault with this development. Young people had the opportunity to earn a little money and to learn how to budget and spend it wisely. They also learned the responsibilities of showing up for work on time and performing tasks that demanded consistent quality and taught new and useful skills. Unfortunately, the reality of the situation proved to be, in many cases, more harmful than beneficial.

The first casualty of high youth employment was school. Several studies showed a strong adverse relationship between the number of hours worked and the grades earned in school. Researchers Ellen Greenberger and Laurence Steinberg found that tenth-graders who worked more than fifteen hours per week and eleventh-graders who worked more than twenty hours had significantly lower grades than students who worked fewer hours. It wasn't simply that less-accomplished students were the ones most likely to work in the first place; another study found that among academically similar students in the tenth grade, those who worked extensively in the following years had lower grades by senior year than those who worked little or not at all. And those who worked long hours beginning at an early age were also at an increased risk of dropping out of school altogether. Students freely admitted this detrimental effect. More than a fourth of employed teenagers surveyed by Greenberger and Steinberg acknowledged that their grades had declined since they began working. More than half reported that working interfered with doing required reading and writing assignments and that it interfered with staying alert during class.

One common tactic of working students was to scale back their class load to the minimum necessary for graduation, which often wasn't much in the laissez-faire schools of the time. Others enrolled in easier courses than they normally would have in order to free up time for their jobs. Educational researcher Linda McNeil found that teachers, in adapting to students' spending less time on their studies due to employment, had gradually reduced their homework demands, simplified their lectures, and made their requirements for papers and presentations less demanding. Of course, the reduced homework load freed up time for students to put in even more hours on the job. For many students, then, school became the part-time job, taking a backseat to employment.

A second consequence of high adolescent employment, largely due to little parental guidance in how their children spent their time and money, was that teenagers simply had the cash to buy certain things they shouldn't have been buying. Specifically, a 1982 study found that teenagers who worked were more likely to drink alcohol, smoke cigarettes, and use marijuana and other drugs, in large part because they could pay for them. An additional link between work and increased drug use is that employed students spend more time around older coworkers who often indulge in such behavior. So while it could be argued that working students were learning to budget their money, they were not all learning to budget it wisely, or even legally.

The greatest irony to increased employment among the Free as teenagers is that instead of fostering respect and appreciation for work, many developed increased cynicism and distaste for the whole enterprise, due to the tedium and mindless repetition of many of their jobs. The most common type of work for teenagers in the new low-skill economy was in the fast-food industry or other service businesses that relied on cheap labor. High-school seniors told researchers that they made little or no use of their skills or abilities at such jobs. It was simply the kind of work people just did "for money."

Greenberger and Steinberg found that while working at these jobs, young people use almost no reading, writing, or mathematical skills. "The average adolescent food service worker," they wrote, "spends only about one minute of every hour on the job using school-taught skills." Nor did the experience much enrich one's life in other ways. The two researchers noted that "wrapping fast-food items in paper containers as fast as one can is unlikely to teach a worker very much about self-reliance or decision making." Getting a pizza there "in thirty minutes or it's free" teaches little (other than perhaps to disregard speed limits and stop signs).

What *is* learned by such mindless tasks is that work is something to be merely endured rather than enjoyed, a boring, distasteful chore rather than an enriching, satisfying endeavor. Perhaps the saddest irony is that the one possible benefit, if it can be called that, of the prevalence of these low-skill, no-future "McJobs" is that this was the type of employment that would be readily available to the Free as they entered the adult workforce.

Perhaps due to the Protestant work ethic that is so ingrained in Americans, or because it presented an opportunity to keep children occupied and out of their hair, parents and other adults apparently weren't too concerned about the negative aspects of overworked teenagers. As increasingly both parents, or the single parent, were out working all day themselves and saw less and less of their children, the youngsters were no more deprived of parental attention by working than they would have been if they had rushed straight home after school. Educators even perceived some interesting side benefits from the phenomenon. One school official described "McDonald's time" to the *Washington Post* as the part of the day when students stream out of school and into the fast-food restaurants to work. An assistant principal told researcher Linda McNeil in 1984 that jobs for students "were good for school discipline in that they help clear seniors out of the halls and away from school grounds during afternoon classes." One incensed mother wrote authors Greenberger and Steinberg that "my son learned more at Burger King than he ever did in high school." The sad fact is that she just may be right.

HARD TIMES

When Congress passed the Fair Labor Standards Act in 1938, it established regulations on how employers could use child workers, with certain tasks prohibited for those under age sixteen and others for those under eighteen. Among these conditions are restrictions against children operating dangerous machinery and regulation of the hours an employer can keep an underage employee on the job. Violations of this law were rare—until the Free entered the workplace in droves during their teenage years.

The General Accounting Office reported that the number of minors found to be illegally employed more than doubled from 1983 to 1989, when 22,500 violations were recorded. This was a higher number of infractions than had been recorded in any year since the 1938 act was legislated. And this figure most likely represents only a fraction of the actual violations. A nationwide 1990 Labor Department sweep of employers found nearly half of the 6,000 workplaces investigated to be in violation of child-labor laws. New York State inspectors estimated that 75,000 children were working illegally in the New York City area alone. Since the problem had been rare until this time, the penalties involved for offending employers were minor. With the skyrocketing number of violations, though, Labor Secretary Elizabeth Dole proposed raising the maximum civil fine for each violation from $1,000 to $10,000 and allowing imprisonment of employers convicted of willful violation of such laws, but penalties for such infractions remain rare, and are seldom severe. In yet another way, the rights of Free children and adolescents seem to have been left unguarded.

MONKEY ON THE BACK

Conservative economists have categorized the eighties as the longest peacetime economic expansion in America's history. However, during that decade, defense spending hit unprecedented levels, and the U.S. fought wars in Grenada and Panama, and left the decade just about to embark on a third in Kuwait. So the "peacetime" label is hardly appropriate. Furthermore, the economic expansion, driven by the new government policy of borrow-and-spend, did little to benefit the younger generation but did leave us foundering in a hole of debt unrivaled in size.

As the Free entered the adult world of work, they found themselves already handicapped by the U.S. economy in ways no other American generation has experienced. From 1970 to 1984, the accumulated debt saddling the federal government, industry, and private households more than quadrupled, from $1.6 trillion to $7.1 trillion. And since 1984, government debt has more than tripled *again*. This debt is money that has been incurred for services already rendered and eventually has to be paid back. So while this burden confronts everyone, it is only the younger generation who never had a chance to use these borrowed funds in a productive way before the payback time. Placing the responsibility of paying off the older generation's debts on the shoulders of the younger generation might be called a surreptitious case of taxation without representation. But un-American as it may be, this idea of billing others later for services provided now seems firmly entrenched in the congressional psyche.

Indicative of the state of the economy as a whole that greeted the Free, 1985 saw a record number of filings for bankruptcy in U.S. courts. The record was then surpassed annually for the next seven years. In 1992 alone, just under 1 million bankruptcy petitions were filed, 92 percent of them personal bankruptcies. Over the eight-year period of record breaking, a total of more than 5 million people decided they just could no longer keep up with their own debt, never mind the national debt. The personal-bankruptcy phenomenon is represented on an international scale as well. Within a few years of the Free's entry in the workforce, the United States went from being the world's largest creditor nation to the world's largest debtor nation—a startling metaphor for the change in environment under which two generations came of age.

The employment climate has also undergone great changes, making it more difficult for first-time job seekers. As a career counselor at Lewis and Clark College explains, "Historically, business organization was highly linear, and people, after they entered the company, were groomed and usually moved up. Now things are much more horizontal, which is good for productivity and good for participatory management but not good for the rookies, the people who don't have experience and want to get in." In the new disposable worker economy, the last in are the first out. Evidence of this phenomenon can be seen in the 1.45 million jobs lost nationally in the recent recession between March 1990 and March 1991. Although sixteen- to twenty-four-year-olds comprised only 17 percent of all workers, according to one Northeastern University economist, this age group suffered 65 percent of the employment loss. Young workers bore *four times* the burden of other age groups.

THE DISAPPEARING JOB

In the 1980 film *Caddyshack,* a young caddy is worrying aloud to a country-clubbing attorney about his fate if he is not awarded a college scholarship. Unsympathetic, the attorney retorts, "The world needs ditch diggers too." Unfortunately, the ditch-digging sector of the economy has hardly expanded to fill the needs left by great loss of opportunity in other areas.

One of the benefits that has long been cited as a coming boon for the Free, due to their smaller numbers, is an imminent labor shortage. The economy swelled to accommodate the numerous Boomers, goes the reasoning, so by the time the next generation entered the job market, there would be so many employment opportunities that they would virtually be able to write their own tickets. Indeed, the economy *did* expand to accommodate the Boomers, but no more. Despite being remembered for the "malaise" that gripped the country, the seventies, the decade that welcomed most Boomers into their careers, was a landmark decade for job creation. After seeing the total number of jobs in the economy increase by a healthy 20 percent during the sixties, the seventies added another astounding 27 percent. The job machine began to grind to a halt at this point, however. According to the Department of Labor, the eighties greeted the Free with job growth of a mere 18 percent, with projections for the nineties at an anemic 13 percent.

The Free are quite conscious of the situation; a 1992 MTV survey of one thousand young adults aged eighteen to twenty-nine found that they considered a lack of jobs or economic opportunity to be the single greatest obstacle facing their generation, with two thirds believing this. They know that it's not the young adults who are scarce, it's *jobs* that are hard to find.

So rather than finding themselves in a wide-open market, the Free have seen fewer job prospects and lower incomes than their predecessors. An additional obstacle placed in front of the Free is simply the enormous number of Boomers directly ahead of them on the career ladder. As twenty-four-year-old Amy, who has a master's degree from Cornell and was working as a traveling fabric salesperson, explained in *Business Week,* "The guy who has the job I want is thirty-four and has a wife and kids. So he's not going anywhere." Novelist Douglas Coupland defines this predicament as "Boomer envy: Envy of material wealth and long-range material security accrued by older members of the baby boom generation by virtue of their fortunate births." Of course, much of the explanation for this situation is that the numbers of the Free are not significantly smaller than the Boomers. But great transformations in the mechanics that drive the economy have also contributed to the situation.

The greatest casualties have been those without a college education. The availability of work that provides the opportunity for such people to earn good wages while developing a career has been in headlong decline for two decades. Stable employment in high-paying sectors such as manufacturing, transportation, and utilities—areas that were previously open to high-school graduates—has fallen sharply. Among male high-school graduates under the age of twenty, for example, 57 percent found work at such employment in 1968; but by 1986, only 36 percent had such good fortune. And whereas young men with a high-school diploma had once gone to work in steel plants and auto factories—and earned decent blue-collar wages suitable for supporting a family—they now face what Brookings Institution economist Gary Burtless bluntly calls "a future of lousy jobs."

The primary driving force behind the declining fortunes of those without a higher education has been a shakeout in the manufacturing sector. During the sixties and seventies, the economy added 5 million manufacturing jobs to its ranks. The young Boomer from a working-class family who graduated from high school during these years could choose from among a number of these relatively high-paying jobs. But in the eighties the bottom dropped out and the economy shed 1.8 million such jobs during the decade—almost one manufacturing job in ten. Since the peak years in the early seventies, the proportion of men under age thirty employed in factories has plunged twice as rapidly as for older workers.

Once a seemingly endless source of steady, good-paying jobs, for example, the Big Three automakers hired virtually no new hourly employees during the decade of the eighties. These developments have prompted incomes-watcher Frank Levy to sadly note that "it is much harder for a male high school graduate to be in 'the Middle Class' now than it was ten years ago." Adds *Business Week* writer Laura Zinn, "This is the generation of diminished expectations—polar opposites of the baby boomers, who grew up thinking anything was possible."

While the situation is most dire for those who haven't attended college, the career prospects for graduates of universities have proven only slightly better. A decade ago, think tanks were anticipating shortages of college graduates, particularly those in technical fields, and envisioning a booming service economy filled with the kind of lower- and mid-level management positions well suited to liberal-arts and business majors. Instead, the buzzword of the nineties, illustrated by enormous layoffs by giants General Motors and IBM, is "downsizing." As *Rolling Stone* magazine commented in 1993, "It appears that the value of the diploma—once a general-admission ticket to the economy—is dropping with each quarter and crop of grads, leaving a lot of people at the door unable to get in."

Robert Ehrman, the director of the Career Development Unit at UCLA, called the business climate the worst labor market he had seen in his twelve years on the job. Victor Lindquist of Northwestern University commented, "This is the most troublesome job market for college graduates in the last twenty-five years." The *New York Times* reported, "This spring's college graduates are facing one of the bleakest job markets in at least two decades." And the *Los Angeles Times* ran a story headed, ENTRY-LEVEL JOB PROSPECTS POOREST SINCE DEPRESSION. What's most notable about these dire reports is that they were all printed during the peak economic years of the mid-eighties—*before* the recession hit a few years later. The idea "that we would go on just having higher levels of college-educated people may have not been very sound," notes one Syracuse University education professor. "We may be seeing the beginning of a saturation level." The gravity of the situation is magnified when one considers the enormous debt with which recent college graduates typically enter the workforce.

The Economic Policy Institute found that wages of college graduates fell 3.1 percent between 1987 and 1991. For those who have managed to get a foot in the door, the institute noted that "having a college degree no longer affords protection against falling wage trends." The inadequate salaries of high-school graduates are starting to trickle up. It's been a popular lament that one in ten college graduates in the sixties was forced to take a job that required no college degree. According to the most recent estimates, *twice* that percentage of eighties graduates were compelled to do so. In fact, the Department of Education estimates that only *22 percent* of the jobs created during the eighties required a college degree. And this situation won't bottom out for years; the Bureau of Labor Statistics (BLS) forecasts that nearly one graduate in *three* from the classes of 1990 through 2005 will be forced to take a job that doesn't require a college degree. Indicative of the trend, *Money* magazine reports that just since 1988 the hiring of college graduates is down 40 percent, and the Labor Department determined in 1990 that 5.8 million people in the economy were "educationally underutilized." As the corporations that have traditionally provided high-paying, stable employment shed jobs, the Free have little choice but to accept the less-promising offers that remain.

MCJOBS AND TEMPS

While the economy did add 21 million new jobs during the eighties, these were overwhelmingly concentrated in the service industry. "We had new jobs," says one Boston College economist, "but the new jobs have been disproportionately in the low-wage sector." *Very* low wage. Forty-four percent of the new jobs created during the eighties paid less than $7,400 a year, which was 30 percent below the poverty-level income for a family of three. And while some have claimed that lots of low-wage "entry-level" service jobs are just what the economy needs, such jobs typically offer few opportunities for advancement. There is often no level past "entry." Economist Bob Kuttner gives the example of the growing fast-food industry: It "employs a small number of executives, and hundreds of thousands of cashiers and kitchen help" who earn minimum wage and have little promise of making headway.

The other areas that have seen enormous gains in employment are part-time jobs and a category that hardly existed before the Free—temporary jobs. According to the Bureau of Labor Statistics, the number of involuntary part-time workers—those seeking a full-time job—more than doubled from 1970 to 1990. The recent economic recovery shows no improvement in this area. It was estimated that half of the jobs that opened up in 1992 were part-time, temporary, or involved some other unconventional arrangement. The BLS reported that a full 90 percent of the jobs created in January of 1993 were for part-time or temporary work. Not only are the hourly wages of part-time employees just 60 percent of full-time workers', only 22 percent of them are covered by employer-sponsored health insurance, less than one third the rate of full-timers. In a possible portent of future trends, the Bank of America has even restructured its entire force of tellers, shifting the majority of them to part-time work specifically to avoid paying such benefits.

By 1992, a nationwide total of nearly 1.5 million "temps" were on the job—although many weren't sure exactly where they would be reporting from one day to the next. During the eighties the number of temporary jobs grew at ten times the rate of full-time jobs, and universities found that as many as 30 percent of their recent graduates were forced into such work. Many companies have completely reorganized around the temporary-worker concept, employing a core of permanent managers and longtime workers, and adding and shedding other workers with the upswings and downturns in the market. Like part-time work, these jobs typically pay much less than full-time, permanent work, but even fewer temporary workers are afforded any benefits. With companies cutting costs wherever possible, the temporary is here to stay.

The Free have grudgingly accepted such work—they have little choice—but they're not happy about it. A 1990 Virginia Slims Opinion Poll of working women found that 61 percent of eighteen- to twenty-nine-year-old women said their work was "just a job" as opposed to "a career." This age group was 20 percent more likely to feel this way than were older women and 33 percent more likely than Boomers, who indicated the greatest satisfaction with their careers. In a survey of five thousand households by the Conference Board, it was found that only 13 percent of all workers aged twenty-five and younger reported being "most satisfied" with their work. Telemarketing or flipping burgers apparently doesn't cultivate a great deal of job satisfaction. Accordingly, in the search for higher pay and better working conditions, the Free have also exhibited the greatest job mobility. As company loyalty has disappeared, employee loyalty has followed.

The immediate future doesn't appear to provide much relief. The Bureau of Labor Statistics recently compiled a list of the types of jobs that are likely to see the greatest growth by the year 2005. The biggest gainers are as follows:

JOB	PROJECTED NUMBER OF NEW JOBS
Retail salespersons	780,000
Registered nurses	765,000
Cashiers	670,000
General office clerks	654,000
Truck drivers	640,000
Waiters, waitresses	637,000
Nursing aides, orderlies	594,000
Janitors, cleaners, maids	540,000
Food preparation workers	524,000
Systems analysts	501,000
Home health aides	479,000

Most of the jobs that are projected to have large numbers of openings are in the service industries and require little education. And few typically present real opportunities for advancement. What's more, even those areas that are projected to be in demand have seen wage declines in the last decade. The Free seem to have two career options: fields that offer few job opportunities, or fields that offer reduced wages.

One particular area of employment that in the recent past afforded abundant entry-level job opportunities is the public sector. Federal, state, and local government employment grew from 7 in 1955 to a zenith of nearly 17 million by 1980. A healthy percentage of those entering the job market in the sixties and seventies were able to find positions in the public arena, jobs that traditionally pay well and offer solid benefits. After 1980, however, the government began to cut back substantially on job offers. Within a few years, government rosters had atrophied down to 15 million employees.

THE GOVERNMENT'S CLOSED-DOOR POLICY

The significance of the freeze in public-sector employment on the wallet is considerable. From 1982 to 1991, public-sector wage increases outpaced those in the private sector by a factor of four. Public employees also received pensions that were twice as generous as those in private industry. During the eighties, government jobs were where the money was to be found, but not where job openings were to be found.

The elimination of public-sector opportunities has most harmed young women and minorities. According to Stanford University economist Martin Carnoy, in 1970, 57 percent of all black male college graduates were employed by the government. In addition, 62 percent of white female college graduates and 79 percent of black female college graduates held public-sector jobs. While the last two decades have seen great gains in the receptivity of private industry to hiring women and minorities, these wages have not increased at the same pace as government jobs, and the fields that have seen the most job growth have been in the lower-paying areas. It could be said that women and minorities have therefore earned the right to the same mediocre jobs that are available to everyone else.

In the area of higher education, largely driven by government support of public universities, job opportunities have also dried up. From 1960 to 1975, the number of professors at work on our college campuses more than doubled. More than half of all professorships that exist today were filled during this fifteen-year period, by individuals who are likely to remain in the ivory tower well into the next century. As Clark Kerr, former University of California chancellor, pointed out as the first Free were considering graduate school, "The Ph.D. candidate in 1960 could not miss; one in 1980 will be lucky to make a hit." With the security and high wages that a tenured university position affords, many of the educators hired during the sixties and seventies are not likely to leave and create an opening for a younger candidate, cutting off one more area of employment. And while it stands to reason that by the time the Free's children are grown there should be a large number of vacancies, the dream of a professorship remains unattainable for many among this generation.

TWO TIERS: THE HIGH-PAYING ONE AND THE FREE ONE

Although membership in labor unions has been on the decline for three decades, unions still tended to protect the interests of all their workers, young and old, equally. That is, until the eighties, when the concept of "two-tiered" contracts gained in popularity. Just as older Americans profited by the spending that resulted in the national debt while younger Americans are obliged to share in repaying it, two-tiered contracts are in effect a means of preserving the wages and benefits of existing employees at the expense of future ones. As an alternative to making more equitable, across-the-board concessions, such contracts generally specify that employees hired after a certain date will be paid less than employees who are already on the job at the time the contract is approved.

In arrangements that maintained the high wages of existing employees, for example, the Associated General Contractors of America signed a contract in 1983 that provided only 60 percent of the prevailing wage to new workers. The Allied Pilots Association agreed with American Airlines on another deal that would provide new pilots with only half the pay of incumbents, who retained their $110,000 annual incomes. New butchers at a California slaughterhouse received only 60 percent of the $10.44 hourly wage of current butchers, although they did the exact same work. And at the electronics firm Motorola, employees are placed in three categories: about 30 percent of them, those with ten years or more of seniority, are guaranteed their jobs even during slow economic periods; 40 percent are regular, permanent employees but have no such guarantees; and the remaining 30 percent—the most recent hirees—are on six-month contracts that the company can terminate on twenty-four hours' notice. Overall, in a survey taken in 1984, more than half of all firms who had engaged in contract negotiations had agreed to at least one two-tiered agreement. The giant Food and Commercial Workers union alone negotiated fifty-five such contracts over a two-year period.

There is a human factor. One package sorter at United Parcel Service complained to a reporter in 1985 that "I get $9.68 an hour, and the guy working next to me makes $13.99 doing exactly the same job." A stewardess with United Airlines was forced to take on additional work since her $1,000 a month base salary was $400 to $500 a month lower than an "A scale" stewardess. A woman working in the hardware department of a department store in Michigan expressed frustration at earning $2 an hour less than a coworker performing the exact same tasks. In this last case, the two-tiered wage agreement saved the company enough money to allow them to expand, but not enough so that the company became strong enough to eliminate the lower wage scale. In other words, everyone benefited from the deal except the younger workers. Young employees in hundreds of corporations as varied as Boeing, Greyhound, and Kroger were affected by the lower tier of union wages. The situation was summed up by a man who had worked for Kroger for thirty-seven years and earned $12.37 an hour. "I made a good living," he said. "I bought my own house, sent my boy through college, and gave the girl a nice wedding. But it won't be that way for the younger people who get our jobs."

OUT OF WORK, OUT OF LUCK

While we've seen how growing unemployment often affects younger workers with greater frequency than those who are older, today's young adults are much less likely to receive any benefits to help them through this period than has pre-

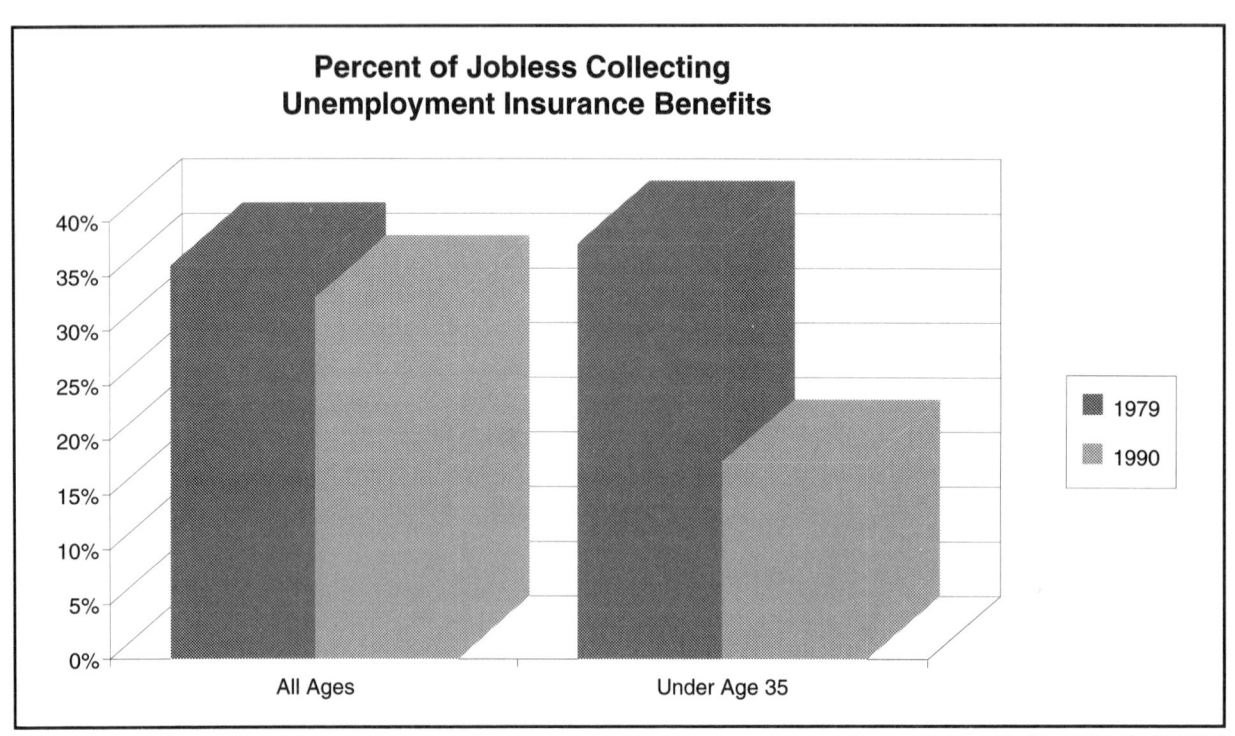

Percent of Jobless Collecting Unemployment Insurance Benefits

■ 1979
■ 1990

SOURCE: BUREAU OF LABOR STATISTICS

viously been the case. In the seventies, younger unemployed workers were slightly *more* likely to be receiving such benefits than older jobless people. Yet today, due primarily to economic trends like the increase in part-time work among the Free, the ranks of those eligible for unemployment benefits has dropped significantly. Fewer than one unemployed young adult in five was receiving any benefits in 1990.

A most surprising reaction to the predicaments that have befallen them is that the Free generally support the trends. They tend to take responsibility for their situation and not to place the blame on the government, their schools, their parents, or any other entity. When the Gallup Organization asked Americans about poverty in general, 45 percent of the Free responded that "lack of effort" is a factor in a person's being poor compared to just 35 percent of older adults. There is a sense among today's young adults that those who can stand on their own two feet should do so. As Theresa Severs, a twenty-year-old unemployed single mother, told the *Washington Post* in 1986, "If you're not employed, you can't put the blame on anybody but yourself. I look at myself," she added. "It's my fault." Or as twenty-five-year-old high-school dropout Roberta Arjes described unemployment compensation, "As long as it's there, they're going to take it." In a small poll taken by Charles Derber at the university where he teaches, he found that three fourths of his students agreed that "it's everyone for himself or herself in the American economy." And even more agreed that "in our society, everyone has to look out for number one." Given the odds that anyone else is going to look out for them in times of need, these students can certainly be considered perceptive if not particularly optimistic.

13

LOW INCOMES AND EXPENSIVE HOMES

Net jobs created from 1988 to 1990   2.7 million
in retail and services   3.1 million
in manufacturing   -974,000

SOURCE: U.S. SMALL BUSINESS ADMINISTRATION

THE INCREDIBLE SHRINKING PAYCHECK

It is an often quoted statistic that incomes have stagnated in the United States over the last two decades. What the statistics usually don't show, however, is that while *on average* incomes have been flat, this phenomenon has not affected all age groups equally. In the last two decades, the median household income of young adults has fallen by more than 27 percent to a level lower than has been seen in more than thirty years.[1] But over this period the incomes of all other age groups have *risen*—considerably, in the cases of the oldest Boomers and the elderly. The reason that incomes have stagnated overall is that the dramatic decreases in the earnings of the Free have offset the gains of everybody else.

To put the significance of these dollar figures into concrete terms: Back in 1963, 60 percent of young men earned enough to keep a family of three out of poverty; by the mid-eighties, only 42 percent could do so. Correspondingly, it's no surprise that the poverty rate for families headed by someone under thirty nearly doubled during these years. After all, the *median income* of a man under age twenty-five in 1986 was more than *33 percent below the poverty level* for a family of three and was even slightly less than the poverty threshold of a single person. The Children's Defense Fund labeled this situation "an economic disaster."

The Free are ten years behind the Boomers with respect to climbing the income ladder toward those in their peak earning years. The primary cause of the enormous drop in household income is simply that young men are earning so much

---

[1] Income comparisons have been adjusted for inflation.

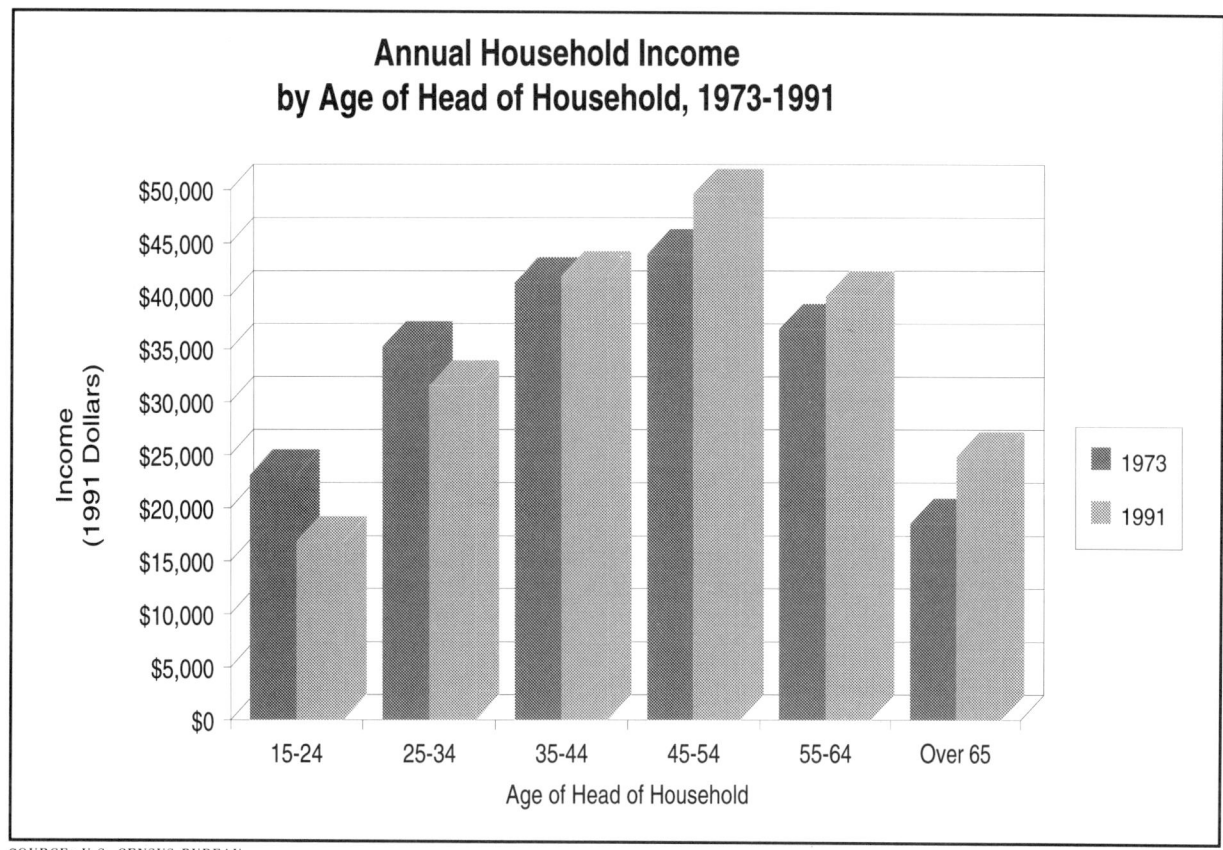

Annual Household Income by Age of Head of Household, 1973-1991

SOURCE: U.S. CENSUS BUREAU

less than did their counterparts of two decades earlier. The typical young male in 1973 could expect to earn over $29,000 a year (in 1991 dollars). In 1991, the salary of a man the same age was only $21,600. With the loss of high-wage manufacturing jobs, young men are forced to take jobs that pay significantly less.

If there is any bright spot in the earnings situation, it is that the first wave of Free women have seen a modest 8-percent gain in annual income compared to twenty years ago, although they still earn only 60 percent of the male wage. Women made significant and consistent strides forward throughout the postwar era, working more and earning more than ever before. But even here the trend has been reversed for younger Free women; the earnings of those in their twenties dropped throughout the eighties—which hasn't happened for women since World War II. Much has been written about the shrinking wage gap between men's and women's earnings, but clearly this narrowing is primarily due to profound drops in men's incomes, and *not* to particularly significant rises in women's.

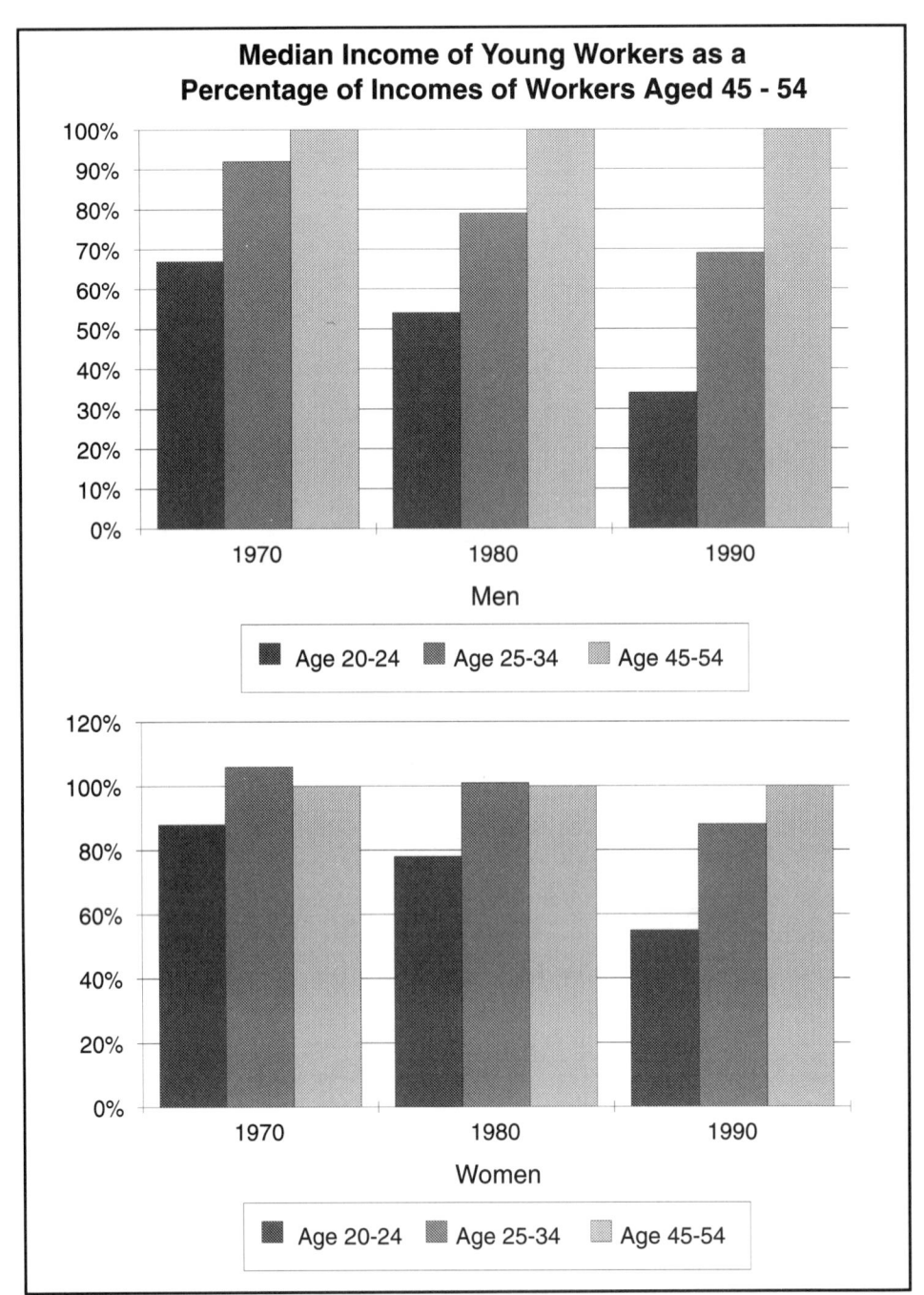

Median Income of Young Workers as a Percentage of Incomes of Workers Aged 45 - 54

Men (1970, 1980, 1990) — Age 20-24, Age 25-34, Age 45-54

Women (1970, 1980, 1990) — Age 20-24, Age 25-34, Age 45-54

SOURCE: U.S. BUREAU OF THE CENSUS

Consistent with just about every other negative trend confronting the Free, minorities have also fared the worst in the income department, perhaps driven in part by the growing discrepancy in educational attainment between blacks and whites. Young black men with a high-school diploma earned 25 percent less in the mid-eighties than their counterparts earned a decade earlier. And even those with a college degree saw a decline of 14 percent. Adding further to the discrepancy in household income is the startling percentage of black families headed by women—58 percent versus 16 percent for whites in 1991. Largely driven by this development, the median income of young black families in that year was a meager $12,000.

Sociologists call the predicament of the diminishing household income "downward mobility," referring to the fact that young adults are unlikely to enjoy the income, status, or lifestyle that their parents had. The expected rise in standard of living from one generation to the next has been a major element of what is known as the American dream, but the Free mark an end to the dream, the first American generation in over a century likely to fail to surpass their parents' living standards. In fact, most would be satisfied if they could even come close.

TRICKLING DOWN

As with other developments that have affected the Free, a good portion of the downturn in their economic situation is due to changes in government policies. The first such change was actually a *failure* to change: The minimum wage, relevant to few other than younger workers, languished at $3.35 for nearly ten years throughout the eighties, the longest period without an increase since the Roosevelt administration. During that time, the figure lost 40 percent of its value to inflation. By 1989, a full-time worker with such an income brought a family of three up to just 70 percent of the poverty level. During debates on increasing the minimum wage, conservative economists argued that raising it to counter the effects of inflation would deprive young people of employment opportunities, as they would be priced out of the market. Armed with such opinions, President Reagan claimed that "the minimum wage has caused more misery and unemployment than anything since the Great Depression." He wasn't entirely mistaken, of course, but the truth in his statement was not what he intended. In fact, the Reagan administration fought for the establishment of a $2.50 an hour subminimum wage termed, in quintessential doublespeak, the "youth opportunity wage."

As the earnings of the Free plummeted, the sums taken from their paychecks and placed in the government coffers were skyrocketing. From the year 1972, when Boomers were beginning to establish their households, to 1987, when the Free were starting to do the same, state and local taxes escalated 520 percent, tripling the inflation rate, and Social Security fees jumped 331 percent, double the pace of inflation. With federal taxes and Social Security factored in, a twenty-five-year-old with a family of four in 1965 earning the median income could expect to pay out about $843. However, two decades later a twenty-five-year-old earning the median income would have to fork over $4,570, nearly twice the amount of two decades earlier, taking inflation into account. (Perhaps it's a small consolation that the odds of that hypothetical 1980s' twenty-five-year-old actually earning the median income were much lower than for his counterpart of the mid-sixties, and he was therefore likely not to be paying so much.) To cite a more realistic example, given the Free's expected income, a family of four earning *poverty-level wages* in 1986 paid more than 10 percent of its earnings in federal taxes alone. In 1979, the same family would have paid only 2 percent.

The eighties saw some landmark tax reforms that added to the financial woes of the Free. The 1981 Economic Recovery Tax Act was hailed as an elixir for the entire population. What it actually accomplished were great decreases in the taxes paid by the relatively affluent share of the population with little or no help for those in the lower income brackets (and thus the young, since statistically there is little difference between the two). Changes to the tax system that would have had a much more beneficial effect for those with lower incomes—increases in personal exemptions and the standard deduction—were not enacted. In addition, the legislation included substantial decreases in the capital-gains and estate taxes, two measures that further added to the disparities in the accumulation of wealth.

The Tax Reform Act of 1986 took the fourteen different tax brackets, the graduated system of taxation that obliges one to pay a greater percentage in taxes as income increases, and replaced them with exactly two tax brackets—15 and 28 percent. Middle-income workers would now pay the same rates as billionaires. With this one feature for providing some equalization in income and wealth largely destroyed, new forms of taxation crept in to make up for lost revenues. States and cities enacted hundreds of new taxes and fees—from excise taxes on alcohol and gasoline to sales-tax hikes and a variety of usage fees—that applied equally to individuals of any income, all of which added to the difficulties borne by young adults struggling to get a foot in the door to the middle class.

As young adults set out on their own, they typically amass more consumer debt than do older people as they purchase their first automobile and set up their households with the necessary appliances. Until 1986, the interest on this debt was tax-deductible, which eased this burden a bit, but with the tax reforms of that year this deduction was eliminated. No longer could a person deduct sales taxes or expenses due to the interest on student loans, automobile loans, or credit cards. This is particularly damaging considering the enormous student-loan debt accumulated by the Free. While the current economic situation of the Free has been compromised by all this new legislation, the financial future looks positively dismal.

SOCIAL INSECURITY

Job Benefits Offered

	1980	1986
Health Care Premiums Paid in Full by Employer	72%	54%
Health Care Coverage Provided for Family	51	35
Employee Covered by Company-Financed Pension Plan	46	37

SOURCE: *MONTHLY LABOR REVIEW*, JULY 1988

Along with the drop in income, the Free have also entered the workforce in a time of declining job benefits. As health-care costs have ballooned, companies are paying a smaller share of health-insurance costs. And though proposed national health care legislation should help the 37 million Americans who are not insured, even this will have its price for the Free. "The vast majority of the Americans watching tonight will pay the same or less for health care coverage," President Clinton noted during a 1993 speech outlining his plan, but he singled out one exception. "If you're a young, single person in your twenties and you're already insured, your rates may go up somewhat" to help pay for those older Americans whose needs are more expensive. As for the Free's financial future, with the rise in service-oriented jobs and the corresponding losses in the industrial sector and in large corporations, fewer young workers are now covered by pension plans than before. As one twenty-six-year-old congressional aide explains, "When we get older, and the boomers have obliterated the Social Security funds, that's when we'll feel the real effect."

Perhaps of more long-term consequence than the drop in income experienced by the Free is the corresponding drop in net worth. With smaller and smaller paychecks coming in, it's much harder to put a little away for a rainy day, or a house, or retirement. In 1973, a typical young family, with the parents in their late twenties, had already amassed a net worth (a home and other assets minus any financial obligations) equal to 60 percent of the average for all families. Boomers were worth more than *twice* as much as the generation before them had been at this age, and still had more than a decade of housing appreciation ahead of them.

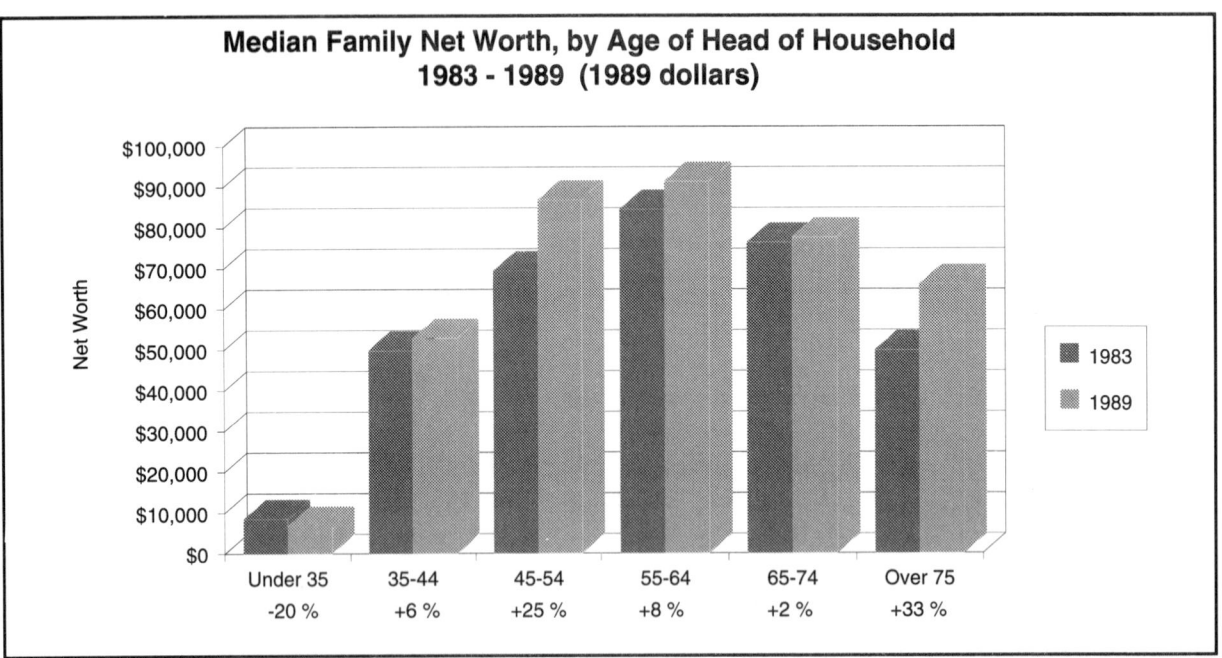

Median Family Net Worth, by Age of Head of Household
1983 - 1989 (1989 dollars)

Age	Change
Under 35	-20 %
35-44	+6 %
45-54	+25 %
55-64	+8 %
65-74	+2 %
Over 75	+33 %

SOURCE: *FEDERAL RESERVE BULLETIN*, JANUARY 1992

By 1989, the picture was quite different. In that year, the typical family headed by someone under the age of thirty-five would have amassed equity totaling only $6,800, a mere 26 percent of the average for all age groups. The youngest families, those under age twenty-five, have seen an even greater drop, with their net worth declining by more than 60 percent compared to Boomers of the same age a decade earlier. In a nutshell, the eighties was the decade when the young became poorer while everyone else became a little bit richer.

In 1971, when Boomers were flocking into jobs, the FICA rate (the portion of each paycheck that went to Social Security) was 4.8 percent, and was applied to their first $9,000 in earnings. Thus the maximum bite would only be $468. Today, Social Security takes 7.65 percent of earnings up to $51,300, for a maximum of $3,924, a 60 percent inflation-adjusted increase in two decades. Since employers match these amounts, the true expenses are actually double these figures, a maximum sum of just under $8,000 per year. Particularly when considered along with the dramatically lower wages of today's young adults, this Social Security burden is crushing to many who are starting out on their own.

Norman Ornstein of the American Enterprise Institute pointed out in a 1992 *New York Times* op-ed piece that the Social Security tax is regressive in not just one, but *three*, ways: "It has a flat tax rate: the same marginal rate for those who earn $1 as for those who earn $1 million. It has an earnings cap, so those who earn $10,000 actually pay a higher percentage of their earnings than those who earn $100,000. And it is a tax on earned income, wages and salaries, exempting income from interest and investments, and thus becoming a tax on employment itself." Ornstein could have added a fourth regressive element: Whereas a married couple with only one worker would have a maximum of $51,300 subject to this tax, a two-earner couple would *each* be accountable up to this amount. Although few Free households earn this much, the overall incongruities apply at all income levels.

Today's high FICA tax rates aren't the worst part of the situation. The future of Social Security looks bleak. While there are supposedly enormous surpluses currently being generated in the system, these surpluses are not put into a separate account for each taxpayer—or even put into a separate account at all. Under current law, Social Security is required to furnish any excesses to the U.S. Treasury to cover current deficits or to refinance the national debt. Therefore the so-called surpluses disappear as soon as they accrue. While in theory, the treasury must repay these funds, the money to do so simply comes from the *taxes* that are collected each year. Whether future taxpayer dollars are earmarked to repay the debt or to repay the Social Security fund is little more than an accounting question. The surpluses are a myth.

With the enormous numbers of Boomers now in the workforce and the only slightly fewer number of Free right behind them, there are today only thirty-one Social Security recipients for every hundred workers. Beginning early in the next century, however, as the Free are entering their peak earning years, the Boomers will begin to retire en masse and will cause unprecedented upheaval in the system. According to the Federal Old-Age, Survivors, and Disability Insurance Trust Fund (OASDI) 1981 report, given the most realistic projections for wage and population growth, by the year 2010 there will already be forty Social Security recipients for every worker, and by 2030, when the youngest Free are at the pinnacle of their careers, there will be sixty-three Social Security recipients per hundred workers.

To pay for this flood of retirees, unless there are drastic cuts in benefits, the projected percentage of workers' income that will go right into the pockets of the elderly is as high as *40 percent*. To top it off, by the OASDI's own estimates, the fund will start running increasingly large deficits after 2010. By the way, while today's retirees can collect full benefits at age sixty-five, Congress has decided that those born after 1959 must wait until age sixty-seven. After paying such exorbitant sums into Social Security, in all likelihood many of the Free will not see their fair share when they need it.

TRUE TAX REFORM

Once all the recent tax changes are taken into account, some interesting truths come to light. One can see exactly how reformed the tax system has become. The Washington-based Tax Foundation determined that in 1990, direct and indirect federal taxes along with state and local charges were taking a record 37.3 cents out of every dollar the typical U.S. family earned. However, the wealthy family with a million-dollar annual income was set back only thirty-five to thirty-six cents on the dollar. So in the wake of the federal government's dismantling of the progressive tax system, the new taxes, fees, and surcharges have countered with a further *regressive* effect.

A study by the government's own Congressional Budget Office came to a similarly disturbing conclusion. The CBO found that from 1977 to 1988, with all the reforms factored in, the effective tax rates for most income groups were essentially unchanged. The aberration from this is felt by two particular groups: The wealthiest 5 percent have seen a substantial decline in their tax rates, and families with the lowest incomes have suffered a significant increase. Unfortunately, the plummeting incomes of the Free have put many of them into the latter category.

THE HOUSING POT O' GOLD

The symbolic achievement of the American dream has long included owning one's home. In the decades following World War II, this element of the dream was realized in ever-increasing numbers, growing steadily from 43.2 percent of all husband-wife households claiming home ownership in 1940, to 79 percent by 1980. In that year, two thirds of *all* Americans were living in their own home, marking the apex of the trend. But in 1980 this trend headed downward for the first time since the Great Depression, and it has continued in this direction. For many among the Free generation, this part of the American dream just may have to remain a dream.

The roots of this decline can be found primarily in the unprecedented increases in home prices during the seventies, a phenomenon that was fueled by the enormous demand of the many young Boomer families. The result of these price increases meant that everyone from the elderly on down to Boomers profited from the price escalation, building substantial equity while experiencing constantly lowered real housing costs as record-high inflation whittled their payments down. As was pointed out in the 1982 Brookings Institution report titled *The Baby Boom Generation and the Economy,* fixed-rate mortgages (the only kind that were universally allowed before 1979) and high inflation bring about great benefits. "Rising prices and mortgage interest rates affect new buyers, but they do not change the payments of existing owners," explained the authors. "For all homeowners, once the purchase is made, the fixed mortgage payments become easier to meet as incomes rise in line with inflation."

With this phenomenon, as well as the tax incentives passed on to homeowners, the rising home prices of the seventies created an illusion of lowered affordability. But as the 1982 report points out: "The truth of the matter was that the cost of home ownership rose less than other prices during the 1970s, despite appearances." Indeed, during that period, since home values did rise faster than the inflation rate—on average 32 percent faster—and since the cost of owning a house declined, buying a home became about as solid an investment as could be found. Home ownership wasn't only easier than in the past; its investment and inflation-busting prospects made it imperative, and any Boomers who failed to act on this very favorable situation simply missed the boat.

And Boomers did react in record numbers. Propelled by the fact that they were earning higher real incomes than any previous generation, young couples bought homes at a particularly rapid rate. For those between twenty-five and thirty-four years old in 1980, despite the enormous demand of their large ranks, the proportion owning the home they lived in increased to 55 percent, a 10-percent rise over the same age group a decade earlier. For younger Boomers, those under twenty-five in 1980, the share of homeowners grew to even higher levels than their older brothers and sisters had achieved ten years before. Whatever might be said about Boomers, they know a smart investment when they see one, and those who seized the opportunity of falling home-ownership costs during the seventies reaped the benefits of a valuable financial cushion.

THE PONZI SCHEME COMES TO AN END

The final tally of the house bidding wars of the seventies is staggering. While inflation caused prices overall to rise by 170 percent from 1972 to 1987, the average price of a new house increased by 294 percent. Since the incomes of today's young people decreased over the same period, however, buying a home has now become even more unattainable than this figure would suggest. In 1973, for example, a young Boomer family with children could expect to spend 23 percent of its income on the mortgage of a newly purchased home. By 1986, a Free family would now have to devote more than *twice* this percentage, a startling 51 percent of its income. An eye-opening illustration of just how dramatically the housing affordability picture has changed is that in the single decade of the eighties, the median age of first-time home buyers rose from twenty-seven to thirty-five—an increase of almost 30 percent. In addition, since 1980 nearly a

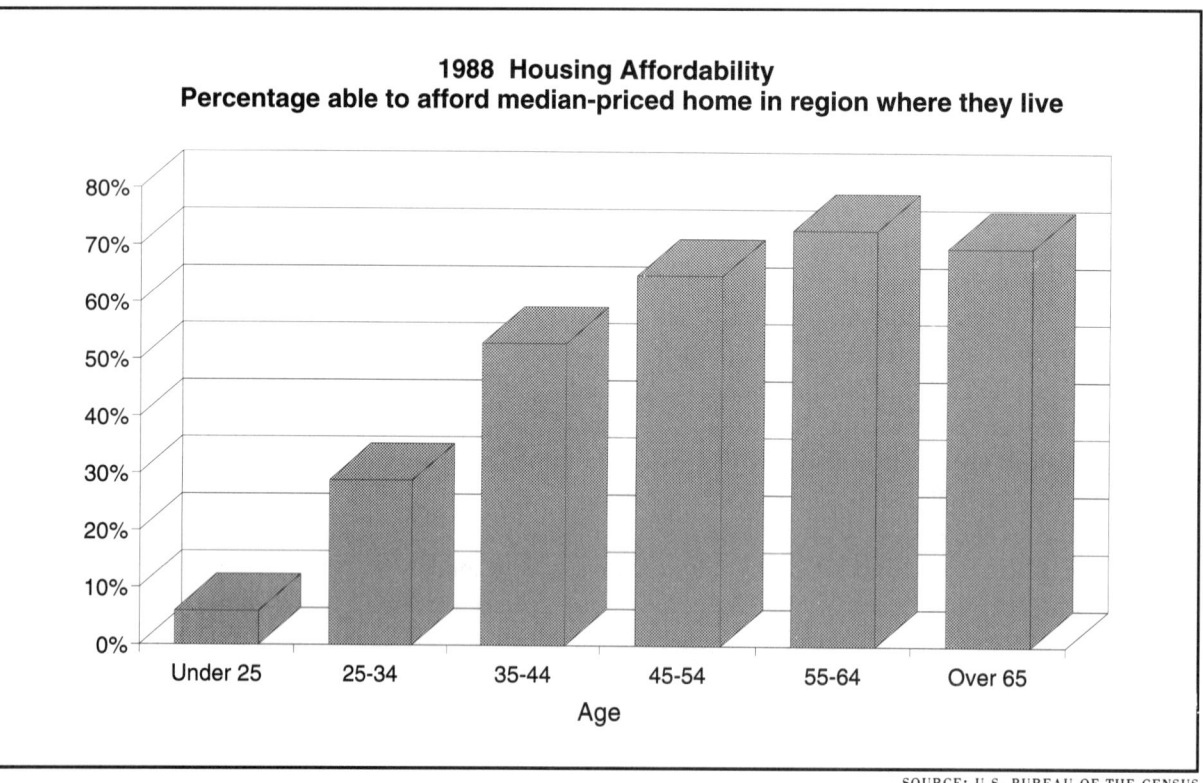

1988 Housing Affordability
Percentage able to afford median-priced home in region where they live

[Bar chart showing percentages by age group: Under 25 ~5%, 25-34 ~27%, 35-44 ~52%, 45-54 ~63%, 55-64 ~72%, Over 65 ~68%]

SOURCE: U.S. BUREAU OF THE CENSUS

quarter of those buying their first homes have needed financial help from parents or other relatives. The median amount of assistance is $5,000—one more addition to the debt load of young adults.

An equally imposing hurdle facing the Free in owning a home is the high down payment required to begin the process. It wouldn't matter if interest rates were zero if a person couldn't come up with the required funds to put down in the first place. Between 1970 and 1985, the typical 20-percent down payment on the average-priced new home nearly quadrupled, rising to $20,160, an increase that has matched the rises in home values in general. Whereas the required down payment took 40 percent of a young family's annual income in the late sixties, it jumped to 60 percent by the eighties. With down-payment requirements soaring at the same time saving is becoming more difficult due to lower earnings and higher taxes, many young families have little chance of ever putting away enough money to satisfy the bank.

Even the increase in closing costs associated with buying a home have added to the burden. Putting the effect of this one cost increase in graphic terms, authors Donald Bartlett and James Steele go back a little further for comparison.

Home Ownership Rates of Young Adults

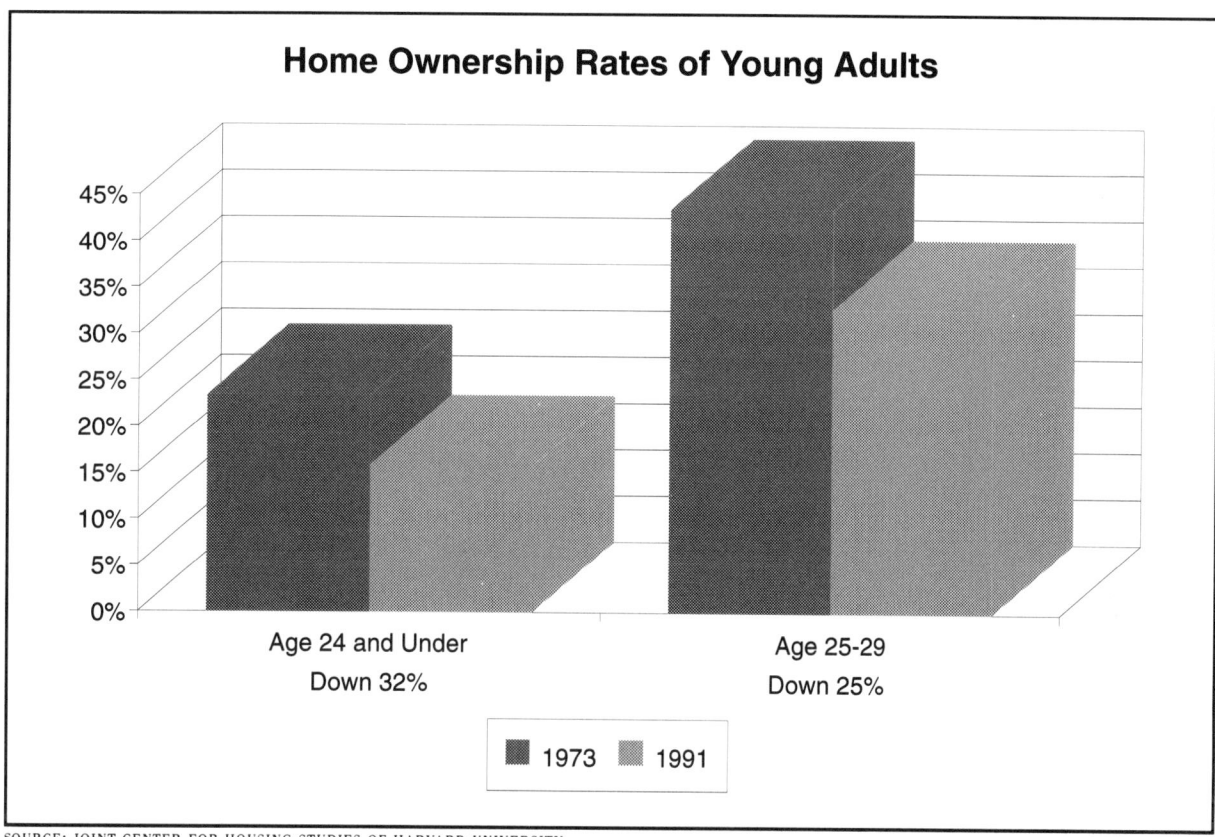

	Age 24 and Under	Age 25-29
1973	~23%	~44%
1991	~15%	~33%
	Down 32%	Down 25%

Legend: ■ 1973 ■ 1991

SOURCE: JOINT CENTER FOR HOUSING STUDIES OF HARVARD UNIVERSITY

The year is 1952, they write, and it's "the opening of Levittown, Pennsylvania, the world's largest planned community, a symbol of the flourishing middle class. It took a factory worker one day to earn enough money to pay the closing costs on a new Levittown house, then selling for $10,000. . . . In 1991, it took a factory worker 18 weeks to earn enough money to pay the closing costs on the same Levittown home, now selling for $100,000 or more." Of course, even those more fortunate of the Free who can scrape together enough for the down payment and closing costs must still face crippling mortgage payments.

Not surprisingly, home ownership among young adults has fallen dramatically in the face of all these trends. In 1973, as the explosion in housing values was just getting under way, 44 percent of those in their mid- to late twenties owned their own homes—44 percent who can now almost retire on their home equity alone. By 1991, the proportion in that age group who owned a home had fallen by a fourth. For those under twenty-five years old, home ownership has seen an even steeper, 32 percent drop. As with income levels, the overall trend of declining home-ownership rates has been almost entirely accounted for by sharp drops in the rates for young adults. Just how important is it to own a home? In 1988, according to the Census Bureau, 43 percent of *all* net worth came from homeowners' equity. For many of those who can do little more than daydream of this aspect of the American dream, a lifetime of living paycheck to paycheck seems to be the likley future.

Of course, if home values would continue to rise faster than inflation forever, each succeeding generation would benefit as much as the previous. But reality generally dictates that an item cannot sustain perpetual increases in value, and the housing market has been no exception. With changes in financing and tax policies described below, the declining trend in the real costs of owning a home in the seventies was abruptly halted, and in 1980 they headed upward. While the years 1965 to 1981 saw an average homeowner realize an inflation-adjusted 6.7-percent annual return on his investment, the eighties saw the returns begin to slow with just a 5 percent increase in real terms over *the entire decade*—not a terrible yield but a far cry from those of the seventies.

And the future looks as if even these slim gains might soon end. N. Gregory Mankiw and David N. Weil of the National Bureau of Economic Research have studied trends in the housing market and concluded that a number of factors, not the least being the fact that most Boomers have already bought their homes, are likely to greatly decrease the investment potential of buying a house. "Housing demand will grow more slowly in the 1990s," they predict, "than in any time in the past forty years. If the historical relation between housing demand and housing prices continues into the future, real housing prices will fall substantially over the next two decades." They estimate that during the next twenty years the real value of housing will decline by 3 percent each year.

Recent data would suggest that these predictions are well founded. After the astronomical price increases from the seventies to the mid-eighties, things began to stall. From 1989 to 1991, the median sales price of new, single-family homes fell by 10 percent in real terms. And even existing homes have fallen slightly in value. We could be seeing the beginning of the first sustained drop in home values in the postwar era.

So those of the Free who have begged, borrowed, and worked overtime to get in on a home are, according to Mankiw and Weil, unlikely to see anything resembling the gains in equity that the previous generations experienced. Furthermore, having grown up during two decades of seemingly limitless housing price rises, a large number of the Free have overextended themselves in the belief that owning a home offers the only protection against inflation. While those who bought homes earlier are also subject to current trends in the market, these homeowners have already built up a good deal of equity and are confronted with payments that inflation has pared down to size. Recent buyers face a more dire situation. With even mortgage-reducing inflation now under control, it's not uncommon for these few to see themselves tied down by their homes, owing much more on them than they could bring in the current market. They see themselves married to their home rather than feeling liberated from paying rent to someone else. As the narrator in Douglas Coupland's novel *Generation X* complains, home ownership isn't what it used to be:

> When someone tells you they've just bought a house, they might as well tell you they no longer have a personality. You can immediately assume so many things; that they're locked into jobs they hate; that they're broke; that they spend every night watching videos . . .

While it generally still makes long-term financial sense to own rather than rent, the benefits have been seriously compromised. Steady prices might make it slightly easier to purchase a house, but the downward trend takes away most of the investment value. To make the situation comparable to what the previous generations profited from, housing prices would have to be cut in half and then begin a long upward climb—an unlikely scenario.

DEREGULATION AND PROTECTING THE HAVES

Once again, much that has affected the trends in the housing market is not merely the result of random changes in demographics and the economy, but has been precipitated by specific legislative actions. Before 1980, the federal government virtually assured that there would be an expanding supply of cheap mortgages. A spate of programs following the Depression, such as those established by the Federal Housing Administration (FHA) and the Veterans Administration (VA), made it easier for buyers who couldn't afford the typical required down payments to qualify for loans. The states, for their part, set ceilings on the rates that lending institutions could charge on mortgages for first-time home buyers. In return, the nation's savings-and-loan institutions were required to dedicate virtually all of their lending to home buyers, but the federal government insured that the lenders who worked through such programs would not have to accept complete liability for a loan in the case of a default. The combination of reduced risks for lenders and little leeway to lend money to anyone other than home buyers contributed to lower mortgage interest rates than would have otherwise prevailed.

The system worked well for more than forty years, making it possible for record numbers to purchase their own homes. However, with the rising inflation rates seen in the seventies, savings-and-loans, who had lent so much over the years at low, fixed rates, found themselves holding mortgage portfolios of ever-diminishing value. By mid-1981, the thrift industry found that on the whole it had lost more than $111 billion on the mortgages that it had previously written to homeowners. In essence, the savings-and-loans and the government had been subsidizing homeowners with interest rates that were lower than the inflation rate. In response to this situation, the government acted to allow the S&Ls to expand into supposedly more profitable areas.

Beginning in 1979, a series of laws were enacted that for the first time since the Great Depression allowed all S&Ls, as well as mutual savings banks, to offer mortgages on which the interest rate varied with the market conditions, eliminating the benefits of high inflation to a borrower. In addition, with deregulation laws passed in 1980, the federal government eliminated the ceilings that states imposed for first mortgages. In separate acts of legislation, Congress authorized savings-and-loans to expand their market by allowing them to invest a certain percentage of their assets in such undertakings as consumer loans and corporate debt securities, as well as in commercial enterprises.

Because the portfolios of the S&Ls were almost exclusively residential mortgages upon enactment of these laws, they could invest as much of their new assets as they wished in non-home-mortgage ventures for a number of years before reaching the maximum allowable percentages. One outcome of this resulting overspending on commercial building at the expense of home loans is that a number of expensive office buildings have simply remained empty. The proportion of office space sitting vacant nationwide zoomed from 4.6 percent in 1980 to 20 percent in 1990.

This overbuilding of income-draining commercial space was just one factor that led to the S&L collapse. Despite President Jimmy Carter's statement upon signing the 1980 legislation that the bill will "help control inflation, strengthen our financial institutions, and help small savers," we've seen how the ensuing mismanagement and speculative actions of the S&Ls made possible by the slackened regulation resulted in a $500 *billion* price tag for the taxpayers. In a nutshell, the new legislation eliminated affordable mortgages while simultaneously allowing S&Ls to risk—and lose—billions of dollars. Not only did the change in the law deprive the Free of the low-cost mortgages that previous generations enjoyed, but they now get to pay for the cleanup of the resulting mess, too.

While the above federal legislation was eliminating the guarantees of cheap mortgage rates, local communities across the country were enacting their own laws designed to benefit existing homeowners at the expense of future buyers. In order to limit growth and thus boost property values, communities across the nation passed increasingly restrictive zoning and land-use ordinances, tacked on expensive building fees, and enacted other measures designed to pass expenses to future buyers. Petaluma, California, and Boulder, Colorado, among others, even went so far as to pass legislation mandating *no growth* at all. Great if you already own a home in such an area—and expensive if you are a prospective buyer.

Rather than raising property taxes on all homeowners equally, many communities decided to attach fees to new home construction to pay for needed services. By 1990, thirty-nine states allowed their municipalities to tax new-home buyers in this way. One county in Maryland, for example, collected $2,629 for roads and schools and $3,000 for sewers for each new home. Fees added $20,000 to the cost of a new house in Southern California. Complaints about such tactics prompted the formation of the federal Advisory Commission on Regulatory Barriers to Affordable Housing, to which one builder griped that his costs had jumped 126 percent in six years because of new levies. While the roads, schools, and sewers built with such funds could be used by all, many cities decided that those young families who were struggling to buy their first home should pay for them.

An even greater inequity can be seen in California, where the tax-revolt-inspired Proposition 13 guaranteed drastically lower property tax rates—but only for those old enough to have bought a home before 1978. Remember that this is the same law that slashed spending on the Free's schools in their youth. In 1992, Stephanie Norlinger took her case challenging Prop 13's inequities all the way to the U.S. Supreme Court. She had bought her modest Los Angeles home in 1988 for $170,000 and was thus paying the maximum annual property tax of $1,700. Meanwhile, her neighbors in nearly identical homes who were longtime residents were paying less than $400 a year. In more affluent Santa Monica, a decade's worth of property taxes could run $51,000 for a recent buyer and as low as $3,000 for a resident in a similar home purchased years earlier. Homeowners over the age of fifty-five, but no one younger, can even take their lower assessment rates with them if they move. Despite the glaring inequality of the law, the Court ruled that the regulation could stand. In essence, Proposition 13 and the other measures that accompanied the tax revolt of the late seventies did nothing to reduce taxes overall. They merely shifted the burden from older homeowners to future generations.

When Congress reformed the tax code in 1986, it eliminated just about every debt-related deduction that taxpayers could claim. The exceptions were the various tax advantages for homeowners, which went largely untouched. So there is a paradox: The one remaining tax break is only available to homeowners, but it's increasingly difficult to become a homeowner for those who aren't already one.

There is one final inconsistency in the logic behind the new tax laws, primarily affecting recent home buyers—those more likely to have seen their investment decline in value. Any gains from a sale of a home are now taxed at the same rate as ordinary income (except for those older than fifty-five, who receive up to a $125,000 exemption from taxes on such capital gains). And while a loss coming from just about any other investment allows a tax write-off, for someone who bought a home at the peak of the market and is now selling at a loss, there is no corresponding tax deduction. In such a case, you lose twice.

RENT FOREVER

The tax laws passed in the early eighties also lowered some of the incentives for investment in rental housing by altering the way landlords depreciate their properties. To compensate for the accompanying loss in deductions, landlords have had to increase the rents they charge tenants. In fast-growing areas like the West, rents rose by 24 percent in real terms over a ten-year period, reaching a median of $427 a month by 1988. According to a study by Harvard University's Joint Center for Housing Studies, rent as a share of the median income of young Americans has jumped by 50 percent since the early seventies. By 1991, those under the age of twenty-five were shelling out 36 percent of their *gross* income on rent.

Since the higher percentage of income devoted to rent makes it that much more difficult to save money for a down payment on a house, young adults face an uphill climb in the pursuit of owning a home. The lower incomes, higher rents, and higher home prices facing the Free prompted the authors of the Harvard study to remark that current trends threaten "to produce a permanent underclass of disadvantaged renters and to jeopardize the long-term financial security of future generations." The housing hole in which the Free find themselves today is deep, and it has steep walls.

THE BOOMERANG EFFECT

The most noticeable result of the lofty housing prices and rents and the corresponding declining incomes of the Free is that more and more of them are returning to their parents' homes to live. By 1988, 61 percent of men and 48 percent of women aged eighteen to twenty-four were living with their parents, more than at any time since the Great Depression. In addition, another 12 to 13 percent were living with other relatives, meaning that only one young man in

Living Arrangements of Young Adults, Age 18-24

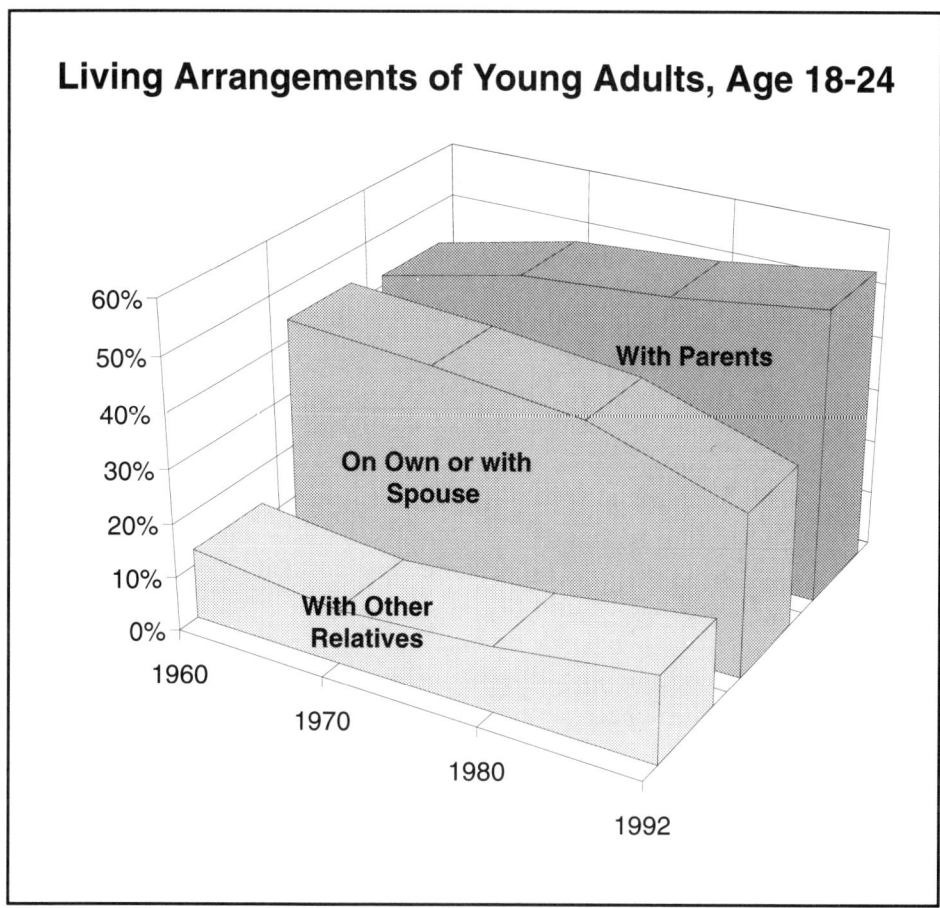

[Chart showing three categories—With Parents, On Own or with Spouse, With Other Relatives—across 1960, 1970, 1980, 1992, with y-axis from 0% to 60%.]

SOURCE: U.S. BUREAU OF THE CENSUS

four and just over one woman in three was living independently in that year. As sociologist Larry Bumpass of the University of Wisconsin noted in 1987, "There is a naive notion that children grow up and leave home when they're eighteen, and the truth is far from that."

Those a little older have also been increasingly unable or unwilling to set out on their own. The proportion of men and women aged twenty-five to thirty-four living with their parents has doubled since 1970. While economic trends are the driving force behind this development, some observers have not been sympathetic to the predicament. Cynthia Graves and Dr. Larry Stockman, authors of *Adult Children Who Won't Grow Up*, categorize such boomerangers as "excessively dependent" and "taking an unhealthy length of time to sever the ties of adolescence." An exasperated parent told the *New York Times* in 1988,

"You think you've done your bit and put them through college and here they come." And in a 1990 article on the subject in *American Demographics* magazine, the writers claimed that there is no reason to feel for the young adults who find themselves in this situation, and rather that "if anyone deserves pity, it's the affluent parent who has feathered such a nice nest that the fledglings won't leave."

Whereas recent graduates in earlier times often stayed home with Mom and Dad for a year to save up for a house or a car, the Free do so to save money to pay off student loans or to simply wait for employment that pays enough for them to afford a place of their own. A good job is certainly the key to being able to live on one's own, but while the stereotype of the lazy freeloader haunts these young adults, who in most cases haven't got the financial resources to live independently, the truth is that more than two-thirds of them *do* work, and most of the rest are in school. Representative of the group is someone like Desmond Moody, two years out of the University of Massachusetts in 1986 and living with Mom and Dad. "College just wasn't the big ticket my parents and I expected it to be," he explained to *U.S. News & World Report*. For the time being, he was at work earning $260 a week at a photocopying store.

Although the economic situation is forcing young adults to stick around their parents' homes for longer periods of time, nearly all eventually do find a way to make it on their own. But with all the trends that are working against them, it takes a bit more diligence, patience, and hard work to be able to make this leap than in past years. The long-term consequences of so many people getting a late career start and the difficulties in saving any portion of their shrinking paychecks remain to be seen.

Part Four

**THE FREE GENERATION
TODAY AND TOMORROW**

14

FREE-STYLE FAMILIES

Births to unmarried mothers as a percentage of all births:

1970—11%

1990—28%

SOURCE: U.S. NATIONAL CENTER FOR HEALTH STATISTICS

WINDS OF CHANGE

The Boomers have often been characterized as being determined to remain teenagers into eternity. The fifties and sixties were fun and exciting times for America's young people, and having virtually invented the youth culture, this generation can often appear to be bent on forever setting the standard of what youth *means*. Evidenced by everything from the omnipresent oldies radio stations to the exploding popularity of plastic surgery, the desire to hold on to their youth is something that seems to be near-universal among Americans currently in their late thirties, forties, and early fifties. The Free, on the other hand, didn't seem to have much of a childhood in the first place, and to them the idea of remaining teenagers forever is something akin to what Dante might have witnessed while strolling through the Inferno.

Once the Free wield some influence in network programming, look for the imminent seventies' and eighties' youth-reminiscence television sitcoms to accentuate the weirdness and the quirky disillusionment rather than the carefree innocence and the-sky's-the-limit optimism depicted in programs like "Happy Days" and "The Wonder Years." Suicidal classmates and drive-by shootings are not the stuff of which nostalgia is made. "For people in my generation," writes David Leavitt, "the goal seems to be to get to thirty as fast as possible, and stay there." For better or worse, we are now arriving at that point, and we have begun to redefine the experience of young adulthood just as radically as we redefined the experience of youth.

LOVE AND MARRIAGE (WELL, MAYBE JUST LOVE)

The Free have seen relationships between men and women undergo complex changes as they enter adulthood. More than ever before, society, particularly among the Free's younger peers, accepts a wide variety of lifestyles—homosexual as well as heterosexual, living together as well as marriage, choosing to remain single, having best friends of the opposite sex. This freedom is one benefit to which we do owe Boomers gratitude and is largely responsible for why I chose to dub this generation the Free, but it has its difficulties and moments of confusion as well. As Nancy Smith of the *Washington Post* writes, "When [Boomers] were young and a man and a woman went out together, it was a 'date.' You had rules. You knew what was going on. That's not true for us. Sometimes when we go out together as a couple—to dinner, to a movie—we're not sure even afterwards what it was. Was it a 'date,' or were we just two friends eating together?" The ambiguity can cause more serious problems as well, as the increasingly familiar discussion of date rape can attest. If one person is thinking "date," while the other is thinking "friend," the misunderstanding can be dangerous. On the plus side, "dating around," or spouse hunting, that ritual that one used to have to endure in order to find a marriage partner in the shortest amount of time, has just about disappeared. You no longer have to sit home alone on a Saturday night if you don't have a date. There's a bigger pool of people to go out with.

There is a sense of detachment toward long-term relationships that now seems to be common, if not predominant, among the Free. "People are afraid to like each other," Leslie Boorstein told *Time* magazine. "Those who belong to no one but themselves can never be abandoned," added one young novelist. Given the often icy environment between the sexes, some, like one nineteen-year-old Bronx woman, seem to have almost given up hope. "Nobody loves nobody anymore," she told the *New York Times*. "And there's no respect, no trust." Perhaps we're merely a group of dreamers, wanting the ideal relationship that might not exist. "Some of us look at [marriage] as giving up the search," writes Nancy Smith. "Settling down means this is as good as it gets, this is as good as I get, this is all I want." Members of the University of New Hampshire Chi Omega sorority related to a reporter from the *Washington Post,* "with some pride," that only one of the twenty-eight senior sisters is engaged to be married. The narrator of Douglas Coupland's novel *Generation X* explains the lack of romance among the young-adult main characters of the story, two men and a woman: "I must say, if nothing else, all of us just being friends *does* simplify life." Simmering below many budding relationships is the question of whether pursuing an amorous union is really worth the possibility of ruining a good friendship. Or as Rick Bruno simply put it in *Time*, "Not getting hurt is a big priority with me."

Of course, the specter of AIDS arrived on the scene to obliterate the phenomenon of "free love" just in time for the Free's entry into adulthood. Adam Glickman, cofounder of a Los Angeles–based chain of condom stores, explained in *Business Week*, "People our age were forming their sexual identity with the understanding that we could die for our actions. No other generation has had to deal with this at this stage of our lives." Gallup polls indicate that the Free regard AIDS as a greater health problem than does any other age group; this is likely due to the fact that the Free constitute most of today's singles' scene (or lack thereof). We also show a greater willingness to deal with it through more education and by allowing condom ads on television. AIDS has cast a mighty blow to the generation that has honed the casual commitment into high art. Discussions of condoms, safe sex, and serial monogamy are commonplace. Through the fear of the consequences, the sexual revolution has largely been replaced by the responsibility revolution.[1] Yet even hidden within the horrors of this plague, some have been able to find a glimmer of hope in the resulting change in our mien. As writer Heather Mackey observes, "If the sixties was the decade of free love, the nineties is the decade of freedom to love."

Some do tie the knot, of course, but not at nearly as young of age as in the recent past. In 1970, among Boomers in their early twenties, nearly half of the men and almost two-thirds of the women were married. If a person hadn't married by the mid-thirties, chances are he or she wasn't going to. Boomers were carrying out a long tradition of dating in their teens and marrying in their twenties. The Free, however, true to their name, have in unprecedented numbers forgone this rite of passage. Today, fewer than one-fourth of the men and only one-third of the women under age twenty-five have married. By age twenty-nine the Free are three times as likely to still be unmarried as first-wave Boomers had been. And the teen bride is all but a thing of the past. This delaying or eschewing altogether of matrimony is particularly a Free phenomenon, as marriage rates for older age groups haven't changed much in the last decade. Of note, despite the lower overall rate of marriage, interracial marriages are nevertheless up by nearly 300 percent since 1970. One barrier is falling.

Some demographers have given the fact that we're staying single longer as the reason so many still live with their parents—nine out of ten who live at home have never married. However, it is debatable which is the cause and which is the effect. Who wants to get married and then move in with the in-laws? And of course, there is the consideration as well that many simply can't afford to get married. Wedlock has traditionally accompanied the couple's starting a career, and as this element is delayed, so is marriage.

---

[1] Although as we saw in chapter six, this isn't necessarily true among teenagers.

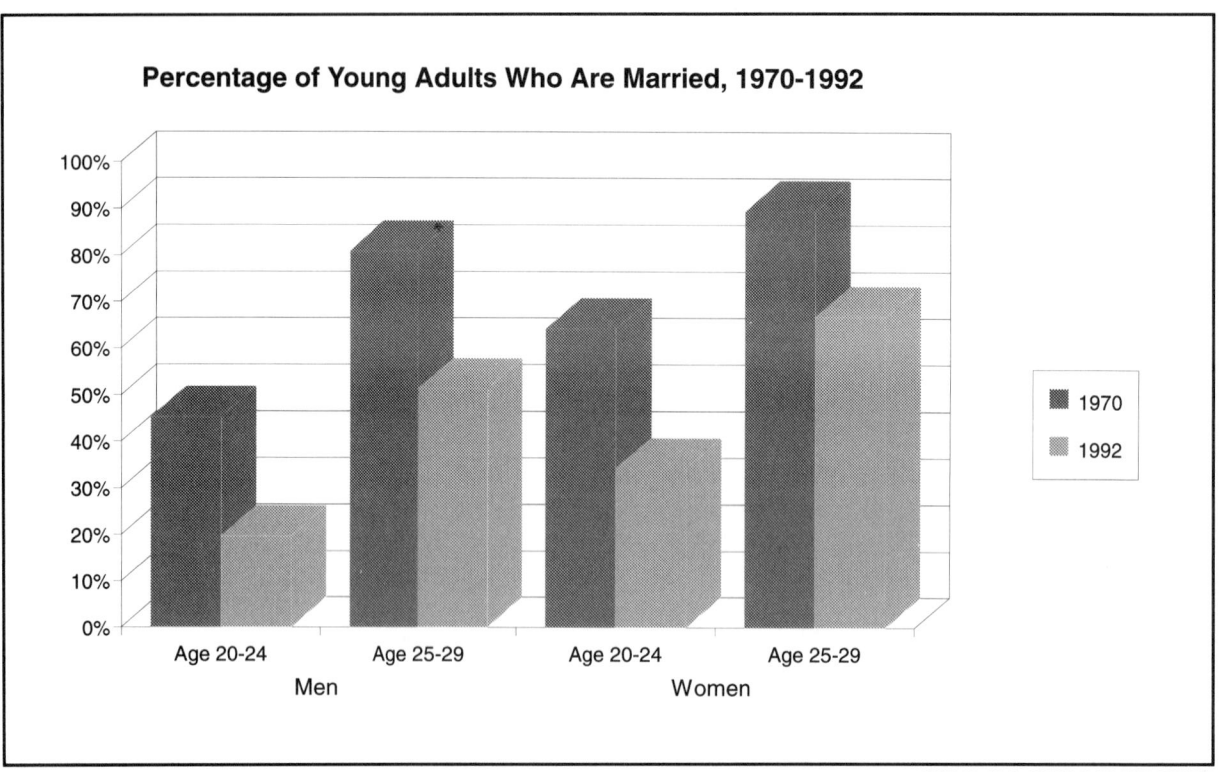

Percentage of Young Adults Who Are Married, 1970-1992

	Age 20-24 (Men)	Age 25-29 (Men)	Age 20-24 (Women)	Age 25-29 (Women)
1970	~45%	~80%	~65%	~88%
1992	~22%	~52%	~37%	~67%

SOURCE: U.S. BUREAU OF THE CENSUS

Seeing their own childhoods, as well as their parents' lives, torn apart by divorce, the Free seem to be determined not to repeat the same mistakes. In a 1990 *Time* magazine poll, 55 percent of the Free reported that they *did not* want a marriage like that of their parents. Women in particular don't want to be in the same vulnerable position as their mothers. "My mother thinks I'm doomed for life because I'm not engaged," Susan Corley told the *Washington Post*. "I would feel just awful if I had to depend on my husband to support me." One twenty-five-year-old told writer Susan Littwin that her mother was married at nineteen and had two children by age twenty-two. She says, "I see myself doing that—if I ever do it—when I'm in my thirties. Now, I have to learn to be single and self-reliant." Jean Smith, a professor at the University of California at Davis, now cautions young married women that because of economic concerns and the consequences of divorce, "it's a foolhardy decision to become a full-time homemaker."

In a nationwide poll a decade ago, researchers asked teenagers, "What do you want most in life?" The top answer was "to be loved" with only the response "to be healthy" even coming close. So even though platonic friendships with the opposite sex are now more commonplace, marriage rates are way down, and there are many more options available, romance is by no means dead. The Free are just experiencing it in their own way. They're more likely to live together outside of marriage than any other age group, for instance. The Census Bureau estimates there were only half a million couples living together in 1970. By 1988 the number had zoomed to 2.6 million. In fact, half of young women who marry today have lived with a man before the wedding. While some consider this merely a "commitment not to be committed," with so many young adults having grown up with the experience of a failed marriage, we know that matrimony is no longer the commitment it used to be. A couple is a couple with or without the ring.

One institution that does seem to have fallen by the wayside as a consequence of the Free testing the waters so thoroughly before marriage is a certain tradition of the wedding night. As *Los Angeles Times* writer Bettijane Levine asked in a recent article, "Is the thrill gone?" When asked about what transpired on her wedding night, one new bride quipped, "What's left to do?" She added, "I wonder if other couples who've been living together do what we did, which is nothing. We were tired from the wedding so we went to sleep. I still feel funny about that. Somehow it doesn't seem right." The thrill of sex isn't gone, it's just that nobody's postponing it anymore. Even Miss Manners has noticed recently that "what newlyweds do on their wedding night is . . . stay at the party. . . . The guests want to do what's proper—wave good-bye, throw some rice, all the traditional things." Barbara Tober, editor-in-chief of *Bride's* magazine, sums up today's wedding couple: "They've lived together. They are best friends. They don't have to lunge at each other behind the hotel-room door." As in so many other aspects of life, the Free have applied their uniquely casual attitude to this traditionally tense situation. Why push it? There's plenty of time to catch up.

THE FREE AS PARENTS?

In a reversal of moves almost as dramatic as the one that marked the advent of the Free, the country now seems to revere children again (witness recent legislation mandating infant car seats, bicycle helmets, and parental advisories about everything from violent television programs to subversive song lyrics). But for those of the Free who have taken on the responsibility of parenthood, many of the grave concerns about children's well-being haven't changed since our own childhood—and some have even worsened.

For instance, while the overall poverty statistics for children began creeping downward by the mid-eighties, the rate for the youngest children, those more

Percentage of Women with No Children, by Age

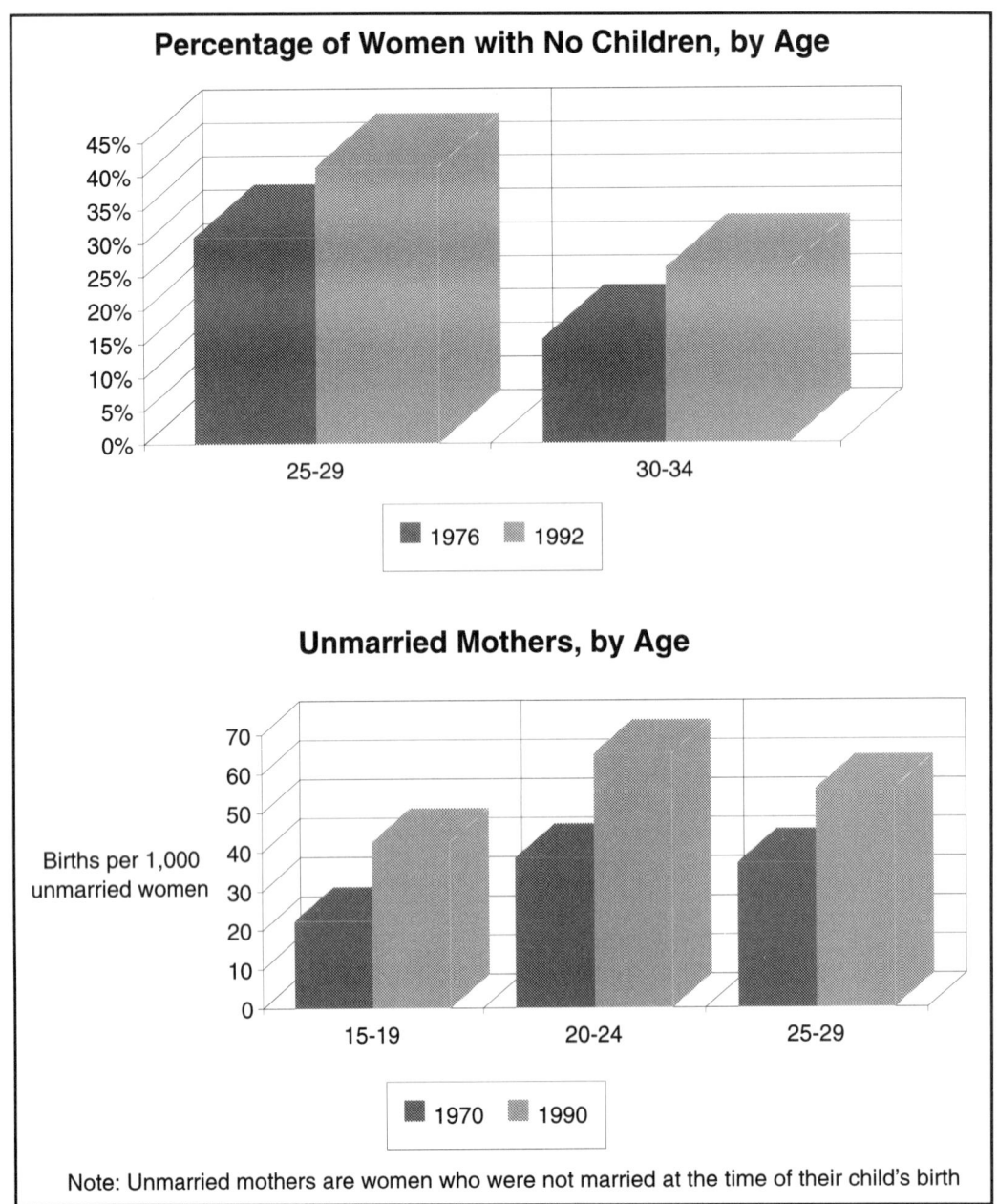

Age	1976	1992
25-29	~31%	~42%
30-34	~16%	~26%

Unmarried Mothers, by Age

Births per 1,000 unmarried women

Age	1970	1990
15-19	~22	~42
20-24	~38	~65
25-29	~37	~56

Note: Unmarried mothers are women who were not married at the time of their child's birth

TOP GRAPH SOURCE: U.S. BUREAU OF THE CENSUS; BOTTOM GRAPH SOURCE: U.S. NATIONAL CENTER FOR HEALTH STATISTICS likely to be the Free's kids, has remained high. In 1990, one young child in three with parents under the age of thirty was living in poverty.

"My generation will be the family generation," predicted one twenty-year-old woman in a 1990 *Time* magazine article. "I don't want my kids to go through what my parents put me through," she added. Although many of us have similarly vowed to do a better job than did our own often unavailable parents, early indications show that we aren't doing much to reverse the downward trends in parenting begun in the sixties. The near-absolute necessity of two incomes to provide for children, the ever more perilous inadequacy of the schools, and the continuing lack of affordable day care have converged to give today's young parents an even steeper hill to climb than was the case two decades ago. Some of the burden we have placed upon ourselves. The single trend that's most perpetuating the poverty situation mentioned above is the continuing increase in unwed mothers. Single motherhood has increased by 50 percent just since 1982, when the first of the Free began having children, today accounting for the households of nearly one white child in five and two thirds of black children. As indicated in chapter two, to say it's difficult to raise a child as a single parent is an understatement. Nearly *two-thirds* of all children under the age of six who live with only their mother are now impoverished.

What's even more dramatic is that those mothers who are divorced are now *less* likely to be working at all than women with children who are married. And mothers who never were married in the first place are the least likely of all to be in the workforce, with over half not seeking any work and another ten percent unemployed. What's more, absent Free fathers don't seem to be any more willing to pay child support than were our own fathers. Since so many of us grew up in families broken by divorce or with only a single parent, despite good intentions we seem to have embraced the idea that a one-parent family can provide for a child just as adequately as one with two parents. Poverty statistics indicate otherwise.

It must also be noted that being married is no longer the guarantee it once was of being able to raise children without being mired in poverty. The share of married couples with children who are impoverished has doubled since 1973 to one in ten. For black and Latino married couples, 20 percent and 30 percent, respectively, are raising their children in poverty. Clearly, the lower income levels that we're attaining have adversely affected even the most traditional of families.

From the word go, many children of the Free are facing an uphill climb. Today the percentage of women of childbearing age who have no medical coverage is up by nearly 50 percent from a decade ago. In public hospitals in large urban areas such as Chicago, Los Angeles, and New York, the number of pregnant women who arrive ready to give birth after having received no prenatal care whatsoever is triple the 1981 rate. Women who haven't received such attention are forty times as likely to lose their babies in the first month of life and are three times as likely to have premature, low-weight babies. Too many of our own children are coming into the world with handicaps that will all but insure a difficult life. Looking toward the future, however, President Clinton, as well as Hillary Clinton, seem to be much more attuned to this situation than were previous administrations. Nineteen ninety-three finally saw the passage of the Family Leave Act, and the Department of Health and Human Services has proposed expanded vaccination programs to insure that all children are immunized against childhood diseases. Perhaps we're seeing the beginnings of a *complete* reversal of the circumstances of our childhood, with additional resources redirected toward the newest members of society.

15

A NEW POLITICAL FORCE

Political Party Affiliation
18- to 29-Year-Olds

	Democrat	Republican	Independent
1980	37	20	not asked
1991	28	35	30

SOURCE: NEW YORK TIMES/CBS NEWS POLLS

A WASTED GENERATION?

A number of columnists have criticized the Free's occasional flippant cynicism toward society. "Where are the young people of America these days?" asked former NBC News president Michael Gartner in a 1989 *Wall Street Journal* editorial. Dewy-eyed, he recalls that "a generation ago, the young people of America wrought major changes in this country and abroad. Postponing their careers, they joined the Peace Corps and spread the good will and smart techniques of this nation. . . . The young people of today . . . know little of war and want, of injustice and inequity." Gartner's view of recent history is somewhat chimerical; no more than fifteen thousand people ever joined the Peace Corps in a single year, for example, and *ten times* that number of young adults were arrested for drug-law violations each year during the sixties and seventies. And, of course, most of this book details the war, want, injustice, and inequity with which the Free are all too familiar.

The barbs have often been even more direct. "Today's youth suffer from herky-jerky brain," opined *New York Times* columnist Russell Baker in 1989. "They can quote fluctuations in the wholesale price of cocaine but they are uncertain how many senators their state sends to Washington," remarked author Susan Littwin. Richard Cohen, in a 1990 *Washington Post* editorial, noted bluntly that "these kids are dumb." Some have even thrown their hands in the air and urged that society simply write this hopeless bunch off. "I'm sorry to say it," commented federal judge Vincent Femia in 1989, "but we've lost a generation of youth to the war on drugs. We have to start with the younger group, concentrate on the kindergartners." Karl Zinsmeister, in a cover story in the *Atlantic,* urged "preventing young criminals from infecting a class of successors" by "putting the full weight of public protection on the sides of babies and schoolchildren." Like a band of lepers, the Free are best kept away from impressionable young ones who may "catch" certain aspects of our characters and our lives.

Americans in general seem to think that the youth of today are a mediocre bunch compared to the Boomers, a belief that has carried through from our births to today. For example, in a 1989 Gallup poll, by a *sixteen-to-one* margin, respondents felt that the Free were more selfish and materialistic than Boomers were at our age. And as a true indicator of the biases we face, two-thirds felt that the group that so loudly denounced the Vietnam War was in its youth *more patriotic* than today's young people.

As detailed in chapter six, the Free have done a few things that indicate we don't always feel so great about ourselves, either. But unlike the rest of society, we don't seem to hold ourselves or each other in contempt for our inadequacies. When the shallowness of yuppie life was featured in news reports during the eighties, many yuppies went to no end to deny that the phenomenon even existed. Meanwhile, business majors in the universities were proclaiming Donald Trump their hero while simultaneously acknowledging the superficiality of their ideals. Boomers flocked to the gym "to get in shape." We went to the gym to have a "good body." "Image is everything," states Andre Agassi's unabashed credo. Sincere even in insincerity and, like George Bernard Shaw's Andrew Undershaft, unashamed. "Mine is a generation perfectly willing to admit its contemptible qualities," wrote David Leavitt in a 1985 *Esquire* essay. He added, "At least we don't pretend we're not wearing costumes." The often brash candor of the Free, expressed everywhere from trash-talking athletes to audacious teenagers, may have arisen from our youth when parents determined they either shouldn't or wouldn't keep some of the unpleasant realities of the world from their kids. With such a frank parental attitude, it's no surprise that frank children would result. This upbringing, with its certain lack of propriety, has bred a generation that may be derided as jaded, devoid of social graces, or even bigoted, but which in truth is no more close-minded or antisocial than other generations. For better or worse, we're just more honest about it.

Those who chastise the Free for not being as selfless and idealistic as the previous generation are recollecting a distorted view of recent history. The sixties was a time of constructive protest but also of senseless destruction. While young adults certainly did win new freedoms, much of this was a selfish self-liberation that advocated a position of "what can I do for me" rather than "what can I do for others." The drug and sexual revolutions that evolved from this attitude may have liberated the middle class of one generation, but they have devastated a significant number of the next.

In addition, the blind rage that was targeted at "the system" often made too little distinction between elements of that system that deserved such condemnation and elements that were worthy of respect and trust. The result is the present state of our institutions, in which the aim is as much to avoid criticism as to provide useful services or to effect change.

The main "system" that was so torn asunder during those years was the system of checks and balances. As the Free try to restore some stability in our own lives, sometimes to the neglect of more profound undertakings, we're derided as prosaic and materialistic. The Free were wasteful mouths to feed in our youth and selfish narcissists as young adults. We may have a chance to redeem ourselves in society's judgmental eyes in the years to come, but it is an uphill climb.

TAKING NOTHING FOR GRANTED

When *Time* magazine devoted a 1990 cover story to "twentysomethings," a number of the young people interviewed complained about the past excesses of Boomers, but rather than addressing these grievances, the writers criticized the Free for taking "for granted many of the real goals of the sixties: civil rights . . . feminism and gay liberation." What the article seemed to overlook, however, was something that was probably quite clear to most of those quoted in the piece: The circumstances that led to the 1992 Los Angeles riots, the continuing pay discrepancies between men and women, and the growing movement among states toward limiting the rights of homosexuals indicate that what's been taken for granted is that the sixties generation ever fully achieved these goals at all. Furthermore, as exemplified by the 1979 Supreme Court *Parham* decision that opened the floodgates to the institutionalizing of teens, many of the rights and privileges that *had* been attained have slowly been stripped away as members of the Free Generation reached an age where they would have profited from the gains.

One of the first of these restrictions was the almost instant whittling away at abortion rights for women. While the 1973 Supreme Court *Roe v. Wade* decision affirmed every woman's right to an abortion, a number of states immediately began enacting restrictions that required a minor to obtain parental consent before being able to undergo the procedure. By the mid-eighties, thirty-five states had such laws on the books, and fourteen were actively enforcing them. A 1990 ABC News/*Washington Post* poll showed that 79 percent of Americans favored this restriction, far more than oppose abortion in general. As described in chapter five, these restrictions often can have grave—even life-ending—consequences for young women.

Similarly, a major freedom-of-speech battle won by Boomers was overturned when the Free came along. A major victory for First Amendment rights was achieved when the Supreme Court ruled in 1969 that high-school students protesting the Vietnam War could not be suspended for wearing black armbands to school. Two decades later, however, the Court had a change of heart. In 1988, it upheld the right of school authorities to delete articles from a high-school student newspaper that they found objectionable. The articles in question concerned the problems of students who are pregnant or whose parents are divorced. In handing down the decision, the Court asserted that the "rights to freedom of speech end at the schoolhouse gate."

Drinking laws are yet another example of Boomer-won civil rights that have since been reversed. In the early sixties, as the first of the Boomers were approaching their twenties, only two states allowed those under the age of twenty to legally drink alcohol. In a parting with precedent, individual states began to lower the legal drinking age until, by 1976, about half the states allowed eighteen- or nineteen-year-olds to drink.

At this point, as the last Boomers entered their twenties, and the first of the Free were now in their teens, everyone soon had a change of heart. In the next decade, states began to increase the drinking age, and in 1986 they were forced to do so by the Department of Transportation under threat of losing federal highway funds. Even as eighteen-year-olds trotted off to fight three wars in a decade, the aging society had decided these youths were too irresponsible to handle alcohol. Fortunately, the right of young adults to vote was codified in the U.S. Constitution, and thus fairly out of harm's way.

As the last wave of the Free are now in their teenage years, many in government seem determined to strip even more of their freedoms away. In October 1993, California Governor Pete Wilson signed into law strict driving regulations affecting those under twenty-one years of age. The legislation inaugurated a "zero-tolerance" policy for monitoring the blood-alcohol content in young-adult drivers. Under the statute, drunk-driving laws for older adults would remain the same—a blood-alcohol level of over .08 percent constituting a violation—but for those under-twenty-one drivers, even having trace amounts of alcohol in their system (this is not illegal despite the person's being under the legal drinking age) would result in the immediate loss of a driver's license. Apparently the legislators don't believe the same regulations need apply to older adults. The National Transportation Board has proposed such legislation nationwide, as well as going so far as to suggest a midnight curfew for all "young novice drivers" under the age of eighteen.

Lastly, one much-discussed idea in recent years has been that of mandatory public service by young adults. Nearly a dozen such proposals were introduced to Congress in 1989 alone. Some leaders, such as Rhode Island Senator Claiborne Pell, have proposed a mandatory year in the service of the poor, the elderly, or urban youths for all young people. President Clinton has begun a program that, while tied to financial aid for education and thus not compulsory, calls for today's students to work at minimum wage in possibly dangerous areas, such as inner-city police departments, as a means of obtaining the same benefits that previous generations received with no strings attached.

It's not that the Free take for granted the efforts and achievements of the sixties; rather, it's that most of us wish we didn't have so many of those same hard-fought battles to fight all over again.

A 1988 Gallup poll about national service brings to light one characteristic of the younger generation. When pollsters asked Americans if they favored a system of *voluntary* national service for young adults, either in the military or in a civilian capacity, the Free were the most enthusiastic age group polled, with 86 percent supporting the idea. However, when pollsters asked about making such a program *compulsory*, the under-thirty crowd showed by far the most distaste, with only 38 percent favoring it. By contrast, Boomers, who had once complained so vociferously about the draft, had a 58 percent approval rate, and those over fifty supported it by more than two to one. The Free have a sense of civic responsibility as firm as anyone else's; we just don't like the idea of being forced into service.

FREE THINKING

We like to keep our options open in general. Writes *Newsweek*, "There are so many choices to make—in relationships, careers, and consumer goods—that [people in their twenties] hate to limit their freedom." Besides being ethnically more diverse than the population at large (there are higher proportions of blacks, Latinos, and Asians in this age group) we're also free of the tribal identity that characterized Boomers and earlier generations. Just as the Boomers' homogeneity engendered the science of "demographics," so has our *lack* of unity spawned the science of "psychographics," or advertisers categorizing people by lifestyles and values rather than age, which they now see as less of a defining characteristic. As consumers, for example, the Free exhibit a tremendous lack of any herd mentality, which is driving demographers and Madison Avenue executives crazy. As far back as 1971, *Advertising Age* cautioned those aiming at the youth market, "Don't try to con them; they'll know when you're fooling." James Truman, editor-in-chief of *Details* magazine, which has successfully carved out a market niche in young male readers, explained to *Business Week* that two decades later "they're tremendously cynical because they know the media is most often talking to them to sell them something." Of course, we usually don't have great financial freedom, and so we can't afford *not* to be discriminating in our purchases.

Despite our disinclination for easy categorization, some general characteristics do seem pervasive among the Free. Many of us share a certain pragmatism and sense of self-reliance—a sort of street-smarts that arguably has its roots in the same unchaperoned, fend-for-oneself childhoods that produced so many cynics among us. Some of the first to notice a character change in today's young generation from the career-driven yuppies who preceded them were corporate executives. "The older managers think that if the shoe doesn't fit, you should wear it and walk funny," explained management consultant Margaret Regan to *Fortune* magazine. The Free, she adds, "say to throw it out and get a new shoe."

Adopting pragmatism as a survival tactic has also bewildered some who can't understand why the young generation is so "serious." Dubbing a group of people in their twenties "the unromantic generation," for example, *New York Times* journalist Bruce Weber remarked, "I'd ask them about love; they'd give me a graph." And despite professional tennis player Jim Courier's rise to the world's number-one ranking in a shorter time than has ever been accomplished before, his restrained, no-nonsense style of play has prompted sports reporters to criticize him for being "too dull, too plain."

But the Free tend to be *selectively* pragmatic—that is, pragmatic when they believe it's worth it. For example, one young woman recently told *Fortune* magazine, "If it came down to career or relationship, I would have to think that the relationship comes first." When one young engineer recently quit his engineering job at a major computer firm so that he could pursue a career in theater, an incredulous management called him into one exit interview after another to try to determine if this was some sort of trend.

The Free have a different view of what's important. With a refreshing clearheadedness, the rock group Jane's Addiction broke up once they had achieved a certain notoriety because, as singer Perry Farrell explained, "I've taken it as far as I can without losing the element of fun." In fact, many of this generation's superstars seem to almost resent their fame, thinking that it serves only to take away from their creativity. Twenty-eight-year-old singer Eddie Vedder explained in *Time* magazine that "sometimes when I see a picture of the band or a picture of my face . . . I hate that guy." The late Kurt Cobain reportedly used to spell *success* s-u-c-k-s-e-g-g-s. Perhaps with so many of the Free identifying with the underdog, they're afraid of being labeled a "sellout" if they enjoy their notoriety too much.

When the Gallup Organization in 1989 asked Americans to rate the importance of "having a sense of accomplishment and lasting contribution," those aged eighteen to twenty-nine were far and away the most likely to answer that this is "very important," with 77 percent responding so. However, many understand that the available employment options in the new McEconomy leave little chance of meaning or a sense of accomplishment for entry-level employees and others. By accepting the limitations of today's economy, a sizable share of this generation is contenting itself with employment that is fulfilling in ways other than a high salary.

The career aspirations of many of the Free are decidedly anti-yuppie. One young investment banker who began his career at a major Wall Street firm in 1988 found the 100-hour workweeks to be senseless. "There were thirty-year-old guys who hadn't had a date since college," he told *Fortune* magazine, "and they thought the problem was that they still weren't making enough money. They forgot how to have a date. That scared the hell out of me." He quit after a year and took a job with a smaller, less high-pressure firm. This early career downshifting is typical, and reflects the realization that with high pay a waning option, the sense of accomplishment will have to come from somewhere besides the office and the paycheck. As financial writer Alan Deutschman has observed about the Free, "Breaking with a long tradition, these business people seem uncommonly capable of finding ego fulfillment outside the office." Numerous polls back up such statements. One 1992 survey of young workers, for example, found that the most important measure of good living had nothing to do with a career or financial success, but required only "a rich family life." And, evidently, the Free don't see the corporation as a family the way their parents' generation did.

Douglas Coupland's best-selling 1991 novel *Generation X* chronicles the daily lives of three young friends who opted out of the search for meaningful work in an economy of bicycle couriers and office temps. "We live small lives on the periphery," relates the narrator. "We are marginalized and there's a great deal in which we choose not to participate." Even the Boomer wannabee who shows up in the novel laments that "by the time goodies like cheap land and hot jobs got to me they just sort of . . . *started running out.*" It's a sentiment echoed coast-to-coast among the Free. A recent University of Vermont graduate, for example, voiced a similarly resigned attitude: "Since I'm not going to make a lot of money anyway, I might as well get a job that rewards me in other ways, where I don't have to work long hours to get ahead."

In his 1991 film *Slacker*, Richard Linklater depicted a subculture that has flowered around college campuses across the country. Linklater created a seemingly endless cast of endearing drifters and dreamers who, unwilling to reduce themselves to an unfulfilling career in telemarketing or the fast-food industry, simply hang around the college town of Austin, Texas, keeping themselves occupied and philosophizing about subjects ranging from pop culture to politics. It's a trend that's reached foreign shores as well: Similar groups of young, self-imposed exiles have sprouted up in the inexpensive neighborhoods of Prague, Budapest, and Warsaw, eking out an existence in the new opportunities of capitalism to be found there. Recognizing that the economy is stacked against them, these young adults have decided either to create their own opportunities from scratch or, in some cases, to refuse to participate at all.

While Boomers, in their youth, also adopted a number of alternative lifestyles, there are some notable differences between them and the current, much-hyped crop. Whereas the young adults who followed Timothy Leary's advice to "turn on, tune in, and drop out" did so because they found the alternative—the aesthetically displeasing, pedestrian lifestyle of their parents—to be undesirable, the Free who have defied tradition and parental expectations have generally done so largely because *there is no alternative.* Despite attempts by many among the Boomer-dominated media to malign the Free for their irresponsibility and lack of discipline, the fact is that in many cases we're simply responding to a failure in the system—a system that's denied us the traditional wealth of opportunities.

AN END TO POLITICS AS USUAL?

Coming out of the "national malaise" that gripped the nation in the years following the Watergate scandal, the Free were quick to embrace the stability that Ronald Reagan represented. Since the upheavals of the sixties and chaos of the seventies were the only political and social environments we had ever known, it isn't hard to see why. Reagan was hailed as a return to normalcy after a decade and a half of turmoil. Speaking of his students, Don Poston of the Texas State Technical Institute observed, "They like Reagan because he says what they want to hear: no more government giveaway programs; an honest day's pay for an honest day's work." Of course, many of us didn't realize that the majority of government programs that were cut were the ones that most benefited families and young people, and that the changing definition of an honest day's pay would force many working people to hover just above poverty level.

Regardless, we loved Reagan, although it's fashionable now to deny this. The 1986 Gallup Youth Survey proved him to be the man most admired by teenagers. In fifteen of sixteen consecutive polls taken during his administration, Reagan garnered a greater share of support from the Free than from any other age group except the oldest of the elderly, and 60 percent of young adults voted for him in the 1984 election. His can-do attitude was likely the prime attraction after a decade of relatively pusillanimous administrations. Speaking of Reagan's decision to bomb Libya in 1986, for example, one young man told the *Washing-*

ton Post, "We don't want to be a bully, but we don't want to be kicked and dragged . . . Reagan doesn't either."

It was Reagan the man, and not his Republican ideology, that romanced the Free. In the 1992 election those under age thirty were the *least* likely to vote for George Bush, with only 33 percent doing so. In fact, we seem to be leery of identifying with any particular political party at all, preferring to look at the individual candidates. In a series of ABC News/*Washington Post* polls in 1986, more eighteen- to twenty-five-year-olds identified themselves as independents than affiliated with either major party. And in the 1992 election, the independent candidate Ross Perot collected nearly a fourth of the Free vote—a 20 percent higher rate than Boomers' and twice the support of the elderly.

On the subject of government involvement in general, the Free seem to prefer that they be left to decide things for themselves. When asked in 1984 whether government had become too intrusive and powerful, 70 percent of those under twenty-five agreed that it had, the highest rate of any age group. Our disdain for government meddling is indicated in other recent polls as well. On the divisive issues of abortion and homosexuality, for example, the Free have consistently indicated higher rates of support for individual choice than have older Americans. And in a 1989 survey on a proposed amendment that would mandate prayer in the public schools, only 20 percent of the Free supported the idea, far fewer than any other group. We generally don't have a problem with allowing people to pray, but we don't approve of making it mandatory, or institutionalized.

However, we are willing to allow the government to interfere when someone else's rights or well-being are at stake. The Free, for example, consistently show the greatest support for legislation that disallows racial and sexual discrimination. In general, the lack of a group identity seems to have engendered the belief that individuals should be given the opportunity to prove themselves without the prejudices of society or the government holding them back.

POSITIVE THINKING?

The Free came of age during an era of widespread corruption and greed, societal attributes that have become so prevalent that we've grown numb to their consequences. From our youth, the oldest of us remember the terrible crimes at Mylai and the Watergate scandal that brought down a president. Then there were the revelations of extensive spying for the enemy by John Walker, Jr., and Aldrich Ames; they betrayed their nation not out of any political conviction, but out of greed for money. The savings-and-loan scandal, as well as the ABSCAM, Wedtech, HUD, and Iran-Contra affairs established that no government official was above suspicion. The two Reagan administrations alone saw more than 240 of their high-level appointees investigated or indicted for criminal or ethical misconduct. Government "for the people" seemed to be a thing of the past. Annual polls conducted by the Center for Political Studies show that in 1980 only one American in four trusted the U.S. government "to do what is right most of the time," a drop of more than half from the sixties. To top it off, even major religious figures proved vulnerable to the depravity bug. Jim Bakker was sentenced for bilking members of his church out of millions; Jimmy Swaggart confessed on national television to visiting a prostitute on a number of occasions; priests from coast to coast have been disciplined for molesting little boys. Is it any wonder that in a 1991 poll of American attitudes, 37 percent of those in their twenties responded that corruption is an "important factor in getting ahead"?

In many ways the Free have absorbed the ever-growing fatalistic attitude of society in general. There is, to be sure, a vein of helplessness that runs through this generation. One college professor who has been teaching English composition for more than twenty years recently noted a marked difference between the plots of her students' fiction today and those of previous students. In the past, she observed, "students plotted their stories so that all kinds of terrible things would happen to their protagonists, but in the end [. . .] everyone, alone or together, would work their way out of danger and get on with their lives." Today, however, "violence enters the story without benefit of plot, as if by metaphysical caprice. Not a caprice of the student writers but of forces way beyond their control."

Student fiction isn't the only area in which this bleak perspective has surfaced. Professional fiction writers, filmmakers, musicians, and visual artists who are in their twenties and early thirties have created their share of despair-laden works as well. In the novels of Bret Easton Ellis, Donna Tartt, Douglas Coupland, Jill Eisenstadt, and others, teenagers and young adults face confusing, empty existences and gloomy futures. They respond with a live-for-the-moment attitude and a variety of violent and self-destructive behaviors. In the mobster films of Rob Weiss and Quentin Tarantino, the urban gang movies of John Singleton and the Hughes brothers, and the films of other young directors like Steven Soderbergh, similarly turbulent lives are depicted, often truncated by tragic, early deaths. In most cases, the protagonists see themselves isolated in a brutal world and yearn for the stability and hope that make life worth living. To no avail.

Why so much gloom and doom? To quote Aristotle's timeless observation, "Art imitates life." The sense that things are getting worse, not better, is validated by Fordham University's annual Index of Social Health. The index compiles statistics on sixteen different social trends, including poverty, child abuse, teen suicide, and income discrepancies between the rich and the poor. Since the study was first published in the early seventies, the "index" has been in a steady decline, hitting a record low in 1991. In contrast to the boom years of the fifties and sixties, growing up in an era of plummeting social well-being has been instrumental in implanting a sense of impotence in the Free, and our art often portrays this.

Yet, despite an uneasy past and evidence such as the daunting job opportunities confronting us, most of us still tend to face the future with a determined steadfastness and even stoicism. In *Time* magazine's 1990 poll of "twentysomethings," an unbelievable 77 percent felt that today's young adults have a *better* chance at a high-paying job than Boomers did when they were our age, and 72 percent feel more likely to obtain an interesting job.

Cynics might argue that this optimism indicates nothing more than naïveté or ignorance. However, this confidence is more likely emblematic of a group that has weathered some rocky trails and now feels that the road ahead could only be comparatively smooth. The Free "are overwhelmingly negative in terms of seeing political institutions as part of the problem," says Gwen Lipsky, head of research at MTV, noting the results of a survey conducted by the network. But we are not wallowing in generational self-pity. "When you ask them about their own options for the future," observes Lipsky, "they feel that through hard work and getting along, they'll be able to get where they want to go."

Indicative of this sense that individual drive can easily overcome any generational handicaps, a 1992 *Fortune* poll of those aged twenty to twenty-nine found that a solid 89 percent of the group felt optimistic about their own career and financial prospects. But only 45 percent felt optimistic about the nation's economic future as a whole. Even with the recognition that things are generally tough—in personal financial concerns, anyway—this is a refreshingly sanguine bunch.

We have tempered our optimism with a sense of realism—the Boomer pipe dream that all of the world's ills can be solved merely with good intentions is widely understood by the younger generation to be a naive fantasy. But we have not thrown in the towel. "Think globally, act locally" is a slogan embraced by this generation's activists, and while many in the media have claimed that today's young adults care for nothing but their own well-being, we have in fact achieved a rather balanced blend of civic-oriented and individualistic concerns. Our approaches toward realizing these goals are just a bit more subtle than those of the sixties.

NO FREE RIDE

The Free's desire to effect social and political change is widespread. We simply use more sophisticated methods and, in many cases, fewer theatrics than preceding generations have. Ralph Nader was recently quoted as saying, "There's a different type of activism today. You don't get the drama of the demonstrations and sit-ins. It's more institutionalized—more joining of groups. But in terms of reporting, researching, and lobbying, there's much more." We've learned that improvements aren't brought about by blanket criticisms of all elements of society, but by working effectively for change within the system. Typical of the new breed of activists is the legal team of the Surfrider Foundation who in 1991, led by thirty-year-old surfing attorney Mark Massara, won a $6 million judgment against two paper mills for violations of the Clean Water Act. Surfers had videotaped and catalogued more than forty thousand violations of the law in order to build their case. As one twenty-five-year-old lobbyist for an antinuclear organization noted, "There are a lot of committed people in Washington who care about arms control and other issues. I think it's different than it was ten years ago. There's more willingness to be in it for the long haul."

Of course, not all of us are activists. A significant minority of the Free seems little concerned with community affairs. Countless articles have been written about the poor voter turnout among young adults, for example. Voter participation among eighteen- to twenty-year-olds has fallen by a third since the 1972 presidential election, while participation by older adults has remained about the same. The Times Mirror Center for the People and the Press completed a study in 1990 (they appropriately titled it *The Age of Indifference*) and found that the under-thirty generation is more apathetic and less informed about important news events than are older Americans. Only *30 percent* of the Free reported that they had read a newspaper the previous day, less than half the number of young people who did so in 1965. Most surprising is that television news hasn't made up the difference, as only 41 percent of the young adults reported that they had watched a news broadcast the previous day. With characteristic bluntness the report concluded that the under-thirty generation "knows less, cares less, and reads newspapers less" than any generation since World War II. Other news reports noted that only 12 percent of the under-thirty group claimed to have paid attention to Congress's handling of the savings-and-loan crisis; high-school teachers have reported being stunned at the utter indifference of their students at the collapse of communism and the tearing down of the Berlin Wall. The conclusion that most arrived at was that the Free are either too stupid, too irresponsible, or too selfish to care.

In their own defense, some young adults have claimed that their "aggressive nonparticipation" is often mistaken for ignorance and indifference. Since no one listens to you anyway, goes their position, what's the use of saying anything? "Withdrawing in disgust is not the same as apathy," says a character in the film *Slacker*. Writes David Leavitt, "If we stand crouched in the shadows of a history in which we refuse to take part, it is because that's exactly where we've chosen to stand." Gary Hart picked up on this sentiment as he tried to woo the younger crowd during his failed 1988 presidential campaign. "All we've had for twenty years is bad news," Hart told the *New York Times Magazine*. "I can't tell you what that's done to a generation, but it's profound." Profound indeed—as evidenced by so many of the Free who, actively or passively, disapprove of political excesses and injustice.

INSIDE JOKE

Despite a fair amount of discontentedness, this is not a brooding bunch. "We are seriously unserious," wrote Nancy Smith in a 1989 *Washington Post* essay. "Our humor is deadpan, even vicious." The Free's sense of humor, which can seem darkly bizarre to older generations, has been with us since our early days. The childhood fads that caught on in our youth were popular largely for their element of double entendre, or for making humorous something that wasn't inherently funny. The first of the Free brought home "pet rocks" to take care of, a product notable only for its stupidity—but that was the whole point. We collected Wacky Packages, collectible cards and stickers touting products like "Lipoff Cup-A-Slop" and "Crust" toothpaste, mocking the items that fill the grocery-store shelves as well as the advertisements that promote them. (They even spoofed themselves with one card featuring "Wormy Packages.") Moronic humor perhaps, but funny to those who at a young age recognized the banality and vapid commercialism omnipresent in our culture.

A few years later came Slime, a green, mucus-like substance that resembled toxic waste. It came packaged, appropriately, in a plastic garbage can. The younger Free delighted in Garbage Pail Kids cards, featuring grotesque cartoon figures like the anorexic "Bony Joanie" and the retching "Up Chuck." And remember the wave of no-arms-and-no-legs jokes? (What do you call a man with no arms and no legs who's been thrown into a swimming pool? Bob.) *Mad* magazine remained popular among twelve-year-olds only by injecting a much more adult brand of satire into its pages than had been the case in earlier decades.

As we've gotten older, our sense of humor has remained pretty much along the same lines. A few years ago, Andrew Dice Clay's twisted, off-color reworkings of nursery rhymes brought sellout crowds to football stadiums. David Letterman's impudence and campy humor makes him a staple in college dorm rooms. Chicago dramatists Jill and Faith Soloway stage *The Real Live Brady Bunch*, featuring actual scripts of the television show, hilarious to those who are familiar with the insipidity of the series, bewildering to those who aren't. Mike Judge's cartoon adolescents Beavis and Butt-head bide their time in a variety of unsupervised and inane activities ranging from watching head-banging music videos to sniffing glue and (in a now infamous early episode) setting animals on fire. Satire and self-aware irony have replaced slapstick. Rather than using humor to escape the inanity and desperation that runs through so many aspects of late-twentieth-century America, the Free often use it to *confront* these problems. Homelessness, suicide, murder, unemployment, even AIDS—all serious issues, but also fodder for humor among a generation so well versed in societal problems large and small.

LONG LIVE ROCK AND ROLL (AND HIP HOP, PUNK, NEW WAVE, RAP . . .)

When the Boomers were taking a Magical Mystery Tour in 1968, *Billboard* magazine tracked the popularity of music in six categories—Rock, Jazz, Country, Soul, Easy Listening, and Classical. A quarter-century later, when the Red Hot Chili Peppers were getting some long-overdue airplay, "topping the charts" was a much less precise term. Reflecting the diversity in the musical tastes of the Free, *Billboard* now keeps track of New Age, World Music, Contemporary Christian, Country, Gospel, R&B, Adult Contemporary, Rap, Album Rock, Modern Rock, Mainstream Rock, Rhythm-Crossover, Heatseekers, three types of Latin music, and two categories of dance tracks. Now, you can be number one and still be unheard of by countless millions.

The explosion of new musical genres reflects the desire among members of this generation to express their individuality. Rock music is one area that the Free seem to play only for the Free. With the exception of a few balladeers like Whitney Houston and Mariah Carey, Boomers seem uneager to embrace younger performers; but new bands don't seem to mind, because this has liberated them from having to abide by the old formulas. While the older generation sustains dinosaur groups from the sixties or "goes country," the Free have flourished with numerous variations on the rock-and-roll theme. Grunge rockers, gangsta rappers, techno-ravers, and funk-rap fusionists don't sell to Boomers, but they're spawning some creative new bands for the next generation.

The key to the new rock and roll is keeping up. While past years have seen their share of faddish performers come and go, now whole genres of music appear out of nowhere, become all the rage, and disappear in a matter of months. When the 1992 movie *Singles* was being filmed, Seattle grunge rock band Pearl Jam was an unknown local act whose members filled in on the screen as supporting backup musicians to a fictional front man. By the time the movie appeared in theaters, Pearl Jam was a platinum act with as much name and face recognition as any of the stars of the film. The Free have yet to produce a rock group with the lasting star power of the mega-bands of the sixties, and perhaps never will. We often forget about a band and move on to the next big thing long before anyone gets to the point of being deified. On the other hand, due to our willingness to give new performers a chance, a number of acts have seen their debut albums reach sales figures that were unheard of for an unknown band twenty years ago. Critics can bemoan our fickleness, but they can't deny our appetite for what's new, unique, and cutting-edge.

Some notable changes in the message of rock music have also sprung up. Rock-and-roll songs have long featured an us-against-them theme, with the idea that through perseverence, ideals, or love, people can change the world. But one notion that runs through many of today's new music acts is me-against-myself, something of a hallmark motif for the Free, in music and elsewhere. Could Morissey have risen to stardom in any other era? "I'm born to lose and destined to fail," sings Social Distortion's Mike Ness. "I'm a creep," moans Radiohead, adding, "I don't belong here." L.A. rocker Beck laments, "I'm a loser, baby, so why don't you kill me?" What hits home with such extremes of self-deprecation is that the listener isn't quite sure if the singer is serious or is just putting us on. While social protest is still a common theme in rock and roll—with particular effectiveness in the songs of many rap artists—our music today, like our humor, often addresses the anguish of life in a more personal way and serves as a form of therapy.

As with rock and roll, the Free have revived another trend of the fifties, amended with a few inimitable twists. Reminiscent of San Francisco's North Beach, which rose to legend status as a haven for the beat poets, coffeehouses and poetry readings are flourishing across the country. A mix of performance art, audience participation, and (occasionally) inspiring poetry, such readings are drawing crowds who want intellectual stimulation, an entertaining evening, or simply something to do while they're waiting for the economy to pick up. As evidence that this new breed of poets aren't taking themselves too seriously, cafés have begun to host "poetry slams" in which judges with scorecards mark each poet à la Olympic gymnastics competitions. The victor of the Superbowl of such events, the International Poetry Slam, earns a top prize of a hundred bucks. Even in poetry, irony reigns supreme.

16

LOOKING AHEAD

Proportion of military enlistees with a high-school diploma:

1963—73%

1989—98%

SOURCE: U.S. DEPARTMENT OF DEFENSE

WAR BETWEEN THE GENERATIONS?

Thomas Jefferson once asserted that each generation has an obligation to leave the following one at least as well off as it had been itself. America had always done a pretty good job of following this maxim until the Free came along, but our story has a lot of chapters yet to be written. Despite a rocky start, we seem to have picked up some traits that just may result in a happy ending after all. But there are a few important issues that will have to be addressed if this is to be so.

It's been considered almost a duty for each American generation to react against the previous one. D. H. Lawrence observed that "we have to hate our immediate predecessors to get free of their authority," and although the Free have never really seemed to care to perpetuate this tradition, recent years have seen indications of a simmering enmity. In a letter to the editor, responding to a *New York Times Magazine* article about the disappearance of morals and the resulting crime wave seen on some college campuses, Jacob Appel of Brown University (class of 1996) replied that the article "neglects to mention the cause of these problems." He follows with a thorough tongue-lashing: "The baby boom generation has crippled our economy with a thirteen-digit debt, depleted our natural resources, permitted our infrastructure to decay, eliminated all standards of common decency, and created a war machine capable of liquidating millions of people in a matter of seconds." Whew! Twenty-year-old Daniel Smith-Rowsey added, in a 1991 *Newsweek* commentary, that "none of you ever told your children, 'someday this will all be yours,' and you're the first middle class to fail that way." A couple of Free-run magazines of political commentary have checked in with their own invectives. The *Next Progressive*, a Washington-based quarterly of political and cultural opinion, ran the story "Why I Hate Boomers" in late 1992, and a cover story of *Diversity and Division* described "How Boomers Ruined America." Even the ordinarily staid *Fortune* magazine acknowledged the burgeoning generational warfare, with a cover story called "Why Busters Hate Boomers."

Other young writers have revealed a sense of claustrophobic repression. Author Richard Blow wrote in a 1992 *Washington Post* essay that "at 28, I've lived under baby boomer cultural domination all my life, which is not unlike trying to breathe with a boulder on my chest." Such opinions are more than extreme exceptions. When *Fortune* asked a sample of the Free "How do you feel about the baby boomers?" four out of five answered that they would not like to be like them. Writer Heather Mackey, in a 1993 feature in the San Francisco–based magazine *The City*, compared the Free-Boomer relationship to the 1992 action film *Under Siege*. The hero "is not part of the power elite, nor is he consciously following anybody's lead. Not James Bond. Not Lieutenant Callahan." He is only "a cook who hangs in a multiracial kitchen and knows that the enemy isn't in some far-off land, but right here in our midst. And the villain wears tie-dye."

But seriously now, despite the fact that they did bring us bell-bottoms and disco, we can't blame this group for *everything* that's wrong.

One area that some economists have speculated might cause real conflict between older and younger Americans in the coming years is the Social Security and health-care demands that will soon be generated when Boomers start retiring en masse. Currently, Boomers are enjoying their peak earning years and contributing great amounts to the system and, as detailed in chapter four, today's elderly are living on the taxes of today's workers. However, economist Philip Longman raises a point that might keep the Boomers from leading any protests about this unfair situation. "As the baby boomers move through midlife," he postulates, "an increasing number will look to the government to support their own aged parents—regardless of need—in hopes of preserving their inheritances." Already indicative that this is on more than a few minds, the amount of a deceased person's estate that is exempt from taxes was raised during the eighties from $175,625 to $600,000, depleting federal revenues by some $9 billion.

While Boomers are earning more than previous generations and have seen healthy increases in the values of their homes, they haven't been saving much else for their retirement. Writes author Ken Dychtwald, "They have made a complete about-face from the traditional Protestant ethic of saving, self-sacrifice, and delayed gratification." Many will likely have little to look forward to other than Social Security, and since the oldest Boomers will themselves begin retiring in just a little more than a decade, they have a vested interest in maintaining the status quo. In addition, the way the Social Security Administration reports its balances gives the impression that the large Boomer cohort is generating huge surpluses that will be there for their retirement.

Even the most absurdly optimistic projections suggest that by the time Boomers have filled the ranks of retirees, the Free—as well as younger Boomers—are going to have to devote a crippling share of their income to the government unless drastic reductions are made in the Social Security benefits allotted. In fact, the longer we wait, the more difficult a fair solution will be. Although today's elderly are taking out many times what they contributed, higher taxes mean that each year's retirees will have paid more and more into Social Security, and they will justifiably be increasingly unwilling to accept any cut in benefits. Thus, when the younger generation finally refuses to shoulder the burden any longer, both old and young will feel cheated, possibly launching all-out generational war. Some in the gray lobby have even tried to foment the conflict by encouraging Boomers to believe that their own cause will be furthered by allotting additional funds for today's elderly.

Although Social Security and Medicare benefits have thus far been sacrosanct, it's important that Boomers and the Free work together now to solve this crisis before it gets to the boiling point, which may be sooner than most people think. A bipartisan commission of legislators formed in 1993 by President Clinton has determined that entitlement spending, primarily Social Security and Medicare, is growing so rapidly that it will consume *nearly the entire federal budget* by the year 2012. As Senator John Danforth, co-chairman of the commission, put it, unless policies are changed dramatically, "there will be no money for national defense, for law enforcement, for the environment, for the highways—that is a very stark finding." Of course it's easier to identify a problem than to solve it, but we all have something at stake here.

Boomers are already forecast as being the "sandwich generation" in the near future. "By 2010, baby boomers will be torn in two directions," predicted Census Bureau statistician Arnold Goldstein in 1989. "Not only will they be looking after their own children, but they'll be looking after their parents too. And some of them won't even have sent their kids through college yet.... For some it could be a real strain." Of course, these predictions will likely apply to the Free as well, but by the time we're ready to retire, the funds will most likely have been drained already. In any case, providing so generously for today's elderly is making it more difficult for both groups to put anything aside for their own retirements.

A number of practical approaches toward Social Security have already been suggested: determine benefits on need rather than past earnings—stop giving generous checks and free health care to the elderly wealthy; base benefits on accumulated wealth rather than current income; eliminate expensive Medicare-funded operations for the oldest old, who are unlikely to live long regardless; have today's elderly wealthy contribute more to the benefits of today's elderly poor; increase the inheritance tax. As was seen, however, by the ferocious attack by the gray lobby on Congress when it enacted the 1988 Medicare Catastrophic Coverage Act, which was only a modest gesture toward a more equitable system—it would have compelled the wealthy elderly to contribute a nominal amount toward assisting the elderly poor—seniors will certainly fight any movement that affects their present cushy situation. Only by using the numbers advantage at the polls can the Free and the Boomers make any headway in correcting these inequities.

WAKING UP?

In spite of the optimism generally expressed by the Free regarding their own financial futures, the recent recession has prompted a growing awareness that things might not be so rosy. The cumulative effects of a stagnant economy and job market, unmanageable government debt, low incomes, and high taxes seem to be finally penetrating the optimistic veneer this generation wears. As far as income is concerned, our saving grace might be our entrepreneurial spirit. Maybe as a result of working so many McJobs in our youth, or our entering the job market in an era of "downsizing," we've realized the advantages of being in business for oneself. The *Washington Post* noticed in 1986 that the Free show "a willingness to take risks and a mistrust of institutions and corporations." Since so many of us have been taking care of ourselves since an early age anyway, we might as well make use of the experience and take care of ourselves in the job market as well. Now is no time to start looking for help from others. As Tom Pirolli, a Philadelphia advertising and promotions executive, succinctly puts it, "The truly intelligent people are looking for their own opportunities. That's more important now because the baby boomers have all the jobs."

The Free have always seemed in a hurry to grow up, and, for better or worse, we're there. We've already taken the baton from the Boomers and begun to show our presence in certain influential areas of society. This generation dominates the ranks of our professional sports. Up-and-coming film directors such as Steven Soderbergh, Jodie Foster, and Quentin Tarantino have shown a talent for developing movies that achieve critical as well as popular acclaim. Young novelists like Tartt, Coupland, and Trey Ellis are writing fiction that is as thought-provoking as it is imaginative. And business tycoons like Michael Dell have shown that plenty of marketing niches still exist for those who are willing to take a good idea and use their savvy to market it well. As we chip away at the Boomers' stronghold on the media and the marketplace, real changes are starting to take shape.

THE CYNICAL GENERATION—PRO AND CON

The cynicism of the Free (sometimes called apathy, superficiality, or bitterness) likely has its origins in the turmoil we witnessed in our youth. We've seen the damage caused by blanket rejection of the whole system. We've seen the long-term effects of irresponsible spending and deferring until later bills that are due today. We've seen what government is capable of doing when left unchecked. For many of this generation, there doesn't seem to be much to believe in.

This cynical outlook can manifest itself in many ways. As apathy, it's shown up in our low Election Day turnouts and general lack of interest in the world around us. As superficiality it's surfaced in a seemingly shallow materialism for which we're often criticized. As bitterness it's appeared in the seemingly random violence that's so prevalent in our cities, most of which is perpetrated by young adults. But the many failed social experiments performed on us as youths have also left us a generation of survivors. We were thrown into the world in a not-so-gentle fashion and told to sink or swim. Most of us are swimming. We may on one hand long for the stability that we lacked as children, but we also know how to get by without it—and are stepping up to the task of righting so many of society's previous wrongs.

This task may seem a bit grand for "the Doofus Generation," but the can-do attitude we've had to develop just to survive will surely help. Cynicism can also engender a healthy skepticism—a tendency to keep a watchful eye on others. Perhaps government scandals like those of the recent past—Watergate, Iran-Contra, ABSCAM—could be avoided if someone were willing to pay enough attention to those in power. The savings-and-loan scandal, too, might have been prevented by more cynical watchdogs. The Free developed a certain shrewdness that should enable us to survive and possibly even prosper.

There are already signs that we may be awakening from the political torpor that has gripped a sizable share of the Free Generation. The eighteen- to twenty-four-year-old age group saw the greatest gains in voter participation of any demographic group during the 1992 election. And a number of local and national organizations championing the Free's causes have begun to spring up in recent years. The United States Student Association, the Student Environmental Action Coalition, and Lead or Leave are among the groups that are now lobbying politicians on a range of issues. Taking a cue from the numerous Boomer manifestos and proclamations of the sixties, one Washington watchdog group has even issued a wake-up call titled the *Third Millennium Declaration.* Even with its broad calls for fiscal responsibility and for cleaning up government corruption, one can sense the collective twinkle in the eyes of the document's framers in its preamble: "Like Wile E. Coyote waiting for a twenty-ton Acme anvil to fall on his head, our generation labors in the expanding shadow of a monstrous national debt." Serious in their intentions, but without the blind bitterness of sixties student organizations, Third Millennium vows to track the votes of Congress on pertinent concerns and let young adults know who is a political ally and who is not.

MIXIN' IT UP

As mentioned in the last chapter, the Free are more ethnically diverse than older generations. But in spite of the sporadic racial unrest of today's youth that the media often chooses to highlight, we respect, accept, and socialize with *each other* much more than older Americans of differing backgrounds do, and this is a source of strength. As evidenced by the 300-percent rise in black-white married couples over the last two decades, what racially based strife exists is primarily aimed not at individuals, but at institutions.

One example of this change in mentality from one generation to the next: Racial integration of our nation's colleges has made a 180-degree spin. In 1963, President Kennedy had to order in National Guard troops to protect two black students wishing to enroll in the all-white University of Alabama. Before this, many blacks wishing to go to college in the South were limited to a few all-black universities, with the occasional exceptions being football players who were recruited for their athletic skills rather than academics. In the years since the Free have begun attending college, however, the number of *white students* choosing to attend historically *black colleges* has increased by more than 5 percent a year so that they now make up one eighth of the student body of those schools. At North Carolina's formerly all-black Johnson C. Smith University, the first white students were enrolled in the early nineties. All were on football scholarships.

Things are moving in the direction of more unity, not less. Writer Michael Small attended a 1992 concert in San Francisco by the incendiary rap group Cypress Hill and was surprised by one element of the show. "To an outsider, it's a bewildering scene," he reported in *Vogue.* "All the inflammatory stereotypes about rap concerts seem realized as the crowd screams gleefully about murder. But at the same time, kids from various races and backgrounds are mingling happily without violence." In many ways with this young generation, members of the different races have more in common with each other than they have differences. When rappers sing about the problems of our urban areas, an entire generation understands what they mean, not just inner-city blacks. Among the Free, hardship and empathy often cross the color lines.

As far as the gender wars go, despite the continuing gap between men's and women's salaries—which is narrowing among younger workers—the barriers between the sexes are also starting to come down, heading toward an equality that the previous generation could only dream about. In the General Social Survey polls taken during the mid-eighties, the Free consistently showed more agreement between the sexes than older Americans on issues ranging from defense spending and space exploration to welfare spending. And researchers say that younger women are much more willing than their older sisters to share parenting duties with men, which bodes well for the youngest generation.

Diversity is not nearly as much of a topic of debate among young adults as it is with older generations, but is simply a fact of life. We've grown up in a more eclectic world, and acceptance of this is woven into the fabric of our being. With our generation more willing to give one another a fair chance—in fact, it's not even a conscious effort for most—the outlook for removing the hurdles that have kept a sizable share of the population from realizing their expectations is bright.

AN EYE TO THE FUTURE

The Free Generation has, to this point, had a history that is in many ways unique and offers a great deal of insight into how some of the often ill-conceived social experiments of the last few decades have fared. Many have weathered some unfortunate experiences, to be sure, but most have arrived with a great deal to offer. While this generation has sometimes seemed paralyzed with indifference or apathy, recent years have seen an increasing willingness to speak out, and, as if a sleeping giant has been woken, our influence in society has begun to accelerate.

One advantage of growing up with limited expectations is that there are no pipe dreams to shatter. In contrast to those who grew up in more idealistic times, we may have developed the wherewithal to work toward long-term goals that have gone unattained without becoming disillusioned in the process. While the past has seen societal trends defined for this generation, the not-so-distant future will see them defined *by* this generation. And given the strengths, flexibilities, and diversity of experiences of the Free, anything can happen.

NOTES

Page 1
"The Doofus Generation"
  Cited in Russell, Cheryl. "What's News With You?" *American Demographics* November 1990: 2.
"The Tuned-Out Generation"
  Zoglin, Richard. "The Tuned-Out Generation." *Time* 9 July 1990: 64.
"A generation of animals"
  Cited in Strauss, William and Howe, Neil. *Generations: The History of America's Future, 1584 to 2069.* New York: William Morrow, 1991: 331.
"The Numb Generation"
  Baker, Russell. "Herky-Jerky Bang-Bang." *New York Times* 30 June 1990: 230
"The Blank Generation"
  Walters, Barry. "Crossing the New Rock Generation Gap." *San Francisco Examiner* 21 March 1993: D1.
A "generation without a soul"
  Quoted in: Blotnik, Srully. "Why Hippies Beget Yuppies." *Forbes* 24 February 1986: 146–7.
"The Unromantic Generation"
  Quoted in: Shames, Lawrence. *The Hunger for More: Searching for Values in an Age of Greed.* New York: Times Books, 1989: 97.
A "generation of self-centered know-nothings."
  Quoted in: Derber, Charles. *Money, Murder and the American Dream: Wilding from Wall Street to Main Street.* Boston: Faber and Faber, 1992: 102.

Page 2
I use these dates
  Strauss, William and Howe, Neil. *Generations: The History of America's Future, 1584 to 2069*: 301.
true children of the 1960s
  Ibid.: 321.
"Third Great Awakening"
  Wolfe, Tom. "The 'ME' Decade and the Third Great Awakening." *New York* 23 August 1976: 26–40.

Page 3
"13er"
  Strauss, William and Howe, Neil. *Generations: The History of America's Future, 1584 to 2069*: 324.
more reckless than our counterparts
  Gallup Poll August 7, 1989, asked "Does the following word apply more to young people in their teens and twenties today or young people in that same age group twenty years ago: Reckless?"
  Today   73%
  Twenty years ago   14
  Both   9
  Neither   1
  No opinion   3

Page 4
one million a year
   Kirst, Michael W. et al., *Conditions of Children in California*, Berkeley: PACE School of Education, UC Berkeley, 1989: 35.
the most incarcerated generation ever
   Strauss, William and Howe, Neil. *Generations: The History of America's Future, 1584 to 2069*: 326.

Page 5
Americans of my generation
   Safire, William. "Cut Them Some Slack." *New York Times Magazine* 3 July 1994: 8.

Page 9
Wolfson case
   Marina Point v. Wolfson, 158 *California Reporter* 669.

Page 10
70 to 90 percent
   Louv, Richard, *Childhood's Future: Listening to the American Family. New Hope for the Next Generation*. Boston: Houghton Mifflin, 1990: 311–2.
a family with children in Dallas
   Simms, Margaret C., The Urban Institute. *Families and Housing Markets: Obstacles to Locating Suitable Housing*. HUD, 1980: 41.
A study conducted in 1979
   Ibid.
apartments constructed during the seventies
   Marans, Robert W., et al. *Measuring Restrictive Rental Practices Affecting Families with Children: A National Survey*. HUD, 1980: 71.
Newer units also tended
   HUD. *Housing Our Families*. 1980, pg. 5–2.

Page 11
median rents for apartments that allowed children
   Simms, Margaret C., The Urban Institute. *Families and Housing Markets: Obstacles to Locating Suitable Housing*: 42.
The judges in the Wolfson case
   Marina Point v. Wolfson: 672.
the policies regarding apartment availability
   A fourth of all apartments nationwide had policies excluding children with another 46 percent accepting them only with certain limitations. HUD. *Housing Our Families*: 5–2.
Michigan survey showed that nearly half
   Ibid. 5–3.
This dilemma crossed all boundaries
   Marans, Robert W., et al. *Measuring Restrictive Rental Practices Affecting Families with Children: A National Survey*: 72.
undesirably long commute
   HUD. *Housing Our Families*: 5–4.

Page 12
The growth of one- and two-person households
   Simms, Margaret C., The Urban Institute. *Families and Housing Markets: Obstacles to Locating Suitable Housing*: 40.

The rationale was that
  Louv, Richard, *Childhood's Future: Listening to the American Family. New Hope for the Next Generation*: 311–2.
The Fair Housing Act
  HUD. *Housing Our Families*: 6–1.
nine different bills
  California Law Review. July 1983: 1324–47.
only eight states had any regulations
  HUD. *Housing Our Families*: 6–3.
(n) the California Supreme Court overturned
  California Law Review. July 1983: 1324–47.
(n) Congress passed an extension
  "Adults-Only Housing Hears the Pitter Patter of Little Feet." *Business Week* 13 March 1989. Senior citizen housing remains exempt from this law.
Richard Hofstadter commented
  Jones, Landon Y. *Great Expectations: America and the Baby Boom Generation*. New York: Coward, McCann & Geoghegan, 1980: 47.

Page 13
Thomas Malthus wrote in 1798
  Malthus, Thomas Robert. *On Population*. New York: Random House, 1960: 9.
he depicts a riot-torn U.S.
  Ehrlich, Paul R. *The Population Bomb*. New York: Ballantine Books, 1968: 52.
The second scenario
  Ehrlich, Paul R. *The Population Bomb*: 71.
In the third
  Ibid.: 74.
Ehrlich suggests a number of baby-prevention measures
  Ibid.: 132.
"The 'Population Bomb' is beginning to usurp"
  Introduction to Malthus, Thomas Robert. *On Population:* xiii.
ZPG grew rapidly
  Back, Kurt W. *Family Planning and Population Control*. Boston: Twayne, 1989: 132.
a host of imitators
  See *Too Many Americans;* Paddock, William and Paul. *Famine, 1975!* Boston: Little, Brown, 1967; Dumont, Rene. *The Hungry Future*. New York: Praeger, 1969; Lader, Lawrence. *Breeding Ourselves to Death*. New York: Ballantine, 1971; Chasteen, Edgar R. *The Case for Compulsory Birth Control*. Englewood Cliffs, NJ: Prentice-Hall, 1971.

Page 14
John Calhoun, decided to test Malthus's original premise
  Jones, Landon Y. *Great Expectations: America and the Baby Boom Generation*: 190.
Life magazine ran an article
  "How 4,000,000 a Year Make Billions in Business." *Life* 16 June 1958: 83.
They signified a drain
  Louv, Richard. *Childhood's Future: Listening to the American Family. New Hope for the Next Generation*: 58.
Life responded to this dire viewpoint
  "Squeezing Into the '70s." *Life* 9 January 1970: 8.
Garret Hardin developed the allegory
  Hardin, Garrett. "Tragedy of the Commons." *Science* 13 December 1968. Of course, the actual moral of this tale is merely that people are selfish!

"Babies are the enemy"
   Sommerville, John. *The Rise and Fall of Childhood.* New York: Vintage, 1982: 7.
the costs of rearing children
   Rivlin, Alice M. "Population Growth and the American Economy." In *Population Ethics*, ed. Francis X. Quinn. Washington, DC: Corpus Books, 1968: 47–8.

Page 15
"we must inevitably be faced with a choice"
   Day, Lincoln H. "The American Fertility Cult." In *The Population Crisis*, ed. Larry K. Y. Ng. Bloomington: Indiana UP, 1965: 124. See also Parsons, Jack. *Population Versus Liberty.* Buffalo: Prometheus, 1973.
"It is, in this sense, *socially irresponsible*"
   Day, Lincoln H. "The American Fertility Cult": 131.
"Make Love, Not Babies"
   Kasindorf, N. "Make Love, Not Babies; Childlessness; Views of the Nathan Freedlands." *Newsweek* 15 June 1970: 111.
"The Population Explosion Is Everybody's Baby"
   Back, Kurt W. *Family Planning and Population Control*: 132.
The percentage of G-rated movies
   Steinberg, Cobbett. *Reel Facts: The Movie Book of Records.* NY: Vintage, 1978: 478.
The Germans have a word
   Louv, Richard, *Childhood's Future: Listening to the American Family. New Hope for the Next Generation*: 58.
"popullution."
   Jones, Landon Y. *Great Expectations: America and the Baby Boom Generation*: 192.
A 1971 survey
   Cited in: Commission on Population Growth and the American Future. "Population Stabilization." In *Population, Environment, and the Quality of Life*, ed. Parker G. Marden and Dennis Hodgson. New York: AMS Press, 1975: 270.
babies were looked upon "like headaches"
   Strauss, William and Howe, Neil. *Generations: The History of America's Future, 1584 to 2069*: 328.
suggested government licensing of children
   Cited in: Jones, Landon Y. *Great Expectations: America and the Baby Boom Generation*: 191.
"Licensing: For Cars and Babies"
   "Licensing: For Cars and Babies." *Bulletin of the Atomic Scientist* November 1970: 15–19.
Senator Robert Packwood
   Wattenberg, Ben. "The Nonsense Explosion: Overpopulation as a Crisis Issue." In *Population, Environment, and the Quality of Life*, ed. Parker G. Marden and Dennis Hodgson: 24.

Page 16
deny college loans
   Jones, Landon Y. *Great Expectations: America and the Baby Boom Generation:* 191.
the most extreme measure
   Wattenberg, Ben. "The Nonsense Explosion: Overpopulation as a Crisis Issue": 24.
The Nixon administration responded
   The Commission on Population Growth and the American Future. *Population and the American Future.* 1972.
rash of publications
   Silverman, Anna and Arnold. *The Case Against Having Children.* New York: David McKay, 1971; Johnson, Stanley. *Life Without Birth.* Boston: Little, Brown, 1970; Peck, Ellen. *The Baby Trap* New York: B. Geis Associates, 1971.

A group of voluntarily childless couples
  Back, Kurt W. *Family Planning and Population Control*: 132.
People wore buttons bearing the slogans
  Jones, Landon Y. *Great Expectations: America and the Baby Boom Generation*: 192.
Betty Rollin summed up the arguments
  Cited in: Jones, Landon Y. *Great Expectations: America and the Baby Boom Generation*: 201.
(n) Further indication of the recent change
  Ehrlich, Paul. *The Population Explosion*; Wattenberg, Ben. *The Birth Dearth*. New York: Pharos, 1987. Also, in a September 1986 cover story, *Newsweek* now declared the *depopulation crisis* a national emergency. Economist Philip Longman has suggested additional taxes on those who *don't* have children since they are providing no future tax base. Smith, Lee. "The War Between the Generations." *Fortune* 20 July 1987: 79.
annual number of babies born
  Vital Statistics of the United States. 1988.
Fertility Rates
  Ibid.

Annual Number of U.S. Births, 1940-1980

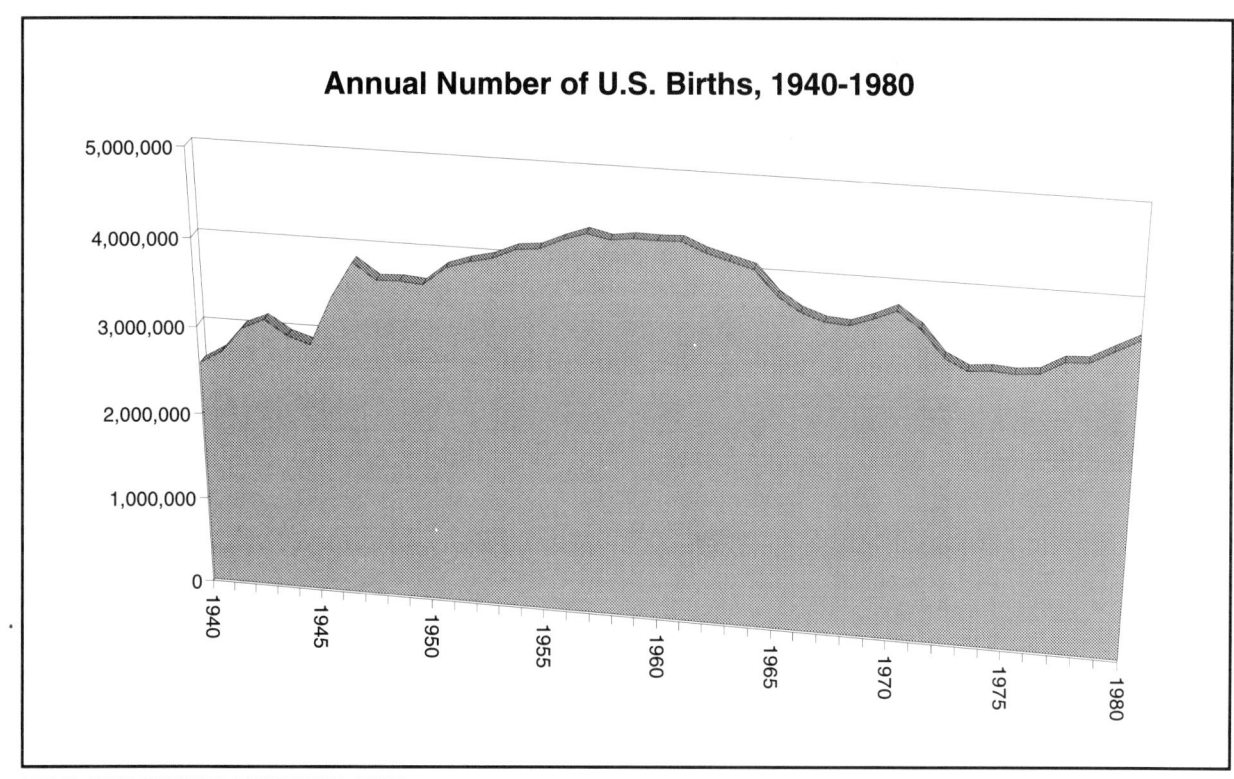

SOURCE: VITAL STATISTICS OF THE UNITED STATES

Page 18
The Cupertino, California, school district
  Dychtwald, Ken and Flower, Joe. *Age Wave: The Challenges and Opportunities of an Aging America.* Los Angeles: Jeremy P. Tarcher, 1989: 12.
New York City closed sixty schools
  Jones, Landon Y. *Great Expectations: America and the Baby Boom Generation*: 302.
eight states in the South and West
  Ibid.
In Utah, the gain was 36 percent
  Ibid.
"child-free"
  Hewlett, Sylvia Ann. *When the Bough Breaks: The Cost of Neglecting Our Children.* New York: Basic Books, 1991: 189.
the number of couples with children
  Otten, Alan L. "Deceptive Picture: If You See Families Staging a Comeback, It's Probably a Mirage." *Wall Street Journal* 25 September 1986: A22.

Page 19
the proportion of married women
  Jones, Landon Y. *Great Expectations: America and the Baby Boom Generation*: 199.
The average male in 1970
  Ibid.: 175.
Jerry Rubin seconded the idea
  Ibid.: 97.
10 percent of married couples
  Jones, Landon Y. *Great Expectations: America and the Baby Boom Generation*: 198.
one fourth of women of reproductive age
  Rayburn, William F. et al. *Every Woman's Pharmacy: A Guide to Safe Drug Use.* St. Louis: C.V. Mosby, 1983: 99.
ten million people
  Yankelovich, Daniel. *New Rules: Searching for Self-Fulfillment in a World Turned Upside Down.* New York: Random House, 1981: xiv.

Page 20
It's speculated that Zero Population Growth
  Mnookin, Robert. *In the Interest of Children: Advocacy Law Reform and Public Policy.* New York: W. H. Freeman, 1985: 164.
The commission also recommended
  The Commission on Population Growth and the American Future. *Population and the American Future.* 1972: 104.
Ann Landers ran a survey
  Jones, Landon Y. *Great Expectations: America and the Baby Boom Generation*: 214.
Parents magazine saw its circulation plummet
  Ibid.: 227.
membership in Parent Teacher Associations
  Dillon, Sam. "Change in Focus for P.T.A.'s: From Status Quo to Advocacy." *New York Times* 13 October 1993, national ed.: A1.

Page 21
in a series of studies on the American family
  63 percent responded affirmatively to the third question. Yankelovich, Daniel. *New Rules: Searching for Self-Fulfillment in a World Turned Upside Down*: 104. In an apparent sense of fairness, in the surveys most parents also acknowledged that while unwilling to sacrifice for

their children themselves, they didn't particularly expect any help from their children in the future either. Two thirds, according to the survey, believed that "children do not have an obligation to their parents regardless of what their parents have done for them." In a single shot the parents of the Free made it known that their kids not only should expect no assistance, but that they didn't want any help from their children either.

an annual survey
   Harris Poll cited in: Strauss, William and Howe, Neil. *Generations: The History of America's Future, 1584 to 2069*: 328.

this particular film
   Elkind, David. *The Hurried Child: Growing Up Too Fast Too Soon*. Reading, MA: Addison-Wesley, 1988: 100.

"Down with childhood!"
   Firestone, Shulamith. *The Dialectic of Sex: The Case for Feminist Revolution*. New York: William Morrow, 1970: 81; Robin Morgan decried children as mere "natural resources" that were being unfairly "mined" from women's bodies. Morgan, Robin. *The Word of a Woman*. New York: W. W. Norton, 1992: 76.

Betty Friedan called the traditions
   Quoted in: Magnet, Myron. "The American Family." *Fortune* 10 August 1992: 45.

Kate Millet suggested that parenthood
   Cited in: Suransky, Valerie Polakow. *The Erosion of Childhood*. Chicago: University of Chicago Press, 1982.

Germaine Greer recommended the founding of a huge baby farm
   Greer, Germaine. *The Female Eunuch*. New York: McGraw-Hill, 1971: 232.

U.S. News & World Report put the total figure
   Cited in: Berman, Eleanor. *The Cooperating Family*. Englewood Cliffs, NJ: Prentice-Hall, 1977: 21.

Page 22
Richard Farson argued that child-labor laws
   Farson, Richard. *Birthrights*. New York: Macmillan, 1974: 166.

He called for an end
   Ibid.: 21, 169.

John Holt wrote
   Holt, John. *Escape from Childhood: The Needs and Rights of Children*. New York: E. P. Dutton, 1974: 145.

He advocated a sort of children's bill of rights
   Ibid.: 3.

"I don't think we should 'protect' children"
   Ibid.: 257.

Jodie Foster began this craze
   "Hooker Hooked." *Time* 23 February 1976: 49.

Brooke Shields did her own nude scene
   Kroll, Jack. "Alice in Brothel-Land." *Newsweek* 10 April 1978: 106–7.

Page 23
Time magazine proclaimed her face
   "Modeling the '80s Look." *Time* 9 February 1981: 84.

Klein himself proclaimed the ads
   Ibid.

When an advertisement ran in the *Village Voice*
   Testimony to the California Assembly Committee on Criminal Justice. "Obscenity and the Use of Minors in Pornographic Material." 31 October 1977.

New York State's highest court
  Meislin, Richard J. "Sexual Portrayals Using Children Legal Unless Obscene, Court Rules." *New York Times* 13 May 1981: A1.

Page 24
"interchange between control and countercontrol."
  Skinner, B. F. *Beyond Freedom and Dignity*. New York: Alfred A. Knopf, 1971: 182–3
Around one thousand of these so-called air cribs
  "Skinner's Utopia: Panacea, or Path to Hell?" *Time* 20 September 1971: 51.
The *New York Times* called
  Cited in: Schrag, Peter and Divoky, Diane. *The Myth of the Hyperactive Child and Other Means of Child Control*. New York: Pantheon, 1975: 43.
Time magazine ran a cover story on Skinner
  "Skinner's Utopia: Panacea, or Path to Hell?" *Time:* 47.
Skinner himself describes this phenomenon
  Skinner, B. F. *Walden Two*. New York: Macmillan, 1976: vi.
As David Elkind wrote
  Elkind, David. *All Grown Up With No Place to Go*. Reading, Ma: Addison-Wesley, 1984: 100.

Page 25
Judy Blume, in defense of her hyperrealistic books
  Quoted in: Strauss, William and Howe, Neil. *Generations: The History of America's Future, 1584 to 2069*: 329.
A divorced New York mother told Marie Winn
  Winn, Marie. *Children Without Childhood*. New York: Pantheon, 1983: 132.
Alayne Yates advised parents
  Yates, Alayne. *Sex Without Shame*. New York: Quill, 1982: 211–2.
Annie Gottlieb, in her groovy Boomer chronicle
  Gottlieb, Annie. *Do You Believe in Magic? The Second Coming of the '60s Generation*. New York: Times Books, 1987: 279.
one therapist confessed
  Franks, Lucinda. "Little Big People." *New York Times Magazine* 10 October 1993: 31.

Page 26
When billionaire banker Seward Prosser Mellon
  Forst, Martin L. and Blomquist, Martha-Elin. *Missing Children: Rhetoric and Reality*. New York: Lexington Books, 1991: 159.
Judith Wallerstein began
  Wallerstein, Judith S. and Blakeslee, Sandra. *Second Chances: Men, Women and Children a Decade After Divorce*. New York: Ticknor & Fields, 1989: 297.
America saw 375,000 divorces
  Kirst, Michael W. et al. *Conditions of Children in California*, Berkeley: PACE School of Education: 35.
more than 40 percent of the Free
  Gross, David M. and Scott, Sophonia. "Twentysomething." *Time* 16 July 1990: 58; Whitehead, Barbara Dafoe. "Dan Quayle Was Right": 50.

Page 27
Graph of annual number of divorces
  U.S. Department of Education. *Youth Indicators*. 1988.

the number of unwed mothers
   Derber, Charles. *Money, Murder and the American Dream: Wilding From Wall Street to Main Street*: 117.
"the adult who sees divorce"
   Wallerstein, Judith S. and Kelly, Joan Berlin. *Surviving the Breakup.* New York: Basic Books, 1980: 37.

Page 28
Many even espoused the belief
   Pruett, Kyle D. *The Nurturing Father.* New York: Warner, 1987: 257.
One *Newsweek* writer observed in a 1967 article
   Waters, Harry F. "The Divorced Woman—American Style." *Newsweek* 13 February 1967: 64.
"The parents who take care of themselves"
   Krantzler, Mel. *Creative Divorce: A New Opportunity for Personal Growth.* New York: M. Evans and Co., 1974: 195.
"children can survive *any* family crisis"
   Krantzler, Mel. *Creative Divorce: A New Opportunity for Personal Growth*: 191.
80 percent of the divorced parents
   Winn, Marie. *Children Without Childhood*: 139.
80 percent "of the youngest children"
   Wallerstein, Judith S. and Kelly, Joan Berlin. *Surviving the Breakup*: 39.

Page 29
a year and a half after their parents' divorce
   Ibid.: 198.
Only one child in five
   Ibid.: 168.
Even after five years
   Ibid.: 198.
"parental care often diminishes"
   Ibid.: 36.
Wallerstein found that only about one in ten
   Ibid.: 41.
the family structure
   Wallerstein, Judith S. and Blakeslee, Sandra. *Second Chances: Men, Women and Children a Decade After Divorce*: 11.
"all too often the adult quest for freedom"
   Whitehead, Barbara Dafoe. "Dan Quayle Was Right": 58.

Page 30
two thirds of the children
   Cited in: Weitzman, Lenore J. *The Divorce Revolution: The Unexpected Social and Economic Consequences for Women and Children in America.* New York: Free Press, 1985: 320.
Michael Rutter has demonstrated
   Cited in: Hewlett, Sylvia Ann. *A Lesser Life: The Myth of Women's Liberation in America.* New York: William Morrow, 1986: 115.
"Anyone who knows children"
   Whitehead, Barbara Dafoe. "Dan Quayle Was Right": 64.
A 1988 survey by the National Center for Health Statistics
   Cited in: Magnet, Myron. "The American Family": 43.
A number of studies have found that the populations of clinics
   Over 80 percent of adolescents admitted for psychiatric reasons come from single-parent fami-

lies. Cited in: Magnet, Myron. "The American Family": 44. See also Luepnitz, Deborah Anna. *Child Custody: A Study of Families After Divorce*: 8.

Page 31
Children living with only one parent
Whitehead, Barbara Dafoe. "Dan Quayle Was Right": 47. In Wallerstein's study, one fourth of the children experienced a severe drop in their standard of living as a consequence of the divorce. Wallerstein, Judith S. and Blakeslee, Sandra. *Second Chances: Men, Women and Children a Decade After Divorce*: 298. And her study was conducted in an upper-middle-class area among families with relatively high incomes. Census Bureau researchers have found that when married couples with children split up, more than one third of white mothers and about half of all black mothers—and of course their children—wind up in poverty. Cited in: McLeod, Ramon G. "Census Finds Clues to Why Couples Split Up." *San Francisco Chronicle* 15 January 1993: A1. Taking into account all single mothers, including those never married in the first place, 41 percent of unwed white mothers were maintaining their households in poverty in 1983 along with 63 percent of black mothers. Bergmann, Barbara R. *The Economic Emergence of Women*. New York: Basic Books, 1986: 230. Only one in ten married couples with children was poor. Whitehead, Barbara Dafoe. "Dan Quayle Was Right": 62.

economists Saul Hoffman and Greg Duncan
Cited in: Faludi, Susan. *Backlash: The Undeclared War Against American Women*. New York: Crown, 1991: 21.

divorce is the single most commonly given reason
Cited in: "Harper's Index" *Harper's Magazine* August 1992.

"Children of divorce feel less protected"
Wallerstein, Judith S. and Blakeslee, Sandra. *Second Chances: Men, Women and Children a Decade After Divorce:* 157.

A staggering 75 percent of single-parent children
Cited in: Magnet, Myron. "The American Family": 43.

a 1977 study by the Carnegie Council on Children
Whitehead, Barbara Dafoe. "Dan Quayle Was Right": 60.

A number of studies indicate
Chicago sociologist James S. Coleman determined in a landmark study of education that student achievement is much more a determination of family background that of any characteristic of the schools themselves. Across a wide range of subjects he noted that "the total effect of home background is considerably greater than the total effect of school variables." Cited in: Hewlett, Sylvia Ann. *When the Bough Breaks: The Cost of Neglecting Our Children*: 19; Wallerstein found that half of the younger children in her study suffered a serious yearlong decline in their school performance. Wallerstein, Judith S. and Blakeslee, Sandra. *Second Chances: Men, Women and Children a Decade After Divorce*: 283. The report by the National Association of Elementary School Principals noted, "One-parent children, on the whole, show lower achievement in schools than their two-parent peers. Among all two-parent children 30 percent were ranked as high achievers, compared to only 17 percent of one-parent children. At the other end of the scale the situation is reversed. 23 percent of two-parent children were low achievers—while fully 38 percent of the one-parent children fell into this category." Apparently students have a difficult time making up for lost time—a survey sponsored by Columbia and Bowling Green Universities found a "dramatic" negative effect even on the SAT scores of students living with only a single parent, a result that held true even when accounting for income disparities. Cited in: Hewlett, Sylvia Ann. *When the Bough Breaks: The Cost of Neglecting Our Children*: 93. One element of Wallerstein's study supported this finding. Although her students came from affluent communities where 75 percent of the graduating classes go on to college, only half of the children in her study managed to stay in school. Wallerstein, Judith S. and Blakeslee, Sandra. *Second Chances: Men, Women and Children a Decade After Divorce*: 18.

A University of Michigan study
   Cited in: Wattenberg, Ben J. *The Birth Dearth.* New York: Pharos, 1987: 76. According to the National Center for Health Statistics, children who live with a mother and stepfather are two to three times as likely to be expelled or suspended from school. Schwartz, Joel. "Healthy Families Make Smarter Children." *American Demographics* February 1992: 13–14.

Page 32
Children in disrupted families also dropped out
   Findings of researcher Nicholas Zill. Cited in: Whitehead, Barbara Dafoe. "Dan Quayle Was Right": 66. Of children who do drop out, those from broken homes were also less likely to eventually get their diplomas or a GED. While one study found a particularly negative effect of divorce on the math scores of college women, most research indicates that boys were the ones who suffered the greatest academic setbacks following a divorce. Cited in: Biller, Henry B. "Father Absence, Divorce, and Personality Development." In *The Role of the Father in Child Development*, ed. Michael E. Lamb. New York: John Wiley & Sons, 1981: 507–9.
"The result of divorce"
   Quoted in: Sidel, Ruth. *Women and Children Last: The Plight of Poor Women in America.* New York: Viking, 1986: 101.
Studies on the Free have shown that after divorcing
   Cited in: Pruett, Kyle D. *The Nurturing Father:* 268.
A large-scale study by University of Pennsylvania sociologists
   Cited in: Hewlett, Sylvia Ann. *When the Bough Breaks: The Cost of Neglecting our Children*: 91. A 1981 study by the National Survey of Children found that nearly half of children between the ages of eleven and sixteen living with just their mothers hadn't seen their fathers in the past year. Cited in: Wingert, Pat with King, Patricia. "And What of Deadbeat Dads?" *Newsweek* 19 December 1988: 66.
A long-term study conducted by Dr. Mavis Hetherington
   Cited in: Biller, Henry B. "Father Absence, Divorce, and Personality Development." In *The Role of the Father in Child Development*: 504; and Warshak, Richard A. *The Custody Revolution: The Father Factor and the Motherhood Mystique.* New York: Poseidon, 1992: 60.
the researchers found that the girls' aggressive behavior
   Cited in: Biller, Henry B. "Father Absence, Divorce, and Personality Development." In *The Role of the Father in Child Development*: 505.
These conclusions were supported
   Ibid.: 506.

Page 33
daughters of single parents are nearly twice as likely
   One study of white families found that daughters of single parents are 53 percent more likely to marry while still teenagers, 111 percent more likely to have children as teenagers, 164 percent more likely to have a child outside of marriage, and 92 percent more likely to dissolve their marriage. Whitehead, Barbara Dafoe. "Dan Quayle Was Right": 62. Another study found that men from divorced families were 35 percent more likely to become divorced themselves and women were 60 percent more apt to do so. Magnet, Myron. "The American Family": 44. As children, the Free's relationships with their parents also suffered from the high divorce rate. In Glynnis Walker's survey of children of divorce, only one fourth of the respondents reported having a good relationship with both parents after a number of years had gone by. An equal number reported a good relationship with *neither* parent. Walker, Glynnis. *Solomon's Children: Exploding the Myths of Divorce.* New York: Arbor House, 1986: 205. Sociologist Alice Rossi has found that among adults with both parents still living, those separated from their fathers during childhood are much less likely to see their father on a regular basis. Whitehead, Bar-

bara Dafoe. "Dan Quayle Was Right": 74. Those who saw their fathers neglect them when they were young seem unwilling to seek a relationship later on in life.

more than 70 percent of all juveniles
  Cited in: Whitehead, Barbara Dafoe. "Dan Quayle Was Right": 77.

Those from fatherless homes
  The 1969 study by Kelly and Baer found a 39 percent recidivism rate among fatherless male delinquents and a 12 percent rate among father-present boys. Cited in: Biller, Henry B. "Father Absence, Divorce, and Personality Development." In *The Role of the Father in Child Development*: 519.

Fortune writer Myron Magnet concludes
  Magnet, Myron. "The American Family": 44.

A study of Peace Corps volunteers
  Cited in: Biller, Henry B. "Father Absence, Divorce, and Personality Development." In *The Role of the Father in Child Development*: 517.

Other studies showed that boys
  A 1970 study by Santrock and Wohlford of fifth-graders found that fatherless boys were more likely to choose an immediately available small candy bar rather than wait for a larger one. Cited in: Biller, Henry B. "Father Absence, Divorce, and Personality Development." In *The Role of the Father in Child Development*: 517.

Educational and economic attainments
  Researchers Mueller and Cooper found that children raised in single-parent families tend to have lower educational, occupational, and economic attainments by young adulthood. Mueller, Daniel P. and Cooper, Philip W. "Children of Single-Parent Families: How They Fare as Young Adults." *Family Relations* January 1986: 169–76.

When pollsters asked fathers
  Cited in: Whitehead, Barbara Dafoe. "Dan Quayle Was Right": 58.

Page 34
1981 Child Support Chart
  Census Bureau data cited in: Mattera, Philip. *Prosperity Lost*. Reading, MA: Addison-Wesley, 1990: 138.

In 1983, the average award
  Bergmann, Barbara R. *The Economic Emergence of Women*: 246.

For black mothers, the average amount
  Cited in: Whitehead, Barbara Dafoe. "Dan Quayle Was Right": 62.

a 1981 Census Bureau study
  U.S. Bureau of the Census, *Current Population Reports*: 60–173.

the women most likely to receive
  Sidel, Ruth. *Women and Children Last: The Plight of Poor Women in America*: 104.

Page 35
the likelihood of children receiving support payments
  Cited in: Strauss, William and Howe, Neil. *Generations: The History of America's Future, 1584 to 2069*: 325.

the average amount of child support
  Cited in: Faludi, Susan. *Backlash: The Undeclared War Against American Women*: 24.

men were more likely to meet their car payments
  Ibid.

many states lowered the top age
  Cited in: Whitehead, Barbara Dafoe. "Dan Quayle Was Right": 74.

a study by Martha Hill
  Cited in: Bergmann, Barbara R. *The Economic Emergence of Women*: 246.

only $5 billion of the $25 billion
  Cited in: Faludi, Susan. *Backlash: The Undeclared War Against American Women*: 25.
Congress passed welfare-reform legislation
  The Federal Family Support Act in 1988. California also can now deny state professional licenses to child support delinquents. Even with the new measures, however, 1990 saw favorable results from only 18 percent of the child support cases that went to court. See Wingert, Pat with King, Patricia. "And What of Deadbeat Dads?": 66; Ellis, Virginia. "Child Support Effort Targets State Licenses." *Los Angeles Times* 24 November 1992: A3; Reid, Jeanne L. "Making Delinquent Dad Pay His Child Support." *Ms.* July–August 1992: 86–9.
fathers fighting for some custody
  Sidel, Ruth. *Women and Children Last: The Plight of Poor Women in America*: 106.

Page 36
20 percent of all children
  Kantrowitz, Barbara and Wingert, Pat. "Step By Step" *Newsweek* Special Issue 1989: 30.
"One of the consistent findings"
  Cited in: Kantrowitz, Barbara and Wingert, Pat. "Step By Step": 27.
more than half of the children
  Wallerstein, Judith S. and Blakeslee, Sandra. *Second Chances: Men, Women and Children a Decade After Divorce*: 248.
Those between nine and fifteen
  Cited in: Kantrowitz, Barbara and Wingert, Pat. "Step By Step": 27.
the most difficult seems to be that between stepmothers and stepdaughters
  Quoted in: Laiken, Deidre S. *Daughters of Divorce: The Effects of Parental Divorce on Women's Lives.* New York: William Morrow, 1981: 152.
stepchildren also have more developmental
  Cited in: Kantrowitz, Barbara and Wingert, Pat. "Step By Step": 27. According to the National Center for Health Statistics, children in stepfamilies are at least as likely as those in single-parent families to have learning disabilities and emotional and behavioral problems. Magnet, Myron. "The American Family": 44.
a study by Canadian researchers
  Cited in: Whitehead, Barbara Dafoe. "Dan Quayle Was Right": 72.
second marriages are even 20 percent more likely to fail
  Cited in: Kantrowitz, Barbara and Wingert, Pat. "Step By Step": 27. Other research conducted at the University of Nebraska has even determined that remarriages involving children are more likely to fail than those in which no children are involved. Analyzing divorce rates over a three-year period, researchers found that the divorce rate for remarriages involving stepchildren involving two previously married partners was 17 percent. Where no children were involved the rate was only 10 percent. "Breaking Up for the Kids." *American Demographics* May 1986: 11.

Page 37
14 percent of the children
  Walker, Glynnis. *Solomon's Children: Exploding the Myths of Divorce*: 153.
"I felt like a carry-over"
  Quoted in: Laiken, Deidre S. *Daughters of Divorce: The Effects of Parental Divorce on Women's Lives*: 161.
"in the second marriage"
  Ibid.
A stepparent's legal right
  Larson, Jan. "Understanding Stepfamilies." *American Demographics* July 1992: 36–40.

One 1972 study found that when a boy's mother remarried
   Cited in: Biller, Henry B. "Father Absence, Divorce, and Personality Development." In *The Role of the Father in Child Development*: 509.
the converse is true for girls
   Cited in: Whitehead, Barbara Dafoe. "Dan Quayle Was Right": 72.
"Happy endings mean hard work from everybody"
   Kantrowitz, Barbara and Wingert, Pat. "Step By Step": 34.

Page 38
In three decades of work
   Quoted in: Whitehead, Barbara Dafoe. "Dan Quayle Was Right": 82. Adds Carl Zinsmeister of the American Enterprise Institute: "There is a mountain of scientific evidence showing that when families disintegrate children often end up with intellectual, physical, and emotional scars for life. . . . We talk about the drug crisis, the education crisis, and the problems of teen pregnancy and juvenile crime. But all these ills trace back predominantly to one source: broken families." Moynihan, Daniel Patrick. "A Landmark for Families." *New York Times* 16 November 1992, national ed.: A13.

Page 39
1983 Median weekly salary
   Cited in: Cronin, Anne. "The Bottom Line: A Reality Check on Salaries." *New York Times* 15 November 1992, national ed.: E2.
" 'just a housewife'—the contemporary nonperson"
   Hewlett, Sylvia Ann. *A Lesser Life: The Myth of Women's Liberation in America*: 253.
12 percent of mothers with preschool children
   Winn, Marie. *Children Without Childhood*: 121.

Page 40
Graph of working mothers
   Bureau of Labor Statistics. Cited in: "A Growing Diversity Among Mothers." *New York Times* 3 October 1992, national ed.: 18.
a majority of even those mothers
   Cited in: Kahn, Alfred J. and Kamerman, Sheila B. *Child Care: Facing the Hard Choices*. Dover, MA: Auburn House, 1987: 11.
among divorced women with children
   Bergmann, Barbara B. *The Economic Emergence of Women*: 53.
"In the mid-1970s the senior management team at IBM"
   Schwartz, Felice N. *Breaking With Tradition: Women and Work, The New Facts of Life*. New York: Warner, 1992: 113.

Page 41
"a policy requiring employers"
   Bergmann, Barbara R. *The Economic Emergence of Women*: 213.
"another disadvantage of long paid maternity leaves"
   Ibid.: 214.
"Decisions aren't made on the basis"
   Quoted in: Adler, Jerry. "Kids Growing Up Scared." *Newsweek* 10 January 1994: 42–50.
Pennsylvania State psychologist Jay Belsky
   Wingert, Pat and Kantrowitz, Barbara. "The Day Care Generation." *Newsweek* Special Issue 1989: 89.
a major study by the Census Bureau
   Cited in: McLeod, Ramon G. "Census Finds Clues to Why Couples Split Up." *San Francisco Chronicle* 15 January 1993: A1.

"You work all day and you come home"
  Minton, Torri. "Working Toward Divorce." *San Francisco Chronicle* 26 January 1993: B3.
(n) A 1986 Gallup poll showed
  Cited in: Hewlett, Sylvia Ann. *When the Bough Breaks: The Cost of Neglecting our Children*: 25.
(n) A 1990 survey by Yankelovich, Clancy, and Shulman
  Cited in: Phillips, Kevin. *Boiling Point*. New York: Random House, 1993: 162.

Page 42
A 1978 study
  Cited in: Winn, Marie. *Children Without Childhood*: 121.
as late as 1990 only 44 percent of employers
  Hewitt Associates study cited in: Schwartz, Felice N. *Breaking With Tradition: Women and Work, the New Facts of Life*: 44.
A Bureau of Labor Statistics study
  Cited in: Schwartz, Felice N. *Breaking With Tradition: Women and Work, the New Facts of Life*: 59.
the median pay for women
  Cited in: Nasar, Sylvia. "Women's Progress Stalled? Just Not So." *New York Times* 18 October 1992, national ed., sec. 3: 1+.
In 1971, Congress seemed to be making
  Morris, Charles R. *A Time of Passion: America 1960–1980,* New York: Harper & Row, 1984: 143.
Reagan nevertheless slashed Title XX funding
  Hewlett, Sylvia Ann. *A Lesser Life: The Myth of Women's Liberation in America*: 119.
the number of day-care centers more than doubled.
  The number of licensed day-care spaces increased from 475,000 to 1,000,000 from 1965 to 1973. Glickman, Beatrice Marden and Springer, Nesha Bass. *Who Cares for the Baby? Choices in Child Care.* New York: Schocken Books, 1978: 74.
In 1977 two thirds of those
  Bergmann, Barbara R. *The Economic Emergence of Women*: 284.
assertions were even made
  Wingert, Pat and Kantrowitz, Barbara. "The Day Care Generation": 87. Jean Curtis told women in her 1976 book *Working Mothers* that mothers with infants who work "encourage a sense of trust" in their babies because of their "eventual reappearance." She added, with no studies cited to substantiate her claim, that "working mothers . . . seem to spend more time with their children on their off hours—evenings and weekends—than nonworking mothers do." They are, she suggested as a strange example of a benefit, "apt to keep their children up later in the evening in order to spend time with them." Curtis, Jean. *Working Mothers*. New York: Doubleday, 1976: 58, 66.

Page 43
"We believe that quality infant day care"
  Evans, E. Belle and Saia, George E. *Day Care for Infants*. Boston: Beacon, 1972: 10.
they were most often conducted
  Wingert, Pat and Kantrowitz, Barbara. "The Day Care Generation": 87.
As the authors of a 1978 book on child care explained
  Glickman, Beatrice Marden and Springer, Nesha Bass. *Who Cares for the Baby? Choices in Child Care*: 93.
While later studies have confirmed
  For a summary of such research, see: Kahn, Alfred J. and Kamerman, Sheila B. *Child Care: Facing the Hard Choices*: 16.

the National Council of Jewish Women
　For more complete details, see: Suransky, Valerie Polakow. *The Erosion of Childhood*: 51; and Sidel, Ruth. *Women and Children Last: The Plight of Poor Women in America*: 124–5.

"Good day care may be good for kids"
　Quoted in: Wingert, Pat and Kantrowitz, Barbara. "The Day Care Generation": 92.

"Children who entered low-quality"
　Cited in: Gay, Kathlyn. *Day Care: Looking for Answers*. Hillside, NJ: Enslow, 1992: 96.

Page 44

He now concludes that infants
　Cited in: Gay, Kathlyn. *Day Care: Looking for Answers*: 94. The costs of child care were also a great obstacle to parents finding good care. The average cost per child was $3,000 a year in 1987. Hewlett, Sylvia Ann. *When the Bough Breaks: The Cost of Neglecting Our Children*: 55. Yet child-care providers earned only $8,000 a year on average, understandably leading to a high turnover among staff. Chapman, Fern Schumer. "Executive Guilt: Who's Taking Care of the Children?" *Fortune* 16 February 1987: 32. This inconsistency is another factor contributing toward the overall poor child-care picture. For example, Marcy Whitebook, project director of the ongoing National Child Care Staffing Study, has determined that children in centers with high turnover spend less time socializing with peers and also have language skills that are less developed. Shell, Ellen Ruppel. *A Child's Place: A Year in the Life of a Day Care Center*. Boston: Little, Brown, 1992: 196.

surveys showed that men averaged
　Cited in: Elkind, David. *The Hurried Child: Growing Up Too Fast Too Soon*: 39. A Gallup poll of February 5, 1990, asked men and women about who does household chores. Percent saying they do all or most of each chore:

	Men	Women
Doing laundry	27%	79%
Preparing meals	26	78
Washing dishes	31	68
Grocery shopping	26	72
Cleaning house	22	69
Caring for children on a daily basis	12	72
Caring for children when sick	10	78

A 1987 Boston University study found
　Cited in: Thomas, Evan with Wingert, Pat. "The Reluctant Father." *Newsweek* 19 December 1988: 64.

in 1976, 63 percent of high-school seniors
　In 1976, 73 percent of boys and 53 percent of girls agreed with this statement. In 1986 the figures were 58 percent for boys and 35 percent for girls. Bachman, Jerald G. "An Eye on the Future." *Psychology Today* July 1987: 6–8.

a *Fortune* magazine survey of working parents
　Chapman, Fern Schumer. "Executive Guilt: Who's Taking Care of the Children?": 35.

Page 45

Taking into account all sources of income
　According to the Census Bureau, figuring in all forms of income and subsidies such as reduced health-care costs, the 1983 poverty rate of the elderly was just over 3 percent. For children, the rate was 17 percent. For those under age six, the rate was 18.2 percent. Cited in: Longman,

Phillip. *Born to Pay: The New Politics of Aging in America.* Boston: Houghton Mifflin, 1987: 240. In 1983, $217 billion in federal funds went to the elderly. Federal outlays for child-oriented programs (AFDC, Head Start, food stamps, child health, child nutrition, and education) totaled $36 billion. Given that there were more children than elderly persons, the eleven-to-one ratio was obtained. Preston, Samuel. "Children and the Elderly in the U.S.": 45.

In 1974, the Free Generation assumed a dubious title
    Howe, Neil and Strauss, William. "America's 13th Generation." *New York Times* 16 March 1991: 23.

"the first society in history"
    Quoted in: Longman, Phillip. *Born to Pay: The New Politics of Aging in America*: 17.

Page 46

Graph of poverty rates
    U.S. Bureau of the Census, *Current Population Survey,* P60, No. 175, tables 2 and 3.

David Eggebeen and Daniel Lechter of Penn State have estimated
    Cited in: Whitehead, Barbara Dafoe. "Dan Quayle Was Right": 77.

In 1983, the Census Bureau reported
    Cited in: Bronfenbrenner, Urie. "Alienation and the Four Worlds of Childhood." *Phi Delta Kappan* February 1986: 433.

Newsweek estimated in 1989
    Kozol, Jonathan. "The New Untouchables." *Newsweek* Special Issue 1989: 49.

Not since the Great Depression
    Kozol, Jonathan. "The New Untouchables": 52.

Page 47

the Family Assistance Plan
    For a complete account of the FAP debate, see Burke, Vincent J., and Burke, Vee. *Nixon's Good Deed: Welfare Reform.* New York: Columbia UP, 1974, and also Morris, Charles R. *A Time of Passion: America 1960–1980*: 142.

grants for AFDC recipients fell 40 percent
    Bernstein, Aaron, et al. "Is Uncle Sam Shortchanging Young Americans?" *Business Week* 19 August 1991: 85.

The maximum AFDC benefit
    Sidel, Ruth. *Women and Children Last: The Plight of Poor Women in America*: 87.

only 12 percent of welfare recipients
    Mattera, Philip. *Prosperity Lost*: 55.

From 1973 to 1982
    Bernstein, Aaron, et al. "Is Uncle Sam Shortchanging Young Americans?": 85.

1981 Omnibus Budget Reconciliation Act
    Sidel, Ruth. *Women and Children Last: The Plight of Poor Women in America*: 86.

benefits for children and families suffered
    Longman, Phillip. *Born to Pay: The New Politics of Aging in America*: 17.

(n) all fifty states denied welfare payments
    Burke, Vincent J., and Burke, Vee. *Nixon's Good Deed: Welfare Reform*: 161.

Page 48

Among those affected by these cuts
    Kozol, Jonathan. "The New Untouchables": 52.

The Children's Defense Fund reports
    Cited in: Weitzman, Lenore J. *The Divorce Revolution: The Unexpected Social and Economic Consequences for Women and Children in America*: 354.

the United States's ranking among nations
   Cited in: Hewlett, Sylvia Ann. *When the Bough Breaks: The Cost of Neglecting Our Children*: 35, 291.
32 billion dollars in federal aid
   Ibid.: 46.
Only one in three renting households
   "The Shape of Housing to Come." *Population Bulletin* January 1986: 31.
families with children saw dramatic increases
   Cited in: Strauss, William and Howe, Neil. *Generations: The History of America's Future, 1584 to 2069*: 98.
from 1960 to the early eighties
   Longman, Phillip. *Born to Pay: The New Politics of Aging in America*: 18.
The federal tax deduction for dependent children
   From 1973 to 1978, the deduction per dependent was $750. In 1979 it was raised to $1,000, where it remained until 1984. To stay even with inflation, the 1984 figure would have had to be $1,750. *Your Federal Income Tax*. IRS Publication No. 17.
a family of four earning poverty-level wages
   Longman, Phillip. *Born to Pay: The New Politics of Aging in America*: 18.

Page 49
tax policy at this time still favored married couples with only one worker
   Bergmann, Barbara R. *The Economic Emergence of Women:* 219. The following table indicates the tax differential among three types of families based on the Tax Reform Act of 1986. Standard deduction is assumed in all cases.

                    Income Taxes in the United States
                              By Marital Status
   1) Married Couple—Both Working
         Man's income $30,000
         Woman's income $20,000
      Their taxes if single ($4,638 + $2,250) $6,888
      Their taxes as a married couple $7,554
   2) Married Couple—One Wage Earner
      Man's income $30,000
      Tax as a single person $4,638
      Tax if married with no children $3,150
   3) Single Parent
      Woman's income $40,000
      Tax with one child (two-person family) $5,712
      Tax of a married couple earning the same (two-person family) $4,854

nearly 30 percent of the over-sixty-five population
   U.S. Bureau of the Census, *Current Population Survey*, P60, No. 175, tables 2 and 3.
the one surviving element
   Burke, Vincent J., and Burke, Vee. *Nixon's Good Deed: Welfare Reform*: 188.
by the end of the eighties
   Hewlett, Sylvia Ann. *When the Bough Breaks: The Cost of Neglecting Our Children*: 36.
a total of $356 billion
   Bernstein, Aaron, et al. "Is Uncle Sam Shortchanging Young Americans?": 85. The granddaddy of elderly programs, Social Security, indexed benefits against inflation in 1973, but the payouts have gone way beyond just staying even. Measured in constant 1982 dollars, the average annual Social Security benefit rose from $2,575 in 1967 to $6,948 in 1989. Given such high monthly payments, the Congressional Research Service has determined that a married

worker retiring at age sixty-five who had paid the maximum Social Security taxes required under the law (the maximum was only $95 a year in 1958) would recover his contributions in just twenty-one months. Low wage earners would recover their contributions in as little as twelve months. Since the average sixty-five-year-old can expect to live about fifteen more years, he or she will collect eight to eleven times the amount contributed to the system. See Hewlett, Sylvia Ann. *When the Bough Breaks: The Cost of Neglecting Our Children*: 139; Chakravarty, Subrata N. with Weisman, Katherine. "Consuming Our Children?" *Forbes* 14 November 1988: 225; Longman, Phillip. *Born to Pay: The New Politics of Aging in America*: 63; Hardy, Dorcas R. and Hardy, C. Colburn. *Social Insecurity*. New York: Villard, 1991: 71.

Philip Longman has noted that only 17 percent of these payments
Longman, Philip. *Born to Pay: The New Politics of Aging in America*: 238.

Page 50
children's share of Medicaid funds
Hewlett, Sylvia Ann. *When the Bough Breaks: The Cost of Neglecting Our Children*: 152.
"In many cases, Congress quite consciously cut programs"
Quoted in: Bernstein, Aaron, et al. "Is Uncle Sam Shortchanging Young Americans?": 85.
one third of the hundreds of billions
Dychtwald, Ken and Flower, Joe. *Age Wave: The Challenges and Opportunities of an Aging America*: 79.
28 percent of the massive Medicare budget
Dychtwald, Ken and Flower, Joe. *Age Wave: The Challenges and Opportunities of an Aging America*: 79. The Medicare system was begun only in 1965 and a decade later was already costing the government $12 billion a year. By 1990 the amount had zoomed to $96 billion, consuming 8 percent of the entire federal budget. A system that had been created with the intent of providing basic care to the neediest of the elderly has grown so that nearly every senior citizen is now covered and over two thirds of their total medical bills are paid out of public funds. And somewhere along the line, Congress reduced the Medicare charge to recipients from 50 percent to 25 percent of the annual cost. All told, Carolyn Davis, former administrator of the Health Care Financing Administration, has estimated that "individuals who became eligible for Medicare in 1983 . . . [will receive] anywhere from ten to 12.5 times their contributions." See Dychtwald, Ken and Flower, Joe. *Age Wave: The Challenges and Opportunities of an Aging America*: 74; Preston, Samuel. "Children and the Elderly in the U.S.": 44; Ginzberg, Eli. "The Health Swamp." *New York Times* 12 November 1992, national ed.: A15; Longman, Phillip. *Born to Pay: The New Politics of Aging in America*: 99.
"society doesn't pay for the education"
Quoted in: Smith, Lee. "The War Between the Generations": 82.
A 1982 Gallup poll showed that 71 percent
Cited in: Preston, Samuel. "Children and the Elderly in the U.S.": 46.
"This is the best time to be a senior citizen"
Quoted in: Sciffres, Manuel with Walsh, Maureen. "Those 24-Karat Golden Years—Can They Last?" *U.S. News & World Report* 18 August 1986: 42. One might sympathize a little more with the inequalities of the benefits shelled out to the old if it weren't for the fact that this growing bloc of voters seems unwilling to share their good fortune. When the Gallup Organization asked Americans in 1983 about their opinions on raising taxes to support our ailing schools, those under age fifty were about evenly split; those older than fifty rejected the idea by more than two to one. In a 1986 survey on welfare spending, which primarily supports families with children, those aged sixty-five and above were overwhelmingly the most likely to respond that we were spending too much (it's notable that in the early seventies, the elderly were the *least* likely to respond thus). Even spreading the wealth more equitably within their own ranks has caused a furor. When Congress passed the Medicare Catastrophic Coverage Act in 1988, it

took a step toward providing additional health care to the elderly poor while obliging the elderly wealthy to pay a modest amount more—only the wealthiest 5 percent would pay the maximum of $800 to support the program, a fraction of their annual Social Security and Medicare benefits. Finding this intolerable, the gray lobby, headed by the giant American Association of Retired Persons with a population larger than that of Canada, leaned heavily on Congress until the house finally repealed the law in October 1989 by a 360 to 66 vote. Given such actions, some lawmakers have privately dubbed the gray lobby the "greedy geezers." See Preston, Samuel. "Children and the Elderly in the U.S.": 48; *Public Opinion Quarterly* Winter 1988; Hewlett, Sylvia Ann. *When the Bough Breaks: The Cost of Neglecting Our Children*: 155–6. By contrast, a 1986 poll by the Yankelovich Group found that among young adults age twenty-one to twenty-nine, 74 percent favored high Social Security benefits for the elderly. Dychtwald, Ken and Flower, Joe. *Age Wave: The Challenges and Opportunities of an Aging America*: 85.

Page 51
In 1967, testimony before a Senate subcommittee
  Michaels, Marguerite with Willwerth, James. "How America Has Run Out of Time." *Time* 24 April 1989: 59.
From 1973 to 1989, productivity increases stalled
  Michaels, Marguerite with Willwerth, James. "How America Has Run Out of Time": 58.
workers in the manufacturing sector
  The average working American put in 1,786 hours on the job in 1969 and was working 1,924 hours by 1989. Schor, Juliet B. "All Work and No Play: It Doesn't Pay." *New York Times* 29 August 1993, national ed.: F9.
A Harris poll indicates that the amount of leisure time
  Cited in: Louv, Richard. *Childhood's Future: Listening to the American Family. New Hope for the Next Generation*: 15.

Page 52
According to the Family Research Council
  Ibid.
In a study conducted by social psychologist Lois Hoffman
  Cited in: Walker, Glynnis. *Solomon's Children: Exploding the Myths of Divorce*: 98.
A study of American fathers
  Cited in: Sommerville, John. *The Rise and Fall of Childhood*: 8.
The average adolescent in 1986
  Phi Delta Kappan February 1986: 417.
parents spent the same amount of time each day
  Cited in: Walker, Glynnis. *Solomon's Children: Exploding the Myths of Divorce*: 99.
nearly all was spent
  Phi Delta Kappan February 1986: 417.
When *Time* magazine asked "twentysomethings"
  Gross, David M. and Scott, Sophonia. "Twentysomething": 62.
Nickelodeon, the cable-television network
  Cited in: Louv, Richard. *Childhood's Future: Listening to the American Family. New Hope for the Next Generation*: 18.

Page 53
"kids understand that they are being cheated"
  Quoted in: Michaels, Marguerite with Willwerth, James. "How America Has Run Out of Time": 64.
In 1982, an estimated 7 million
  Sommerville, John. *The Rise and Fall of Childhood*: 8.

An additional half-million *preschool* children
   Chapman, Fern Schumer. "Executive Guilt: Who's Taking Care of the Children?": 37.
a 1987 Louise Harris poll found
   Cited in: Louv, Richard. *Childhood's Future: Listening to the American Family. New Hope for the Next Generation*: 84.
The 1988 Census Bureau report, "After-School Care of Children"
   Ibid.
A number of cities established telephone support lines
   "Telephone Support for Latchkey Children." *Child Welfare* January–February 1988: 49–59.
Typically, older youths in the eighties
   Phi Delta Kappan February 1986: 417.

Page 54
As Pauline Kael wrote in *The New Yorker*
   Cited in: Schultze, Quentin J. et al. *Dancing in the Dark: Youth, Popular Culture and the Electronic Media*. Grand Rapids, MI: William B. Eerdmans, 1991: 228.
Milpitas case compiled from:
   Abramson, Pamela. "Bitter Memories of a Murder." *Newsweek* 22 June 1987: 25; "Coast Police Say 'Callous' Youths Viewed Girl's Body and Stoned It." *New York Times* 25 November 1981; "California Youth Pleads Guilty to Death He Boasted About." *New York Times* 21 July 1982: 12; King, Wayne. "Youths' Silence on Murder Victim Leaves a California Town Baffled." *New York Times* 14 December 1981: D11; "Coast Youth Who Boasted of Killing Girl Is Sentenced." *New York Times* 5 December 1982: 26; "Teen-Ager Found Guilty in Concealment of Body." *New York Times* 28 January 1982: 14.

Page 55
indicates that in 75 percent of the cases
   Quoted in: Frymier, Jack. "Understanding and Preventing Teen Suicide." *Phi Delta Kappan* December 1988: 293.
leaving their kids alone after school facilitated
   Chapman, Fern Schumer. "Executive Guilt: Who's Taking Care of the Children?": 37.
A 1981 nationwide survey of teenagers
   Norman, Jane and Harris, Myron. *The Private Life of the American Teenager*. New York: Rawson, Wade, 1981: 255.

Page 56
A 1989 study of five thousand eighth-grade students
   Cited in: Hewlett, Sylvia Ann. *When the Bough Breaks: The Cost of Neglecting Our Children*: 83.
"seem to develop a lot of anger"
   Quoted in: Winn, Marie. *Children Without Childhood*: 141.
a 1987 Harris poll
   Cited in: Louv, Richard. *Childhood's Future: Listening to the American Family. New Hope for the Next Generation*: 89.
Studies done in the early eighties
   Cited in: Postman, Neil. *The Disappearance of Childhood*: 79.
Elementary-school teachers often complained
   "Sweet 16 and Ready for Work." *The Economist* 30 January 1988: 21.
Becky Bell case compiled from:
   Bell, Bill. "Dear Becky." *Seventeen* March 1991: 184–5; Marcus, Erin. "After Daughter's Death, Parents Campaign Against Abortion Consent Laws." *Washington Post* 8 August 1990:

A3; Mann, Judy. "Illegal Abortion's Deadly Price." *Washington Post* 3 August 1990: C3; "Abortion" *Rolling Stone* 9 August 1990: 43.

Page 58
Newspapers reported the death
 Louv, Richard. *Childhood's Future: Listening to the American Family. New Hope for the Next Generation*: 29.
Joel Best, a sociology professor
 Ibid.
And what of the deaths
 Ibid.
The 1983 television docudrama "Adam"
 Forst, Martin L. and Blomquist, Martha-Elin. *Missing Children: Rhetoric and Reality*: 58.

Page 59
There were other widely reported incidents
 Compiled in: Forst, Martin L. and Blomquist, Martha-Elin. *Missing Children: Rhetoric and Reality*: 56–7.
A 1983 U.S. Department of Health and Human Services report
 Forst, Martin L. and Blomquist, Martha-Elin. *Missing Children: Rhetoric and Reality*: 30.
Jay Howell, then executive director
 Ibid.: 31.
Senator Paula Hawkins
 Ibid.: 95.
a Chicago television station circulated
 Louv, Richard. *Childhood's Future: Listening to the American Family. New Hope for the Next Generation*: 378.
the FBI's data
 Forst, Martin L. and Blomquist, Martha-Elin. *Missing Children: Rhetoric and Reality:* 31.

Page 60
The National Child Safety Council led a campaign in 1985
 Ibid.: 73.
Only eleven children
 Ibid.
a program sponsored by the U.S. Department of Justice
 Ibid.: 38.

Page 61
Between 1980 and 1984, the researchers determined
 Ibid.: 39.
"Missing children," they write, "became a symbol"
 Quoted in: Forst, Martin L. and Blomquist, Martha-Elin. *Missing Children: Rhetoric and Reality*: 292.
the Department of Justice researchers estimated
 Forst, Martin L. and Blomquist, Martha-Elin. *Missing Children: Rhetoric and Reality*: 40.

Page 62
The American Humane Association has been compiling data
 Ibid.: 49.
Each year, about forty thousand of these children were injured
 Gaines, Donna. *Teenage Wasteland: Suburbia's Dead End Kids*. New York: Pantheon, 1990: 247.

Neil Postman has hypothesized that
   Postman, Neil. *The Disappearance of Childhood*: 136.
the age group that felt the largest-percentage increase
   Jones, Landon Y. *Great Expectations: America and the Baby Boom Generation*: 212.
only one in ten murder victims
   Forst, Martin L. and Blomquist, Martha-Elin. *Missing Children: Rhetoric and Reality*: 52.

Page 63
Number of drunk-driving arrests nationwide
   FBI. *Uniform Crime Reports,* annual.
offered a sad portrait
   Elkind, David. *All Grown Up With No Place to Go*: 3.
It was estimated in the eighties
   Strauss, William and Howe, Neil. *Generations: The History of America's Future, 1584 to 2069*: 326.
A national survey of more than forty thousand teenagers
   Cited in: Kolodny, Robert C., et al. *How to Survive Your Adolescent's Adolescence.* Boston: Little, Brown, 1984: 17; and Light, Paul C. *Baby Boomers.* New York: W. W. Norton, 1988: 141.

Page 64
Pamela Douglas, a teacher of screenwriting
   Littwin, Susan. *The Postponed Generation: Why American Youth Are Growing Up Later*: 243.
Brown University students voted
   Leavitt, David. "The New Lost Generation." *Esquire* May 1985: 91.
Writer David Leavitt responded to this question
   Leavitt, David. "The New Lost Generation": 91.
Nineteen-year-old Shellie Wilburn told the *Washington Post*
   Jordan, Mary and Maraniss, David. "An Upbeat Generation Looking Out for Itself": A8.
a Gallup poll showed
   A Gallup poll, February 20, 1991, asked, "Do you favor or oppose the U.S. use of tactical nuclear weapons in the Persian Gulf war?" Age eighteen to twenty-nine, 73 percent opposed; age thirty to forty-nine, 67 percent opposed; age fifty and over, 60 percent opposed.
a 1993 Gallup poll found that one Free teenager in three
   Cited in "Harper's Index" *Harper's Magazine* February 1994: 13.
an interesting question in 1981 to 100 young track-and-field athletes
   Goldman, Bob. *Death in the Locker Room.* South Bend, IN: Icarus, 1984: 32.

Page 65
Bob Goldman polled weight lifters
   Goldman, Bob. *Death in the Locker Room*: 32.
the University of Wisconsin Hospital reports
   Brumberg, Joan Jacobs. *Fasting Girls.* Cambridge: Harvard UP, 1988: 12.
afflicting as many as one young woman in twenty
   Hewlett, Sylvia Ann. *When the Bough Breaks: The Cost of Neglecting Our Children*: 71.
the country's first residential facility
   Brumberg, Joan Jacobs. *Fasting Girls*: 21.
they do seem to agree on
   Ibid.: 24.
"anorexia is an attempted solution"
   Orbach, Susie. *Hunger Strike.* New York: W. W. Norton, 1986: 103.

Page 66
"the 'anorectic generations,' particularly those born since 1960"
    Brumberg, Joan Jacobs. *Fasting Girls*: 266.
"often the girl who becomes bulimic"
    Maloney, Michael, M.D. and Kranz, Rachel. *Straight Talk about Eating Disorders*. New York: Facts on File, 1991: 83. See also Shisslak, Catherine, et al. "Family Disfunction in Normal Weight Bulimics and Bulimic Anorexic Families." *Journal of Clinical Psychology* March 1990: 185, and "Parent Talk Shapes Teen Body Image (Anorexia Nervosa and Bulimia in Teenage Girls)" *Tufts University Diet and Nutrition Letter* February 1992: 7.
"Mother's increasing presence in the workplace"
    Quoted in: Hewlett, Sylvia Ann. *When the Bough Breaks: The Cost of Neglecting Our Children*: 71.
A 1981 study of college women
    Brumberg, Joan Jacobs. *Fasting Girls*: 264.
recent studies indicate that the affliction rate of anorexia
    "Bulimia, Anorexia Fading Away." *USA Today Magazine* October 1990: 6.
A study done in the mid-eighties
    Cited in: Hewlett, Sylvia Ann. *When the Bough Breaks: The Cost of Neglecting Our Children*: 71.

Page 67
Graph of teenage drug use
    Annual University of Michigan surveys cited in: Treaster, Joseph B. "Drug Use by Younger Teen-Agers Appears to Rise, Counter to Trend." *New York Times* 14 April 1993: A1.
The American Academy of Pediatrics called overweight children
    Kock, Joanne Barbara and Freeman, Linda Nancy. *Good Parents for Hard Times*. New York: Fireside, 1992: 87.
an A. C. Nielson survey showed that kids of that age
    Cited in: Kock, Joanne Barbara and Freeman, Linda Nancy. *Good Parents for Hard Times*: 87.
a study conducted by the National Institute on Drug Abuse
    Cited in: Elkind, David. *All Grown Up With No Place to Go*: 187.
The Department of Health, Education and Welfare determined
    Ibid.: 186.
Cocaine, which rose in popularity
    National Institute on Drug Abuse statistics cited in: Barringer, Felicity. "What Is Youth Coming To?" *New York Times* 19 August 1990: E1.

Page 68
In 1966, 19 percent of high-school students
    "Administration Cites Drop in Teen Drug Use." *Alcoholism and Drug Abuse Week* 30 January 1991: 5.
The proportion had more than tripled
    Compilation of a series of surveys cited in: Elkind, David. *All Grown Up With No Place to Go*: 185.
a survey of junior-high-school students
    Cited in: Elkind, David. *All Grown Up With No Place to Go*: 6.
A survey conducted by the *Weekly Reader*
    Cited in: Kock, Joanne Barbara and Freeman, Linda Nancy. *Good Parents for Hard Times*: 20.
Although alcohol has long been synonymous
    "Campus Drinking: Who, Why and How Much." *U.S. News & World Report* 20 June 1994: 20.

Page 69
"No longer can teen births be written off"
  Becklund, Laurie. "I Wanted Somebody to Love." *Los Angeles Times* 14 March 1993: E1.
only 26 percent of women in 1971
  Mnookin, Robert. *In the Interest of Children: Advocacy Law Reform and Public Policy*: 156.
In 1978 alone there were more than 1.1 million teenage pregnancies
  Perry, Nancy J. "Why It's Tough to Be a Girl." *Fortune* 10 August 1992: 82.
more than one teenage girl in ten
  Kantrowitz, Barbara et al. "Kids and Contraceptives." *Newsweek* 16 February 1987: 58.
The rate of births to teenage mothers dropped steadily
  Vinovskis, Maris A. *An "Epidemic" of Adolescent Pregnancy?* New York: Oxford University Press, 1988: 25; and Census Data cited in: *USA by Numbers*: 74.

Page 70
Graph of young women's sexual activity
  Cited in: Barringer, Felicity. "What Is Youth Coming To?": E1.
The ratio of abortions to births
  Mnookin, Robert. *In the Interest of Children: Advocacy Law Reform and Public Policy*: 158.
Over a half-million teenage girls each year
  Family Planning Perspectives. The Alan Guttmacher Institute. Cited in: *USA by Numbers*: 83.
(n) the teenage birth rate also took a turn for the worse
  McLeod, Dara. "Teen-Age Births in U.S. Hit Highest Level in 15 Years." *Los Angeles Times* 13 December 1991: A21.

Page 71
mothers who were not married
  Kantrowitz, Barbara et al. "Kids and Contraceptives": 54.
Only eighty-seven thousand babies were born to unwed teens in 1960
  Census Data cited in: *USA by Numbers*: 74.
"a sense that they alone call the shots"
  Quoted in: Williams, Lena. "Teen-Age Sex: New Codes Amid the Old Anxiety." *New York Times* 27 February 1989: A1.
"They're little kids with grown-up problems"
  Kantrowitz, Barbara et al. "Kids and Contraceptives": 65. Girls in particular seem to seek sex as a substitute for a lack of familial affection. See Perry, Nancy J. "Why It's Tough to Be a Girl": 82.
An often volatile debate
  Kantrowitz, Barbara et al. "Kids and Contraceptives": 64.
"squeal law"
  Vinovskis, Maris A. *An "Epidemic" of Adolescent Pregnancy?*: 109.
only 28 percent of the fathers of teenage girls
  Kirst, Michael W. et al. *Conditions of Children in California*, Berkeley: PACE School of Education: 357.
In San Diego County, adult men fathered 85 percent
  Louv, Richard. *Childhood's Future: Listening to the American Family. New Hope for the Next Generation*: 154.
"This used to be called statutory rape"
  Quoted in: Louv, Richard. *Childhood's Future: Listening to the American Family. New Hope for the Next Generation*: 154.

Page 72
Two and a half million adolescents a year
   Leary, Warren E. "Gloomy Report on the Health of Teenagers." *New York Times* 9 June 1990: 24.
The Alan Guttmacher Institute estimates
   Barringer, Felicity. "Report Finds 1 in 5 Infected by Viruses Spread Sexually." *New York Times* 1 April 1993: A1.
those aged twenty to twenty-nine accounted for 21 percent
   Louv, Richard. *Childhood's Future: Listening to the American Family. New Hope for the Next Generation*: 156.
despite a decade of AIDS awareness
   Perlman, David. "Unsafe Sex Common Among Bay Area Gays." *San Francisco Chronicle* 8 August 1994: A3.
As one nineteen-year-old explained
   Cited in: Jones, Robert A. "Dangerous Liaisons." *Los Angeles Times Magazine* 25 July 1993: 10.
The incidence of gonorrhea
   Goleman, Daniel. "Teen-Agers Called Shrewd Judges of Risk." *New York Times* 2 March 1993: B5.
The Centers for Disease Control found
   "Health Report." *Time* 30 August 1993: 16. If not detected early, gonorrhea can lead to heart and joint problems, infertility, and can also increase the risk of HIV infection.

Page 73
"Never before has one generation of American teenagers"
   Cited in: Leary, Warren E. "Gloomy Report on the Health of Teenagers": 24.
an eighteen-year-old freshman at the University of Massachusetts
   Finder, Alan. "Like Russian Roulette, But with Elevators." *New York Times* 17 April 1990: B1.
The activity, called "tracking,"
   Sims, Calvin. "Youths Playing Deadly Game in Subway." *New York Times* 23 January 1991: B1.

Page 74
Like the football hero of a movie
   Hinds, Michael DeCourcy. "Not Like the Movie: A Dare to Test Nerves Turns Deadly." *New York Times* 29 October 1993, national ed.: A1.
callers to the Palm Beach County Probation Department
   Sterling, Bruce. *The Hacker Crackdown*. New York: Bantam, 1992: 99–102.

Page 75
some six thousand computers linked by the Internet system
   Sterling, Bruce. *The Hacker Crackdown*: 88.
the Legion of Doom
   Ibid.: 282.
The Southern Bell inquiry alone
   Ibid.: 99.
Gallup poll asked Americans who was more reckless
   August 7, 1989.
Dr. Mimi Mahon has observed
   Hinds, Michael DeCourcy. "Not Like the Movie: A Dare to Test Nerves Turns Deadly": A1.
One recent study of 199 youths aged twelve to eighteen and their parents
   Goleman, Daniel. "Teen-Agers Called Shrewd Judges of Risk": B5.

Page 76
a tragic event in March 1987
   Martz, Larry et al. "The Copycat Suicides." *Newsweek* 23 March 1987: 28–9.

Page 77
Suicide chart
   Statistical Abstract of the United States, 1992: Table No. 126.

Page 78
second leading cause of death
   Hewlett, Sylvia Ann. *When the Bough Breaks: The Cost of Neglecting Our Children*: 91.
the rate for ten- to fourteen-year-olds
   Results of a study by Johns Hopkins University researchers cited in: Louv, Richard. *Childhood's Future: Listening to the American Family. New Hope for the Next Generation*: 166.
five thousand teenagers a year were committing suicide
   Elkind, David. *All Grown Up With No Place to Go*: 7.
According to the CDC Youth Risk Behavior Survey
   Cited in: "Attempted Suicide Among High School Students—United States, 1990." *Journal of the American Medical Association* 9 October 1991: 1911.
the suicide rates for all other age groups
   The rate among the older boomers aged thirty-five to forty-four in 1988, for example, has fallen by about 12 percent since 1970, and the rate for those aged forty-five to fifty-four fell by 25 percent. *Statistical Abstract of the United States, 1992*: Table No. 126.
the adolescent term "doing it,"
   Gaines, Donna. *Teenage Wasteland: Suburbia's Dead End Kids*: 247.
During a seventeen-month period ending in 1980
   "Suicide Belt." *Time* 1 September 1980: 56.
A single Washington, D.C., youth home
   Engel, Margaret. "8 Suicide Attemts Reported at D.C. Youth Home Since January." *Washington Post* 30 May 1986: A1.
the director of the D.C. Receiving Home for Children
   Engel, Margaret. "8 Suicide Attempts Reported at D.C. Youth Home Since January": A1.
Bergenfield's police chief described the four teenagers
   Martz, Larry et al. "The Copycat Suicides": 28–9.
one out of every three adolescents
   Results of a CDC survey cited in: Louv, Richard. *Childhood's Future: Listening to the American Family. New Hope for the Next Generation*: 166.

Page 79
depression has been cited as a factor
   DenHouter, Kathryn V. "To Silence One's Self: A Brief Analysis of the Literature on Adolescent Suicide." *Child Welfare* January 1981: 2–11.
between 6 and 8 percent of junior- and senior-high-school students
   Frymier, Jack. "Understanding and Preventing Teen Suicide": 290.
A 1988 study of 752 families by researchers
   Cited in: Hewlett, Sylvia Ann. *When the Bough Breaks: The Cost of Neglecting Our Children*: 91. Another study, by Emile Durkheim, also showed a strong correlation between suicide and family stability: The highest rates of attempted and successful suicides were found among families with single, divorced, or widowed parents, whereas the lowest rates were generally associated with a strong family life. DenHouter, Kathryn V. "To Silence One's Self: A Brief Analysis of the Literature on Adolescent Suicide": 3.

Page 80
Amount spent
U.S. Department of Health and Human Services, *Health United States*, 1993: table 140.
Richard Nixon made a foreboding request
Quoted in: Schrag, Peter and Divoky, Diane. *The Myth of the Hyperactive Child and Other Means of Child Control*: 3.
Hutschnecker maintained that studies
Ibid.: 4.
proposed that every child
Ibid.: 6.

Page 81
a number of school systems across the nation
Schrag, Peter and Divoky, Diane. *The Myth of the Hyperactive Child and Other Means of Child Control*: 7.
The wave of special-education laws
Ibid.: xii.
it purportedly afflicted as many as 40 percent of all children
Brutten, Milton et al. *Something's Wrong With My Child*. New York: Harcourt, Brace, Jovanovich, 1973: 10.
task force organized by the Public Health Service
Hughes, Richard and Brewin, Robert. *The Tranquilizing of America: Pill Popping and the American Way of Life*. New York: Warner Books, 1987: 134.

Page 82
the numbers had already risen
Schrag, Peter and Divoky, Diane. *The Myth of the Hyperactive Child and Other Means of Child Control:* 35.
"But it's not the broken marriage that causes the LD"
Quoted in: Schrag, Peter and Divoky, Diane. *The Myth of the Hyperactive Child and Other Means of Child Control*: 52.
Psychiatrist Camilla Anderson
Cited in: Schrag, Peter and Divoky, Diane. *The Myth of the Hyperactive Child and Other Means of Child Control*: 52.
Ms. Anderson's recommendation to sterilize all MBD victims
Ibid.
the drugs of choice were Ritalin
Schrag, Peter and Divoky, Diane. *The Myth of the Hyperactive Child and Other Means of Child Control*: 71.
one hundred and fifty thousand children
Cited in: Hughes, Richard and Brewin, Robert. *The Tranquilizing of America: Pill Popping and the American Way of Life*: 130.
The number climbed to almost half a million
Coles, Gerald. *The Learning Mystique: A Critical Look at "Learning Disabilities."* New York: Pantheon, 1987: 92.
Authors Richard Hughes and Robert Brewin estimate
Hughes, Richard and Brewin, Robert. *The Tranquilizing of America: Pill Popping and the American Way of Life:* 130.
The drugs were recommended for children
Ibid.: 128.

"The MBD Child: A Guide for Parents"
    Cited in: Schrag, Peter and Divoky, Diane. *The Myth of the Hyperactive Child and Other Means of Child Control*: 58.

Page 83
The National Easter Seal Society heralded the benefits
    Hughes, Richard and Brewin, Robert. *The Tranquilizing of America: Pill Popping and the American Way of Life*: 135.
"the affliction of geniuses."
    Related in: Coles, Gerald. *The Learning Mystique: A Critical Look at "Learning Disabilities"*: 123.
"Future teachers will be trained in a school"
    Cited in: Hughes, Richard and Brewin, Robert. *The Tranquilizing of America: Pill Popping and the American Way of Life*: 321.
"schoolteachers are very impressed with drug therapy"
    Ibid.: 143.

Page 84
the experience of a family
    Cited in: Schrag, Peter and Divoky, Diane. *The Myth of the Hyperactive Child and Other Means of Child Control*: 74.
Dr. Nancy Durant, a New Jersey child psychiatrist
    Hughes, Richard and Brewin, Robert. *The Tranquilizing of America: Pill Popping and the American Way of Life*: 146.
One Fordham University sociologist explained
    Ibid.: 138.
"the smart pill"
    Ibid.: 137.

Page 85
"the best testament to the effectiveness of chemotherapy"
    Alabiso, Frank P. and Hansen, James C. *The Hyperactive Child in the Classroom*. Springfield, IL: Charles C. Thomas, 1977: 47.
the original 1966 Public Health Service task force
    Hughes, Richard and Brewin, Robert. *The Tranquilizing of America: Pill Popping and the American Way of Life*: 134.
"of the 756 reports on the psychotropic medication of children"
    Schrag, Peter and Divoky, Diane. *The Myth of the Hyperactive Child and Other Means of Child Control*: 84.
Dr. Gerald Coles reviewed every study
    Coles, Gerald. *The Learning Mystique: A Critical Look at "Learning Disabilities"*: 94.
A representative study published
    Reprinted in: Milliman, Howard L. et al. *Therapies for School Behavior Problems*. San Francisco: Jossey-Bass, 1980.
This controlled five-year study
    Hughes, Richard and Brewin, Robert. *The Tranquilizing of America: Pill Popping and the American Way of Life*: 149.

Page 86
"after decades of research"
    Coles, Gerald. *The Learning Mystique: A Critical Look at "Learning Disabilities"*: xii.

there was "no significant difference"
: While this study had found a hopeful clue to the biological origins of the real hyperactivity that afflicts a small percentage of the population, it found no connection between these possible metabolic differences and learning disabilities. Zametkin, Alan J., M.D., et al. "Cerebral Glucose Metabolism in Adults with Hyperactivity of Childhood Onset." *New England Journal of Medicine* 15 November 1990: 1365.

the FDA finally ordered it eliminated
: Hughes, Richard and Brewin, Robert. *The Tranquilizing of America: Pill Popping and the American Way of Life*: 132.

MBD was removed from the 1980 edition
: Coles, Gerald. *The Learning Mystique: A Critical Look at "Learning Disabilities"*: 93.

The use of psychoactive drugs on kids dropped off
: Hughes, Richard and Brewin, Robert. *The Tranquilizing of America: Pill Popping and the American Way of Life:* 149. As of 1988, it was estimated that 800,000 children were on Ritalin, although the drug is now generally prescribed as part of a complete process involving the entire family, the school, and the physician. Says Dr. J. H. Satterfield, director of research for the National Center for Hyperactive Children, "We switched from the notion that stimulant medication treatment alone is adequate treatment for these children a long time ago." See Cowart, Virginia S. "The Ritalin Controversy: What's Made This Drug's Opponents Hyperactive?" *Journal of the American Medical Association* 6 May 1988: 2521–3.

"the 'enlightened' answer to spanking"
: Schrag, Peter and Divoky, Diane. *The Myth of the Hyperactive Child and Other Means of Child Control*: 71.

One mother relates how her five-year-old son was affected
: Hughes, Richard and Brewin, Robert. *The Tranquilizing of America: Pill Popping and the American Way of Life*: 128.

Other adverse reactions include
: Ibid.: 330.

Ritalin had been banned in Sweden and Japan
: A Johns Hopkins study by Doctors Daniel Safer and Richard Allen of the University's Division of Child Psychiatry found that the use of dextroamphetamine, one commonly prescribed drug for hyperactivity in children, caused a "drop of 38 percent in weight and 25 percent reduction in height. Ritalin has also produced a 17 percent drop in growth and some weight loss over the same period of time." Cited in: Wooden, Kenneth. *Weeping in the Playtime of Others.* New York: McGraw-Hill, 1976: 66.

Dr. Gerald Coles cites as an example a series of studies
: Coles, Gerald. *The Learning Mystique: A Critical Look at "Learning Disabilities"*: 30.

Page 87

other studies showed that a simple change in the child's diet
: This concept was developed by Dr. Ben F. Feingold. This approach has been found to work with some, but not all, children. Hughes, Richard and Brewin, Robert. *The Tranquilizing of America: Pill Popping and the American Way of Life:* 154. A 1983 study by Susan Pollard found that among children diagnosed as hyperactive, parent training was found to be equally effective to methylphenidate (Ritalin) in producing improvements in the child's behavior. Pollard, Susan, et al. "The Effects of Parent Training and Ritalin on the Parent-Child Interactions of Hyperactive Boys." *Child and Family Behavior Therapy* Winter 1983: 51–69.

"some kids even learn to ask for their pills"
: Granger, Lori and Granger, Bill. *The Magic Feather: The Truth About "Special Education."* New York: Dutton, 1986: 95.

"The drugs hid the child's real personality"
    Quoted in: Hughes, Richard and Brewin, Robert. *The Tranquilizing of America: Pill Popping and the American Way of Life*: 157.
"an entire generation is slowly being conditioned"
    Schrag, Peter and Divoky, Diane. *The Myth of the Hyperactive Child and Other Means of Child Control*: xvii.
a blue-ribbon panel assembled in Washington
    Hughes, Richard and Brewin, Robert. *The Tranquilizing of America: Pill Popping and the American Way of Life*: 139.
One study that tracked a group of 103
    In this study of white, middle-class youths begun in the mid-seventies by researchers at the Long Island Jewish Medical Center and the New York State Psychiatric Institute, it was found that 4 percent of an unmedicated control group of boys later developed drug-abuse problems compared to 16 percent of the boys who had been treated for hyperactivity. The drugs hardly assisted in educational attainment either, as 25 percent of the treated boys had dropped out of high school compared with just 2 percent of the control group. Cited in: Cowley, Geoffrey with Cooper, Joshua. "The Not-Young and the Restless." *Newsweek* 26 July 1993: 48–9.

Page 88
there were a number of medical breakthroughs
    Schrag, Peter and Divoky, Diane. *The Myth of the Hyperactive Child and Other Means of Child Control*: i.
One author explains that terms like MBD and LD
    Coles, Gerald. *The Learning Mystique: A Critical Look at "Learning Disabilities"*: 196.
more than 4 *billion* Valium and Librium
    Hughes, Richard and Brewin, Robert. *The Tranquilizing of America: Pill Popping and the American Way of Life*: 20.

Page 89
Parham v. J.R.
    442 U.S. 584, 99 S. Ct. 2493
Lois Weithorn, a psychologist and lawyer
    Quoted in: Hewlett, Sylvia Ann. *When the Bough Breaks: The Cost of Neglecting Our Children*: 126.
there were only 6,500 minors nationwide
    Hewlett, Sylvia Ann. *When the Bough Breaks: The Cost of Neglecting Our Children*: 124.
the number had already doubled
    Gelman, David et al. "Treating Teens in Trouble." *Newsweek* 20 January 1986: 52–4.
shot up 350 percent to nearly 50,000
    Gelmen, David et al. "Treating Teens in Trouble": 52–4.
the figure had reached nearly 200,000.
    Hewlett, Sylvia Ann. *When the Bough Breaks: The Cost of Neglecting Our Children*: 124. The average age of admission had also dropped over the two-decade period. Louv, Richard. *Childhood's Future: Listening to the American Family. New Hope for the Next Generation*: 166.
nebulous conditions like "conduct disorder"
    Gelman, David et al. "Treating Teens in Trouble": 52–4; Lyon, Banning. "You're Sane Now." *New York Times* 13 October 1993, national ed.: A13.
House Select Committee on Children, Youth and Families
    Gelman, David et al. "Treating Teens in Trouble": 52–4.

A recent University of Michigan study
   Cited in: Hewlett, Sylvia Ann. *When the Bough Breaks: The Cost of Neglecting Our Children*: 125.

Page 90
most of the children studied had been hospitalized
   Louv, Richard. *Childhood's Future: Listening to the American Family. New Hope for the Next Generation*: 166.
Between 1969 and 1982, private ownership
   Gelman, David et al. "Treating Teens in Trouble": 52–4.
growing by 20 percent a year
   Hewlett, Sylvia Ann. *When the Bough Breaks: The Cost of Neglecting Our Children*: 127.
The *Chicago Tribune* reported a contest
   Cited in: Hewlett, Sylvia Ann. *When the Bough Breaks: The Cost of Neglecting Our Children*: 127.
thirteen states had mandated that insurance plans
   Gelman, David et al. "Treating Teens in Trouble": 52–4.
"There are a lot of options available"
   Quoted in: Gelman, David et al. "Treating Teens in Trouble": 52–4.
the length of a patient's stay
   Hewlett, Sylvia Ann. *When the Bough Breaks: The Cost of Neglecting Our Children*: 127. Insurance fraud was likely a significant contributor to the explosive growth of such facilities, as the hospitals gleaned enormous profits by inflating claims and keeping teens confined as long as payments were flowing. In late 1993, National Medical Enterprises, which owned 132 psychiatric hospitals, agreed to pay insurers Aetna, Metropolitan Life, and Cigna $125 million to settle charges that it had fraudulently filed over $700 million in bogus claims. Lyon, Banning. "You're Sane Now": A13.
"divorce and single parenthood"
   Hewlett, Sylvia Ann. *When the Bough Breaks: The Cost of Neglecting Our Children*: 125.
more than 80 percent of children confined
   Magnet, Myron. "The American Family": 42–7.

Page 91
"Hospitals may be the most"
   Quoted in: Gelman, David et al. "Treating Teens in Trouble": 52–4.

Page 92
children who set off on their own
   A quote by Cynthia Myers of the National Runaway Switchboard in: Elkind, David. *All Grown Up With No Place to Go*: 194.
most estimates put the figure
   Forst, Martin L. and Blomquist, Martha-Elin. *Missing Children: Rhetoric and Reality*: 34.
This was roughly double the number of 1970
   An estimated 600,000 children were runaways in 1970. Cited in: Elkind, David. *All Grown Up With No Place to Go*: 194.

Page 93
Los Angeles officials estimated
   Forst, Martin L. and Blomquist, Martha-Elin. *Missing Children: Rhetoric and Reality*: 35. It's estimated that about 12 percent of runaways are so-called cross-country runners. Hughes, Della. "Running Away: A 50-50 Chance to Survive?" *USA Today* September 1989: 65.

125,000 a year, according to one 1988 study
   Forst, Martin L. and Blomquist, Martha-Elin. *Missing Children: Rhetoric and Reality*: 42.
offenses such as misbehaving, getting pregnant
   Kolodny, Robert C., et al. *How to Survive Your Adolescent's Adolescence*: 239.
a 1989 House committee put the total number of throwaways
   Rich, Spencer. " 'Discarded' Child Population Put at Nearly 500,000." *Washington Post* 12 December 1989: A1.
The House panel, for example, cited the growing problems
   Rich, Spencer. " 'Discarded' Child Population Put at Nearly 500,000": A1. Della Hughes, chairman of the National Network of Runaway and Youth Services, notes that coming from a divorced, single-parent, or blended family greatly increases the chances that a young person will take off in search of help outside of the home. Hughes, Della. "Running Away: A 50-50 Chance to Survive?": 65.
the vast majority were victims of physical or sexual abuse
   A 1987 survey conducted by the National Network of Runaway and Youth Services found that 61 percent of the teens served in U.S. shelters were victims of abuse. Hughes, Della. "Running Away: A 50-50 Chance to Survive?": 64.
About one in five panhandled
   Forst, Martin L. and Blomquist, Martha-Elin. *Missing Children: Rhetoric and Reality*: 197.
"Runaways in the streets for more than a month"
   Quoted in: Elkind, David. *All Grown Up With No Place to Go*: 196.
a major cause of death among boys
   Elkind, David. *All Grown Up With No Place to Go*: 197.
a *Newsweek* reporter found
   "Throwaway Kids." *Newsweek* 25 April 1988: 65.

Page 94
An estimated five thousand kids a year
   Ibid.: 64–8.
youth shelters remained woefully understaffed
   Taylor, Ronald B. *The Kid Business: How It Exploits the Children It Should Help*: 34.
a tendency toward building more jails and institutions
   Hughes, Della. "Running Away: A 50-50 Chance to Survive?": 66.
we were incarcerating our population
   Terry, Don. "The Glamour of the Big House: Doing Time in Prison Has Become a Macho Rite of Passage in the Inner City." *San Francisco Chronicle* 11 October 1992: This World Section.
Juvenile arrests were on the decline
   For example, there were 85,418 juvenile arrests for violent crime and 733,775 arrests for property crime nationwide in 1975. There were just 64,344 juvenile arrests for violent crime in 1984, along with 570,919 property crime arrests. FBI Uniform Crime Reports, 1975, 1984.
In California
   In California, 127,842 juveniles were arrested for felonies in 1975. But there were only 73,521 such arrests in 1985, a drop of nearly half. Even when the slightly smaller size of the Free population is taken into account, there was still a 36 percent decline in the share of the juvenile population arrested. However, even though the number of juveniles arrested was nearly halved from 1975 to 1985, the population of the California Youth Authority's state detention facilities *rose* by 50 percent! In addition, the number of juveniles on probation increased by 66 percent, and the number in county detention centers was up by 24 percent. Kirst, Michael W. et al. *Conditions of Children in California, Berkeley: PACE School of Education*: 261, 266, 375; Louv, Richard. *Childhood's Future: Listening to the American Family. New Hope for the Next Generation*: 396.

Police forces across the country began planting "moles"
  Banks, Sandy. "Students Held in Drug Sweeps at 9 Schools." *Los Angeles Times* 15 November 1983: II-1.

Page 95
Graph of homicide rates
  Butterfield, Fox. "Seeds of Murder Epidemic: Teen-Age Boys With Guns." *New York Times* 19 October 1992, national ed.: A8.
on any given day, there were almost eight thousand young people
  Quoted in: Wooden, Kenneth. *Weeping in the Playtime of Others*: 27.
California *alone* could claim this many teenage inmates.
  In 1987 California housed 8,385 in its California Youth Authority institutions. Kirst, Michael W. et al. *Conditions of Children in California, Berkeley: PACE School of Education*: 375.
one young black man in four
  Cited in: Terry, Don. "The Glamour of the Big House: Doing Time in Prison Has Become a Macho Rite of Passage in the Inner City": This World Section.

Page 96
the greatest increase in the overall crime rate
  While the total number of juvenile arrests of boys increased by 3.1 percent from 1982 to 1991, arrests of girls rose by 15 percent. For violent crimes, the number of girls arrested soared by 62 percent. FBI Uniform Crime Reports, 1992, Table 33.
the arrest rates of older adults
  Butterfield, Fox. "Seeds of Murder Epidemic: Teen-Age Boys With Guns": A8.
"it was fun"
  Quoted in: Baker, Susan and Gore, Tipper. "Some Reasons for 'Wilding.'" *Newsweek* 29 May 1989: 6.
four Chicago youths were murdered by fellow teenagers
  Darnton, Nina. "Street Crimes of Fashion." *Newsweek* 5 March 1990: 58.
Three 1988 New York City prep-school graduates
  Carlson, Margaret. "Five Friends in a Car." *Time* 11 July 1988: 20.
sealed court records
  Murray, Charles. *Losing Ground: American Social Policy 1950–1980*: 171.
Cameron Kocher of Kunkletown, Pennsylvania
  In late 1992, Cameron Kocher arranged to enter a no-contest plea to involuntary manslaughter and was placed on probation until age twenty-one. Anderson, Charles-Edward. "Grown-up Crime, Boy Defendant." *ABA Journal* November 1989: 26–7; Lowry, Tom. "The Little Boy with a Gun." *Ladies Home Journal* April 1991: 124; Raske, Henry J. "Kocher Enters Plea; Avoids Adult Trial for Playmate's Killing." *ABA Journal* December 1992: 21.

Page 97
laws were changed so that children
  Postman, Neil. *The Disappearance of Childhood*: 135.
Nationwide, a total of 61,253 children
  Forer, Lois G. *Unequal Protection: Women, Children, and the Elderly in Court*. New York: W. W. Norton, 1991: 116. Judge Lois Forer notes a number of discrepancies that remain in the system that, while allowing for trying a child as an adult, don't allow the same rights accorded to adults. For instance, the courts can detain an alleged juvenile offender without a warrant, deny him the right to bail, and refuse other constitutional protections such as the right to a speedy trial. Since most cases involving adolescents originate in the juvenile courts, where rights are not as explicit, before being transferred to adult court, protections such as these are allowed to slide during the period in between. Other rights denied juveniles whose cases are later referred

to adult court are entitlement to a police lineup, rights to examine police records, and the right to have an attorney present during questioning.

While the average sentence of a young person convicted
    1975 statistics from U.S. Bureau of Prisons Annual Statistical Report. 1991 statistics from U.S. Bureau of Justice Statistics, Federal Criminal Case Processing, 1980–89, October 1991.

eighteen-year-old Ronald Harmelin was ordered in 1986
    Greenhouse, Linda. "Life Sentence Upheld for First-Time Drug Possession." *San Francisco Chronicle* 28 June 1991: A19.

prison became so commonplace in the inner cities
    Terry, Don. "The Glamour of the Big House: Doing Time in Prison Has Become a Macho Rite of Passage in the Inner City": This World Section.

Terry Roach was all of seventeen
    Stengel, Richard. "Young Crime, Old Punishment." *Time* 20 January 1986: 22–3.

Page 98
Paula Cooper became the youngest female on death row
    Landau, Elaine. *Teens and the Death Penalty*. Hillside, NJ: Enslow, 1992: 91.

author Ronald Taylor described the mood
    Taylor, Ronald B. *The Kid Business: How It Exploits the Children It Should Help*: 112.

In 1986 there were thirty-one prisoners on death row
    Cited in: Stengel, Richard. "Young Crime, Old Punishment": 23.

Amnesty International found that
    Landau, Elaine. *Teens and the Death Penalty*: 102.

In 1988, the Supreme Court barred executions
    "Reprieved. Paula Cooper." *Time* 24 July 1989: 49.

Ronald Ward thus had his sentence modified to life imprisonment
    "Young Death Row Inmate Gets New 'Life' Sentence." *Jet* 21 March 1988: 24.

"Won't nobody have to drag me in there"
    Quoted in: Stengel, Richard. "Young Crime, Old Punishment": 22.

As he sat strapped in the chair
    Landau, Elaine. *Teens and the Death Penalty*: 63.

A 1987 Gallup poll showed
    Poll published on December 4, 1988, asked, "Do you favor or oppose the death penalty for persons convicted of murder?" Age 18–29, 83 percent were in favor; age 30–49, 80 percent were in favor; age 50 and over, 77 percent were in favor.

Page 99
Recent college surveys
    In the 1985 American Council on Education survey of college freshman, only 27 percent opposed the death penalty and 69 percent felt there was too much concern for the rights of criminals. In 1969 the figures were 56 percent and 52 percent. Cited in: Schwartz, Joe. "From Ban the Bomb to Benetton." *American Demographics* September 1987: 58–60.

From the mid-seventies to the mid-eighties
    Fingerhut, Lois A., et al. "Firearm and Nonfirearm Homicide Among Persons 15 Through 19 Years of Age: Difference by Level of Urbanization, United States, 1979 Through 1989." *Journal of the American Medical Association* 10 June 1992: 3048.

81 percent of the victims of all violent crime
    Cited in: Baker, Susan and Gore, Tipper. "Some Reasons for 'Wilding.'"

For all teenagers
    Fingerhut, Lois A., et al. "Firearm and Nonfirearm Homicide Among Persons 15 Through 19 Years of Age: Difference by Level of Urbanization, United States, 1979 Through 1989": 3048.

in *four out of five* cases
: Between the ages of fifteen and twenty-four. Cited in: Derber, Charles. *Money, Murder and the American Dream: Wilding from Wall Street to Main Street*: 112.

Edna Williams of Newark, New Jersey, explained
: Nieves, Evelyn. "Young Newark Shooting Victim Becomes a Symbol of Conflict With Police." *New York Times* 9 October 1992, national ed.: A15.

Page 100

Fordham University Index of Social Well-Being
: Steinberg, Jacques. "U.S. Social Well-Being Is Rated Lowest Since Study Began in 1970." *New York Times* 5 October 1992, national ed.: 16; "Researchers Say U.S. Social Well-Being Is 'Awful.' *New York Times* 18 October 1993, national ed.: A12.

identified the following on an unlabeled map
: Taylor, Ronald A., et al. "Which Way Is the Pacific Ocean?" *U.S. News & World Report* 8 August 1988: 11.

Page 106

"For the first time in the history of our country"
: Cited in: Littwin, Susan. *The Postponed Generation: Why American Youth Are Growing Up Later*: 42.

"Traditional became synonymous with bad"
: Bigler, Philip and Lockard, Karen. *Failing Grades: A Teacher's Report Card on Education in America.* Arlington, VA: Vandamere Press, 1992: 136.

"old" values such as structured learning and professionalism
: Ravitch, Diane. *The Schools We Deserve: Reflections on the Educational Crises of Our Time.* New York: Basic Books, 1985: 36.

"schools should be a place where children learn"
: Holt, John. *How Children Fail.* New York: Delacorte, 1964: 289.

"Teachers' questions," wrote Holt, "like their tests, are *traps.*"
: Ibid.: 253.

"To a very great degree, school is a place"
: Ibid.: 263.

"Teachers," wrote Illich, "more often than not"
: Illich, Ivan. *Deschooling Society.* New York: Harper & Row, 1970: 29.

"School leads many to a kind of spiritual suicide."
: Ibid.: 60.

the sentiment wasn't only that teachers have failed to teach
: Ravitch, Diane. *The Schools We Deserve: Reflections on the Educational Crises of Our Time*: 68. The disdain, or at least indifference, toward teachers' roles in education is indicated in the utterances of James Allen, U.S. Commissioner of Education, as he launched the national "Right to Read" program in 1970. In proclaiming national literacy in the seventies as "education's moon," he called on the backing of a wide-ranging and diverse segment of the public: "Necessary will be committed participation and support of the Congress; state and local political leaders and legislative bodies; business, industry, and labor; civic and community groups; publishers; advertising organizations; television, radio, and the press; research and scientific organizations; foundations; the entertainment industry; the sports world; and perhaps most essential of all, the understanding and support of the enlightened and enthusiastic public." Apparently everyone's help was being solicited except teachers and their students. Smith, Frank. *Insult to Intelligence: The Bureaucratic Invasion of Our Schools.* New York: Arbor House, 1986: 88. Even in 1990, not a single teacher was invited to George Bush's educational summit.

this custom had largely been reversed
> In constant 1970 dollars, average teacher pay rose from $4,799 in 1950 to $8,840 in 1970. *Historical Statistics of the United States Colonial Times to 1970*: Series H, 520–530.

Teachers saw a decade-long salary decline during the seventies
> The average public school teacher salary was $15,000 in 1979, a drop of over 7 percent from 1970 after inflation. National Education Association. *Estimates of School Statistics, 1982–83*. Over the same period, salaries of other city employees remained about even, and even the beleaguered manufacturing sector was able to increase wages by 8 percent. U.S. Bureau of the Census. *City Employment,* series GE, No. 2, annual; U.S. Bureau of Labor Statistics, *Employment and Earnings,* monthly.

the average beginning salaries of teachers declined even more steeply
> Cited in: Farber, Barry A. *Crisis in Education: Stress and Burnout in the American Teacher*. San Francisco: Jossey-Bass, 1991: 64.

the number of educational professionals
> Bigler, Philip and Lockard, Karen. *Failing Grades: A Teacher's Report Card on Education in America*: 13.

During New York City's 1976 budget crisis
> Hiss, Tony. "The End of the Rainbow." *New Yorker* 12 April 1993: 51.

Chicago's Board of Education moved into its new headquarters
> Bennett, William J. *The Devaluing of America: The Fight for Our Culture and Our Children*. New York: Summit, 1992: 41.

Page 108
the reforms implemented by these new administrators
> Farber, Barry A. *Crisis in Education: Stress and Burnout in the American Teacher*: 137.

One popular program, called "DISTAR,"
> Smith, Frank. *Insult to Intelligence: The Bureaucratic Invasion of Our Schools*: 89.

Principals ordered mandatory exam review days
> Bigler, Philip and Lockard, Karen. *Failing Grades: A Teacher's Report Card on Education in America*: 54.

From 1969 to 1982, the number of parents
> Boyer, Ernest L., *The Carnegie Foundation for the Advancement of Teaching. High School: A Report on Secondary Education in America.* New York: Harper & Row, 1983: 154.

Nearly one in five 1970 college freshmen
> Ravitch, Diane. *The Schools We Deserve: Reflections on the Educational Crises of Our Time*: 94.

When a 1989 nationwide Gallup poll asked teachers
> Cited in: Farber, Barry A. *Crisis in Education: Stress and Burnout in the American Teacher*: 51. A poll published in 1991 asked teachers to respond to the statement "I feel that parents have made things easier for me." Three fourths of urban teachers replied either "never" or "rarely" to this as did two thirds of those in suburban schools. Farber, Barry A. *Crisis in Education: Stress and Burnout in the American Teacher*: 256.

In 1981, a full third of high-school teachers
> Boyer, Ernest L. *The Carnegie Foundation for the Advancement of Teaching. High School: A Report on Secondary Education in America*: 159.

A national sample of teachers who began their careers
> Cited in: Farber, Barry A. *Crisis in Education: Stress and Burnout in the American Teacher*: 111. A RAND Corporation study came to even more disheartening conclusions reporting that while at least 80 percent of new teachers stay for a second year, there is a steady attrition in subsequent years. Fewer than 30 percent of males and 50 percent of females were still teaching six years after they had begun.

the last few decades have seen primarily lower-achieving students
Preston, Samuel. "Children and the Elderly in the U.S.": 49. What's worse, even with lower-achieving students entering the teaching profession in the first place, the highest-scoring among these are the ones most likely to leave it. A study that followed students beginning with their senior year in high school found that the mean SAT score of those who enter the field of teaching and then leave it is forty-two points higher than those who enter it and stay. Thus, those who end up remaining permanently in the profession averaged a combined SAT score that was 118 points lower than those who never taught at all.
Eric A. Hanushek of the University of Rochester reviewed 130 studies
Preston, Samuel. "Children and the Elderly in the U.S.": 48.

Page 109
School Opinion Chart
Gallup, George. "Gallup poll of the Public's Attitudes Toward the Public Schools." *Phi Delta Kappan* September 1981: 35.
A 1955 Gallup poll found that two thirds of Americans
Gallup polls cited in: Boyer, Ernest L. *The Carnegie Foundation for the Advancement of Teaching. High School: A Report on Secondary Education in America*: 19.
Only four dollars in ten
U.S. National Center for Education Statistics. *Bond Sales for Public School Purposes*, annual.
Californians voted by a two-to-one margin for Proposition 13
Issel, William. *Social Change in the United States 1945–1983*. New York: Schocken Books, 1985: 151.

Page 110
Prop 13 precipitated drastic cuts
Speich, Don F. and Weiner, Stephen S. *In the Eye of the Storm: Proposition 13 and Public Education in California*: 34.
A 1983 survey of 100 school districts
Boyer, Ernest L. *The Carnegie Foundation for the Advancement of Teaching. High School: A Report on Secondary Education in America*: 294. From 1960 to 1987 the proportion of urban school budgets spent on building maintenance decreased from 9.6 percent to just 3.5 percent. See Farber, Barry A. *Crisis in Education: Stress and Burnout in the American Teacher*: 67, and Boyer, Ernest L. *The Carnegie Foundation for the Advancement of Teaching. High School: A Report on Secondary Education in America*: 294.
nearly twice the *total* federal funding
Total federal spending in 1983 on primary and secondary education was $14.5 billion. U.S. National Center for Education Statistics. *Federal Support for Education, Fiscal Years 1980 to 1984.* June 1985. According to the National Center for Education Statistics, the total expenditures per pupil in American schools rose by 82 percent from the beginning of the 1950s to the end of the decade. This trend continued in the sixties with a 58-percent increase over that ten-year period. Then things began to dry up with the seventies and eighties seeing funding rise by less than half this rate, while at the same time schools were asked to perform a great number of additional tasks—all costing money. Programs were mandated for special education, free school lunches, and accommodating handicapped students, among others, all justifiable additions, but all costly and demanding more funding than was allocated, forcing resources from traditional classroom studies. See: Odden, Allen R. *Rethinking School Finance: An Agenda for the 1990s*. San Francisco: Jossey-Bass, 1992.
a movement swept the country
Ravitch, Diane. *The Schools We Deserve: Reflections on the Educational Crises of Our Time*: 84.

Page 111
(n) the U.S. lagged behind
"U.S. Is Said to Lag in School Spending." *New York Times* 16 January 1990: A23.
Classroom walls were literally torn down
Boyer, Ernest L., *The Carnegie Foundation for the Advancement of Teaching. High School: A Report on Secondary Education in America*: 56.
"The idea was no longer to 'educate' the child"
Ravitch, Diane. *The Schools We Deserve: Reflections on the Educational Crises of Our Time*: 86.
At least five major national studies
See: Passow, Harry A. "Reforming America's High Schools." *Education Digest* October 1975: 2–5.
A group of business executives in California calling themselves the California Roundtable
Ravitch, Diane. *The Schools We Deserve: Reflections on the Educational Crises of Our Time*: 65.

Page 112
The vast majority of high schools established special smoking areas
Bigler, Philip and Lockard, Karen. *Failing Grades: A Teacher's Report Card on Education in America*: 46.
he would feel the flush of self-worth
Honig, Bill. *Last Chance For Our Children: How You Can Help Save Our Schools.* Reading, MA: Addison-Wesley, 1985: 74.
"The most important job in junior high"
Quoted in: "Choice Politics." *Wall Street Journal* 15 October 1993: A12.
the researchers found that teachers often made little association
Powell, Arthur G., et al. *The Shopping Mall High School.* Boston: Houghton Mifflin, 1985: 58.
"failure comes from not attending"
Powell, Arthur G., et al. *The Shopping Mall High School*: 59.

Page 113
the parents of the Free didn't even consider academic work
Polls show that students feel the same way. Cited in: Powell, Arthur G., et al. *The Shopping Mall High School:* 303.
Berkeley, California, instituted a series of experimental minischools
Collier, Peter and Horowitz, David. *Destructive Generation: Second Thoughts About the '60s.* New York: Summit, 1989: 207. Directly affecting a larger number of students, a Washington, D.C., federal judge ordered school administrators in 1967 to abandon ability grouping—a conventional practice of assigning similarly skilled children to a common work group. The judge deemed that such a practice discriminated against black students. Superintendents complained of hundreds of court orders regulating every aspect of schooling, hiring, promotion, curriculum, and financing. Minority-rights advocates in particular persuaded the courts that the high failure and suspension rates had nothing to do with student shortcomings caused by a wide range of factors, but were blatant examples of racism. Hands tied by the ensuing court orders, public education reduced itself to the lowest common denominator so as to exhibit no biases whatsoever. The weak programs instituted on behalf of disadvantaged students ended up as ineffectual for all, but particularly for just those students most in need. See: Ravitch, Diane. *The Schools We Deserve: Reflections on the Educational Crises of Our Time.*
In a ruling handed down in Ann Arbor, Michigan
Honig, Bill. *Last Chance For Our Children: How You Can Help Save Our Schools*: 76.
Average High School Grades of College Freshmen
The Higher Education Research Institute, UCLA. *The American Freshman: National Norms,* annual.

Page 114
the Ann Arbor mandate was dropped after only a few years
   Ravitch, Diane. *The Schools We Deserve: Reflections on the Educational Crises of Our Time*: 265.
international math test given to thirteen-year-olds
   Finn, Chester E., Jr. "A Nation Still at Risk": 49.
"The homework habit is disgraceful"
   Neill, A. S. *Summerhill: A Radical Approach to Child Rearing*. New York: Hart Publishing, 1960: 378.
A 1979 survey by the California Department of Education
   Honig, Bill: *Last Chance For Our Children: How You Can Help Save Our Schools*: 139.
the average amount of time high schoolers devoted to homework
   The average time was cut from ten hours a week to five. Cited in: Hewlett, Sylvia Ann. *When the Bough Breaks: The Cost of Neglecting Our Children*: 94.
A math teacher explained his position
   Powell, Arthur G., et al. *The Shopping Mall High School*: 80.
Another teacher complained to the *Los Angeles Times*
   Armbruster, Frank E. *Our Children's Crippled Future: How American Education Has Failed*. New York: Quadrangle, 1977: 105.
a new school policy mandated that the four novels assigned
   Powell, Arthur G., et al. *The Shopping Mall High School*: 80.

Page 115
From 1970 to 1977 alone, enrollments in nonsectarian private schools
   Boyer, Ernest L., *The Carnegie Foundation for the Advancement of Teaching*. *High School: A Report on Secondary Education in America*: 282.
an estimated nine out of ten parents who could afford it
   Derber, Charles. *Money, Murder and the American Dream: Wilding From Wall Street to Main Street*: 124.
nearly half of Chicago's public-school teachers
   Bennett, William J. *The Devaluing of America: The Fight for Our Culture and Our Children*: 64.
A 1982 report by sociologist James Coleman
   Coleman, James S., et al. *High School Achievement: Public, Catholic, and Private High Schools Compared*. New York: Basic Books, 1982. Despite the greater academic attainment in private schools, Coleman noted that those in public schools nevertheless earn higher grades than their counterparts.
Universities dramatically lowered their academic requirements
   Ravitch, Diane. *The Schools We Deserve: Reflections on the Educational Crises of Our Time*: 52. A 1979 study by the College Board found only 56 percent of four-year public colleges requiring even a single high-school English class for incoming freshman. Only 51 percent demanded a mathematics course, and barely a third required completing any type of physical-science course. Boyer, Ernest L. *College: The Undergraduate Experience in America*. New York: Harper & Row, 1987: 30.
Requisite courses had been so thoroughly eliminated
   Boyer, Ernest L., *The Carnegie Foundation for the Advancement of Teaching*. *High School: A Report on Secondary Education in America*: 252, and Boyer, Ernest L. *College: The Undergraduate Experience in America*: 26. Requirements hadn't been completely eliminated, but their nature certainly changed after the sixties. The 1984 "Path Study" conducted by a Stanford University team found that of the few subjects California's schools did require, 42 percent were nonacademic in nature. Physical education, consumer education, and driver's training pro-

vided the bulk of these. Honig, Bill. *Last Chance For Our Children: How You Can Help Save Our Schools*: 44. In thirteen other states, over half of a typical high school student's credits came from electives such as these. Magnet, Myron. "How to Smarten Up the Schools." *Fortune* 117 1988: 86–90+. Reprinted in *The State of U.S. Education.* Robert Emmet Long Ed. New York: H. W. Wilson, 1991: 35.

Only one college in four even considered
Boyer, Ernest L. *The Carnegie Foundation for the Advancement of Teaching. High School: A Report on Secondary Education in America*: 252.

Page 116
it was determined that the requirements themselves
Ravitch, Diane. *The Schools We Deserve: Reflections on the Educational Crises of Our Time*: 68.

The 1982 California Roundtable study noted
Ravitch, Diane. *The Schools We Deserve: Reflections on the Educational Crises of Our Time*: 65.

the U.S. Department of Education studied transcripts
Boyer, Ernest L. *The Carnegie Foundation for the Advancement of Teaching. High School: A Report on Secondary Education in America*: 73. For decades, high schools have offered students three basic areas of study to pursue, college preparatory, vocational, or the "general" track. Those following the college prep route customarily take a heavy concentration of the traditional subjects such as English, mathematics, science, and a foreign language. The vocational programs typically equipped a student with skills for a particular career, with less emphasis on academics and more hands-on experience. But it is the vague, open-ended, "general" track, allowing a great number of electives, that saw tremendous growth from the Boomers to the Free. Whereas 12 percent of high-school students were enrolled in the general track in the late sixties, a decade later, 43 percent were following this route. Boyer, Ernest L. *The Carnegie Foundation for the Advancement of Teaching. High School: A Report on Secondary Education in America*: 79.

The top-ten growth areas
Boyer, Ernest L. *The Carnegie Foundation for the Advancement of Teaching. High School: A Report on Secondary Education in America*: 73.

"time spent learning to cook and drive"
Cited in: Greenberger, Ellen and Steinberg, Lawrence. *When Teenagers Work.* New York: Basic Books, 1986: 189.

Page 117
A 1988 Gallup survey of Americans aged eighteen to twenty-four
Taylor, Ronald A., et al. "Which Way is the Pacific Ocean?" *U.S. News & World Report* 8 August 1988: 11.

The percentage of students who took pure geography courses
Taylor, Ronald A., et al. "Which Way is the Pacific Ocean?": 11.

The new educational authorities, like E. D. Hirsch
Strauss, William and Howe, Neil. *Generations: The History of America's Future, 1584 to 2069*: 321. Real reforms have been slow, however. Even in 1993, a team of reporters in Los Angeles paying a visit to one middle school found classes in baseball card collecting, jigsaw puzzles, and crocheting. "Choice Politics." *Wall Street Journal* 15 October 1993: A12.

"Most young people learn pretty much"
Finn, Chester E., Jr. "A Nation Still at Risk": 51.

the seniors favored *more* emphasis on academic subjects
Boyer, Ernest L. *The Carnegie Foundation for the Advancement of Teaching. High School: A Report on Secondary Education in America*: 22.

the percentage wishing for more stress on academics
> The 1972 survey showed that 47 percent of the seniors felt so; in 1980 the percentage was 67 percent. Boyer, Ernest L. *The Carnegie Foundation for the Advancement of Teaching. High School: A Report on Secondary Education in America*: 78.

66 percent of black children
> Honig, Bill. *Last Chance For Our Children: How You Can Help Save Our Schools*: 75.

identify those traits that "make a teacher good."
> Norman, Jane and Harris, Myron. *The Private Life of the American Teenager*: 131.

Page 118
The number of states that required the exams
> Ravitch, Diane. *The Schools We Deserve: Reflections on the Educational Crises of Our Time*: 48.

the following questions intended to test reading comprehension
> Boyer, Ernest L. *The Carnegie Foundation for the Advancement of Teaching. High School: A Report on Secondary Education in America*: 30.

Page 119
sixteen schools were found to have cheated
> Louv, Richard. *Childhood's Future: Listening to the American Family. New Hope for the Next Generation*: 336.

all fifty states reported above-average scores
> Louv, Richard. *Childhood's Future: Listening to the American Family. New Hope for the Next Generation:* 336. By the late eighties, educators were finally beginning to take actions at the front end of the educational process rather than offering poor attempts to demonstrate the schools' credibility by testing at the back end. As of 1988, thirty-two states had adopted policies mandating that beginning *teachers* pass competency tests before receiving certification. Even though these tests have been criticized for being far too easy, some states nevertheless experienced rather high failure rates, keeping many unqualified teachers out of the classroom who otherwise would have been in charge of teaching the nation's children. In California, for example, 24 percent of white takers of the 1985 exam failed, as did 61 percent of Hispanics and 74 percent of blacks. Anrig, Gregory R. "Teacher Education and Teacher Testing: The Rush to Mandate." *Phi Delta Kappan* February 1986: 447–51.

Page 120
the mix of students taking the SAT
> Ravitch, Diane. *The Schools We Deserve: Reflections on the Educational Crises of Our Time*: 48.

the number and proportion of high-scoring students
> In 1972, 53,800 students (5.3 percent) scored over 650 on the verbal portion of the exam. By 1980, only 29,000 students (2.9 percent) could make this claim. Ravitch, Diane. *The Schools We Deserve: Reflections on the Educational Crises of Our Time*: 48.

researchers Annegret Harnischfeger and David E. Wiley analyzed
> Ravitch, Diane. *The Schools We Deserve: Reflections on the Educational Crises of Our Time*: 49. Another study of math capabilities found that American students were equal to their counterparts in China and Japan in first grade but were already far behind by fifth grade. Stevenson, Harold W., et al. "Mathematics Achievement of Chinese, Japanese, and American Children." *Science* 14 February 1986.

8 percent of seventeen-year-old white children were functionally illiterate
> The National Assessment of Educational Progress survey, cited in: Ravitch, Diane. *The Schools We Deserve: Reflections on the Educational Crises of Our Time*: 47.

William Brock, Ronald Reagan's Secretary of Labor
> Hewlett, Sylvia Ann. *When the Bough Breaks: The Cost of Neglecting Our Children*: 66.

When the first International Mathematics Study
   Ibid.
In the 1988 international Gallup survey
   Taylor, Ronald A., et al. "Which Way Is the Pacific Ocean?": 11.
As the lower grades fail to educate the young
   Powell, Arthur G., et al. *The Shopping Mall High School*: 108.

Page 121
SAT Chart
   U.S. Department of Education. *Digest of Education Statistics, 1993*.
half the students entering the state university and college system
   Ravitch, Diane. *The Schools We Deserve: Reflections on the Educational Crises of Our Time*: 65.
"Perhaps high schools teach students what they most need to know"
   Powell, Arthur G., et al. *The Shopping Mall High School*: 303.
(n) the biggest loser
   Report of the Comparison of the Skills of the Average Work Force. *America's Choice: High Skills or Low Wages!* Rochester, NY, 1990: 23.

Page 122
Number of humor magazines
   "Demomemo." *American Demographics* May 1987: 8.
only 18 percent of U.S. public-school students
   U.S. National Center for Education Statistics. *Digest of Education Statistics*, annual.
more than 44 percent of all Boomers
   Jones, Landon Y. *Great Expectations: America and the Baby Boom Generation*: 310.

Page 123
Graph of Tuition Rates
   U.S. National Center for Education Statistics. *Digest of Education Statistics*, Table 301, 1992; and Celis, William. "Colleges Increase Student Fees Again, But at Lowest Percentage in Decades." *New York Times* 7 April 1993, national ed.: B7.
Top schools such as Stanford and Harvard
   "Cost of Public Colleges Rises 10%." *New York Times* 14 October 1992, national ed.: B8.
Wesleyan University made the ability to pay
   Edmondson, Brad. "Colleges Conquer the Baby Bust." *American Demographics* September 1987: 55.
Ivy League universities found themselves enmeshed in the scandal
   Barrett, Paul M. "U.S. Charges 8 Ivy League Universities and MIT with Fixing Financial Aid." *Wall Street Journal* 23 May 1991: A16.
a top Boomer student in 1972 from a low-income family
   Edmondson, Brad. "Colleges Conquer the Baby Bust." *American Demographics* September 1987: 55.

Page 124
the average college undergraduate was taking more than six years
   U.S. Bureau of the Census. *Current Population Reports* Series: 70-32.
the average candidate could expect to spend ten and a half years
   Anderson, Martin. *Imposters in the Temple: American Intellectuals Are Destroying Our Universities and Cheating Our Students of Their Future*. New York: Simon & Schuster, 1992: 73.
In fact, a federal study by the Department of Education
   The high school class of 1972 saw 15 percent of its members earn a bachelor's degree within the next four years. Only 7 percent of the class of 1982 could claim such an accomplishment.

Cited in: Putka, Gary. "College Completion Rates Are Said to Decline Sharply." *Wall Street Journal* 28 July 1989: B1.

a greater proportion of the Free to *begin* college

Fifty-nine percent of 1988 high-school graduates enrolled in college in the fall. Riche, Martha Farnsworth. "The Boomerang Age." *American Demographics* May 1990: 30.

Page 125

The percentage of middle-income black men

Wingert, Pat. "Fewer Blacks on Campus: A Disturbing New Report on a Troubling Trend." *Newsweek* 29 January 1990: 75. Overall the percentage of black students going on to college from high school dropped from 34 percent in 1976 to 26 percent in 1985. Coontz, Stephanie. *The Way We Never Were: American Families and the Nostalgia Trap.* New York: Basic Books, 1992: 234.

The rate of dropping out

D'Souza, Dinesh. *Illiberal Education: The Politics of Race and Sex on Campus.* New York: The Free Press, 1991: 267. 52 percent of all students fail to graduate after five years. Lederman, Douglas. "College Athletes Graduate at Higher Rate than Other Students, but Men's College Basketball Players Lag Far Behind, a Survey Finds." *Chronicle of Higher Education* 27 March 1991: A1.

"Never has a higher education been more important"

Chakravarty, Subrata N. with Weisman, Katherine. "Consuming Our Children?": 222.

The wage gap between those with college degrees and those without

Male college graduates over age 25 in 1970 earned 28 percent more than nongraduates; women graduates had a 32-percent advantage. In 1980 the gap was 20 percent for men, 24 percent for women. By 1990 the gap had reached 32 percent for men and 35 percent for women. U.S. National Center for Education Statistics. *Digest of Education Statistics*, Table 367. 1992.

a member of the Free Generation with a college degree

Gross, David M. and Scott, Sophonia. "Twentysomething": 60.

"The college graduate will earn $640,000 more"

"Bennett in the Breach." *National Review* 13 March 1987: 20.

Page 126

Rather than bidding up salaries of college graduates

Samuelson, Robert J. "The Value of College." *Newsweek* 31 August 1992: 75.

a Pell Grant, awarded to the neediest students

Hewlett, Sylvia Ann. *When the Bough Breaks: The Cost of Neglecting Our Children*: 249.

Support for students at the state level

Kerr, Clark. *The Great Transformation in Higher Education 1960–1980.* Albany, NY: State University of New York Press, 1991: 362. At the University of California, for example, the state's share of the operating budget fell from 65 percent in 1959 to just 41 percent by 1992. "Facing 4th Year of Cuts, Berkeley Chancellor Leads Budget Revolt." *New York Times* 12 May 1993, national ed.: B7.

The first program to go was the $2 billion paid through Social Security

Mattera, Philip. *Prosperity Lost:* 132.

by 1990, they were covering less than a third

Hewlett, Sylvia Ann. *When the Bough Breaks: The Cost of Neglecting our Children*: 249.

assistance that used to come in the form of grants

When one talked about financial aid in the 1970s, in 70 percent of the cases, that meant scholarships or grants. In the 15-year span from 1977 to 1992, however, the proportion of assistance in the form of loans, which of course must be paid back, rose from just 17 percent to 50 percent. Further adding to the true cost of college financing was that the 1986 tax reforms eliminated the tax deduction that had previously been allowed on the interest on student loans. Ginsberg, Edward and Ginsberg, Susan. "Student Loan Default." *Phi Delta Kappan* March 1989: 557; Mattera, Philip. *Prosperity Lost:* 132; McGrath, Anne. "A Tax Course Not Taught in School." *U.S. News & World Report* 17 November 1986: 60–1.

federal subsidies for students fell by 20 percent
Mattera, Philip. *Prosperity Lost*: 132.

the schools themselves were forced
The amount of aid offered by colleges rose by 80 percent, adjusted for inflation, from 1980 to 1988. Mattera, Philip. *Prosperity Lost*: 132.

"Colleges raise costs because they can"
"Time to End Student-Loan Subsidies?" *U.S. News & World Report* 1 December 1986: 8.

Page 127
Graph of student loan debt
U.S. National Center for Education Statistics. *Digest of Education Statistics*, Table 345. 1993.

A 1986 study by the Joint Economic Committee of Congress
Mattera, Philip. *Prosperity Lost:* 132.

A recent graduate of a four-year undergraduate program
Louv, Richard. *Childhood's Future: Listening to the American Family. New Hope for the Next Generation*: 382.

"I myself have taken out $18,000"
Minton, Torri. "An Education in Debt and Stress." *San Francisco Chronicle* 9 March 1993: B3.

Page 128
Goals of College Freshmen
Russell, Cheryl. "Meet the Next Generation." *American Demographics* April 1990: 2; Kate, Nancy Ten. "College Students Favor Activism, Drug Tests." *American Demographics* January 1991: 12.

Free students indicated a dramatic shift to the right
Schwartz, Joe. "From Ban the Bomb to Benetton": 60; Boyer, Ernest L. *College: The Undergraduate Experience in America*: 205.

Even concern for issues like environmental problems
Russell, Cheryl. "Meet the Next Generation": 2.

"important reasons for going to college"
Boyer, Ernest L. *College: The Undergraduate Experience in America*: 12.

Degrees in Selected Fields
Cited in: Boyer, Ernest L. *College: The Undergraduate Experience in America*: 104.

Page 129
four out of five college students believed
Blotnik, Srully. "Why Hippies Beget Yuppies." *Forbes* 24 February 1986: 146.

Fully 40 percent of the 1986 Yale graduating class
Lewis, Michael. *Liar's Poker: Rising Through the Wreckage on Wall Street*. New York: W. W. Norton, 1989: 24.

Two Stanford University researchers
Katchadourian, Herant A. and Boli, John. *Careerism and Intellectualism Among College Students*. San Francisco: Jossey-Bass, 1985: appendix IV, table 1.

Companies weren't even looking at liberal-arts majors
Boyer, Ernest L. *College: The Undergraduate Experience in America*: 104.

a group of students at UC-Berkeley
  Barber, Benjamin R. *An Aristocracy of Everyone: The Politics of Education and the Future of America.* New York: Ballantine, 1992: 220.

Page 130
A 1984 survey of college faculty
  Boyer, Ernest L. *College: The Undergraduate Experience in America*: 75.
nearly half the Free who attended college
  Forty-three percent of those who entered college in 1984 failed at least one course by 1990. Woodward, Kenneth L. "Young Beyond Their Years." *Newsweek* Special Issue 1989: 60.
Helen S. Astin wrote in *Educational Record*
  Boyer, Ernest L. *College: The Undergraduate Experience in America*: 76.
A 1984 survey showed that more than half
  Boyer, Ernest L. *College: The Undergraduate Experience in America*: 161.
Four of the top-ten best-selling books
  McDowell, Edwin. "What Students Read When They Don't Have To." *New York Times* 7 July 1990: C16.
UCLA's annual nationwide survey of incoming freshmen
  Kate, Nancy Ten. "College Students Favor Activism, Drug Tests": 12.

Page 131
a 1983 Indiana University survey
  Horowitz, Helen Lefkowitz. *Campus Life.* New York: Alfred A. Knopf, 1987: 270.
A later survey reported in the *Boston Globe*
  Cited in: Sommers, Christine Hoff. "Teaching the Virtues." *Chicago Tribune Magazine* 12 September 1993: 14–18.
seventy-three students in an introductory computer-science course
  Derber, Charles. *Money, Murder and the American Dream: Wilding From Wall Street to Main Street*: 101.
Professors reported students coming to their offices
  For a satirical account of how one professor would handle the situation, see Borkat, Roberta F. "A Liberating Curriculum." *Newsweek* 12 April 1993: 11.
Dr. Barbara McGowan
  Littwin, Susan. *The Postponed Generation: Why American Youth Are Growing Up Later*: 51.
At the University of Maryland
  Ibid.
Dr. Samual Klagsburn
  Ibid.

Page 132
As historian Christopher Lasch observed
  Lasch, Christopher. *The Culture of Narcissus: American Life in an Age of Diminishing Expectations.* New York: W. W. Norton, 1978: 148.
no one had actually proved that it was not "relevant"
  Douglas, George H. *Education Without Impact.* New York: Birch Lane, 1992: 108.
a Carnegie Foundation report
  Kerr, Clark. *The Great Transformation in Higher Education 1960–1980*: 331.
course requirements were greatly reduced
  Ibid.: 280.
college students should be able to study whatever they please
  Sheils, Merrill et al. "Crisis in the Liberal Arts." *Newsweek* 6 February 1978: 69–70. Despite the overwhelming evidence that Free students were entering universities greatly lacking basic

knowledge that one expects of a college student, the universities saw no need to try to sincerely remedy these deficiencies. A 1988 report found that it was possible to graduate from 37 percent of American colleges without taking a single course in history. One could earn a degree from 45 percent of schools without having completed an American or English literature course, from 62 percent without studying any philosophy whatsoever, and from 77 percent without studying a foreign language. Cited in: D'Souza, Dinesh. *Illiberal Education: The Politics of Race and Sex on Campus:* 15.

University of Illinois professor George Douglas related
   Douglas, George H. *Education Without Impact*: 122.

Duke's English department added courses
   King, Nina. "Classroom Notes: A Controversial English Department Deserves High Marks for Teaching." *Washington Post* 7 April 1991: R12.

Temple University's American Studies department
   Hinds, Michael deCourcy. "Taking U.F.O.'s for Credit and for Real." *New York Times* 28 October 1992, national ed.: A16.

When Pete Schaub, a University of Washington at Seattle business major
   D'Souza, Dinesh. *Illiberal Education: The Politics of Race and Sex on Campus*: 202.

Page 133

What enabled nonacademic or pseudoacademic classes to survive
   General education requirements from 1992–93 course catalogs for Duke, Temple, Washington, and UC Davis.

Richard Sabot and John Wakeman-Linn of Williams College
   The schools studied were Amherst College, Duke University, Hamilton College, Haverford College, Pomona College, the University of Michigan, the University of North Carolina, and the University of Wisconsin. Samuelson, Robert J. "The Value of College": 75.

Page 134

Nearly *half* of the Williams College class of 1993
   Shanker, Albert. "Competing for Customers." Advertisement, *New York Times* 27 June 1993: E7.

the National Endowment for the Humanities gave a multiple-choice test
   "Ignorance Is No Bliss." *Los Angeles Times* 10 October 1989: sec. 2, pg. 6.

GRE score graph
   Graduate Record Examination Board and U.S. Department of Education National Center for Education Statistics

Page 135

"the nation's colleges are more successful in credentialling"
   Boyer, Ernest L. *College: The Undergraduate Experience in America*: 2.

Allan Bloom's runaway best-seller
   Bloom, Allan. *The Closing of the American Mind: How Higher Education Has Failed Democracy and Impoverished the Souls of Today's Students*. New York: Simon and Schuster, 1987.

"college seems to be a place"
   Sullivan, Robert E., Jr. "Greatly Reduced Expectations." *Rolling Stone* Spring 1993 On Campus: 32.

Page 136

senior graduate students on the verge
   Douglas, George H. *Education Without Impact*: 119.

At Ohio State University
   Anderson, Martin. *Imposters in the Temple: American Intellectuals Are Destroying Our Universities and Cheating our Students of Their Future*: 54.

Even those at the nation's most elite
    Anderson, Martin. *Imposters in the Temple: American Intellectuals Are Destroying Our Universities and Cheating Our Students of Their Future*: 55. At Stanford, Martin Anderson tallied the percentage of TAs handling the teaching load in the various departments as follows: economics (25 percent), philosophy (31 percent), sociology (32 percent), mathematics (34 percent), physics (38 percent), chemistry (40 percent), political science (43 percent), history (48 percent), German (48 percent), psychology (50 percent), religious studies (53 percent), English (59 percent), Spanish (73 percent), and freshman English (100 percent).

When 2,200 student teachers at the University of Massachusetts
    Anderson, Martin. *Imposters in the Temple: American Intellectuals Are Destroying Our Universities and Cheating Our Students of Their Future*: 54.

During a strike a year later at Berkeley
    Herscher, Elaine. "UC Explains How Finals Will Be Graded in Strike." *San Francisco Chronicle* 9 December 1992: D6.

the professors who won this prize were nonetheless denied tenure and fired
    Anderson, Martin. *Imposters in the Temple: American Intellectuals Are Destroying Our Universities and Cheating Our Students of Their Future*: 199.

Professor Allan Bloom complained
    Bloom, Allan. *The Closing of the American Mind: How Higher Education Has Failed Democracy and Impoverished the Souls of Today's Students*: 341.

Wendy Kaminer of Radcliffe wrote
    Kaminer, Wendy. *I'm Dysfunctional, You're Dysfunctional.* Reading, MA: Addison-Wesley, 1992: 41.

And Robert Bellah, professor of sociology at Berkeley
    Woodward, Kenneth L. "Young Beyond Their Years": 60.

Page 137
Middlebury College professor Jay Parini wrote
    D'Souza, Dinesh. *Illiberal Education: The Politics of Race and Sex on Campus*: 18.

the danger of any exploitation of the university
    Kerr, Clark. *The Great Transformation in Higher Education 1960–1980:* 153.

This statement ordained as punishable offenses
    D'Souza, Dinesh. *Illiberal Education: The Politics of Race and Sex on Campus*: 142.

Page 138
District Judge Avern Cohn ruled as unconstitutional the entire Michigan policy
    Ibid.: 144.

At Emory
    Barringer, Felicity. "Campus Battle Pits Freedom of Speech Against Racial Slurs." *New York Times* 25 April 1989: A1.

The University of Conecticut warned of penalties
    D'Souza, Dinesh. *Illiberal Education: The Politics of Race and Sex on Campus*: 9.

Tufts created three levels
    Russo, Melissa. "Free Speech at Tufts: Zoned Out." *New York Times* 27 September 1989: A29.

At Michigan and Berkeley
    Leo, John. "The Class That Deserves Cutting." *U.S. News & World Report* 29 May 1989: 58.

Page 139
A whole new set of colloquialisms
    Harvey, Miles. "Politically Correct Is Politically Suspect." *In These Times* 25 Dec–14 Jan 1991–92: 146.

An Occidental College student
  Baker, Bob. "Free Speech or Vulgarity?" *Los Angeles Times* 1 March 1992: B1.
a Yale sophomore
  Salholz, Eloise. "Everything but Shouting Fire: Colleges Grapple with the Limits of Free Speech." *Newsweek* 20 October 1986: 70.
UCLA fraternity Theta Xi
  Gordon, Larry. "Fraternity Faces Sanctions for Offensive Songbook." *Los Angeles Times* 2 October 1992: B1.
A Brown University student was expelled
  Harvey, Miles. "Politically Correct Is Politically Suspect": 144.
Connecticut attempted to kick a student out
  D'Souza, Dinesh. *Illiberal Education: The Politics of Race and Sex on Campus*: 145.
Stanford ejected a student
  Barringer, Felicity. "Campus Battle Pits Freedom of Speech Against Racial Slurs": A1.
The University of Pennsylvania shut down a fraternity house
  D'Souza, Dinesh. *Illiberal Education: The Politics of Race and Sex on Campus*: 133.
A Michigan student was reprimanded
  "Colleges Take 2 Basic Approaches in Adapting Anti-Harassment Plans." *Chronicle of Higher Education* 4 October 1989: A38.

Page 143
number of personal bankruptcies
  Administrative Office of the U.S. Courts. *Annual Report of the Director.*
a series of blue-ribbon commissions
  Greenberger, Ellen and Steinberg, Lawrence. *When Teenagers Work*: 1.
James Coleman warned
  Woodward, Kenneth L. "Young Beyond Their Years": 54–60.
"Rarely have the recommendations of social scientists"
  Greenberger, Ellen and Steinberg, Lawrence. *When Teenagers Work*: 1.
in earlier generations
  Elkind, David. "When Teenagers Work." *Parents* June 1987: 168.

Page 144
Several studies in the early eighties showed
  Cited in: Greenberger, Ellen and Steinberg, Lawrence. *When Teenagers Work*: 8.
the highest rates were among those
  A 1981 study showed that children from families with incomes of less than $7,000 were the least likely to hold jobs; those from families with incomes over $25,000 were the most likely. Cited in: Greenberger, Ellen and Steinberg, Lawrence. *When Teenagers Work*: 74.
The great majority of working adolescents
  Greenberger and Steinberg found that over 80 percent of working high-school seniors saved "none" or a "little" of their earnings. Greenberger, Ellen and Steinberg, Lawrence. *When Teenagers Work*: 106. In a 1981 poll of American teenagers, only 7 percent of sixteen- to eighteen-year-olds answered "no" to the question "Do your parents allow you to spend and manage your money as you wish?" Norman, Jane and Harris, Myron. *The Private Life of the American Teenager*: 182.
nearly $50 billion in 1985
  Cited in: Hornblower, Margot. "Madison Avenue Adapts To Generation of Skeptics." *Washington Post* 29 May 1986: A1.
David Elkind warned
  Elkind, David. "When Teenagers Work": 168.

The proportion of teenagers who worked
: 33 percent of boys and 22 percent of girls aged sixteen and seventeen worked in 1960. 45 percent of boys and 42 percent of girls this age worked in 1980. Cited in: Greenberger, Ellen and Steinberg, Lawrence. *When Teenagers Work:* 11.

between two thirds and three fourths
: According to the University of Michigan's Institute for Social Research 1985 survey. Cited in: "Teenagers Still Pursuing the American Dream." *USA Today* April 1986: 2–3.

In the western part of the country
: Kirst, Michael W. et al. *Conditions of Children in California, Berkeley: PACE School of Education*: 139.

In a 1981 survey
: Cited in: Greenberger, Ellen and Steinberg, Lawrence. *When Teenagers Work*: 21.

Page 145

This amount of work brought
: "Sweet 16 and Ready for Work": 21.

Several studies showed a strong adverse relationship
: Cited in: Greenberger, Ellen and Steinberg, Lawrence. *When Teenagers Work*: 117.

those who worked long hours
: Quoted by Ellen Greenberger in: Louv, Richard. *Childhood's Future: Listening to the American Family. New Hope for the Next Generation*: 91.

More than a fourth of employed teenagers
: Greenberger, Ellen and Steinberg, Lawrence. *When Teenagers Work*: 118.

More than half reported
: Ibid.: 121.

One common tactic of working students
: Ibid.: 120.

Educational researcher Linda McNeil found
: Cited in: Greenberger, Ellen and Steinberg, Lawrence. *When Teenagers Work*: 120.

a 1982 study found that teenagers who worked were more likely
: Ibid.: 132.

Page 146

An additional link between work and increased drug use
: Bachman, Jerald G. "An Eye on the Future." *Psychology Today* July 1987: 8.

The most common type of work for teenagers
: "The Latest Worry for Parents of Teens." *Fortune* 2 February 1987: 10.

they made little or no use of their skills or abilities
: Bachman, Jerald G. "An Eye on the Future": 6.

young people use almost no reading, writing, or mathematical skills
: Greenberger, Ellen and Steinberg, Lawrence. *When Teenagers Work*: 66.

"wrapping fast-food items in paper containers"
: Ibid.: 67.

the youngsters were no more deprived of parental attention
: "Sweet 16 and Ready for Work": 21.

One school official described "McDonald's time"
: Quoted in: Louv, Richard. *Childhood's Future: Listening to the American Family. New Hope for the Next Generation*: 91.

An assistant principal told researcher Linda McNeil
: Cited in: Greenberger, Ellen and Steinberg, Lawrence. *When Teenagers Work*: 192.

Page 147
One incensed mother wrote authors Greenberger and Steinberg
"The Latest Worry for Parents of Teens": 10.
the number of minors found to be illegally employed
Cited in: Mattera, Philip. *Prosperity Lost*: 148.
This was a higher number of infractions
Louv, Richard. *Childhood's Future: Listening to the American Family. New Hope for the Next Generation*: 91.
A nationwide 1990 Labor Department sweep
Swoboda, Frank. "Secretary Dole: Stiffer Child Labor Penalties." *Washington Post* 29 June 1990: A8.
New York state inspectors estimated
Mattera, Philip. *Prosperity Lost*: 148.
Labor Secretary Elizabeth Dole proposed raising
Swoboda, Frank. "Secretary Dole: Stiffer Child Labor Penalties."
a hole of debt unrivaled in size
As a percentage of GNP, the federal debt fell throughout the years of Boomer youth and entry into the workforce, dropping from 130 percent of GNP to 31 percent by 1980. In the eighties, however, the federal debt ballooned reaching 55 percent of the GNP by 1990. "The Numbers Behind the Budget: Federal Debt." *Washington Post* 30 August 1990: A21.

Page 148
From 1970 to 1984, the accumulated debt
Over this same period, the real value of the nation's productive facilities, those which produce jobs and capital, rose only 1.6-fold. Longman, Philip. *Born to Pay: The New Politics of Aging in America*: 176.
since 1984, government debt
U.S. Bureau of the Census, *Government Finances*, series GF, No. 5.
1985 saw a record number of filings for bankruptcy
Administrative Office of the U.S. Courts. *Annual Report of the Director*.
the United States went from the world's largest creditor nation
Phillips, Kevin. *The Politics of Rich and Poor: Wealth and the American Electorate in the Reagan Aftermath*. New York: Random House, 1990: 7.
"Historically, business organization was highly linear"
Quoted in: Sullivan, Robert E., Jr. "Greatly Reduced Expectations." *Rolling Stone* Spring 1993 On Campus: 32.
Although sixteen- to twenty-four-year-olds comprised only 17 percent
Bernstein, Aaron, et al. "What Happened to the American Dream?" *Business Week* 19 August 1991: 84.

Page 149
there would be so many employment opportunities
See Gross, David M. and Sophonia, Scott. "Twentysomething": 57.
After seeing the total number of jobs in the economy
"The Good Old Malaise Days." *Time* 27 September 1993: 17.
a 1992 MTV survey
Dunn, William. *The Baby Bust: A Generation Comes of Age*. Ithaca, NY: American Demographics Books, 1993: 122.
"The guy who has the job I want"
Quoted in: Zinn, Laura et al. "Move Over, Boomers." *Business Week* 14 December 1992: 74.

"Boomer envy"
  Coupland, Douglas. *Generation X.* New York: St. Martin's Press, 1991: 21.

Page 150
Among male high-school graduates under the age of twenty
  Grant, William T. Commission. "The Forgotten Half: Pathways to Success for America's Youth and Young Families": 282.
"a future of lousy jobs"
  Quoted in: Phillips, Kevin. *Boiling Point*: 190.
the economy added 5 million manufacturing jobs
  Kuttner, Bob. "The Declining Middle." *The Atlantic Monthly* July 1983: 60.
the economy shed 1.8 million such jobs
  Bartlett, Donald L. and Steele, James B. *America: What Went Wrong*: xi.
the proportion of men under age thirty
  From 1973 to 1989, the proportion of male workers aged thirty to sixty-two who worked in manufacturing fell from 30 percent to 25 percent. The percentage of men under age thirty fell from 28 percent to 19 percent. Bernstein, Aaron, et al. "What Happened to the American Dream?": 82. For the youngest workers, those twenty-years-old or less, the proportion was cut in half from 44 percent to 22 percent. "Non-College Youth Face Uncertain Future." *USA Today Magazine* July 1988: 9.
the Big Three automakers
  Deutschman, Alan. "What 25-Year-Olds Want." *Fortune* 27 August 1990: 45.
"it is much harder for a male high school graduate"
  Phillips, Kevin. *Boiling Point*: 31.
"This is the generation of diminished expectations"
  Zinn, Laura et al. "Move Over, Boomers": 77.
think tanks were anticipating shortages of college graduates
  Sullivan, Robert E., Jr. "Greatly Reduced Expectations": 29.
As *Rolling Stone* magazine commented
  Ibid.: 31.
Robert Ehrman, the director of the Career Development Unit at UCLA
  Job market headlines reprinted in: Littwin, Susan. *The Postponed Generation: Why American Youths Are Growing Up Later*: 27.

Page 151
notes one Syracuse University education professor
  Quoted in: Putka, Gary. "College Completion Rates Are Said to Decline Sharply." *Rolling Stone* Spring 1993 On Campus: B1.
the Economic Policy Institute found
  Cited in: Phillips, Kevin. *Boiling Point*: 12.
one in ten college graduates in the sixties
  Sullivan, Robert E., Jr. "Greatly Reduced Expectations." *Rolling Stone* Spring 1993 On Campus: 31.
the Department of Education estimates
  Dunn, William. *The Baby Bust: A Generation Comes of Age*: 79.
the Bureau of Labor Statistics (BLS) estimates
  Rataan, Suneel. "Why Busters Hate Boomers." *Fortune* 4 October 1993: 56–62.
Money magazine reports
  "Smart Ways to Help Your Child Land a Job." *Money* June 1993: 18.
the Labor Department determined
  Sullivan, Robert E., Jr. "Greatly Reduced Expectations": 31.

"We had new jobs"
   Quoted in: Brophy, Beth with Walsh, Maureen. "Middle-Class Squeeze." *U.S. News & World Report* 18 August 1986: 38.
Forty-four percent of the new jobs
   Derber, Charles. *Money, Murder and the American Dream: Wilding From Wall Street to Main Street*: 123.
while some have claimed
   Kuttner, Bob. "The Declining Middle": 62.

Page 152
Economist Bob Kuttner
   Ibid.
According to the Bureau of Labor Statistics
   Coontz, Stephanie. *The Way We Never Were: American Families and the Nostalgia Trap*: 64.
the hourly wages of part-time employees
   Ibid.
the Bank of America has even
   Burdman, Pamela. " 'Flexible' Jobs on the Rise." *San Francisco Chronicle* 10 August 1992: C1; Howe, Kenneth. "B of A Slashing Hours of Thousands of Tellers." *San Francisco Chronicle* 5 February 1993: A1. Bank of America is not the only bank to cut costs by eliminating full-time jobs with benefits. Wells Fargo, First Interstate, and others have adopted similar strategies. See Howe, Kenneth. "B of A Cut in Job Hours Follows Trend." *San Francisco Chronicle* 11 February 1993: A1.
a nationwide total of nearly 1.5 million "temps"
   Kilborn, Peter T. "New Jobs Lack the Old Security In Time of 'Disposable Workers.' " *New York Times* 15 March 1993: A1.
the number of temporary jobs grew
   Ibid.
Many companies have completely reorganized
   Ibid.
A 1990 Virginia Slims Opinion Poll
   Cited in: "American Women Get Mad." *American Demographics* August 1990: 32.
In a survey of five thousand households by the Conference Board
   Linden, Fabian. "Good Jobs." *American Demographics* December 1987: 4.
the Free have also exhibited the greatest job mobility
   Riche, Martha Farnsworth. "The Boomerang Age": 52.

Page 153
jobs that are likely to see the greatest growth
   Kilborn, Peter T. "Home Health Growing in Size and Patient Appeal." *New York Times* 30 August 1994, national ed.: A1.
Federal, state, and local government employment
   Light, Paul C. *Baby Boomers*: 260.
Public sector wage increases
   Koretz, Gene. "Fat Paychecks Got States and Cities Deep in Hock . . . While Federal Employees Stayed Ahead of the Pack." *Business Week* 23 September 1991: 26. In 1990 the average annual pension of federal employees was $12,966, of state and local employees, $9,068, and of private sector employees, $6,512. U.S. Census Bureau data cited in: Bartlett, Donald L. and Steele, James B. *America: What Went Wrong*: 12. Since employee compensation accounts for over half of all state and local government expenditures—paid, of course, from various tax receipts—the consequences of the disproportionately high earnings of public-sector employees

have been doubly harsh. While those so employed have certainly benefited, everyone else has been forced to foot the bill. Thus, the Free have been compelled to pay for these higher-priced public employees, but they have been shut out from securing such jobs. Koretz, Gene. "Fat Paychecks Got States and Cities Deep in Hock . . . While Federal Employees Stayed Ahead of the Pack": 26.

Page 154
According to Stanford University economist Martin Carnoy
    Kuttner, Bob. "The Declining Middle": 71.
the number of professors at work
    Anderson, Martin. *Imposters in the Temple: American Intellectuals Are Destroying Our Universities and Cheating Our Students of Their Future*: 35.
"The Ph.D. candidate in 1960 could not miss"
    Kerr, Clark. *The Great Transformation in Higher Education 1960–1980*: 137.

Page 155
the Associated General Contractors of America
    Seaberry, Jane. "Two-Tiered Wages: More Jobs vs. More Worker Alienation." *Washington Post* 7 April 1985: G1.
New butchers at a California slaughterhouse
    "Labor Letter." *Wall Street Journal* 9 July 1985: A1.
at the electronics firm Motorola
    Mattera, Philip. *Prosperity Lost*: 80.
more than half of all firms
    Seaberry, Jane. "Two-Tiered Wages: More Jobs vs. More Worker Alienation": G1.
"I get $9.68 an hour"
    Quoted in: Mattera, Philip. *Prosperity Lost*: 113.
A stewardess with United Airlines
    Brophy, Beth with Walsh, Maureen. "Middle-Class Squeeze": 41.
A woman working in the hardware department
    Seaberry, Jane. "Two-Tiered Wages: More Jobs vs. More Worker Alienation": G1.
"I made a good living"
    Quoted in: Mattera, Philip. *Prosperity Lost*: 114.

Page 156
Unemployment Insurance Graph
    Cited in: Bernstein, Aaron, et al. "Is Uncle Sam Shortchanging Young Americans?": 85.
When the Gallup Organization asked Americans
    Gallup poll, 1989
"If you're not employed, you can't put the blame"
    Quoted in: Schmidt, Susan. "The Jobless Take the Blame." *Washington Post* 28 May 1986: A1.

Page 157
"As long as it's there"
    Quoted in: Vobejda, Barbara and Klose, Kevin. "In Illinois, Making Their Own Breaks." *Washington Post* 29 May 1986: A12.
a small poll taken by Charles Derber
    Derber, Charles. *Money, Murder and the American Dream: Wilding From Wall Street to Main Street*: 100.

Page 158
Net jobs creation from 1988 to 1990
  U.S. Small Business Administration.
60 percent of young men earned enough
  Coontz, Stephanie. *The Way We Never Were: American Families and the Nostalgia Trap*: 261.
the poverty rate for families headed by someone under 30
  "It's a Struggle." *American Demographics* February 1990: 10.
the *median income* of a man under age twenty-five
  Median income of males that age was $6,565 while the poverty level was $5,701. U.S. Bureau of the Census. *Money Income of Households, Families and Persons*. Table B-15, 1991; U.S. Bureau of the Census. *Current Population Reports*, P-60, No. 175.
The Children's Defense Fund labeled this
  Mattera, Philip. *Prosperity Lost*: 12.

Page 159
1973–1991 Graph of Income by Age Group
  U.S. Bureau of the Census. *Money Income of Households, Families and Persons*. Table B-10, 1991.
The typical young male in 1973
  U.S. Bureau of the Census. *Money Income of Households, Families and Persons*. Table B-15, 1991.

Page 160
Graph of Median Incomes of Younger Workers as a Percentage of Incomes of Workers Aged Forty-five to Fifty-four, Men and Women
  Ibid.

Page 161
Young black men with a high-school diploma
  Levy, Frank and Michel, Richard C. *The Economic Future of American Families: Income and Wealth Trends*. Washington, DC: Urban Institute, 1991: 30.
percentage of black families headed by women
  Bernstein, Aaron, et al. "What Happened to the American Dream?": 83.
the median income of young black families
  Ibid.
"downward mobility"
  Littwin, Susan. *The Postponed Generation: Why American Youth Are Growing Up Later*: 37.
The minimum wage
  Barash, David P. *The L Word*. New York: William Morrow, 1992: 128.
a full-time worker with such an income
  Mattera, Philip. *Prosperity Lost*: 149.
"the minimum wage has caused more misery"
  Quoted in: Mattera, Philip. *Prosperity Lost*: 148.
"youth opportunity wage"
  Mattera, Philip. *Prosperity Lost*: 149.
state and local taxes escalated
  Cited in: Light, Paul C. *Baby Boomers*: 46.

Page 162
a twenty-five-year-old with a family of four in 1965
  Brophy, Beth with Walsh, Maureen. "Middle-Class Squeeze": 37.

a family of four earning *poverty-level wages* in 1986
   Longman, Phillip. *Born to Pay: The New Politics of Aging in America*: 18.
The 1981 Economic Recovery Tax Act
   Mattera, Philip. *Prosperity Lost*: 49.
The Tax Reform Act of 1986
   The top bracket was later raised to 31 percent. This tax act did correct a few of these inequities—the standard deduction, the earned income tax credit, and the personal exemption were all increased. Mattera, Philip. *Prosperity Lost*: 51.
this deduction was eliminated
   J. K. Lasser's What the New Tax Law Means to You. New York: Pocket Books, 1986: 50.

Page 163
Job Benefits Offered
   Mattera, Philip. *Prosperity Lost*: 122.
the proposed national health plan
   Transcript of President Clinton's September 22, 1993 speech. "From the President's Address to Congress on Health Care." *New York Times* 23 September 1993, national ed.: A16–17.
"When we get older, and the boomers"
   Quoted in: Bernstein, Aaron, et al. "What Happened to the American Dream?": 84.
In 1973, a typical young family
   Levy, Frank and Michel, Richard C. *The Economic Future of American Families: Income and Wealth Trends*: 52.
Boomers were worth more than *twice* as much
   Ibid. 53.

Page 164
Graph of median net worth by age
   Board of Governors of the Federal Reserve System. *Federal Reserve Bulletin* January 1992.
their net worth declining by more than 60 percent
   Levy, Frank and Michel, Richard C. *The Economic Future of American Families: Income and Wealth Trends*: 53.
In 1971, when Boomers were flocking into jobs
   Hardy, Dorcas R. and Hardy, C. Colburn. *Social Insecurity*: 12.
Today, Social Security takes 7.65 percent
   Phillips, Kevin. *Boiling Point*: 43.
Norman Ornstein of the American Enterprise Institute pointed out
   Ornstein, Norman. "The Payroll Tax Is Getting Out of Hand." *New York Times* 8 November 1992, national ed.: F13.

Page 165
Social Security is required to furnish any excesses to the U.S. Treasury
   Longman, Phillip. *Born to Pay: The New Politics of Aging in America*: 78.
there are today only thirty-one Social Security recipients
   Russell, Louise B. *The Baby Boom Generation and the Economy*: 151.
by the year 2010 there will already be forty Social Security recipients for every worker
   Ibid. 153.
the projected percentage of workers' income
   Smith, Lee. "The War Between the Generations": 79.
the fund will start running increasingly large deficits
   Hardy, Dorcas R. and Hardy, C. Colburn. *Social Insecurity*: 15.

those born after 1959 must wait until age sixty-seven
    Loeb, Marshall. *Marshall Loeb's 1993 Money Guide.* Boston: Little, Brown, 1993: 599.

Page 166
The Washington-based Tax Foundation determined that in 1990
    Phillips, Kevin. *Boiling Point*: 104.
A study by the government's own Congressional Budget Office
    Mattera, Philip. *Prosperity Lost*: 52.
growing steadily from 43.2 percent of all husband-wife households
    Russell, Louise B. *The Baby Boom Generation and the Economy*: 112.

Page 167
"Rising prices and mortgage interest rates affect new buyers"
    Russell, Louise B. *The Baby Boom Generation and the Economy*: 115.
"The truth of the matter was that the cost of home ownership"
    Ibid.
home values did rise faster
    Malabre, Alfred L., Jr. *Beyond Our Means.* New York: Random House, 1987: 45.
earning higher real incomes than any previous generation
    Russell, Louise B. *The Baby Boom Generation and the Economy*: 164.
the proportion owning the home they lived in
    Ibid.: 112.
the average price of a new house increased
    Light, Paul C. *Baby Boomers:* 46.
a young Boomer family with children
    Louv, Richard. *Childhood's Future: Listening to the American Family. New Hope for the Next Generation*: 49.
the median age of first-time home buyers
    Newman, Katherine S. *Declining Fortunes: The Withering of the American Dream.* New York: Basic Books, 1993: 32.
nearly a quarter of those buying their first homes
    Whitehead, Barbara Dafoe. "Dan Quayle Was Right": 74.

Page 168
Graph of median home affordability by age
    U.S. Bureau of the Census. *Who Can Afford to Buy a House?* May 1991, Table 3.
down payment on the average-priced new home nearly quadrupled
    Brophy, Beth with Walsh, Maureen. "Middle-Class Squeeze": 37.

Page 169
"the opening of Levittown, Pennsylvania"
    Bartlett, Donald L. and Steele, James B. *America: What Went Wrong*: 20.
the overall trend of declining home-ownership rates
    Homeownership Trends in the 1980's. Bureau of the Census, 1990. In the last twenty years, due primarily to great gains among the elderly, the overall home ownership rate has remained at about 64 percent. Barringer, Felicity. "Younger Baby Boomers Are Found Less Well Off." *New York Times* 4 January 1992: 26.
In 1988, according to the Census Bureau
    Phillips, Kevin. *Boiling Point*: 180.
in 1980 they headed upward
    Russell, Louise B. *The Baby Boom Generation and the Economy*: 118.

the years 1965 to 1981 saw an average homeowner
   Longman, Phillip. *Born to Pay: The New Politics of Aging in America*: 58.
the eighties saw . . . just a 5-percent increase
   Koretz, Gene. "The 1980s' Surge in Home Prices Was Mostly a Mirage." *Business Week* 23 September 1991: 26.
"Housing demand will grow more slowly in the 1990s"
   Cited in: Levy, Frank and Michel, Richard C. *The Economic Future of American Families: Income and Wealth Trends*: 88–9.

Page 170
Graph of home-ownership rates
   Joint Center for Housing Studies of Harvard University. Cited in Dunn, William. *The Baby Bust: A Generation Comes of Age*: 169.
From 1989 to 1991, the median sales price
   The median sales price of a new, single-family home was $120,000 in both 1989 and 1991, a 10-percent decline adjusted for inflation. U.S. Bureau of the Census and U.S. Department of Housing and Urban Development. *Current Construction Reports*, series C25; *Characteristics of New Housing*, annual; *New One-Family Houses Sold*, monthly. In the Northeast, the median sales price of an existing single-family home was $145,200 in 1989 and $141,900 in 1991, a 12-percent decline adjusted for inflation. National Association of Realtors. *Home Sales*, monthly, and *Home Sales Yearbook: 1990*.

Page 171
When someone tells you they've just bought a house
   Coupland, Douglas. *Generation X*: 143.
Before 1980, the federal government virtually assured
   Longman, Phillip. *Born To Pay: The New Politics of Aging in America*: 54.
A spate of programs following the Depression
   The Housing Finance System and Federal Policy: Recent Changes and Options for the Future. Congressional Budget Office, 1983: 31.
the federal government insured that the lenders
   For example, the VA and FHA programs, as well as the Federal Home Loan Mortgage Corporation and the Government National Mortgage Association, greatly reduced the liability of lending institutions in making home loans. Wilson, Stephen Delos. *The Bankruptcy of America.* Germantown, TN: Ridge Mills Press, 1992: 103.

Page 172
the combination of reduced risks
   The Housing Finance System and Federal Policy: Recent Changes and Options for the Future. Congressional Budget Office, 1983: 4.
it had lost more than $111 billion
   Longman, Phillip. *Born To Pay: The New Politics of Aging in America*: 55.
a series of laws were enacted
   The Housing Finance System and Federal Policy: Recent Changes and Options for the Future. Congressional Budget Office, 1983: 8.
with deregulation laws passed in 1980
   The 1980 Depositor Institutions Deregulation and Monetary Control Act. While they did include a clause allowing the states to reinstate the ceilings by a certain date, only Kansas chose to do so. Twelve states took advantage of the clause that allowed them to reinstate ceilings at a later date. *The Housing Finance System and Federal Policy: Recent Changes and Options for the Future.* Congressional Budget Office, 1983: 31.

In separate acts of legislation
  The 1980 Depository Institutions Deregulation and Monetary Control Act, and the 1982 Garn–St. Germain Depository Institutions Act. *The Housing Finance System and Federal Policy: Recent Changes and Options for the Future.* Congressional Budget Office, 1983: 36.
The proportion of office space sitting vacant
  In only four years, the vacancy rate jumped from 4.6 percent to 15.5 percent. ONCOR International's *National Office Market Report* and *International Office Market Report.*
"help control inflation"
  Quoted in: Farnsworth, Clyde H. "Far-Reaching Banking Legislation Signed by President." *New York Times* 1 April 1980: 1.
$500 *billion* price tag for the taxpayers.
  Bartlett, Donald L. and Steele, James B. *America: What Went Wrong*: 43.

Page 173
In order to limit growth
  Longman, Phillip. *Born to Pay: The New Politics of Aging in America*: 47.
many communities decided to attach fees
  Examples cited in: Phillips, Kevin. *Boiling Point*: 121.
Stephanie Norlinger took her case challenging Prop 13's inequities
  Kinsey, Michael. "Beverly Hills Grandfather." *Washington Post* 12 March 1992: A27.
the Court ruled
  "California Property Tax Cap Upheld." *Facts on File* July 1992: 503.

Page 174
The exceptions were the various tax advantages for homeowners
  Malabre, Alfred L., Jr. *Beyond Our Means*: 43.
Any gains from a sale of a home
  Wilson, Stephen Delos. *The Bankruptcy of America*: 100.
lowered some of the incentives for investment
  The 1981 Economic Recovery Tax Act accelerated the rate of depreciating investments. The 1982 Tax Equity and Fiscal Responsibility Act reduced tax deductions on income-producing properties. *The Housing Finance System and Federal Policy: Recent Changes and Options for the Future.* Congressional Budget Office, 1983: 40.
To compensate for the accompanying loss in deductions
  Zelizer, Viviana A. *Pricing the Priceless Child: The Changing Social Value of Children.* New York: Basic Books, 1985: 32.
rents rose by 24 percent
  Mattera, Philip. *Prosperity Lost*: 127.
"to produce a permanent underclass of disadvantaged renters"
  Quoted in: Phillips, Kevin. *Boiling Point*: 159.

Page 175
By 1988, 61 percent of men
  Riche, Martha Farnsworth. "The Boomerang Age." *American Demographics* May 1990: 25.
another 12 to 13 percent
  Ibid.: 26.
"There is a naive notion that children grow up"
  Quoted in: Toufexis, Anastasia. "Show Me the Way to Go Home." *Time* 4 May 1987: 106.
The proportion of men and women aged twenty-five to thirty-four
  McLeod, Ramon G. "27% of Adults under 35 Live With Parents": A1.

Cynthia Graves and Dr. Larry Stockman, authors
   Stockman, Dr. Larry V. and Graves, Cynthia. *Adult Children Who Won't Grow Up.* Chicago: Contemporary Books, 1989: 24.
An exasperated parent told the *New York Times*
   Quoted in: Mattera, Philip. *Prosperity Lost*: 127.
"if anyone deserves pity, it's the affluent parent"
   Riche, Martha Farnsworth. "Mysterious Young Adults": 43.
Whereas recent graduates in earlier times
   Walsh, Liesel. "Why the Baby Bust Won't Spend." *American Demographics* December 1992: 14.
more than two thirds of them *do* work
   Riche, Martha Farnsworth. "The Boomerang Age": 27.
most of the rest are in school
   In 1987, 74 percent of men and 75 percent of women aged twenty to twenty-four who were attending school lived with their parents. Riche, Martha Farnsworth. "Mysterious Young Adults": 41.
"College just wasn't the big ticket"
   Brophy, Beth with Walsh, Maureen. "Middle-Class Squeeze": 36.

Page 176
Graph of Living Arrangements of Young Adults, Age Eighteen to Twenty-four
   McLeod, Ramon G. "27% of Adults under 35 Live With Parents." *San Francisco Chronicle* 12 February 1993: A1.

Page 179
"For people in my generation"
   Leavitt, David. "The New Lost Generation": 94.

Page 180
As Nancy Smith of the *Washington Post* writes
   Smith, Nancy. "25 and Pending": C1.
"People are afraid"
   Gross, David M. and Sophonia, Scott. "Twentysomething": 59.
"Those who belong to no one but themselves"
   Leavitt, David. "The New Lost Generation": 91.
one nineteen-year-old Bronx woman
   Henneberger, Melinda with Marriott, Michel. "For Some, Youthful Courting Has Become a Game of Abuse." *New York Times* 11 July 1993, national ed.: A1.
"Some of us look at [marriage] as giving up"
   Smith, Nancy. "25 and Pending": C1.
Members of the University of New Hampshire
   Cohn, D'Vera and Kiernan, Laura A. "Lacking Group Identity, Students Focus on Selves." *Washington Post* 28 May 1986: A1.
"I must say, if nothing else"
   Coupland, Douglas. *Generation X*: 61.
"Not getting hurt"
   Gross, David M. and Scott, Sophonia. "Twentysomething": 59.

Page 181
"People our age were forming their sexual identity"
   Quoted in: Zinn, Laura et al. "Move Over, Boomers": 77.
Gallup polls indicate that the Free regard AIDS
   Gallup poll on May 15, 1991, asked "What would you say is the most urgent health problem

facing this country at the present time?" Sixty percent of those aged eighteen to twenty-nine responded that AIDS was the most urgent, compared to 44 percent of those thirty to forty-nine, and 35 percent of those fifty and over.

We also show a greater willingness to deal with it

Gallup poll on November 22, 1991 concerning AIDS issues asked, "Do you think the major television networks should or should not accept advertising from condom manufacturers for broadcast?" 87 percent of those aged eighteen to twenty-nine responded that yes, they should accept such advertising. 76 percent of those thirty to forty-nine responded so as well as 54 percent of those fifty and over.

"If the '60s was the decade of free love"

Mackey, Heather. "The Sixties: Hey San Francisco, Get Over It." *The City* February 1993: 28.

Page 182

the teen bride is all but a thing of the past

In 1989, 2.8 percent of men and 9.5 percent of women aged eighteen to nineteen were married. U.S. Bureau of the Census. *Current Population Reports*, series P-20, No. 445.

marriage rates for older age groups

For example, in 1975, only 7.2 percent of men and 4.8 percent of women aged forty to forty-four had never been married. In 1989, 8.3 percent of men and 6.3 percent of women of this age were never married. U.S. Bureau of the Census. *Current Population Reports*, series P-20, No. 445.

interracial marriages are nevertheless up

McLeod, Ramon G. "27% of Adults under 35 Live With Parents."

nine out of ten who live at home

Riche, Martha Farnsworth. "Mysterious Young Adults": 42.

In a 1990 *Time* magazine poll

Gross, David M. and Scott, Sophronia. "Twentysomething": 60.

Graph of marriage rates

U.S. Bureau of the Census. *Current Population Reports*, series P-20, No. 444.

"My mother thinks I'm doomed for life"

Quoted in: Cohn, D'Vera and Kiernan, Laura A. "Lacking Group Identity, Students Focus on Selves": A1.

"I see myself doing that—if I ever do it"

Littwin, Susan. *The Postponed Generation: Why American Youth Are Growing Up Later*: 69.

"it's a foolhardy decision"

"Housewives Devastated by Divorce." *San Francisco Chronicle* 23 March 1993: B5.

In a nationwide poll

Norman, Jane and Harris, Myron. *The Private Life of the American Teenager*: 289.

Page 183

They're more likely to live together

Age nineteen to twenty-four are the most likely to live together, according to Cornell University demographer Linda Jacobsen. Riche, Martha Farnsworth. "The Boomerang Age": 27.

there were only half a million couples living together

Cited in: Woodward, Kenneth L. "Young Beyond Their Years": 57.

half of young women who marry

Cited in: Levine, Bettijane. "Is the Thrill Gone?" *Los Angeles Times* 16 December 1992: E1.

Los Angeles Times writer Bettijane Levine asked

Levine, Bettijane. "Is the Thrill Gone?": E1.

In 1990, one young child in three

Cited in: Hewlett, Sylvia Ann. *When the Bough Breaks: The Cost of Neglecting Our Children*: 36.

Page 184
Childless Women Graph
   U.S. Bureau of the Census. *Current Population Reports*, P20-476.
Single Mothers Graph
   U.S. National Center for Health Statistics. *Monthly Vital Statistics Report*.

Page 185
"My generation will be the family generation"
   Gross, David M. and Sophronia, Scott. "Twentysomething": 58.
Single motherhood has increased by 50 percent
   U.S. Census Bureau. Cited in: "Single-Parent Families: On the Rise." *New York Times* 5 October 1992, national ed.: 16. See also DeParle, Jason. "Census Reports a Sharp Increase Among Never-Married Mothers." *New York Times* 14 July 1993, national ed." A1.
Nearly *two thirds* of all children under the age of six
   In 1987, 10.4 percent of children living with a married couple were in poverty compared to 51.2 percent of those living with just their mother. 61.4 percent of children under age six living with only their mothers were living in poverty. National Center for Children in Poverty, Columbia University. And despite the very modest rise in women's incomes in the last two decades, other trends have caused those with children to continue to face worsening difficulties. For example, only one single-parent family in twenty could afford payments on their own homes in 1987, less than half the 1973 rate. Grant, William T. Commission. "The Forgotten Half: Pathways to Success for America's Youth and Young Families": 282.
mothers who are divorced are now *less* likely to be working
   As of March, 1991, 55.8 percent of mothers with children under age six living with their husband were working, compared to 52.2 percent of divorced mothers and 38.1 percent of never-married mothers. Cited in: "A Growing Diversity Among Mothers": 18.
absent Free fathers
   In 1989, only 25.5 percent of custodial single mothers were awarded child support and received the full amount. Waldman, Steven. "Deadbeat Dads": 46.
The share of married couples with children who are impoverished
   National Center for Children in Poverty, Columbia University.
the percentage of women of childbearing age
   Cited in: Hewlett, Sylvia Ann. *When the Bough Breaks: The Cost of Neglecting Our Children*: 170.

Page 187
Political Party Affiliation
   Ifill, Gwen. "Seeking Electoral Edge, Parties Court the Young." *New York Times* 14 October 1991: A20.
"Where are the young people of America these days?"
   Gartner, Michael. "Youth and Revolution, Everywhere but Here." *Wall Street Journal* 30 November 1989: A15.
ten times that number of young adults were arrested
   FBI Uniform Crime Reports, annual.
"Today's youth suffer"
   Baker, Russell. "Herky-Jerky Bang-Bang."
"They can quote fluctuations"
   Littwin, Susan. *The Postponed Generation: Why American Youth Are Growing Up Later*: 230.
Richard Cohen, in a 1990 *Washington Post*
   Cohen, Richard. "Johnny's Miserable SATs." *Washington Post* 4 September 1990: A19.
"I'm sorry to say it"
   Quoted in: Strauss, William and Howe, Neil. *Generations: The History of America's Future, 1584 to 2069*: 337.

Page 188
Karl Zinsmeister, in a cover story
   Ibid.
in a 1989 Gallup poll
   Gallup poll of August 7, 1989.
"Mine is a generation perfectly willing to admit its contemptible qualities"
   Leavitt, David. "The New Lost Generation": 94.
"At least we don't pretend"
   Ibid.: 90.

Page 189
taking "for granted"
   Gross, David M. and Scott, Sophonia. "Twentysomething": 61.
thirty-five states had such laws on the books
   Bell, Bill. "Dear Becky": 184.
A 1990 ABC News/*Washington Post* poll
   Marcus, Erin. "After Daughter's Death, Parents Campaign Against Abortion Consent Laws." *Washington Post* 8 August 1990: A3.

Page 190
a major freedom-of-speech battle won by Boomers
   Forer, Lois G. *Unequal Protection: Women, Children, and the Elderly in Court*: 205.
only two states allowed those under the age of twenty
   World Almanac 1966: 779.
by 1976, about half the states
   World Almanac 1976: 124.
they were forced to do so by the Department of Transportation
   Rose, Frank. "If It Feels Good, It Must Be Bad." *Fortune* 21 October 1991: 96.
In October 1993, California Governor Pete Wilson signed into law
   "Law Punishes Minors Who Drink and Drive." *New York Times* 8 October 1993, national ed.: A17.
The National Transportation Board has proposed
   "Board Advises Curfews for Young Drivers." *San Francisco Chronicle* 3 March 1993: A4.
Nearly a dozen such proposals were introduced to Congress
   Duffey, Joseph. "Reconstituting America Through National Service." *Vital Speeches* 15 October 1989: 26.

Page 191
Senator Claiborne Pell, have proposed a mandatory year
   Bacard, Andre. "Sparking Life Into Our Youth." *The Humanist*: July/August 1987 46.
A 1988 Gallup poll on the national service idea
   Gallup poll published January 24, 1988.
"There are so many choices to make"
   Woodward, Kenneth L. "Young Beyond Their Years": 57.
there are higher proportions of blacks, Latinos, and Asians
   In 1992, of those aged eighteen to twenty-nine, 14 percent were black, 12.3 percent were Latino, and 3.9 percent were Asian. In the population as a whole, 12.4 percent were black, 9.5 percent were Latino, and 3.3 percent were Asian. Cited in: Zinn, Laura et al. "Move Over, Boomers": 77.
the science of "psychographics,"
   Hornblower, Margot. "Madison Avenue Adapts to Generation of Skeptics": A1.

"Don't try to con them"
　Reprinted in: Mitchell, Susan. "Generation X." *San Diego Union-Tribune* 30 May 1993: G1.
"they're tremendously cynical"
　Zinn, Laura et al. "Move Over, Boomers": 78.

Page 192
"The older managers think that if the shoe doesn't fit"
　Deutschman, Alan. "What 25-Year-Olds Want": 44.
"I'd ask them about love"
　Cited in: Shames, Lawrence. *The Hunger for More: Searching for Values in an Age of Greed*: 97.
"too dull, too plain"
　Muscatine, Alison. "Great Tennis Is Not Enough." *San Francisco Chronicle* 22 June 1992: C3.
"If it came down to career or relationship"
　Quoted in: Deutschman, Alan. "What 25-Year-Olds Want": 43.
Eddie Vedder explained
　Farley, Christopher John. "Rock's Anxious Rebels." *Time* 25 October 1993: 60.
Gallup Organization in 1989 asked Americans
　Gallup poll February 26, 1989. 67 percent of those aged thirty to forty-nine, and 65 percent of those fifty and over agreed with this sentiment.

Page 193
"There were thirty-year-old guys"
　Quoted in: Deutschman, Alan. "What 25-Year-Olds Want": 47.
"Breaking with a long tradition"
　Deutschman, Alan. "What 25-Year-Olds Want": 44.
One 1992 survey of young workers
　Deutschman, Alan. "The Upbeat Generation." *Fortune* 13 July 1992: 47.
"We live small lives on the periphery"
　Coupland, Douglas. *Generation X*: 11.
"by the time goodies like cheap land and hot jobs got to me"
　Ibid.: 90.
"Since I'm not going to make a lot of money anyway"
　Walsh, Liesel. "Why the Baby Bust Won't Spend." *American Demographics* December 1992: 14.

Page 194
"They like Reagan because he says what they want to hear"
　Quoted in: Jordan, Mary and Maraniss, David. "An Upbeat Generation Looking Out for Itself": A1.
The 1986 Gallup Youth Survey
　Cited in: "Exploding the Myths about Teenagers." *U.S. News & World Report* 10 February 1986: 80.
In fifteen of sixteen consecutive polls
　Cited in: Strauss, William and Howe, Neil. *Generations: The History of America's Future, 1584 to 2069*: 326.
60 percent of young adults voted for him
　Cohn, D'Vera and Kiernan, Laura A. "Lacking Group Identity, Students Focus on Selves": A1.

Page 195
"We don't want to be a bully"
　Quoted in: Jordan, Mary and Maraniss, David. "An Upbeat Generation Looking Out for Itself": A1.

In the 1992 election
   Network exit polls. Cited in: Roberts, Jerry. "Clinton Will Have Opportunity to Stumble or Soar." *San Francisco Chronicle* 15 January 1993: A4.
In a series of ABC News/*Washington Post* polls
   Jordan, Mary and Maraniss, David. "An Upbeat Generation Looking Out for Itself": A1.
the independent candidate Ross Perot
   Network exit polls. Cited in: Roberts, Jerry. "Clinton Will Have Opportunity to Stumble or Soar": A4.
70 percent of those under twenty-five agreed that it had
   Cited in: Light, Paul C. *Baby Boomers*: 195.
higher rates of support for individual choice
   Gallup poll of January 22, 1989 asked if the Supreme Court should overturn the *Roe v. Wade* decision. 69 percent of those aged eighteen to twenty-nine responded "no" compared to 57 percent aged thirty to forty-nine, 51 percent aged fifty to sixty-four, and 48 percent aged sixty-five and over; Gallup poll of October 25, 1989 asked, "Do you think homosexual relations between consenting adults should or should not be legal?" 61 percent of those aged eighteen to twenty-nine responded that they should be legal compared to 53 percent aged thirty to forty-nine, and 32 percent aged fifty and over; Gallup poll of May 5, 1991 asked, "Do you generally favor or oppose using federal funds to enable poor women to have abortions?" 54 percent of those aged eighteen to twenty-nine favored the idea compared to 50 percent aged thirty to forty-nine, and 48 percent aged fifty and over; Gallup poll of June 5, 1991 asked, "Do you think abortions should be legal under any circumstances, legal only under certain circumstances, or illegal in all circumstances?" 39 percent of those aged eighteen to twenty-nine responded that it should be legal under any circumstances compared to 30 percent of those aged thirty and over.
And in a 1989 survey on a proposed amendment
   20 percent of those aged thirty-five and under supported the prayer amendment compared to 32 percent aged thirty-six to fifty, 46 percent aged fifty-one to sixty-five, and 53 percent aged sixty-six and over. *Public Opinion Quarterly* Spring 1989: 48.
legislation that disallows racial and sexual discrimination
   Gallup poll of August 21, 1988. 66 percent of those aged eighteen to twenty-nine felt that discrimination in private clubs based on sex should not be legal compared to 59 percent aged thirty to forty-nine, and 47 percent aged fifty and over.
extensive spying
   Magnet, Myron. "The Money Society." *Fortune* 6 July 1987: 28.

Page 196
The two Reagan administrations alone
   Cited in: Derber, Charles. *Money, Murder and the American Dream: Wilding From Wall Street to Main Street*: 57.
Annual polls conducted by the Center for Political Studies
   "America the Cynical." *Time* 19 July 1993: 17.
a 1991 poll of American attitudes
   Cited in: "Harper's Index" *Harper's Magazine* October 1992: 11.
One college professor
   Howe, Fanny. "The Plot Sickens." *Lear's* December 1992: 30–32.
Fordham University's annual Index of Social Health.
   Steinberg, Jacques. "U.S. Social Well-Being Is Rated Lowest Since Study Began in 1970": 16; "Researchers Say U.S. Social Well-Being is 'Awful' ": A12.

Page 197
an unbelievable 77 percent felt that today's young adults
   Gross, David M. and Sophonia, Scott. "Twentysomething": 61.
Gwen Lipsky, head of research at MTV
   Quoted in: Farley, Christopher John. "Taking Shots at the Baby Boomers." *Time* 19 July 1993: 31.
a 1992 *Fortune* poll of those aged twenty to twenty-nine
   Deutschman, Alan. "The Upbeat Generation": 48.
we have not thrown in the towel
   66 percent of those aged eighteen to thirty felt so compared to 50 percent of the population as a whole. Cited in: Littwin, Susan. *The Postponed Generation: Why American Youth Are Growing Up Later*: 39. A Gallup poll of November 14, 1992, asked, "In general, are you satisfied or dissatisfied with the way things are going in the United States at this time?" Though only 33 percent of those aged eighteen to twenty-nine were satisfied, this was still 33 percent higher than any other age group.

Page 198
"There's a different type of activism today"
   Quoted in: Littwin, Susan. *The Postponed Generation: Why American Youth Are Growing Up Later*: 234.
the Surfrider Foundation
   Shao, Maria. "Hey Dude, No More Toxic Beach Party." *Business Week* 16 September 1991: 38.
"There are a lot of committed people in Washington"
   Quoted in: Littwin, Susan. *The Postponed Generation: Why American Youth Are Growing Up Later*: 234.
Voter participation among eighteen- to twenty-year-olds
   U.S. Census Data Bureau. Cited in: Berke, Richard. "Is the Vote, Too, Wasted on Youth?" *New York Times* 30 June 1991 sec 4: E2.
a study in 1990
   Cited in: Zoglin, Richard. "The Tuned-Out Generation": 64.
Other news reports noted that only 12 percent
   Zoglin, Richard. "The Tuned-Out Generation." *Time* 9 July 1990: 64.
high-school teachers have reported being stunned
   Strauss, William and Howe, Neil. *Generations: The History of America's Future, 1584 to 2069*: 333.

Page 199
Writes David Leavitt
   Leavitt, David. "The New Lost Generation": 94.
"All we've had for twenty years is bad news"
   Reprinted in: Littwin, Susan. *The Postponed Generation: Why American Youth Are Growing Up Later*: 234.
"We are seriously unserious"
   Smith, Nancy. "25 and Pending": C1.

Page 200
Chicago dramatists Jill and Faith Soloway
   Hollander, Nicole. "Here's a Story about a Bunch Named Brady . . ." *New York Times* 21 April 1991: H31.
Grunge rockers, gangsta rappers, techno-ravers, and funk-rap fusionists
   See, for example, Walters, Barry. "Crossing the New Rock Generation Gap." *San Francisco Examiner* 21 March 1993: D1.

Page 201
The victor of the Superbowl of such events, the International Poetry Slam
    Smith, Gregory B. "Full-Contact Free Verse." *San Francisco Examiner Image Magazine* 18 April 1993: 20.

Page 202
Proportion of military enlistees
    Selected Manpower Statistics. U.S. Department of Defense, 1979, 1990.
D. H. Lawrence observed
    Quoted in: Farley, Christopher John. "Taking Shots at the Baby Boomers": 31.
Jacob Appel of Brown University (class of 1996) replied
    "Letters to the Editor." *New York Times Magazine* 28 March 1993: 6.
Daniel Smith-Rowsey added, in a 1991 *Newsweek* commentary
    Smith-Rowsey, Michael. "The Terrible Twenties." *Newsweek* 10 July 1991: 10.
A couple of Free-run magazines of political commentary
    Cited in: "A New Crowd Learns the Ropes." *San Francisco Chronicle* 14 January 1993: B5.

Page 203
Fortune magazine acknowledged the burgeoning generation warfare
    Rataan, Suneel. "Why Busters Hate Boomers": 56–70.
Richard Blow wrote in a 1992 *Washington Post* essay
    Blow, Richard. "Twentynothing." *Washington Post* 13 December 1992: C5.
"How do you feel about the baby-boomers?"
    Deutschman, Alan. "The Upbeat Generation": 53.
Heather Mackey
    Mackey, Heather. "The Sixties: Hey San Francisco, Get Over It": 29.
Philip Longman raises a point
    Longman, Philip. *Born to Pay: The New Politics of Aging in America*: 253.
the amount of a deceased person's estate
    Lewin, Marion Ein and Sullivan, Sean. *The Care of Tomorrow's Elderly.* Washington, D.C.: American Enterprise Institute for Policy Research, 1989: 119.
"They have made a complete about-face"
    Dychtwald, Ken and Flower, Joe. *Age Wave: The Challenges and Opportunities of an Aging America*: 277.

Page 204
Some in the gray lobby
    Beck, Melinda. "The Geezer Boom." *Newsweek* Special Issue 1989: 66.
A bipartisan commission
    Rosenblatt, Robert A. "Panel Says Entitlement Will Eat Up Federal Budget by 2012." *San Francisco Chronicle* 9 August 1994: A3.
"By 2010, baby boomers will be torn in two directions"
    Quoted in: Beck, Melinda. "The Geezer Boom": 63.

Page 205
The *Washington Post* noticed in 1986
    Hornblower, Margot. "Madison Avenue Adapts to Generation of Skeptics": A1.
"The truly intelligent people"
    Walcoff, Christina. "Watch Out Boomers!" *Marin Independent Journal* 10 May 1993: D1.

Page 206
The eighteen to twenty four-year-old age group saw the greatest gains
    Farley, Christopher John. "Taking Shots at the Baby Boomers.": 31.

Page 207
the *Third Millennium Declaration*
    Ibid.: 30.
Writer Michael Small attended a 1992 concert in San Francisco
    Small, Michael. "Rap's Bad Rap." *Vogue* March 1993: 228.

Page 208
In the General Social Survey polls taken during the mid-eighties
    "What Men and Women Think." *American Demographics* August 1987: 36.
And researchers say that younger women
    Blackman, Ann, et al. "Bringing Up Father." *Time* 28 June 1993: 58.

INDEX

abduction of children, 58–62
ableism, 139
abortion, 19–20
   death from, 56–57
   opposition to, 189–91
   parental consent, 57
   teenage pregnancy, 69–73
   See also health
abuse of children, 36, 62
Adam, 58
Adult Children Who Won't Grow Up (Graves/Stockman), 175
adults-only apartments, 9–12
Advertising Age
   on the youth market, 191
Agassi, Andre
   on image, 188
Age of Indifference, The, 198
Aid to Families with Dependent Children (AFDC), 47–48
AIDS, 72
   Free Generation and, 181
   runaways and, 93–94
Alabiso, Frank P.
   and hyperactive children, 85
Alan Guttmacher Institute
   on STDs, 72
   on teenage pregnancy, 69–73
alcoholism, 68
All Grown Up with No Place to Go (Elkind), 24–25, 63
Allen, James
   and delinquent tendencies, 80–81
allowable speech, 138
Alsalam, Nabeel
   on college standards, 135
American College Test (ACT), 120
American Demographics magazine
   on living with parents, 176
American Humane Association, 62
American Journal of Orthopsychiatry, 85
American Medical Association, 72–73
Ames, Aldrich, 195
anorexia nervosa, 65–67
anti-intellectualism, 132–35
Appel, Jacob
   on Boomers, 202
Aristotle, 196
Arjes, Roberta
   on unemployment, 156–57
Astin, Helen S.
   on admissions policies, 130
athletes and fatal drugs, 64–65
Atlantic magazine
   on protecting children from the Free Generation, 188

Baby Boom Generation and the Economy, The (Brookings Institute report), 166
Baby Boomers
   date boundaries, 1–2
   and employment, 149
   fathers and, 32
   vs. Free Generation, 202–205
   and home ownership, 166–67
   pop-culture icons, 100–102, 179
   and student aid, 126
   as terminology, 1–2
Baker, Russell
   on Free Generation intelligence, 187
Bartlett, Donald
   and home ownership, 168–69
Basic Educational Opportunity Grants (Pell Grants), 126
Beavis and Butthead, 200
Bell, Becky, death of, 56–57
Bell, Bill and Karen, 57
Bellah, Robert
   on student standards, 136–37
Belsky, Jay
   on child care, 41, 43–44
Bennett, William
   on the benefits of sexual abstinence, 71
   on city schools, 107
   on education and employment, 125
Bergmann, Barbara
   on paid leave for women, 40–41
Best, Joel
   on Halloween terrorism, 58
Beyond Freedom and Dignity (Skinner), 24
Billboard magazine
   and changing music tastes, 200
birth control
   abortion and, 19–20
   and the Free Generation, 2
   oral contraception, 19

Birthrights (Farson), 21–22
Black English, 113
blacks
    employment, 154
    minority collage students, 124, 125
    minority high school students, 113–14, 117, 120
    parents, 185
    racial integration, 207–208
    rap, 207–208
Blake, William, 4
Bliley, Thomas, Jr.
    on throwaway children, 93
Blomquist, Martha-Elin
    on missing children, 61
Bloom, Allan
    on cultural literacy, 117, 135, 136
Bloomingdale, Stephanie
    on student loans, 127
Blue Lagoon, The, 54
Blume, Judy
    on protecting children, 25
Boli, John
    and career-oriented majors, 129
books
    feminist, 21, 28
    and the Free Generation, 2–3
    Free Generation novelists, 196, 205
    high school reading lists, 114
    and overpopulation, 13
    See also media; film and television
Boorstein, Leslie
    on relationships and the Free Generation, 180
Bosco, James
    teaching with drugs, 83
Boston Globe
    on cheating, 131

Bouling, Kenneth
    children, government licensing of, 15
Bow, Richard
    on Boomers, 203
Boyer, Ernest
    on high schools, 109
Brennan, William
    children, confinement of, 88
Brewin, Robert
    and MBD treatment, 82
Brock, William
    on functional illiteracy, 120–21
Bronfenbrenner, Urie
    on adolescent employment, 143
Broussard, Anthony Jacques, 54–55
Brumberg, Joan Jacobs
    on anorexia, 66
Bruno, Rick
    on relationships and the Free Generation, 180
bulimia, 65, 66. *See also* anorexia nervosa
Bumpass, Larry
    on living with parents, 175
Bundy, Ted, 59
Burress, Cheryl, suicide of, 76
Burtless, Gary
    on employment expectations, 150
Bush, George, 195
Business Week
    on the youth market, 191

Calhoun, John
    overpopulation testing, 14
California Roundtable, 116, 121
capital punishment, 97, 98–99
Carey, Mariah, 200

Carnegie Council on Children, 31
Carnoy, Martin
    on black student employment, 154
Carr, Jessica Ann, murder of, 96–97
Carter, Jimmy, 24
    and the S&L collapse, 172
Centers for Disease Control (CDC)
    and STDs, 72
    Youth Risk Behavior Survey, 78
cheating, 131
Chicago Tribune
    on the psychiatric admissions contest, 90
child abduction, 58–62
Child Development Act, 42
child labor laws, 21–22, 147
child support, 33–35
childlessness, benefits of, 16
children
    abduction of, 58–62
    abuse of, 36, 62
    afterschool supervision, 53
    confinement of, 88–91
    cost of raising, 21–22
    day-care centers and, 42–44
    divorce and, 29–31
    feminist movement and, 21
    foster children, 94
    government response to, 16, 42, 45–50, 94
    hyperactivity, 83–88
    negative film depiction, 15
    and poverty, 45–50
    as a priority, 20–22
    as sex objects, 22–23
    tried as adults, 97–98
    See also fathers; mothers; parents

children (discrimination against)
　anti-child sentiment, 15–16
　apartments, 9–12
　government licensing of, 15
Children Without Childhood (Winn), 25
children's bill of rights, 22
Children's Defense Fund, 48
Ciba-Geigy, 82, 85, 88
City magazine
　Free Generation vs. Baby Boomer, 203
Clay, Andrew Dice, 199
Clinton, Bill, 5
　on abortion, 20
　and entitlement, 204
　and the needs of children, 186
Clinton, Hillary, 186
Closing of the American Mind, The (Bloom), 117, 135
Cobain, Kurt
　on success, 192
　suicide of, 79
cocaine, 67–68
Cohen, Richard
　on Free Generation intelligence, 187
Cohn, Avern
　on college political correctness, 138–40
Coleman, James
　on private education, 115
Coles, Dr. Gerald
　on studies of stimulant drugs, 85–86, 86–87
collective parenthood, 21
college education, *See* education (college)
Commission on Population Growth and the American Future, 16, 20

Conrad, Marcy, murder of, 54–55
Cooper, Paula, death sentence of, 98
Corley, Susan
　marriage, expectations of, 182
Cosmopolitan magazine
　Brooke Shields and, 23
Coupland, Douglas, 196, 205
　on Boomer envy, 149
　on career aspirations, 193
　and home ownership, 170
　on the lack of romance, 180
Courier, Jim
　style of, 192
Cox, Kim
　on sex and intimacy, 71
Creative Divorce: A New Opportunity for Personal Growth (Krantzler), 28
crime
　capital punishment and, 97, 98–99
　delinquent tendencies, tests for, 80–81
　drug use, 67–68, 94–96, 97
　and fatherless families, 33
　hacker crimes, 74–75
　juveniles tried as adults, 97–98
　life-threatening behavior, 73–74
　murder, 54–55, 96, 96–97, 99
　prostitution, 93
　teenagers, 92, 94–96, 97–98
　vandalism and violence, 55–56, 96
　wilding, 96
Cultural Literacy (Hirsch), 117
Culture of Narcissus, The (Lasch), 132

custody battles, 26
Cylert, 82
Cypress Hill, 207

Daly, Martin
　on sexual abuse, 36
Danforth, John
　on entitlements, 204
Davis, John Blake
　on the cost of education, 15
Day, Lincoln
　on population control, 15
day-care centers, 42–44
Day Care for Infants (Evans/Saia), 43
Dell, Michael, 205
Derber, Charles
　on employment expectations, 157
Deschooling Society (Illich), 107
Details magazine, 191
Deutschman, Alan, 193
Dexedrine, 82
Diagnostic and Statistical Manual of Mental Disorders, 86
Disappearance of Childhood, The (Postman), 62
discarded children, 93
DISTAR (education reform program), 108
Diversity and Division
　on Boomers, 203
Divoky, Diane
　and hyperactive children, 84, 85, 86, 87
divorce
　child support, 33–35
　and children 29–31, 90
　crime and fatherless families, 33
　custody battles, 26
　and the Free Generation, 26–38

INDEX 279

divorce (*cont.*):
   and psychiatric admissions of children, 90
   stepfamilies, 36–38
   Wallerstein study, 26–28, 29, 36
   women's income and, 31
Dialectic of Sex, The (Firestone), 21
Do You Believe in Magic? (Gottlieb), 25
Dole, Elizabeth
   and child-labor laws, 147
Douglas, George, 132
   on student anti-intellectualism, 132–35
Douglas, Pamela, 64
drugs
   and athletes, 64–65
   crime and, 94–96, 97
   and emotional problems, 80–91
   and hyperactivity, 83–88
   illegal use of, 67–68
   stimulant drugs, studies of, 85–86
   teaching with, 83
D'Souza, Dinesh
   on college political correctness, 138–40
Duncan, Greg
   on divorce and women's income, 31
Durant, Dr. Nancy
   and hyperactive children, 84
Durenberger, David
   on education vs. Medicare, 50
Dychtwald, Ken
   Free Generation vs. Baby Boomers, 203
Dylan, Bob, 18

Economic Policy Institute, 151
Economic Recovery Tax Act, 162
Edison, Thomas
   and learning disability, 83, 87
education (college)
   academic requirements, 115, 124, 130
   anti-intellectualism, 132–35
   cheating, 131
   conservativeness of students, 122, 128–30
   cost of, 21, 122–24
   degrees and earnings, 125–26
   dropping out, 125
   and employment, 125
   four-year vs. six-year, 124–25
   Free Generation and, 128–30
   grading, 133–34
   Graduate Record Exam (GRE) score, 134
   intellectuals vs. careerists, 129, 132–35
   literacy, 136–37
   minority students, 124, 125
   political correctness, 132–34, 138–40
   remedial courses, 130
   student aid programs, 125, 126–27
   student attitude, 130–31, 132–35
   teaching assistants, 136–37
   test scores, decline in, 134–35
   Woman's Studies, 132–33
education (high school)
   city schools, 107
   competency tests, 118–19
   curriculum devaluation, 115–16, 116–17
   curriculum specialists, 106–108
   desire to learn, 117–18
   deterioration of, 105–106
   and functional illiteracy, 120–21
   grades, 112–13
   graduation requirements, 115–16
   homework, abolition of, 114–15
   minority students, 113–14, 117, 120
   organizational experiments, 110–12
   private education, 115
   property taxes and, 109–10
   reforms, 106–108
   scholastic aptitude tests, 108–109, 120–21
   student self-esteem, 112–14
   teachers, esteem for, 108–10
   teachers' pay, 107
   teaching with drugs, 83
Education Without Impact (Douglas), 132
Educational Record (Astin), 130
Eggebeen, David
   on the child poverty rate, 46
Ehrlich, Paul
   on overpopulation, 13–14
Ehrman, Robert
   on employment expectations, 150
Einstein, Albert
   and learning disability, 83, 87
Eisenstadt, Jill, 196
elevator surfing, 73
Elkind, David
   on children and innocence, 24–26

on *Kramer vs. Kramer,* 21
on premature adulthood, 63
on teenage consumption, 144
Ellis, Bret Easton, 196, 205
emotionally disturbed children, 80–91
confinement of, 88–91
delinquent tendencies, tests for, 80–81
hyperactivity, 83–88
insurance and, 90
learning disabilities, 81–88
MBD (minimal brain dysfunction), 81–88
psychiatric admissions contest, 90
Ritalin and, 82–83, 83–88
student stress, 131
employment, 143–57
adolescents and, 143–47
career aspirations, 193–94
expectations, 149–50
Fair Labor Standards Act, 147
low-wage and service jobs, 151–53
minority, 154
McDonald's time, 146–47
public sector, 153–54
and school, 145–47
temporary jobs, 152
unemployment, 148, 155–57
unions and, 154–55
U.S. economy and, 147–48
women and, 152
See also income
Enovid 10 and the Free Generation, 2
Escape from Childhood (Holt), 22

Esquire magazine
on image, 188

Fair Labor Standards Act (1938), 147
Family Assistance Plan (FAP), 47, 49
Family Leave Act, 186
Family Research Council of Washington, D.C., 52
Farrell, Perry
on the breakup of Jane's Addiction, 192
Farson, Richard
on child labor laws, 21–22
fast food jobs, 152
Fast Times at Ridgemont High, 54
Fasting Girls (Broussard), 66
fatherless families and crime, 33
fathers
and child support, 33–35
children, caring for, 44
collective parenthood, 21
crime and fatherless families, 33
Federal Housing Administration (FHA), 171
Federal Old-Age, Survivors, and Disability Insurance Trust Fund (OASDI), 165
Femia, Vincent
on Free Generation intelligence, 187–88
Feminine Mystique, The (Friedan), 28
feminist movement and children, 21
film and television, 179
on adolescent subculture, 54
children, negative depiction of, 15
children, sexual exploitation of, 23–24
the Cleavers, 27, 39
and dangerous behavior, 74
Free Generation film directors, 205
and hacker crimes, 75
slasher films, 54
See also books; media
Finn, Chester
on learning, 117
Firestone, Shulamith
on childhood, 21
Forbes magazine
on education and employment, 125
Forst, Martin
on missing children, 61
Fortune magazine
on Boomers, 203
on career aspirations, 193
on Free Generation optimism, 197
on the youth market, 192
Foster, Jodie, 22, 205
foster children, 94
Free Generation, 208
and anorexia, 65–67
anti-intellectualism of, 132–35
vs. Baby Boomers, 202–205
birth control and, 2
and capital punishment, 97, 98–99
crime and, 94–99
divorce and, 26–38
drug use, 67–68
and emotional problems, 80–91
and impetuous behavior, 73–76
marriage, 33
music of, 200–201
and the nuclear threat, 63–65

Free Generation (*cont.*):
   pop-culture icons, 100–102, 179
   vs. senior citizens, 50
   and stepfamilies, 36–38
   and suicide, 76–79, 99
   teenage pregnancy, 69–73
   as terminology, 3–5
   See also books; education; employment; film and television; income; lifestyle; media; politics
Friedan, Betty, 28
   on marriage and motherhood, 21
Fry Guy (hacker crime), 74–75
functional illiteracy, 120–21
Furstenberg, Frank
   on stepparenthood, 36

Gacy, John Wayne, 59
Garbage Pail Kids, 199
Garbarino, James
   on child development, 41
Garfinkel, Dr. Barry
   on parents/teens relationship, 55
   on teenage suicide, 79
Gartner, Michael
   on Free Generation intelligence, 187
Generation X
   as terminology, 3
   See also Free Generation
Generation X (Coupland), 171, 180, 193
Generations (Howe/ Strauss), 3
Ginsberg, Ruth Bader
   and opportunities for women, 39
Glickman, Adam
   on AIDS, 181
Goldman, Bob
   on athletes and fatal drugs, 64–65

Goldstein, Arnold
   on entitlements, 204
gonorrhea, 72
Gottlieb, Annie
   on "Boomer" parenting, 25
Gould, Dr. Robert
   on dangerous behavior, 74
Graduate Record Exam (GRE), 134
Granger, Lori and Bill
   and learning disabilities, 87
Grannan, Nancy, suicide of, 76–77
Graves, Cynthia
   on living with parents, 175
Greenberger, Ellen
   on working students, 145–47
Greenstein, Robert
   on children vs. senior citizens, 50
Greer, Germaine
   on baby farms, 21
Guerrier, Jean
   and tracking, 73–74

hacker crimes, 74–75
Halloween candy tampering, 57–58
Hansen, James C.
   and hyperactive children, 85
Hanushek, Eric A.
   on student achievement, 108–109
Happy Days, 39
Hardin, Garret
   and overpopulation, 14
Harmelin, Ronald, drug sentence of, 97
Harnischfeger, Annegret
   on aptitude tests, 120
Harris, Myron
   students on teachers, 117

Hart, Gary
   on the Free Generation, 198
Hawkins, Paula
   on missing children, 59–60
health
   AIDS, 72, 93–94, 181
   alcoholism, 68
   anorexia nervosa, 65–67
   athletes and fatal drugs, 64–65
   bulimia, 65, 66
   drug use, 67–68
   hyperactivity, 83–88
   learning disabilities, 81–88
   MBD (minimal brain dysfunction), 81–88
   Medicaid and children, 50
   Medicare, 204–205
   obesity, 66–67
   psychiatic admissions contest, 90
   runaways and, 93–94
   sexually transmitted diseases (STDs), 72–73
   teenage pregnancy, 69–73
   See also abortion; emotionally disturbed children
Herndon, James
   school organizational experiments, 110–12
Hetherington, Dr. Mavis, 32
Hewlett, Sylvia Ann
   and psychiatric admissions of children, 90
   teenage girls, effect of divorce on, 39
Himmelfarb, Gertrude
   on overpopulation, 13
Hirsch, E. D.
   on cultural literacy, 117

Hoffman, Lois
  on mothers and preschool children, 52
Hoffman, Saul
  on divorce and women's income, 31
Hofstadter, Richard
  and the "overvalued child," 12
Holt, John
  on the exploitation of children, 22
  on reform of education, 106
home ownership, 166–74
  affordability, 167–71
  Boomers and, 166–67
  Levittown houses, 169
  mortgages, 171–74
  parents, living with, 174–76
  property taxes, 173–74
  and renting, 174
  S&Ls and, 172
homelessness and children, 46–47
Honig, Bill
  on curriculum, 115
Houston, Whitney, 200
How Children Fail (Holt), 106
Howe, Neil
  on Baby Boomers, 2
Howes, Carollee
  on child care, 43
Hughes, Richard
  and MBD treatment, 82
Hughs brothers, 196
humor and the Free Generation, 199–200
Hunger Strike (Orbach), 65
Hurried Child, The (Elkind), 63
Hutschnecker, Arnold A.
  delinquent tendencies, tests for, 80–81

Hyperactive Child in the Classroom, The (Alabiso/Hansen), 85
hyperactivity, 83–88

Illich, Ivan
  on educational reform, 107, 110
income, 158–76
  Free Generation vs. Boomers, 158–61, 166–67
  and home ownership, 166–67, 167–74
  and the minimum wage, 161
  and Social Security, 163–65, 203–205
  tax and, 161–63, 166
  wage and population growth, 165
  wealthy vs. poor, 166
  See also employment
insurance and disturbed children, 90
intellectuals vs. careerists, 129

Jane's Addiction (rock group), 192
Jefferson, Thomas
  on obligation, 202
Judge, Mike, 200
juveniles tried as adults, 97–98

Kael, Pauline
  on *Fast Times at Ridgemont High*, 54
Kaminer, Wendy
  on student standards, 136
Katchadourian, Herant A.
  and career-oriented majors, 129
Kerr, Clark
  on employment expectations, 154

Kid Business, The (Taylor), 98
KIDLINE, 53
Kirsten, Judy
  on statutory rape, 71–72
Klagsburn, Dr. Samual
  on student stress, 131
Klein, Calvin, 23
Kocher, Cameron
  and Jessica Ann Carr's murder, 96–97
Koop, C. Everett
  and condom distribution, 71
Kozol, Jonathan
  school organizational experiments, 110–12
Kramer vs. Kramer, 21
Krantzler, Mel
  on the adaptability of children, 28, 30
Kranz, Rachel
  on anorexia, 66
Krisberg, Barry
  on the inevitability of prison, 97

Laiken, Deidre S.
  and stepparents, 37
Landers, Ann
  on parenting, 20
Lasch, Christopher
  on student anti-intellectualism, 132–35
laughism, 139
Lawrence, D. H.
  on earlier generations, 202
learning disabilities, 81–88
Leary, Timothy, 194
Leave It to Beaver, 27, 39
Leavitt, David
  on Free Generation activism, 198
  on image, 188
  on nuclear disaster, 64
  on young adulthood, 179

Lechter, Daniel
    on the child poverty rate, 46
Letterman, David, 56
    humor of, 199–200
Levine, Bettijane
    on Free Generation marriage, 183
Levittown houses, 169
Levy, Frank
    on employment expectations, 150
Librium, 88
Life magazine
    on children and economics, 14
lifestyle (Free Generation), 179–87
    the lack of romance, 180–81
    marriage, expectations of, 182–83
    parenthood, 183–86
    parents, living with, 174–76
    relationships, 180–83
    renting, 174
    rock music, 192
    See also employment; income; home ownership
Linklater, Richard, 193
Linquist, Victor
    on employment expectations, 150
Lipsky, Gwen
    on Free Generation optimism, 197
Little Darlings, 54
Littwin, Susan
    on Free Generation intelligence, 187
Logan, Karen, suicide of, 76–77
Longman, Philip
    Free Generation vs. Baby Boomer, 203
    and Social Security, 49

Look magazine
    on motherhood, 16
lookism, 139
Los Angeles Times
    on employment expectations, 151
    on teenagers and AIDS, 72
Lost Generation, 45
Lourie, Dr. Ira
    on insurance and disturbed children, 90
LSD, 67

McDonald's time, 146–47
McGowan, Dr. Barbara
    on student stress, 131
Mackey, Heather
    Free Generation vs. Baby Boomer, 203
    on love, 181
McMillan, Walter
    and elevator surfing, 73
McNeil, Linda
    on working students, 145–47
Mad magazine, 199
Magic Feather: The Truth about "Special Education," The (Granger/Granger), 87
Magnet, Myron
    crime and fatherless families, 33
Mahon, Dr. Mimi
    and teenage impetuous behavior, 75
Malle, Louis, 22
Maloney, Dr. Michael
    on anorexia, 66
Malthus, Thomas
    on overpopulation, 13
Mankiw, N. Gregory
    and home ownership, 170
marijuana, 67
Massara, Mark

    on Free Generation optimism, 197
MBD (minimal brain dysfunction), 81–88
"MBD Child: A Guide for Parents, The" (Ciba-Geigy publication), 82
media
    childlessness, benefits of, 16
    children, sexual exploitation of, 24
    children, violence against, 62
    and dangerous behavior, 74
    on employment expectations, 151
    and the Free Generation, 1–2, 192
    Free Generation magazines, 203
    on Halloween terrorism, 58
    and parents, 20
    television watching, 67
    See also books; film and television
Medicaid and children, 50
Medicare, 204–205
Mellin, Laurel
    on anorexia, 66
Mellon family divorce, 26
Menaker, Dr. Esther
    on stepmothers and stepdaughters, 36
"Mental Health: The Hidden System of Adolescent Social Control" (USC study), 90–91
Milken, Michael
    as Free Generation hero, 130
Millet, Kate
    on collective parenthood, 21

Minnesota Scholastic Aptitude Test, 120
Minton, Torri
  on working mothers, 41–42
Mirkin, Dr. Gabe
  on athletes and fatal drugs, 64–65
Missing Children (Forst/Blomquist), 61
Money magazine
  on employment expectations, 150
Moody, Desmond
  on living with parents, 176
Morris, Robert
  and hacker crimes, 75
mothers
  collective parenthood, 21
  feminist movement and, 21
  and maternity provisions, 40
  stepmothers and stepdaughters, 36
  working, 41–42
  See also children; fathers; parents
Moynihan, Daniel Patrick
  and the Family Assistance Plan, 47
  on youth and poverty, 45
music and the Free Generation, 200–201
murder, 99
  juveniles tried as adults, 97–98
  and teenagers, 54-55, 96, 96–97
Myth of the Hyperactive Child, The (Schrag/Divoky), 84, 85, 87

Nader, Ralph
  on Free Generation activism, 198

Nathanson, Gayle Wilson
  on teenage pregnancy, 69–73
Nation at Risk, A (NCEE report), 106, 111, 116–17
National Association of Secondary School Principals (NASSP), 111
  report of, 121
National Association of State Boards of Education, 72
National Center for Health Statistics, 30
National Center for Missing and Exploited Children, 59
National Child Safety Council, 60
National Council of Jewish Women, 43
National Defense Student Loans, 126
National Endowment for the Humanities, 134
National Institute on Drug Abuse, 67
National Panel on High Schools and Adolescent Education, 111
national service, 191
Neill, A. S.
  and educational reform, 107, 110
  on homework, 114
Ness, Mike, 201
New York Times
  on employment expectations, 151
  on living with parents, 175–76
  on relationships and the Free Generation, 180
  on Social Security, 164–65
  on student stress, 131
New Yorker magazine, 54

Newsweek magazine
  on children in poverty, 46
  on divorce, 28
  on the Free Generation, 191
  on Free Generation vs. Baby Boomer, 202–203
  on insurance and disturbed children, 90
  on overpopulation, 15
  on runaways and AIDS, 93–94
  on stepfamilies, 37
Next Progressive quarterly
  on Free Generation vs. Baby Boomer, 203
Nickelodeon, 52–53
Nielson, A. C.
  on television watching, 67
Nixon, Richard
  and the Child Development Act, 42
  delinquent tendencies, tests for, 80–81
  and the Family Assistance Plan, 47
NON (National Organization for Non-Parents), 16
Norlinger, Stephanie
  and Prop 13, 173
Norman, Jane
  students on teachers, 117
nuclear threat, 63–65
Nurturing Father, The (Pruett), 35

obesity, 66–67
Olton, Thomas, suicide of, 76
Operation Outreach, 93
oral contraception, 19
Orbach, Susie
  on anorexia, 65
Ornstein, Norman
  on Social Security, 164–65

INDEX 285

overpopulation
   abortion and, 19–20
   declining birth rate, 16–18
   fear of, 9, 12–18
   government response to, 16

Packwood, Robert
   on children and tax exemption, 15–16
parent-child role-reversal movies, 29–30
parenthood, collective, 21
parents, 51-62
   and abortion, 56-57
   and diminished supervision, 73–74
   Free Generation, 183–86
   living with, 174–76
   marriage, Free Generation expectations of, 182–83
   minority, 185
   and prescription drugs, 88
   single-parent families, 37–38
   See also children; fathers; mothers
Parents magazine, 20
   on teenage consumption, 144
Parham v. J.R., 88–89, 189
Pearl Jam, 200–201
Pell, Claiborne
   and mandatory public service, 191
Pell Grants, 126
Perot, Ross, 195
"Physician's Handbook: Screening for MBD" (Ciba-Geigy publication), 82
Pirolli, Tom
   on the Free Generation, 205

Planned Parenthood, 19
poetry slams, 201
political correctness, 132–34, 138–40
politics (Free Generation), 187–201
   abortion, opposition to, 189–91
   Boomers, complaints about, 189–91
   and civil rights, 189, 190–91, 195
   conservativeness of students, 122, 128–30
   cynicism of, 187–89, 195–96
   and George Bush, 195
   national service, 191
   racial integration, 207–208
   and Ronald Reagan, 194–95
   and Ross Perot, 195
   social and political change, 198–99
pop-culture icons, 100–102
Popenoe, David
   on single-parent families, 37–38
Population Bomb, The (Ehrlich), 13
Postman, Neil
   on childhood innocence, 62
Poston, Don
   on the Free Generation and Ronald Reagan, 194–95
poverty and age, 45–50
Pretty Baby, 22
Program, The, 74
property taxes, 109–10, 173–74
Proposition 13, 109–10, 173
Pruett, Kyle
   on nurturing fathers, 35

psychiatric admissions contest, 90
pushouts, 93

Quann, Patricia
   and teenage suicide, 78

racial integration, 207–208
   See also blacks
Rader, Dotsin
   on runaways and prostitution, 93
Ravitch, Diane
   on educational reform, 110
reading comprehension, testing, 118–19
Reagan, Ronald
   and benefits for children, 48
   and day-care funding, 42
   Free Generation and, 194–95
   and the minimum wage, 161
Reagan administration
   and the "squeal law," 71
Real Live Brady Bunch, The (Soloway/Soloway play), 200
Red Hot Chili Peppers, 200
Regan, Margaret
   on the youth market, 192
Renfrew Center, 65
Ritalin, 82
   and hyperactivity, 83–88
   side effects, 86–88
   studies on, 85–86, 86–88
River's Edge, The, 55
Rizzo, Thomas, suicide of, 76
Roach, Terry, sentence of, 97, 98
rock music and the Free Generation, 192
Roland, Dr. Alan
   and child support, 37

Rollin, Betty
   on motherhood, 16
Rolling Stone magazine
   on employment expectations, 150
Rubin, Jerry, 18
Rubin, Dr. Lillian
   on sexual behavior, 71
runaways, 92–94
   and AIDS, 93–94
   and prostitution, 93
Rutter, Michael
   on children and divorce, 30

S&Ls, 172–73
Sabot, Richard
   and grading, 133–34
San Francisco Chronicle
   on student loans, 127
Schaub, Pete
   and Woman's Studies, 132–33
Schmidt, Benno C.
   and political correctness, 139
Scholastic Aptitude Test (SAT), 108–109
   lowering scores, 120–21, 134
Schools We Deserve, The (Ravitch), 111
Schrag, Peter
   and hyperactive children, 84, 85, 86, 87
Schwartz, Felice
   and maternity provisions, 40
Science and Human Behavior (Skinner), 24
Science magazine, 14
Sellers, Herbert A.
   on elevator surfing, 73
senior citizens vs. Free Generation, 50
Severs, Theresa
   on unemployment, 156

sex
   and abstinence, 71
   and condom distribution, 71
   government and, 71–72
   and intimacy, 71
   statutory rape, 71–72
   See also abortion
sex objects, children as, 22–23
Sex Without Shame (Yates), 25
sexual revolution, 69–73
sexually transmitted diseases (STDs), 72–73
Shaw, George Bernard, 188
Shields, Brooke, 22–23
single-parent families, 37–38
   and psychiatric admissions of children, 90
Singles, 200
Singleton, John, 196
Sixteen Candles, 54
Skinner, B. F.
   on freedom, 24
Slacker (Linklater film), 193, 199
slasher films, 54
Slime, 199
Small, Michael
   on Cypress Hill, 207
Smith, Jean
   on marriage, expectations of, 182
Smith, Nancy
   on Boomer dating, 180
   on Free Generation humor, 199
Smith-Rowsey, Daniel
   on Free Generation vs. Baby Boomers, 202–203
Social Security
   Baby Boomers and, 203–205
   Free Generation and, 163–65

   and the poor, 49
Soderbergh, Steven, 196, 205
Soloway, Jill and Faith, 200
Sommerville, John
   on babies as the enemy, 14
speech zones, 138
Sportsmedicine Book, The (Mirkin), 65
Steele, James
   and home ownership, 168–69
Steinberg, Laurence
   on working students, 145–47
stepfamilies, 36–38
stepmothers and stepdaughters, 36
Stewart, Mark
   on children and behavioral drugs, 87
stimulant drugs, studies on, 85–86
Stockman, Dr. Larry
   on living with parents, 175
Straight Talk About Eating Disorders (Kranz/Maloney), 66
Strauss, William
   on Baby Boomers, 2
student self-esteem, 112–14
Suicidal Tendencies (rock group), 91
suicide, 76–79, 99
Sullivan, Louis
   on child abuse, 62
Summerhill (Neill), 114
Surfrider Foundation, 198

Taps, 54
Tarantino, Quentin, 196, 205
Tartt, Donna, 196, 205
Tax Reform Act (1986), 162
Taxi Driver, 22

Taylor, Ronald
   on juvenile punishment, 98
teachers
   esteem for, 108–10
   pay, 107
   teaching with drugs, 83
   See also education
teaching assistants, 136–37
"Teaching with Drugs" (Bosco paper), 83
teenage pregnancy, 69–73
   black girls and, 69
   statutory rape, 71–72
teenagers
   cause of death, 99
   confinement of, 88–91
   crime and, 92, 94–96, 97–98
   and emotional problems, 80–91
   employment, 143–57
   and hacker crimes, 74–75
   and impetuous behavior, 73–76
   murder and, 54–55, 99
   runaways, 92–94
   and sexually transmitted diseases, 72–73
   and suicide, 76–79, 99
   throwaways, 93
   vandalism, 55–56
television. *See* film and television
temporary jobs, 152
Third Millennium Declaration, 207
Thomas, Lewis
   on nuclear disaster, 64
Thompson, Wayne, sentence of, 97, 98
Thorazine, 82, 85
throwaways, 93
Time magazine
   Boomers, Free Generation complaints about, 189–91

on Brooke Shields, 22–23
on Free Generation income expectations, 197
on Free Generation parenthood, 185
marriage, Free Generation expectations of, 182–83
and parenting, 51, 52
on relationships and the Free Generation, 180
tracking, 73–74
Tranquilizing of America, The (Hughes/Brewin), 83–84
Truman, James
   on the youth market, 191
Trump, Donald
   as Free Generation hero, 130, 188

Under Siege, 203
unemployment, 148, 155–57
U.S. News & World Report
   college education, cost of, 21
   on living with parents, 176
   on senior citizens, 50

vandalism and teenagers, 55–56, 96
Vedder, Eddie
   on success, 192
vehicle accidents, death from, 99
Veterans Administration (VA), 171
Village Voice, 23

Wacky Packages, 199
Wakeman-Linn, John
   and grading, 133–34
Waldon Two (Skinner), 24
Walker, Glynnis
   on divorced families, 37
Walker, John, Jr., 195
Wall Street Journal

on the Free Generation, 187
Wallerstein, Judith
   economic security of children, 31
   on the effects of divorce, 26–29
   on stepfathers, 36
Walsh, Adam, abduction of, 58–59, 61, 62
Ward, Ronald, sentence of, 97, 98
Washington Post
   on the Free Generation, 205
   Free Generation vs. Baby Boomer, 203
   on Free Generation expectations, 64
   on Free Generation intelligence, 187
   on Free Generation marriage, 182
   on the Free Generation and Ronald Reagan, 194–95
   on "McDonald's time," 146–47
   and teenage suicide, 78
Weber, Bruce
   on the Free Generation and romance, 192
Weekly Reader
   on student alcoholism, 68
Weil, David N.
   and home ownership, 170
Weiss, Dr. Gabrielle
   side effects of Ritalin, 85
Weiss, Rob, 196
Weithorn, Lois
   children, confinement of, 89
When Teenagers Work (Bronfenbrenner), 143
When the Bough Breaks: The Cost of Neglecting Our Children (Hewlett), 90

Whitehead, Barbara Dafoe
   on the conservativeness of children, 30
   on divorce, 29
Wilburn, Shellie
   on the expectations of nuclear catastrophe, 64
wilding, 96
Wiley, David E.
   on aptitude tests, 120
Williams, Edna
   on the killing of children, 99
Williams, Wayne, 59
Wilson, Margo
   on sexual abuse, 36
Wilson, Pete
   and driving regulations, 190
Winn, Marie
   on latchkey children, 56
   and protecting children, 25
Wolfe, Tom, 2
Wolfson, Lois and Stephen
   and apartment discrimination, 9–12
women
   child support, 33–35
   day-care centers and, 42–44
   divorce and income, 31
   economic opportunities, 39–44
   and employment, 152
   government and, 185–86
   median pay for, 42
   working mothers, 41–42
women's studies, 132–33

Yankelovich, Skelly, and White studies, 20–21
Yates, Alayne
   on children and sex, 25

Zero Population Growth, Inc. (ZPG), 13
   and abortion, 19–20
Zigler, Edward
   and absent parents, 53
Zinn, Laura
   on employment expectations, 150
Zinsmeister, Karl
   on protecting children from the Free Generation, 188